THE ILLUSTRATED HISTORY OF
ENGLISH FOOTBALL

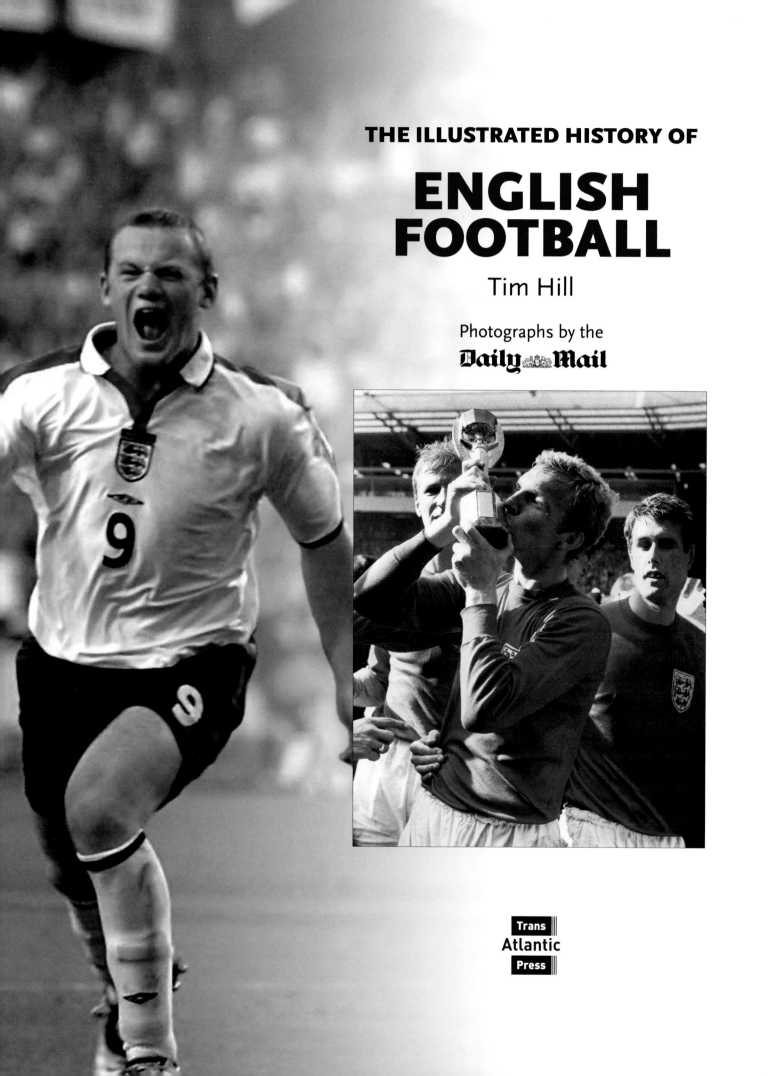

THE ILLUSTRATED HISTORY OF

ENGLISH FOOTBALL

Tim Hill

Photographs by the
Daily Mail

**Trans
Atlantic
Press**

For Laura and Jenny

Published by Transatlantic Press in 2009

Transatlantic Press
38 Copthorne Road
Croxley Green
Hertfordshire, WD3 4AQ, UK

© Atlantic Publishing
Photographs © Associated Newspapers Archive

A catalogue record for this book is available from the British Library.

ISBN 978-1-907176-04-3
Printed in China

Contents

Introduction

The Beautiful Game

'The world turns around a spinning ball'. In those words the esteemed Uruguayan writer Eduardo Galeano encapsulated football's unique place on the cultural landscape. No other pursuit crosses international borders and cultural boundaries like the Beautiful Game.

It was a visiting English professor who introduced football to the land of Galeano's birth in 1882, a pattern that was replicated the world over. The game that developed on the playing fields of England's public schools and universities spread apace to the industrial heartlands, and thence to all four corners of the globe.

This book chronicles the landmarks and watershed moments in the history of English football, from the birth of the Football Association in 1863 to Manchester United's record-equalling 18th championship success of 2008-09. It charts the sequence of events that set football and rugby on divergent paths; the founding of the FA Cup and the era of the gentleman-amateur; the rise of professionalism and the establishment of league football. The great teams of each era are highlighted, and there are profiles of the star players who have held fans in thrall with their virtuosity. Dazzling skills made for valuable commodities, and when Alf Common joined Middlesbrough for £1000 in 1905 – the first four-figure transfer – it provoked intakes of breath every bit as sharp as those that followed Cristiano Ronaldo's £80 million move from Manchester United to Real Madrid 104 years later. What's more, Boro splashed out on a star striker in a desperate bid to stave off relegation. Plus ca change...

Lavishly illustrated using over 450 photographs from the archives of the *Daily Mail*, *The Illustrated History of English Football* also includes a detailed statistical record that will settle many arguments, and spark off many more. Football is often described as having its own international language; this book comprehensively chronicles the A to Z of the country that brought the game to the world.

The New Dribbling Sport

The beginnings of football cannot be dated exactly.
A rudimentary form of the game was played in China as early as 200
BC, and the ancient Greeks and Romans also had their own versions.
Suffice to say that throughout history inflated animals' bladders, indeed
any spherical objects that would serve the purpose, have been kicked,
thrown and headed in the name of sporting endeavour.

Britain was just one of many countries that absorbed football into its cultural fabric. It is said that after the Anglo-Saxons repelled an attack by the Danes in the early Middle Ages, a celebratory game of football was played using the head of one of the vanquished as a ball. Entire villages would participate in long attritional sporting battles with their neighbours, often on Shrove Tuesday or other public holidays. One such took place between the Derbyshire villages of All Saints and St Peter's and gave rise to the expression "local derby". Several monarchs, including Edward III and Richard II, attempted to ban football, fearing that their subjects were spending too much time honing their ball skills at the expense of their dexterity with the longbow. The Puritans were equally concerned, regarding football as a form of revelling that the country could well do without. Needless to say, all these efforts came to nought.

Public schools and universities lead the way

It wasn't until the 19th century that a number of games which could all be loosely united under the umbrella of "football" finally spread their wings and stood alone. Diversification was the new Zeitgeist, and it was not achieved without a degree of acrimony.

The game of football in the eighteenth and early nineteenth centuries was championed by the elite educational institutions. Thomas Arnold, the headmaster of Rugby School in the 1830s, took the progressive view that football ought to be positively encouraged, not suppressed. He felt that exercising both mind and body were equally important, and football was far preferable to drinking and gambling as a leisure pursuit. Many other public schools and universities took the same view, and it was here that the game flourished, although each institution developed its own version of the game.

William Webb Ellis "disregards the rules"

Ironically, a fictitious event at Rugby School a decade before Arnold took up his post remains a key date in the annals of sport. In 1823 William Webb Ellis is

supposed to have shown "a fine disregard for the rules of football" by picking up the ball and running with it. This landmark event is almost certainly nothing more than an apocryphal tale, but it did usher in a period in which a number of distinct sports emerged from a plethora of broadly similar ball games.

Contrary to the view expressed in the William Webb Ellis commemorative plaque, which speaks of his celebrated exploit "originating the distinctive feature of the rugby game", it was those who wanted to play only a dribbling, kicking game who were the real innovators. All the other football-derived sports

- including Australian Rules, American football and hurling, as well as rugby itself - embraced handling as a key element. It was these sports which represented a link with the past. In the mid-19th century, it was Association football that was the brand new package on offer, although the term itself had not yet been coined.

Hacking becomes the key issue
It wasn't simply a case of a handling game versus a dribbling game, however. Proponents of the latter, including those at Eton and Charterhouse, wanted to do away with hacking - kicking an opponent's shins. This was the issue

of greatest concern. The hacking that went on at that time made the on-field misdemeanours of the modern era seem tame by comparison. Broken limbs were commonplace, and fatalities not unknown. Etonians and Carthusians were in the vanguard of those who wanted a game in which the ball - and only the ball - was kicked. There were many who harrumphed at the idea; the aggression that was central to the game of rugby football was the stuff on which Great Britain had built her empire. A more "civilised" game, so the argument ran, risked the country's pre-eminence as a military power.

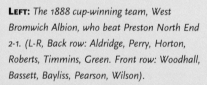

LEFT: *The 1888 cup-winning team, West Bromwich Albion, who beat Preston North End 2-1. (L-R, Back row: Aldridge, Perry, Horton, Roberts, Timmins, Green. Front row: Woodhall, Bassett, Bayliss, Pearson, Wilson).*

ABOVE: *An illustration dating from the 1860s shows a group of boys playing "football". Public schools such as Eton and Winchester had taken up the game but each team played according to its own set of rules making competition almost impossible.*

OPPOSITE PAGE: *A recent re-enactment of the famous occasion in 1823 when William Webb Ellis decided to pick up the ball and run with it. In 1839 Queen Adelaide, widow of William IV, visited Rugby School and watched a game on the famous sporting field. The boys had been given a tasselled cap to commemorate the visit, and some of them wore the headgear on the field of play. That didn't catch on, but the idea of presenting caps as a way of honouring international appearances did.*

Football Association formed

When Old Etonians of the 1840s moved on to Cambridge University, they continued to express their opposition to the version of football as played at Rugby School. The battle lines were drawn, and the battle itself would be fought over the rules. In 1848 some of the proponents of the dribbling game drew up the Cambridge Rules, which were forerunners of those of Association Football. This was a key event, despite the fact that these rules were not widely taken up. Even within the walls of Rugby School itself there had been no standard set of rules. There were no inter-collegiate fixtures, and so the students themselves could make up and amend rules on a whim. A revised version of the Cambridge Rules was drafted in 1862. The time was fast approaching when the rival camps would have to face each other and thrash the issue out once and for all.

Historic decision

On 26 October 1863 representatives from eleven leading football clubs met at the Freemasons' Tavern, Great Queen Street, London. Of the dribbling game's champions in academia, only Charterhouse School was represented. The decision to form a new body, the Football Association, was uncontroversial. Some six weeks later, at the fifth meeting, the laws of the game were up for discussion and the temperature rose. The majority view favoured outlawing handling the ball and hacking. A vocal minority, led by Blackheath FC, would not countenance what they perceived as a bastardisation of their beloved game. Once again, the objectors were more concerned over the abandonment of hacking than they were at the prospect of seeing running with the ball in hand outlawed. Having lost the vote 13-4, Blackheath's representatives resigned and withdrew, hardly realising the historic significance of their decision.

BOTTOM: *Richmond rugby team pictured in the 1890s. In 1863 eleven southern clubs formed the Football Association. Blackheath refused to accept the majority decision and left the FA, eventually forming the Rugby Football Union.*

BELOW: *An early advertisement for boots mentions both rugby and 'association', but a clear distinction between the two games was not properly made until the second half of the 19th century.*

The "new" dribbling game

There were many clubs who chose to follow Blackheath and stick with the traditional handling game. But these were far outnumbered by those who subscribed to the "new" kicking and dribbling sport. And so, ironically, the traditional roughhouse working man's game of rugby lost out in the popularity stakes to a perceived less manly code whose champions had been public schoolboys! Association football quickly established itself as the sport of the masses, while rugby became something of an elitist pursuit. In a remarkably short space of time, orthodoxy had been stood on its head.

Hybrid games still common

Football in 1863 still retained many of the elements of rugby. Hacking had gone, but handling the ball was still permissible, and a kick at goal could be won by touching down over the opposition's goal-line. Nor did the formation of the FA have an immediate unifying effect on the game that was played up and down the country. Many clubs played "soccer" - a word coined from Association football - others played rugby, while it was common to see games that were a hybrid of the two codes. When the FA was formed, Sheffield FC had already been in existence for at least five years. But this club had devised its own rules and when it sought FA membership, the Association did not even

deign to reply. Notts County, established in 1862, thus became the oldest club among the founding members of the Football League. That was still a long way off, however. During the 1860s and 1870s the FA's priorities were consolidation and standardisation, amending the laws and, in 1871, establishing a cup competition.

Rule changes

Rule changes that made the game far more recognisable as the one we know today included the introduction of goal kicks (1869) and corner kicks (1872). Offside was integrated into the laws, with three defenders required between the attacking player and the goal. In the mid-1860s tape was stretched between the posts at a height of 8 feet; a decade later it was replaced by a crossbar. In 1871 the term "goalkeeper" made its first appearance in the game's legislative framework, and sealed the end of handling the ball for the outfield players. 11-a-side games became the norm and the rules were enforced by an umpire. Thus, by the time the Rugby Football Union was formed in 1871, the two codes had diverged dramatically.

BELOW: *The 1889 cup winners, Preston North End, who beat Wolverhampton Wanderers 3-0. L-R, Back row: Drummond, Howarth, Russell, Holmes, Graham, Mills-Roberts. Front Row: Gordon, Ross, Goodall, Dewhurst, Thompson.*

BELOW: *Not every match was played according to the regulations but the rules of the game gradually expanded from the 14 agreed upon by the FA in 1863. In 1865 the height of the tape which formed the crossbar of the goal was set at 8 feet although nets were not compulsory until 1891. Goalkeepers were first mentioned in the rules in 1871 and the penalty kick was introduced in 1891.*

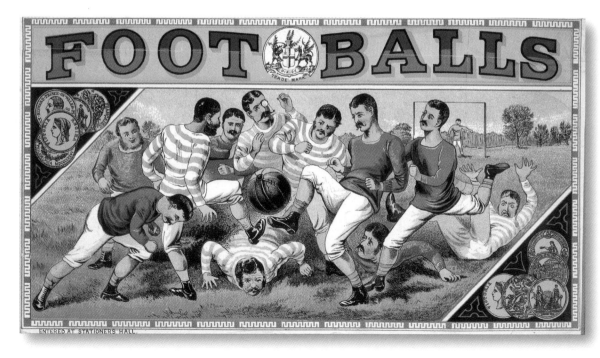

The birth of the FA Cup

One of the key events in this period was not a change in the way the game was played but an administrative appointment. Charles Alcock was an Old Harrovian who, along with his elder brother James, had helped to found the Forest club. Forest was among those clubs represented at the historic meeting at the Freemasons' Tavern, although Alcock himself was not present. James Alcock became an FA Committee member when it was first constituted, but within three years Charles had replaced him and it was he who became one of the most influential figures of the day. Alcock was a driving force in the effort to establish a unified game throughout the land. In 1870 he was appointed Secretary to the FA, a position he held for 25 years. His greatest contribution came just one year into that appointment, when he was the prime mover in the birth of the FA Cup.

15 clubs enter inaugural FA Cup

It was at an FA Committee meeting on 20 July 1871 that Alcock proposed the following motion: "That it is desirable that a Challenge Cup should be established in connection with the Association, for which all clubs belonging to the Association should be invited to compete". The idea was probably based on the inter-house competitions he had participated in during his time at Harrow.

As there were no league matches at this time, fixtures were an ad hoc mish-mash cobbled together between club secretaries with varying degrees of success. A Cup competition suddenly gave football a focal point, and it quickly caught the imagination of the clubs. By this time some fifty of them were affiliated to the FA, yet logistical problems meant that only 15 entered the inaugural competition, held in the 1871-72 season. There was an overwhelming southern

bias, 13 of the entrants coming from that region, including eight from the environs of the capital. Donington Grammar School in Lincolnshire was England's most northerly participant, while Queen's Park ignored a daunting travel schedule and flew the flag for Scotland. With the aid of two byes and a walk-over - after Donington scratched - Queen's Park found themselves in the semi-finals without having kicked a ball! They funded their trip to London to play the Wanderers from public subscription. The game ended in a goalless draw, and as the Scottish club's resources wouldn't stretch to a replay, it was the Wanderers who went on to contest the Final.

BELOW: *Cambridge University football team in 1894. Until the 1880s football was dominated by the gentlemen-amateur teams coming mainly from the public schools and universities of the south. In 1881 Old Etonians played Old Carthusians for the Cup, the last time two amateur sides appeared in the final.*

LEFT: *12,000 spectators assembled at the Oval to witness Blackburn Rovers win the FA Cup final in 1884 when they beat Queen's Park 2-1. (L-R Back row: Lofthouse, McIntyre, Beverley, Arthur, Suter, Forrest. Front Row: Douglas, Sourbutts, Brown, Inglis, Hargreaves.)*

BOTTOM: *The 1892 winning cup team West Bromwich Albion beat local rivals Aston Villa 3-0. (L-R: Bassett, Nicholson, Reynolds, McLeod, Reader, Nicholls, Perry, Pearson, Groves, McCulloch, Geddes).*

RIGHT: *By the 1880s the game was more structured. Rules were recognised nationally and the FA Cup was a well-established competition. In 1888 William McGregor, a director of Aston Villa, took the initiative and invited 11 teams to join his club in the formation of a league.*

ASTON VILLA

League Champions 1893-94 Winners of English Cup 1886-87.

Oh What a Scorcher "REYNOLDS"

Wanderers win the first Cup Final

The captain of the Wanderers was none other than Charles Alcock himself. Alcock had founded the club, which had no ground of its own and played its home matches at Battersea Park. That meant early kick-offs in winter, as the park closed its gates at 4.00 p.m.!

The Wanderers' opponents in the inaugural Cup Final were the Royal Engineers, the latter being installed as warm favourites. The match took place at Kennington Oval on 16 March 1872 in front of a 2000-strong crowd who had paid a shilling each for the privilege. The Wanderers upset the odds and ran out 1-0 winners. The goal was scored by Matthew Betts, who had been a registered member of the Harrovian Chequer club which had scratched earlier in the competition. He turned out for the Wanderers under an assumed name, a clear breach of the regulations. The first FA Cup Final thus saw the deciding goal scored by a player who really shouldn't have been on the pitch. If that weren't bad enough, the Royal Engineers had been handicapped by the fact that one of their players,

Lieutenant Cresswell, was nursing a broken collarbone for most of the match. Nearly a hundred years before the era of substitutes, players had to be made of stern stuff.

Clash with the Boat Race

Wanderers went on to win the Cup four more times in the 1870s, although this was not a feat that could be compared to the modern era. In 1873, for example, the club was given a bye to the Final as cup holders. That match, in which Wanderers beat Oxford University 2-0, took place at 11.00 a.m. to avoid a clash with the Boat Race. For all the strides football had made, the latter remained a much more prestigious event in the sporting calendar.

Of more significance was the fact that gentlemen-amateurs, the leisured classes, dominated the competition in the early years. The Wanderers had the cream of the players from the public school and university systems. Old Etonians appeared in five Finals in that first decade, finally winning the trophy in 1879. Oxford University beat Royal Engineers to lift

the Cup in 1874 and were also beaten finalists in 1873 and 1877. Clearly football in the elite educational institutions was still strong enough to get the better of the teams from the industrial Midlands and North. One of the stars of the day was Arthur Kinnaird, who was said to have been a dynamic, skilful performer in any position on the field. He appeared in nine FA Cup Finals, picking up winners' medals with Old Etonians in 1879 and 1882, and adding three more victories to his tally with Wanderers in 1873, 1877 and 1878.

BELOW: *In the late 19th century football teams sprang up all over the country. Some of these, such as Bolton, Southampton, Wolves and Everton, originally called St Domingo's, were established by churches. Others, like Spurs and the two Sheffield sides, were offshoots from cricket clubs. Newton Heath, later re-named Manchester United, began life as a works team started by employees of the Lancashire and Yorkshire Railway Company.*

The rise of professionalism

In 1879 Lancashire side Darwen almost produced an upset of seismic proportions. In their 4th-round match against Old Etonians at Kennington Oval they came back from 5-1 down to force a draw. Darwen were in the ascendancy at the end of the match, and the Old Etonians' captain hastily declined the offer to play extra time. There was no question of the Old Etonians heading north for a replay, so Darwen had to make another trip to the capital. That game finished level too, and although Old Etonians prevailed in the third clash, it was clear that dominance of the gentlemen-amateurs was under threat.

End of the road for the gentleman-amateur

The pendulum swung after 1881, when Old Carthusians beat Old Etonians in the last all-amateur Final. By then, many future illustrious clubs had been formed. Some had their roots in church schools, including Aston Villa, Woverhampton Wanderers and Everton. Others, such as Newton Heath and Stoke City sprang up as works teams. Sheffield Wednesday and Preston North End were among those formed as offshoots of existing sports clubs, often ones for which cricket was the chief pursuit. But it was the town of Blackburn which ushered in the new era. Rovers reached the Cup Final in 1882, with Old Etonians providing the opposition. Blackburn boasted several classy Scottish players and, like many other clubs, was covertly organised along professional lines. One of the players' fathers was so confident of the result that he bet a row of houses on a Blackburn victory. It was an expensive gamble, for Old Etonians won the match 1-0. But the writing was on the wall. This would be the last time that an amateur club would lift the trophy.

The Cup goes north

The following year, Blackburn Olympic took the Cup north for the first time. The backbone of the team was made up of weavers and spinners, plumbers and sheet-metal workers. It also included players who appeared to earn their living purely from football, professionals in all but name. Olympic had a player-manager, Jack Hunter, who used advanced methods to prepare the team, including taking the players away to Blackpool to get them into peak physical and mental condition for the Final, in which they were up against the holders. Blackburn won the match 2-1 after extra time. For Old Etonians, a sixth Final appearance in twelve years was to be their last. They, together with the other clubs spawned from academia and the military, represented the old guard. And the shift in footballing power was not just away from the gentleman-amateur to artisans and professionals; it was also from the Home Counties to the industrial heartlands of the Midlands and the North. In the next 37 years the Cup would return to the south-east just once.

PLAYER'S CIGARETTES

NICHOLSON · McCULLOCH · READER · REYNOLDS · GROVES · PERRY · BASSETT · GEDDES · NICHOLLS · McLEOD · PEARSON

ASSOCIATION CUP WINNERS
WEST BROMWICH ALBION, 1892

ABOVE: *West Bromwich Albion appeared in the Cup Final on five occasions between 1886 and 1895, winning once against Preston in 1888 and later defeating Aston Villa in 1892.*
RIGHT: *The 1896 cup-winning team Sheffield Wednesday who beat Wolverhampton Wanderers 2-1. J. Massey, M.J Earp, A. Langley, H. Brandan, T.H Crawshaw, C. Petrie, A. Brash, A. Brady, L. Bell, H. Davies, F. Spiksley.*

"Shamateurism"

By the 1870s it was clear that what would later be dubbed "shamateurism" was rife. Teams were vying for the best players, and it was inevitable that inducements would be offered. There was a game of cat-and-mouse between the clubs and the Football Association. The clubs found all manner of means to reward their players. These included giving nominal jobs which required little, if any, work to be done; putting money into players' boots on match days; and having phoney sets of accounts which would suggest to any enquiring eyes that everything was above board.

For a time the FA stood firm. In 1882 the Association reaffirmed its commitment to an amateur game, with payments strictly limited to out-of-pocket expenses. While the clubs made it difficult for the authorities to prove any underhand dealings, they did sometimes slip up. One of the victims was Accrington, who were thrown out of the FA after being found guilty of paying one of their players. Another was Preston, who were disqualified from the FA Cup after brazenly admitting to a misdemeanour that virtually every club was guilty of. The same issue was affecting rugby, and along the same geographical lines. In the case of the handling code, the rival camps became so entrenched that many northern clubs eventually broke away and established a new professional game; Rugby League was born.

FA relents

Football came close to suffering the same kind of split which divided rugby down the middle. Manual workers at that time might have earned one or two pounds a week, and although more liberal employment laws had been introduced, for many Saturday was still just another working day. Matters came to a head in October 1884, when a number of northern clubs banded together with a view to setting up a professional football league. In July the following year the FA relented. The administrators initially tried to impose caveats and restrictions, imposing a two-year residence rule to prevent clubs from importing star players for Cup matches. But the door was now ajar and it was soon fully opened. The age of the professional footballer had officially begun.

England's first international

The 1870s also saw international football take off. Five England-Scotland matches were staged between 1870 and 1872, but these took the form of London-based players from north and south of the border taking part in representative fixtures. Once again it was Charles Alcock who was the driving force behind these encounters. The first international proper between the two countries took place on 30 November 1872. Alcock initially set a midweek date for the match, rearranging it for a Saturday when he realised that Scottish players and spectators might not

have the same independent means that he and his team enjoyed.

The match took place at the West of Scotland cricket ground, Partick. At that time cricket enjoyed a higher profile than football in Scotland and the formation of the SFA was still a year away. One of the country's leading clubs, Queen's Park, thus took responsibility for organizing the team to take on England. A crowd of just over 2000 paid a shilling apiece to watch the match, which ended in a goalless draw. The embryonic state of Scottish football was illustrated by the fact that the photographer who was due to record the event wanted a guarantee that he would be able to sell his prints. No guarantee was forthcoming and the photographer thus withdrew, seeing little market for such pictures. Nevertheless, the game created a lot of interest in Scotland. It wasn't long before football, which could be played on almost any patch of ground, supplanted cricket as both a participation and spectator sport.

Scots influence English game

The Scots came to the Oval for a return match on 8 March 1873. Alexander Bonsor, who played for Old Etonians and the Wanderers, wrote his name into the history books as the scorer of England's first international goal. England won the game 4-2, and it became a fixture on the sporting calendar thereafter.

As well as promoting the game in their own country, the top Scotttish players of the day influenced the development of English football too. Dribbling was a feature of the English game, a legacy of the public schools and universities, which concentrated on individual skills rather than teamwork. It was the Scots who saw the advantage of playing a passing game. Many were recruited by clubs in the north of England, a practice that had gone on long before the FA embraced professionalism. They were usually the star players. Fergus Suter and James Love, the leading lights in the Darwen team that had given Old Etonians such a scare, were prime examples of this trend. It was the influence of Suter, Love and their ilk which made English clubs realise that packing a team with dribblers was not the way forward.

> **12 TEAMS THAT FOUNDED THE LEAGUE IN 1888**
>
> **Accrington Stanley**
> **Aston Villa**
> **Blackburn Rovers**
> **Bolton Wanderers**
> **Burnley**
> **Derby County**
> **Everton**
> **Notts County**
> **Preston North end**
> **Stoke City**
> **West Bromwich Albion**
> **Wolverhampton Wanderers**

Villa man proposes league football

By the late 1880s professional footballers were playing international matches and clubs were competing for the FA Cup. Rule changes had given the game all its distinctive features. The last big piece of the jigsaw was league competition.

At the time fixtures were often anything but "fixed". Shambolic was a more apposite description. Postponements or cancellations were commonplace, and the game was crying out for organised fixture lists, not least because spectators who turned up to find there was no game were bound to feel aggrieved. Regular matches were also vital to meet a club's overheads, which now included players' wages. The establishment of a competitive league was the brainchild of William McGregor, a Scot who had relocated from Perthshire to Birmingham and ran a draper's shop. McGregor had no track record as a player, but his decision to join the board of his local club, Aston Villa, was to have a profound effect on the game.

12 teams contest new league competition

On 2 March 1888 McGregor wrote to Blackburn, Bolton, Preston and West Bromwich Albion about the prospect of forming a league, and naturally he also sounded out his own club on the idea. Throughout the spring of 1888 a series of meetings took place to thrash out the details and agree a name for the new body: the Football League. 12 teams were incorporated as founder members. These were the original five clubs that McGregor contacted, together with Accrington, Burnley, Everton, Derby County, Notts County, Wolverhampton Wanderers and Stoke. Other clubs, including Nottingham Forest, had also been keen to join, but the dates set aside for the matches, which were to be held on a home and away basis, meant that only 12 teams could be accommodated. Teams would be awarded two points for a win and one for a draw, a system which was to endure for almost a hundred years. McGregor became the Football League's first president, and the opening matches were played on 8 September 1888.

Opposite: The victorious Aston Villa team who defeated Everton 3-2 in the 1897 FA Cup final. (L-R Back row: Spencer, Whitehouse, Evans, Crabtree. Front row: Jas. Cowan, Athersmith, Campbell, Devey, Wheldon, John Cowan, Reynolds.)
Left: The 1894 cup-winning team, Notts County, who beat Bolton Wanderers 4-1 in front of 32,000 at Everton's ground. (L-R Back row: Bramley, Harper, Calderhead, Toone, Hendry, Shelton. Front row: Watson, Donnelly, Logan, Bruce, Daft).
Above: The original FA trophy

"Invincibles" of Preston set the standards

Preston set the standards in the early years, winning the league in the first two seasons and finishing runners-up in the following three campaigns. The inaugural season, 1888-89, was the most remarkable, Preston remaining unbeaten on their way to the championship, and not conceding a goal in the FA Cup, which they won by defeating Wolves 3-0 in the Final. Quite justifiably they were dubbed the "Invincibles". The team's star striker was a Scot, John Goodall. Goodall had previously shone for Great Lever, and representatives from Deepdale all but kidnapped him to acquire his services. Apart from his goalscoring feats, Goodall was also noteworthy for the fact that despite his roots he played international football for England by dint of residence.

Goodall left to join Derby after Preston's Double-winning campaign.

Rise of Sunderland
Supremacy passed from Preston to Sunderland. The Wearside club had replaced founder-members Stoke in the 1890-91 season and finished in mid-table in their first campaign. They would have finished fifth but had two points deducted for fielding 'keeper Ned Doig before his move from Arbroath was sanctioned. In the next four years Sunderland lifted the title three times and were runners-up once. Of the 116 games played during those four campaigns the "team-of-all-talents" won 81, drew 13 and were beaten just 22 times. Their success was based on a phenomenal home record; the team lost

just once in six years on their own ground.

The first of Sunderland's championships came in 1891-92, when the league was also extended to 14 clubs. Stoke were back, and Darwen were admitted. These clubs occupied the bottom two places, and Darwen had the dubious honour of becoming the first-ever team to suffer relegation to the newly-formed Second Division. The following year saw the league expanded again, to 16 clubs. Nottingham Forest were finally admitted, and ended their debut season in mid-table. The other debutants didn't fare quite so well. Newton Heath, the team that would eventually be reconstituted as Manchester United, propped up the table five points adrift of their nearest rivals.

Promotion and relegation

Promotion and relegation were not automatic, however; a series of "test matches" was held between the bottom three clubs of Division One and the top three in the new Second Division to decide the issue. Newton Heath survived that year but weren't so lucky the next. After finishing bottom in 1893-94 too, Newton Heath went down 2-0 to Division Two champions Liverpool, and the two teams swapped places. For Liverpool it meant promotion to the top flight at the first time of asking. Having had considerable success in the Lancashire League, the club had applied for a place in the Second Division after hearing that Accrington Stanley had resigned. Another club which achieved league status in the same year was Woolwich Arsenal. The Gunners had been formed in 1886, turned professional in 1891 and had already undergone three name changes. The team didn't quite have the same impact as the men from Anfield, but they had the honour of becoming the first southern club to be elected to the Football League.

Villa win the Cup - and lose it
In 1893-94 Aston Villa prevented Sunderland from making it a hat-trick of league titles, finishing six points ahead of the Wearside club. Villa went on to win the championship four more times in the next six seasons. They added the FA Cup to their trophy cabinet in 1895

and 1897, and were also runners-up in 1892. By completing the Double in 1896-97, Villa matched Preston's feat of eight years earlier. The Midlanders did lose four league games that season, yet still equalled Preston's achievement of finishing 11 points clear of the field. A thrilling 3-2 win over Everton completed the Double, an achievement that would prove elusive for the next 64 years.

Villa were also involved in a major off-field drama. Following the club's 1-0 FA Cup win over West Bromwich Albion in 1895, the trophy was put on display at a Birmingham bootmaker's shop belonging to William Shillcock. It was stolen on 11 September and never recovered. As a result, the FA fined Villa £25 and put the money towards a replacement trophy.

Townley the hat-trick hero
Following their three successive FA Cup wins in the mid-1880s, Blackburn Rovers notched two more successes at the start of the next decade. In 1890 Blackburn thumped Sheffield Wednesday 6-1, the biggest margin of the 19 finals that had taken place thus far. Blackburn had finished third in the championship and were hot favourites to beat Wednesday, despite the fact that the Yorkshire club had taken three league scalps in previous

rounds. Blackburn winger William Townley hit three of the goals, becoming the first player to score a hat-trick in the final.

The following year Notts County thought they had a better chance of beating Blackburn, having just thrashed them 7-1 on their own ground in the league. But three first-half goals at the Oval meant that the Lancashire club lifted the trophy for the fifth time in eight years.

OPPOSITE ABOVE: *1895 works team Woolwich Arsenal was founded in 1886 as Dial Square FC and played their home matches on Plumstead Common. In 1893 it was admitted to the newly-formed Second Division becoming the first southern club to be admitted to the league.*
ABOVE: *Nottingham Forest, who beat Derby County 3-1 in 1898. (L-R Back row: Mr. H. Hallam (secretary), McInnes, Mr. T. W. Hancock, Ritchie, Allsopp, Mr. B. Winter, Scott, Mr. H.S. Harford, Spouncer, G. Bee (trainer). Front row: Richards, Frank Forman, McPherson, Wragg, Capes, Benbow (on ground).*
OPPOSITE BELOW: *Fans head through London towards Crystal Palace, the venue for the Cup Final from 1895.*
LEFT: *In 1895 Aston Villa won the FA Cup for the second time. While on display in Birmingham the trophy was stolen and is believed by some to have been melted down to be made into counterfeit coins. Three more trophies have been used since this time, the most recent being introduced in the early 1990s.*

Cup Final moves north to Goodison

West Bromwich Albion put Rovers out in 1892 and went on to beat their much-fancied neighbours Aston Villa in the Final. There was another upset in 1893, when Wolves beat Everton 1-0. This match took place at Fallowfield, Manchester, after Surrey County Cricket Club expressed concerns that the Oval might not be able to cope with the huge numbers that the Cup Final now regularly attracted. Wolves' first victory prompted the club to award miniature replicas of the trophy to the players. This proved very handy two years later after the Cup was stolen; it meant that an identical replacement could be made.

1893-94 was a bitter-sweet year for Notts County. Having been relegated the previous year, the team won through to face Division One side Bolton in the final, which was staged at Goodison Park. County were unhappy about the choice of venue, feeling that it favoured their opponents. They needn't have worried as they ran out 4-1 winners, with Jimmy Logan grabbing a hat-trick to equal William Townley's feat of four years earlier. Notts County failed to make it a Cup-promotion double, though. Having finished third in Division Two, they were beaten 4-0 by Preston in the play-off.

Glory for Sheffield clubs

The Cup Final returned to the capital in 1895, Crystal Palace hosting the clash between Aston Villa and WBA. It was the third time in nine years that these two clubs had met in the Final, both having registered a win each. There was no upset this year. Form side Villa won 1-0, the goal scored by the captain John Devey after just 40 seconds. This remains the fastest goal ever scored in an FA Cup Final.

The city of Sheffield briefly enjoyed a spell in the limelight in the late 1890s. Wednesday beat Wolves by the odd goal in the 1896 Cup Final, neither club having set the league alight. The following year United finished as championship runners-up to Villa in the latter's Double-winning season. The Blades went one better in 1897-98, becoming only the fifth club to win the title. Their league form slumped dramatically in the next campaign, and they narrowly avoided relegation. But

they made it to the Cup Final, where they faced Derby County, whose side boasted goal ace Steve Bloomer. United managed to shackle him, although they did find themselves a goal down at half-time. A storming second half saw the Blades hit four goals without reply for a famous victory. Full-back Harry Thickett was the hero of the hour, having played the game out with two broken ribs.

Automatic promotion and relegation

The "test match" system was scrapped at the end of the 1897-98 season. A suspicious play-off prompted the Football League to adopt automatic promotion and relegation. Stoke and Burnley, who had finished bottom of Division One and top of Division Two respectively, played out a tame goalless draw which saw both teams secure top-flight status the following season. At the end of the 1898-99 season, Manchester City and Glossop were the first beneficiaries of the new two-up, two-down system, with Bolton and Sheffield Wednesday becoming the first clubs to suffer the drop without the lifeline of a play-off.

ABOVE: *The popularity of football among the masses had grown rapidly. By the turn of the century an estimated 7 million spectators watched league matches each year and in the 1890s the first newspaper devoted to sport was published. At the same time manufacturers saw the opportunity to make money by producing football equipment and began to advertise their products.*

BELOW: *Sheffield United went a goal behind in the 1899 cup final but a header from Bennett and strikes from Beers, Almond and Priest won the game 4-1.*

A new century dawns

As the new century dawned, the interest in football continued to grow exponentially. An aggregate of seven million people turned out to watch two 18-strong leagues battle it out for supremacy. And in less than thirty years the FA Cup had grown into one of the pre-eminent events of the sporting calendar. A record 73,833 crowd watched Sheffield United's win over Derby in 1899; attendances would soon comfortably exceed the six-figure mark. It was the showpiece event of the people's game, and had come a long way since the day it was moved to accommodate the Boat Race.

LEFT: *Bury defeated Southampton 4-0 to become champions at the turn of the century. The opening of the war in South Africa was the first time football had been interfered with by a conflict as many prominent players had departed for the front. (L-R Back row: Darroch, Thompson, Davidson. Middle row: Pray, Leeming, Ross. Front row: Richards, Wood, McLuckie, Sagar, Plant).*

FOOTBALL LEAGUE 1888-1899 TOP 10 LEAGUE POSITIONS

1888-89
1 Preston — 40
2 Aston Villa — 29
3 Wolverhampton W. — 28
4 Blackburn Rovers — 26
5 Bolton Wanderers — 22
6 West Bromwich A. — 22
7 Accrington — 20
8 Everton — 20
9 Burnley — 17
10 Derby County — 16

1889-90
1 Preston — 33
2 Everton — 31
3 Blackburn Rovers — 27
4 Wolverhampton W. — 25
5 West Bromwich A. — 25
6 Accrington — 24
7 Derby County — 21
8 Aston Villa — 19
9 Bolton Wanderers — 19
10 Notts County — 17

1890-91
1 Everton — 29
2 Preston — 27
3 Notts County — 26
4 Wolverhampton W. — 26
5 Bolton Wanderers — 25
6 Blackburn Rovers — 24
7 Sunderland — 23
8 Burnley — 21
9 Aston Villa — 18
10 Accrington — 16

1891-92
1 Sunderland — 42
2 Preston — 37
3 Bolton Wanderers — 36
4 Aston Villa — 30
5 Everton — 28
6 Wolverhampton W. — 26
7 Burnley — 26
8 Notts County — 26
9 Blackburn Rovers — 26
10 Derby County — 24

1892-93
1 Sunderland — 48
2 Preston — 37
3 Everton — 36
4 Aston Villa — 35
5 Bolton Wanderers — 32
6 Burnley — 30
7 Stoke — 29
8 West Bromwich A. — 29
9 Blackburn Rovers — 29
10 Nottingham Forest — 28

1893-94
1 Aston Villa — 44
2 Sunderland — 38
3 Derby County — 36
4 Blackburn Rovers — 34
5 Burnley — 34
6 Everton — 33
7 Nottingham Forest — 32
8 West Bromwich A. — 32
9 Wolverhampton W. — 31
10 Sheffield United — 31

1894-95
1 Sunderland — 47
2 Everton — 42
3 Aston Villa — 39
4 Preston — 35
5 Blackburn Rovers — 32
6 Sheffield United — 32
7 Nottingham Forest — 31
8 The Wednesday — 28
9 Burnley — 26
10 Bolton Wanderers — 25

1895-96
1 Aston Villa — 45
2 Derby County — 41
3 Everton — 39
4 Bolton Wanderers — 37
5 Sunderland — 37
6 Stoke — 30
7 The Wednesday — 29
8 Blackburn Rovers — 29
9 Preston — 28
10 Burnley — 27

1896-97
1 Aston Villa — 47
2 Sheffield United — 36
3 Derby County — 36
4 Preston — 34
5 Liverpool — 33
6 The Wednesday — 31
7 Everton — 31
8 Bolton Wanderers — 30
9 Bury — 30
10 Wolverhampton W. — 28

1897-98
1 Sheffield United — 42
2 Sunderland — 37
3 Wolverhampton W. — 35
4 Everton — 35
5 The Wednesday — 33
6 Aston Villa — 33
7 West Bromwich A. — 32
8 Nottingham Forest — 31
9 Liverpool — 28
10 Derby County — 28

1898-99
1 Aston Villa — 45
2 Liverpool — 43
3 Burnley — 39
4 Everton — 38
5 Notts County — 37
6 Blackburn Rovers — 36
7 Sunderland — 36
8 Wolverhampton W. — 35
9 Derby County — 35
10 Bury — 35

1900-1919
The People's Game

Football in the Edwardian era continued to provide rich entertainment for very little outlay. Sixpence was the typical entrance fee, and working men in their droves flocked to matches. Lifelong allegiances were developed, passions aroused. These sometimes manifested themselves in ways that earned rebuke. An over-exuberant crowd invaded the pitch in a Cup-tie between Spurs and Villa in 1904, causing the match to be abandoned. The FA ordered a replay at Villa Park and fined the London club £350. Some years later, when Europe was plunged into war, politicians expressed concern that munitions workers were preoccupied by football when their minds should have been on the war effort.

Meredith leads players' challenge against maximum wage

Burgeoning interest inevitably meant that football was no longer simply sport and entertainment but also big business. Some of the top clubs started to show extremely healthy balance sheets, and it wasn't long before players began to demand a bigger slice of the cake. In April 1901 a new maximum wage of £4 a week was introduced. This compared favourably with other skilled tradesmen of the day, but players began to recognise their worth and started to express dissatisfaction. Matters came to a head in 1907 with the formation of a Players' Union. The league and FA were worried about footballers becoming organised, possibly even affiliating to the Trades Union movement. They threatened to impose a ban on players who took up union membership. Manchester United star Billy Meredith was one of a vociferous group unwilling to be browbeaten. While many players lost their nerve and fell into line, Meredith led a group of players who threatened to withdraw all their labour. Prior to the 1909-10 season they began training independently under the banner of The Outcasts. Just before the season got under way the authorities caved in. The maximum wage was subsequently increased to £5 a week. The principle of player power was established.

First £1000 transfer

Another manifestation of the way in which

football was now a huge enterprise was in the transfer market. 1905 saw Sunderland and England inside-forward Alf Common join Middlesbrough for £1000, the first four-figure fee. This landmark deal polarised opinion. Boro fans were jubilant after Common helped the club finish clear of relegation. But to some the buying and selling of players in such a way smacked of human trafficking, something that was morally questionable. The game's administrators may not have taken such an extreme view, but they were apprehensive. In 1908 the league tried to impose a £350 cap on transfers. It lasted just four months. The authorities realised that the ruling was unenforceable. Pragmatism won the day, as it had over the issue of professionalism some 20 years earlier.

OPPOSITE ABOVE: *The Accrington Stanley team of 1907-08. Accrington were one of the original founders of the Football League in 1888.*

OPPOSITE BELOW: *Supporters of Everton and Sheffield had a long way to travel for the 1907 Cup Final at Crystal Palace. Here supporters are going past St Paul's as they make their way to South London. 84,000 fans watched Wednesday win the match 2-1.*

ABOVE: *At the end of the 19th century, Sunderland, dubbed "team of all the talents" was the most successful club in the north east. However by 1900 Newcastle United began to make its mark. Like its neighbour, the Newcastle team contained many Scottish players. In the 1901-2 season Sunderland regularly fielded 9 Scots.*

BELOW: *The Sheffield Wednesday team 1909-1910.*

Billy Meredith

"The Welsh Wizard"
Billy Meredith, "the Welsh Wizard", is widely regarded as the game's first superstar. Meredith came from Welsh mining stock, and he himself was working underground by the age of 12. His parents were eventually persuaded to allow him to pursue a career in football and Meredith joined Manchester City in 1894. He quickly established himself as a skilful, free-scoring winger, and became known for the fact that he never took to the field without a toothpick to chew on. By 1904 30-year-old Meredith was City's captain, and scored the only goal of the game in that year's FA Cup Final win over Bolton. Meredith was banned for eight months after allegedly attempting to bribe an Aston Villa player before a vital league match in April 1905. He denied the charge and when the ban was lifted he moved across the city to join Manchester United. He helped United to win the FA Cup in 1909 and the championship in 1910-11. He rejoined Manchester City in 1921 as a player-coach. He finally hung up his boots three years later, when he was four months short of his 50th birthday. His swansong came in City's 1924 FA Cup semi-final defeat by Newcastle. He had played 48 times for Wales between 1895 and 1920, winning the last of his caps when he was 45. Meredith was at the forefront of a campaign to end the £4 maximum wage that was in force in the early 1900s. That figure was increased to £5 as a result, and the roots of the PFA can be traced back to the Welshman's early efforts to establish a Players' Union.

LEFT: *Billy Meredith, a tough, talented and controversial player who captained Wales and played for both Manchester City and Manchester United in a 30-year career which ended in 1924. Instrumental in setting the foundations for a Players' Union, he was also banned for a season for reportedly attempting to bribe an Aston Villa player in a match-fixing scandal.*
BELOW: *An FA Cup fourth round match played on March 10, 1906. Woolwich Arsenal beat Manchester United 3-2. United would go on to win their first league title just two years later.*

Newcastle dominant

On the field of play one team stood out in the early years of the new century: Newcastle United. In the 13 seasons 1899-1900 to 1911-12 Newcastle finished in the top 6 eleven times and won the championship on three occasions, in 1905, 1907 and 1909. Their Cup record was, if anything, even more remarkable. Between 1905 and 1911 they reached the Final five times. In 1909 the team went down to Manchester United in the semis, so 1907 was the only year in which the club failed to reach the last four. And that season of "failure" was dramatic indeed - a home defeat by Crystal Palace, then a Southern League outfit.

Unfortunately, Newcastle's record after reaching the Final was not so impressive. Crystal Palace, the venue for each of them, was not a happy hunting ground. Newcastle failed to record a single victory in five attempts. Their best effort came in 1910, when they managed a 1-1 draw with Second Division Barnsley before beating the Yorkshire side in a replay at Goodison Park.

Villa thwart Double hopes

1904-05 saw Newcastle come agonisingly close to the Double. Aston Villa spoiled the party in the Cup Final. Villa were not quite the force they'd been in the 1890s, but spearheaded by new young striking sensation Harry Hampton they ran out 2-0 winners. Hampton scored both goals. Newcastle picked themselves up and won 3-0 at Middlesbrough on the last day of the season, enough to pip Everton for the championship by a point.

BELOW: *A scene from the 1907 Cup Final between Everton and Sheffield Wednesday. Just one year earlier Everton were 1-0 victors over Newcastle, but on this occasion were beaten 2-1 by Wednesday. The middle years of the decade were highly successful for both Merseyside teams. Alec Young's goal gave Everton the FA Cup in 1906 and Liverpool's Scottish centre-half Alex Raisbeck helped them secure victory in the league in the same year.*

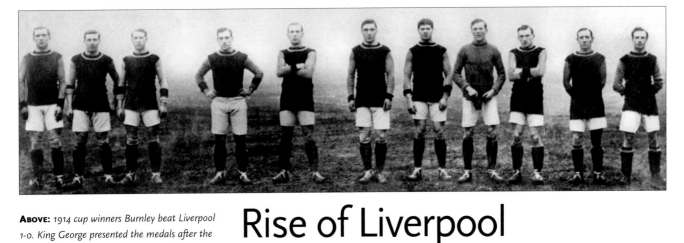

ABOVE: *1914 cup winners Burnley beat Liverpool 1-0. King George presented the medals after the game - the first time the monarch had done so. (L-R: Halley, Watson, Lindley, Boyle, Bamford, Freeman, Taylor, Dawson, Nesbitt, Hodgson, Mosscrop).*

BELOW: *Spectators climb trees to watch the 1912 Cup Final between Barnsley and West Bromwich Albion, that ended in a no-score draw. Second Division Barnsley finally defeated West Brom by a single goal scored during extra time in the replay. Three successive drawn Cup Finals convinced the FA to change the rules of the competition to allow extra time to be played should the first match be tied.*

Rise of Liverpool and Manchester United

Liverpool and Manchester United also made their mark in this period, winning the title four times between them.

Liverpool had come a long way since their League baptism in 1893. Just six years later they were on course for the Double, but were hammered 5-0 by Villa in a title showdown, then lost an FA Cup semi-final to Sheffield United. That was the year that Liverpool changed their colours from blue-and-white quarters to red. It didn't help them then, but two years later, 1900-01, the title went to Anfield for the first time. On that occasion, instead of riding high then falling away, as they had done two years earlier, the team went on a tremendous late run which included nine wins and three draws in 12 games. A 1-0 victory at relegated West Bromwich Albion clinched the championship.

Raisbeck stars at Anfield

Liverpool's star was Alex Raisbeck. In his third season at the club, the Scottish international was tigerish in the tackle and outstanding in the air, despite standing only 5ft. 9in. tall. Raisbeck was still the linchpin when Liverpool won their second title five years later, 1905-06. The intervening period had been something of a rollercoaster, the club having been relegated in 1903-04. But they made their mark in the record books by winning the Second and First Division championships in consecutive seasons. 1905-06 was also noteworthy for the fact that Everton beat Newcastle in the FA Cup Final; Liverpool's journalists made much capital out of their city's footballing supremacy that year.

LEAGUE DIVISION ONE 1900-1919 TOP 10 LEAGUE POSITIONS

1899-1900
1	Aston Villa	50
2	Sheffield United	48
3	Sunderland	41
4	Wolverhampton W	39
5	Newcastle United	36
6	Derby County	36
7	Manchester City	34
8	Nottingham Forest	34
9	Stoke	34
10	Liverpool	33

1900-01
1	Liverpool	45
2	Sunderland	43
3	Notts County	40
4	Nottingham Forest	39
5	Bury	39
6	Newcastle United	38
7	Everton	37
8	The Wednesday	36
9	Blackburn Rovers	33
10	Bolton Wanderers	33

1901-02
1	Sunderland	44
2	Everton	41
3	Newcastle United	37
4	Blackburn Rovers	36
5	Nottingham Forest	35
6	Derby County	35
7	Bury	34
8	Aston Villa	34
9	The Wednesday	34
10	Sheffield United	33

1902-03
1	The Wednesday	42
2	Aston Villa	41
3	Sunderland	41
4	Sheffield United	39
5	Liverpool	38
6	Stoke	37
7	West Bromwich A.	36
8	Bury	35
9	Derby County	35
10	Nottingham Forest	35

1903-04
1	The Wednesday	47
2	Manchester City	44
3	Everton	43
4	Newcastle United	42
5	Aston Villa	41
6	Sunderland	39
7	Sheffield United	38
8	Wolverhampton W	36
9	Nottingham Forest	31
10	Middlesbrough	30

1904-05
1	Newcastle United	48
2	Everton	47
3	Manchester City	46
4	Aston Villa	42
5	Sunderland	40
6	Sheffield United	40
7	Small Heath	39
8	Preston	36
9	The Wednesday	33
10	Woolwich Arsenal	33

1905-06
1	Liverpool	51
2	Preston	47
3	The Wednesday	44
4	Newcastle United	43
5	Manchester City	43
6	Bolton Wanderers	41
7	Birmingham City	41
8	Aston Villa	40
9	Blackburn Rovers	40
10	Stoke	39

1906-07
1	Newcastle United	51
2	Bristol City	48
3	Everton	45
4	Sheffield United	45
5	Aston Villa	44
6	Bolton Wanderers	44
7	Woolwich Arsenal	44
8	Manchester United	42
9	Birmingham City	38
10	Sunderland	37

1907-08
1	Manchester United	52
2	Aston Villa	43
3	Manchester City	43
4	Newcastle United	42
5	The Wednesday	42
6	Middlesbrough	41
7	Bury	39
8	Liverpool	38
9	Nottingham Forest	37
10	Bristol City	36

1908-09
1	Newcastle United	53
2	Everton	46
3	Sunderland	44
4	Blackburn Rovers	41
5	The Wednesday	40
6	Woolwich Arsenal	38
7	Aston Villa	38
8	Bristol City	38
9	Middlesbrough	37
10	Preston	37

1909-10
1	Aston Villa	53
2	Liverpool	48
3	Blackburn Rovers	45
4	Newcastle United	45
5	Manchester United	45
6	Sheffield United	42
7	Bradford City	42
8	Sunderland	41
9	Notts County	40
10	Everton	40

1910-11
1	Manchester United	52
2	Aston Villa	51
3	Sunderland	45
4	Everton	45
5	Bradford City	45
6	The Wednesday	42
7	Oldham	41
8	Newcastle United	40
9	Sheffield United	38
10	Woolwich Arsenal	38

1911-12
1	Blackburn Rovers	49
2	Everton	46
3	Newcastle United	44
4	Bolton Wanderers	43
5	The Wednesday	41
6	Aston Villa	41
7	Middlesbrough	40
8	Sunderland	39
9	West Bromwich A.	39
10	Woolwich Arsenal	38

1912-13
1	Sunderland	54
2	Aston Villa	50
3	The Wednesday	49
4	Manchester United	46
5	Blackburn Rovers	45
6	Manchester City	44
7	Derby County	42
8	Bolton Wanderers	42
9	Oldham	42
10	West Bromwich A.	38

1913-14
1	Blackburn Rovers	51
2	Aston Villa	44
3	Oldham	43
4	Middlesbrough	43
5	West Bromwich A.	43
6	Bolton Wanderers	42
7	Sunderland	40
8	Chelsea	39
9	Bradford City	38
10	Sheffield United	37

1914-15
1	Everton	46
2	Oldham	45
3	Blackburn Rovers	43
4	Burnley	43
5	Manchester City	43
6	Sheffield United	43
7	The Wednesday	43
8	Sunderland	41
9	Bradford PA	41
10	West Bromwich A.	40

WHAT A CLINKER
"McCARTNEY."

Steve Bloomer

Steve Bloomer was the most prolific marksman of his day. An inside-forward with a deadly accurate shot, Bloomer began his career as an 18-year-old with Derby in 1892. He ended his career at the age of 40 in 1914 at the same club, although he did have a four-year spell at Middlesbrough along the way. These 22 years yielded a remarkable 352 League goals in 598 appearances. It was not until the 1936-37 season that Dixie Dean set a new mark, and only a handful of players have outscored him since. Bloomer's record 28 goals in just 23 games for England stood even longer, until the 1950s. The FA presented him with a portrait of himself when he won his 21st cap, which was a record at the time. After hanging up his boots, Bloomer took up a coaching job in Germany and was interned for the duration of the First World War.

FA CUP FINALS

1900	Bury	v	Southampton	4-0
1901	Tottenham H.	v	Sheffield United	3-1
1902	Sheffield United	v	Southampton	2-1
1903	Bury	v	Derby County	6-0
1904	Manchester City	v	Bolton Wanderers	1-0
1905	Aston Villa	v	Newcastle United	2-0
1906	Everton	v	Newcastle United	1-0
1907	Sheffield W.	v	Everton	2-1
1908	Wolverhampton W	v	Newcastle United	3-1
1909	Manchester Utd	v	Bristol City	1-0
1910	Newcastle United	v	Barnsley	2-0
1911	Bradford City	v	Newcastle United	1-0
1912	Barnsley	v	West Bromwich A.	1-0
1913	Aston Villa	v	Sunderland	1-0
1914	Burnley	v	Liverpool	1-0
1915	Sheffield United	v	Chelsea	3-0
1916-1919				no competition

BELOW: *The 1911 Cup Final played at Crystal Palace ended in a 2-2 draw forcing a mid-week replay at newly-completed Old Trafford. Newcastle were unlucky again being defeated by Bradford by one goal to nil. The Tyneside team had reached the Final 5 times in the last 7 years but had only lifted the trophy once - in 1910. During the 1909-10 season Manchester United took up residence at Old Trafford and Arsenal's new stadium at Highbury was completed in 1913.*

Newton Heath reformed as Manchester United

Manchester United also scaled the heights after some lean times at the turn of the century. By 1901 the Newton Heath club was in a parlous state, both on and off the field. The team was languishing in the Second Division and facing crippling debts. A winding-up order was issued and the team had to rely on fund-raising through bazaars and the like in order to fulfil its fixtures. In 1902 things improved dramatically when some wealthy local businessmen pumped much-needed funds into the club. The Phoenix-like revival prompted a call for a new name. Manchester Celtic and Manchester Central were considered; Manchester United was settled upon.

Mangnall masterminds title win

Legendary manager Ernest Mangnall arrived the following year, and after three top six finishes in Division Two, United won promotion in 1905-06 and made their debut in the top flight the following season. The team that was promoted already boasted Charlie Roberts, one of the outstanding half-backs of his day. Apart from his dominance on the pitch, Roberts was noted for bucking the usual trend regarding length of shorts, preferring to wear his well above the knee. This act of rebelliousness, together with

his vocal support of the Players' Union, was said to be one of the reasons why he won only three caps.

Mangnall knew he had to strengthen the team for an assault on the championship. He signed Billy Meredith from neighbours Manchester City, one of the transfer coups of the period. Meredith, who had scored the goal which beat Bolton in the 1904 Cup Final was an established star but arived at United under a cloud. There had been allegations of illegal payments at Manchester City and Meredith himself was implicated in a bribery scandal. All that was forgotten two years later when Manchester United became champions for the first time. Ten straight wins early in the 1907-08 season, including a 6-1 thrashing of defending champions Newcastle, gave United a lead that proved decisive. As champions, United took part in the inaugural Charity Shield match, in which they faced Southern League winners Queen's Park Rangers. The match took place at Stamford Bridge, United winning 4-0 after a replay.

United relocate to Old Trafford

The following season was disappointing as far as the league went, but it brought a first FA Cup success. In the Final United

beat mid-table side Bristol City 1-0, but along the way they had accounted for Newcastle, Everton and Blackburn, who occupied three of the top four places in the league that year.

1909-10 saw United finish empty-handed but it was noteworthy as the season in which the club took up residence at Old Trafford. The move to the new stadium, which cost £60,000 and could hold 100,000, was timely; for as United played host to Liverpool on 19 February 1910 to mark the beginning of a new era, part of the old Bank Street ground collapsed in a gale. In 1910-11, United's first full season at Old Trafford, they were crowned champions for the second time.

Teams from the Midlands and the North continued to dominate. Sunderland, Sheffield Wednesday, Blackburn and Everton were the other clubs which won league titles between 1900 and 1915. In that final campaign before war brought a 4-year hiatus, one of Lancashire's lesser lights very nearly made it to the top of the tree. Oldham would have won the championship had they beaten Liverpool in their final match; they lost and Everton snatched the title by a point.

BELOW: *A record crowd of over 120, 000 gather outside the Crystal Palace ground for a view of the 1913 FA Cup Final between Aston Villa and Sunderland.*

BOVRIL

Spurs set new record

For the emerging teams from the South success was sporadic. However, in 1901 it was a London team which created a record that will surely remain unequalled. Spurs, then in the Southern League, won the FA Cup, the only non-league side ever to win the trophy. They disposed of three Division One sides en route, Preston, West Bromwich Albion and holders Bury. They faced Sheffield United in the final, and most observers thought they were on the receiving end of a bad decision when 'keeper Clawley was adjudged to have made a save behind his line. A goal was given and the game ended 2-2. A 3-1 victory in the replay at Bolton meant that any error hadn't been too costly. Sandy Brown was the Spurs' hero, netting a record 15 times during the Cup run, including three in the two Finals. 110,000 watched the first encounter at Crystal Palace, a record that has been beaten only twice since. Some commentators did note that the team consisted entirely of players from the provinces and Scotland, and as such the victory could hardly be regarded as a revival of the capital's footballing fortunes. Spurs were elected to the league in 1908, winning promotion to Division One at the first attempt.

Arsenal's rise was more steady. It wasn't until 1904-05 -11 years after becoming a League club - that the Gunners made it into the top flight. Several seasons of consolidation followed before the club was relegated in 1912-13.

This proved to be a blessing in disguise, as it precipitated Chairman Henry Norris's decision to relocate to Highbury. New neighbours Spurs were none too pleased with the decision, creating a rivalry that continues unabated.

Chelsea win league status in five months

Chelsea's entry into the league was remarkable in itself. At the start of 1905 the club didn't exist, yet just five months later it was elected to Division Two. Founder Gus Mears was behind this amazing rise up the ladder. He acquired the Stamford Bridge Athletic ground, signed a group of players and then, in May, saw the club's application to join the Second Division accepted. Both divisions were expanded from 18 to 20 clubs, and Chelsea joined the ranks with a club that would have rather less of an impact on the game, Clapham Orient. Chelsea finished third in their debut season, while Clapham Orient propped up the table. Chelsea were promoted to the First Division the following year.

BELOW: *The 1914 Cup Final in which Burnley defeated Liverpool by one goal scored in the 58th minute. This was the fourth year in succession that the Final had ended with a 1-0 scoreline.*

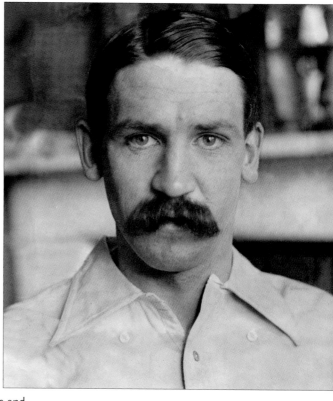

ABOVE: *Kenneth Hunt was born in Oxford in 1884. While studying for a degree he played football for Oxford University. In 1906 he signed for Wolverhampton Wanderers and played a significant part in the 3-1 defeat of hot favourites Newcastle United in the 1908 Cup Final when he scored the opening goal. After 40 minutes a poor clearance went straight to Hunt who fired a tremendous shot past United keeper Lawrence. Hunt remained an amateur player and played his first game for England against Italy in 1907. He was also selected to play for England in the 1908 Olympic Games in London. England won the gold medal by beating Denmark 2-0 on 24th October, 1908.*

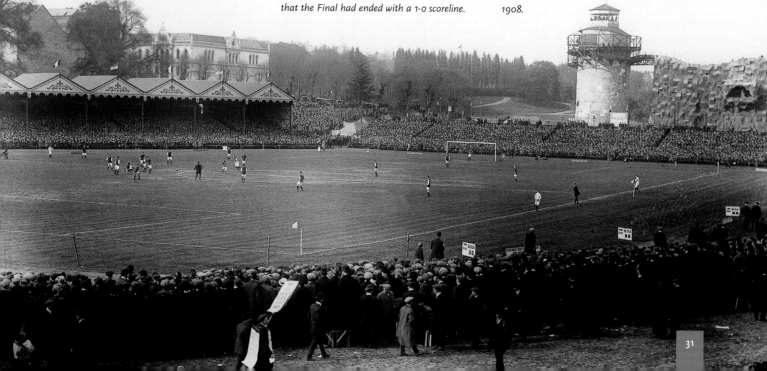

"Khaki Final"

In 1914-15 Chelsea finished second from bottom in the league but reached their first Cup Final. They failed to reproduce their best form, however, and went down 3-0 to Sheffield United. The Yorkshire club hoisted a brand-new trophy aloft, the third in the competition's history. The design of the previous cup had been copied by a regional competition, and the FA decided to present it to Lord Kinnaird for his services to the game and have a new one made.

The Chelsea-Sheffield United match was dubbed "The Khaki Final" because of the number of uniformed spectators present. Football had come in for a lot of criticism for completing the 1914-15 programme, hostilities having broken out the previous August. Questions had been asked in the House of Commons over the issue, but the game did serve as an effective recruiting sergeant. Rousing speeches were made at matches, and both players and supporters enlisted in droves, long before conscription was introduced. At the end of the Khaki Final Lord Derby gave a speech, saying: "You have played with one another and against one another for the Cup. Play with one another for England now".

Brief moment in the limelight

The period immediately prior to World War One saw some unheralded clubs enjoy a brief moment in the spotlight. Apart from Oldham's agonising experience in the 1914-15 championship race, Bradford City and Barnsley also tasted success. In 1910-11 Bradford finished 5th in the league and beat Newcastle in the Cup Final. Division Two side Barnsley made it to two Finals in three seasons, losing to Newcastle in 1910 and beating West Brom in 1912. Between those two appearances the club had finished 19th in Division Two and been forced to apply for re-election.

Both of Barnsley's Cup appearances and Bradford's 1911 victory had gone to replays, prompting the FA to institute extra time from 1913. It wasn't needed that year - a 1-0 win for Villa over Sunderland - or the next, when Burnley ran out 1-0 winners over Liverpool. That 1914 Final marked the first time that a reigning monarch attended football's showpiece. King George V handed Burnley's skipper Tommy Boyle the Cup and at the same time rang down the curtain on the Crystal Palace as a final venue.

BELOW: *Tottenham Hotspur, winners of the FA Cup 1901, the only non-league side to win the trophy since the league was founded in 1888. In the first years of the new century the northern clubs still dominated league and Cup football. The 'great eight' comprised Everton, Sheffield Wednesday, Newcastle, Sunderland, Liverpool, Aston Villa and both Manchester clubs. Arsenal was the first southern side to be admitted to the First Division in the 1903-4 season with Chelsea following on in 1907.*

BOTTOM: *1913 FA Cup finalists Sunderland. Despite winning the league that year, the team lost the cup final 1-0 to Aston Villa. (L-R, Back row: J. Butler, F. Cuggy, H.M. Ness, J. Richardson, H. Martin, W. Tinsley, J. Mordue. Front row: W. Cringan, C. Gladwin, C.M Buchan, C. Thompson, H.F. Low, G. Holly).*

Decline of gentlemen-amateurs

Until the early 1900s the England side invariably included a number of amateurs. The cream of the public school and university systems could still hold their own against the professionals. Players such as Charles Burgess Fry and Gilbert Oswald Smith were outstanding performers. The latter was rated a better goalscorer than the legendary Steve Bloomer.

Many of the top gentlemen-amateurs turned out for Corinthians, who regularly beat the top league sides they came up against. In 1900 Corinthians put eight past Wolves and in 1904 thrashed Cup holders Bury 10-3. In March 1902 England fielded just one amateur in the side that drew with Wales in Wrexham. In April 1905 Spurs' centre-forward Vivian Woodward was the sole amateur in the side which beat Scotland 1-0 at Crystal Palace. The decline of the amateur international was hastened in 1907, when the FA sought to bring all players under their jurisdiction. The amateurs demurred and formed the Amateur Football Association. This marked a parting of the ways, and as top sides

such as Corinthians were now prevented from testing themselves against league opposition, they soon lost their edge and a proud tradition was consigned to the history books.

Ibrox disaster

On the international front this period is remembered chiefly for a tragedy. When Scotland and England met at Ibrox Park on 5 April 1902, 25 people were killed when a section of the stand collapsed. The game eventually continued and ended 1-1 but the result was later expunged from the record books.

BELOW: *1914 FA Cup finalists Liverpool were beaten 1-0 by Burnley at Crystal Palace. (L-R, Back row: D. McKinley, E. Longworth, K. Campbell, T. Fairfoul, R. Purcell, T. Miller. Front Row: J. Sheldon, W. Metcalf, R. Ferguson, H.C. Lowe, W. Lacey, J. Nicholl.)*

BOTTOM: *Among the crowd at the 1914 Cup Final was King George V, the first monarch ever to attend the event. The route between Buckingham Palace and Crystal Palace was lined with cheering crowds. Ironically, the public schools that had done so much to develop the game of football had now adopted rugby as their sport and football was the passion of the working classes.*

The 1913 Cup Final brought together two of the
most successful clubs in the league: Aston Villa
and Sunderland. In the 1912-13 season both sides
had the potential of winning the Double, which
Aston Villa had succeeded in doing in 1896-7.
In the event, Sunderland took the league title
and Villa won the Cup, defeating Sunderland by
one goal to nil in front of a record crowd of over
120,000. The scores might have been higher since
the Birmingham team were without their keeper
for part of the second half and Villa's Charlie
Wallace missed a penalty, only the second ever
awarded in an FA Cup Final.

STAND D.N° 106 to 705
(GREY CARDS.

STAND D.N° 1 to 405
(GREY CARDS.

Football becomes Olympic sport

International football was still largely confined to fixtures against the other home nations. But in 1908 football made its official debut as an Olympic sport. An England side was chosen to represent the United Kingdom and took the gold medal. England retained the Olympic crown in 1912; on both occasions the beaten finalists were Denmark.

FIFA founded

Bohemia had sought entry into the 1912 Olympic tournament but had been unable to compete since the country was not a member of FIFA. The Federation International de Football Association had been formed in Paris on 21 May 1904. France, Belgium, Switzerland, Denmark, the Netherlands, Sweden and Spain were the founding members of world football's new governing body, England joining the following year.

BELOW: *Over 70,000 people officially attended the Cup Final in 1914 but many preferred to spectate from vantage points outside the ground. This was the last time that Crystal Palace was to play host to the Final, the first time being in 1895 when Aston Villa's John Devey scored a goal forty seconds into the game.*

LEFT: *Sheffield United defeated Chelsea 3-1 in the 1915 FA Cup final. Little did the public realise that five years of grim tragedy would elapse before another final would be played. (L-R, Back row: English, Gough, Brelsford, Sturgess. Middle: Cook, Fazackerley, Utley, Masterman, Evans. Front: Simmons, Kitchen).*

Football in the trenches

As the 1914-15 season drew to a close it was clear that football could not continue. The decision to suspend the League and Cup competition came as no surprise, and the global conflict brought forth the heroic and less seemly side of the footballing fraternity. The unsavoury element occurred in a game between Manchester United and Liverpool on 2 April 1915. The political uncertainties prompted a number of players to conspire and rig the result - a 2-0 win for United - and make a killing at the bookmaker's. Suspicions were aroused and the subsequent inquiry resulted in eight players receiving life bans. After the war the Football League took a more charitable view of those who had fought for their country. The exception was Manchester United's Enoch "Knocker" West, whose ban remained in force after he continued to deny all charges.

Greater nobility was shown in the famous Christmas Day truce of 1914, when German and British soldiers played an impromptu game in No-Man's-Land. And even in the height of battle football was often used as a morale booster. Members of some regiments invoked the names of their beloved clubs as they advanced, and even dribbled balls onto the battlefield. Back in England, regional football replaced the traditional competitions between 1915 and 1918. These were low-key affairs and fixtures were organised so as not to interfere with the war effort. After Armistice Day on 11 November 1918 the appetite of both clubs and supporters to reinstate the official programme was huge. There was even talk of getting a truncated FA Cup competition off the ground immediately. In the end the authorities decided in favour of starting afresh the following season, and 1919-20 thus became the first postwar campaign.

BELOW: *The 1915 Cup final was a subdued affair, held in Manchester on a damp afternoon before a crowd of only 50,000, many of whom were servicemen displaying signs of the injuries sustained in battle.*

1920-1929
A New Structure

Once the Great war was over, the appetite to quickly
reinstate the league and Cup competitions proper was huge.
The early months of 1919 saw all the clubs take stock.
After a four-year interruption they had to assess their playing
staffs and effect repairs to their stadiums. The administrators
were also busy. Divisions One and Two were immediately
expanded to 22 clubs, and within two years two regional
Third Divisions had been formed. This meant that the Football
League in 1921-22 comprised 86 clubs compared with just
40 prior to World War One.

Controversy as 5th-placed Arsenal gain promotion

The way in which Division One was expanded in 1919-20 got the new era off to a controversial start. The expectation was that the top two Second Division sides from the 1914-15 season, Derby and Preston, would simply be promoted. But the Football League decided that Arsenal would go up too. The Gunners had finished only 5th in that final pre-war season, and Chairman Henry Norris was said to have engaged in some feverish behind-the-scenes lobbying in order to get the club elected to the top table. Three promoted teams meant that a First Division club had to go. Tottenham had

finished bottom in 1914-15 and they were the obvious candidates. It took Spurs just one season to bounce back, but the circumstances in which they had swapped places with their north London rivals did nothing to promote harmony between the two clubs.

OPPOSITE BELOW: *A typical band of cup-tie enthusiasts who paraded the streets on their way to Stamford Bridge plentifully bedecked with rosettes and ribbons, and keeping up their spirits with rattles and other noisy instruments. Stamford Bridge, an impressive stadium built in 1904 by Chelsea with a capacity of 100,000 was to be the venue for the postwar Cup Finals until Wembley Stadium was completed in 1923.*

BELOW: *Aston Villa play Huddersfield in the 1920 Cup Final. Villa's winning goal was scored by Kirton who had joined the Birmingham side from Leeds City after the club had been forced to sell off its entire squad.*

OPPOSITE ABOVE: *The Aston Villa squad in 1921. (L-R, Back row: Ducat, Hampton, Boyman, Hardy, Edgley, Dorrell, Weston. Front row: Wallace, Kirton, Harrod, Stephenson, Thompson). Left: Aston Villa collect the Cup at Stamford Bridge in 1920.*

1919-20 DIVISION ONE		
1	West Bromwich Albion	60
2	Burnley	51
3	Chelsea	49
4	Liverpool	48
5	Sunderland	48
6	Bolton Wanderers	47
7	Manchester City	45
8	Newcastle United	43
9	Aston Villa	42
10	The Arsenal	42
11	Bradford PA	42
12	Manchester United	40
13	Middlesbrough	40
14	Sheffield United	40
15	Bradford City	39
16	Everton	38
17	Oldham	38
18	Derby County	38
19	Preston	38
20	Blackburn Rovers	37
21	Notts County	36
22	The Wednesday	23

Leeds expelled over illegal payments

The early drama of the 1919-20 campaign took place off the field, when Second Division side Leeds City were expelled from the league for making illegal payments. City, managed by Herbert Chapman, had won the Northern regional championship in 1918 and seemed to be a team on the up. After the allegations were made Chapman chose to put a match to the club's books rather than submit them for scrutiny. He was suspended and Port Vale took over Leeds' fixtures. For

Chapman and Leeds it was the parting of the ways, though both would rise again after a brief period in the wilderness. In 1920 the club reconstituted itself as Leeds United and returned to the fold. That same year Chapman, after a short spell with an engineering firm, also returned to the game. Over the next 14 years, first with Huddersfield Town and then with Arsenal, Chapman would take club management into a different realm.

ABOVE RIGHT: *Supporters of both Aston Villa and Huddersfield seemed full of confidence on their way to the 1920 Cup Final. Villa, who eventually won a closely fought contest 1-0 after extra time, had now won the Cup six times. They would only win the competition once more in the twentieth century - beating Manchester United in 1957.*

BELOW: *Cantrell, the Spurs centre-forward, and Bliss (right) inside-left, battling with defenders in the Wolves' goalmouth during the 1921 Cup Final.*
RIGHT: *Bliss gets past Woodward as the defender slips on the muddy surface. Heavy rain had created poor playing conditions and spectators were disappointed that the quality of the football suffered. Spurs' 1-0 win was the first southern victory in the Cup since 1901 when the London club last won the trophy.*

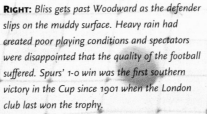

The rise of Huddersfield

In 1920 Huddersfield were in dire straits. The club was the poor relation to the town's rugby league side, and had even contemplated relocating lock, stock and barrel to Leeds. Things improved after the club acquired several of the players auctioned off by Leeds City. Huddersfield then made the most important signing of all: Herbert Chapman himself. In 1920 Huddersfield won promotion to the top flight for the first time and also made it to the FA Cup final, in which they went down 1-0 to Aston Villa. This was no flash in the plan; the best was yet to come. Chapman set to work using his uncanny knack for buying the right player at the right time and moulding individuals into a formidable unit. Probably the key acquisition was Villa's inside-forward Clem Stephenson, who arrived in March 1921 in a £4000 deal. Many thought 30-year-old Stephenson's best years were behind him, but Chapman made him captain and in the autumn of his career he enjoyed a golden period as he led Huddersfield on an extraordinary run of success. The first silverware came in 1922, when the Yorkshire club lifted the FA Cup. It was a dour affair, with Preston providing the opposition. The only goal came from the penalty spot after Huddersfield winger Billy Smith was brought down. Preston

seemed to have a legitimate case that the foul had been committed outside the box, but the referee waved this away and Smith himself stepped up to score. This game marked the last of three postwar finals to be contested at Stamford Bridge. By the following April the new Wembley Stadium would be ready.

Mathematicians needed to determine championship

In the next six seasons Huddersfield finished no lower than third in the league, and the club's remarkable run included a famous hat-trick of championships starting in 1923-24. This first league title was also the most dramatic. At the end of the season Huddersfield and Cardiff both had 57 points. Huddersfield's goals column read 60-33, Cardiff's 61-34. This

was an era in which goal average decided such issues and Huddersfield's was superior by a wafer-thin 0.024. Cardiff would not have needed to trouble the mathematicians had they converted a last-minute penalty in their final match at Birmingham. But a nervous Len Davies fired wide, the game ended in a goalless draw and Cardiff had to settle for the runners-up spot. Under the modern goal difference system, of course, the placings would have been reversed, Cardiff having scored one more goal than their rivals.

BELOW: *King George V presenting the cup to Arthur Grimsdell, captain of Tottenham Hotspur, after the 1921 Cup Final at Stamford Bridge.*
BOTTOM: *Herbert Chapman (back row, left) pictured with Huddersfield Town in 1921. Chapman is one of a select group of managers who have won the league championship with different clubs: Huddersfield Town in 1924 and 1925, Arsenal in 1931 and 1933.*

1920-21 DIVISION ONE

1	Burnley	59
2	Manchester City	54
3	Bolton Wanderers	52
4	Liverpool	51
5	Newcastle United	50
6	Tottenham Hotspur	47
7	Everton	47
8	Middlesbrough	46
9	The Arsenal	44
10	Aston Villa	43
11	Blackburn Rovers	41
12	Sunderland	41
13	Manchester United	40
14	West Bromwich Albion	40
15	Bradford City	39
16	Preston	39
17	Huddersfield	39
18	Chelsea	39
19	Oldham	33
20	Sheffield United	30
21	Derby County	26
22	Bradford PA	24

Chapman moves to Arsenal

Huddersfield retained their title in 1924-25, conceding just 28 goals all season. No club had ever won the championship with a better defensive record than that. Wednesday had been equally miserly in 1903-04 but that was in the days of a 34-match season.

Herbert Chapman laid the foundations for Huddersfield's hat-trick of league titles but before the third crown had been claimed he had taken up a new challenge. It would take him longer to shape his new club, Arsenal, into a championship-winning side, but by the end of the decade the Gunners would be setting the standards all other clubs had to measure themselves by.

ABOVE AND BELOW: *Going for goal: Decades before Denis Law perfected the art Bliss executes an overhead kick for Tottenham in the Cup Final against Wolverhampton Wanderers. Later in the game he tries a more conventional shot at goal.*
LEFT: *With his rosettes and cockerel, Tottenham's emblem, this fan left no doubt as to which side he supported.*
OPPOSITE ABOVE: *Stamford Bridge 1922: The Duke of York shakes hands with the Huddersfield team with Prince George and Wilson, the Huddersfield captain, behind him. Chapman's most important addition to his new team was Aston Villa's inside-forward Clem Stephenson for whom he paid £4000.*
OPPOSITE BELOW: *W.H. Smith of Huddersfield scores the winning goal from a disputed penalty in the 1922 final. Smith had been brought down by the Preston defence but it was generally agreed that the action took place outside the box.*

Rise and fall of West Brom and Burnley

Huddersfield apart, no club enjoyed a sustained period of success in the 1920s. West Bromwich Albion won the first postwar championship, 1919-20, for the only time in their history. Long before the decade was out the Midlands club was languishing in the Second Division. Burnley had finished runners-up to West Brom, and they took over the mantle in 1920-21. A 30-match unbeaten run - 21 wins and 9 draws - between early September and late March carried the Lancashire club to its first title. But once again decline quickly set in. After six seasons in the bottom half of the table Burnley finally suffered the drop in 1929-30.

Scott marshals mean Liverpool defence

Liverpool were the only club apart from Huddersfield to win two championships in this period. The team's success was built on a resilient defence, with the huge Irish goalkeeper Elisha Scott performing heroics and establishing himself as an Anfield legend. In 1921-22 Liverpool found the net just 63 times. Six teams had bettered that but none could match the 36 in the Goals Against column. The following year Liverpool held off the challenge of a skilful Sunderland side to retain their crown, and this time their defence was even more impenetrable: only 31 goals conceded in their 42 games, a new record. Liverpool didn't suffer the same fate as West Bromwich Albion and Burnley thereafter, but their form for the rest of the 1920s was erratic and they didn't mount another serious title challenge.

Gallacher becomes toast of Tyneside

Huddersfield then took charge, and their vice-like grip on the league was not broken until Newcastle claimed their 4th title in 1926-27. Their star was diminutive Scottish striker Hughie Gallacher, widely regarded as the greatest finisher of his era. Gallacher, who had joined Newcastle from Airdrie for £5500, hit 36 of the team's 96 league goals. Having missed four matches, this very nearly gave him a scoring ratio of a goal a game.

LEFT: *Frank Moss pictured in 1924. Moss played for Aston Villa and England and went on to captain both teams.*

1921-22 DIVISION ONE

1	Liverpool	57
2	Tottenham Hotspur	51
3	Burnley	49
4	Cardiff	48
5	Aston Villa	47
6	Bolton Wanderers	47
7	Newcastle United	46
8	Middlesbrough	46
9	Chelsea	46
10	Manchester City	45
11	Sheffield United	40
12	Sunderland	40
13	West Bromwich Albion	40
14	Huddersfield	39
15	Blackburn Rovers	38
16	Preston	38
17	The Arsenal	37
18	Birmingham City	37
19	Oldham	37
20	Everton	36
21	Bradford City	32
22	Manchester United	28

BELOW: *A panoramic photograph of the last Cup Final at Stamford Bridge before the move to Wembley. Smith's winning penalty kick for Huddersfield was the first to decide a Cup Final. Preston's goalkeeper, James Mitchell, had tried to distract Smith as he prepared to take the kick by moving about on the goal line. Following this incident, the rule was brought in which required the goalkeeper to remain still until the ball was kicked.*

Herbert Chapman

Herbert Chapman was the most successful manager of the 1920s and early 1930s, his influence on the game continuing long after his death in 1934. He had had an undistinguished playing career at Northampton, Sheffield United and Spurs, standing out more for his trademark yellow boots than for the quality of his play. He made his name during the First World war as manager of Leeds City, but in 1919 he was suspended over financial irregularities. He took over an ailing Huddersfield Town side in 1920 and within four years he transformed the club into championship winners. After retaining the title, Chapman moved to Highbury in 1925. Along with veteran inside-forward Charlie Buchan, Chapman reacted to a change in the offside law by introducing a fluid WM system, replacing the rigid 2-3-5 formation that most teams played. This involved the centre-half dropping into a purely defensive role, abandoning his usual role of providing the link between defence and attack. That "schemer's" job was filled by an inside forward, which meant a revolutionary 3-3-4 formation.

Chapman had an uncanny knack for spotting potential. He signed Cliff Bastin and paid a world record £10,890 for David Jack. It is said that when he met his opposite number at Bolton to discuss Jack's transfer, he arranged for the hotel waiter to to keep the drinks coming - but instructed that his own glass should contain nothing alcoholic. By the time the men got down to business the atmosphere was very convivial. Bolton did get a world record fee but Chapman still thought his underhand tactic had given him the better of the deal.

Alex James was acquired for slightly less than Jack, but it was his arrival from Preston in 1929 that sparked a phenomenal run of success.

With James playing that key schemer's role, Arsenal went on to win the championship three times in four years, and finished runners-up to Everton in 1931-32. There was also an FA Cup victory over Chapman's former club, Huddersfield, in 1930.

Chapman died just before Arsenal confirmed their third championship, but all the pieces were in place for further success. The Gunners' league titles of 1935 and 1938, together with another FA Cup victory in 1936, also owed much to the groundwork Chapman laid. His influence also spread to the international side, notably when England beat Italy in November 1934. Chapman's Arsenal provided seven of the players who beat the reigning world champions 3-2.

ABOVE LEFT: *Herbert Chapman made his name as manager of Leeds City during the First World War. After transforming Huddersfield he went on to even greater success at Arsenal.*

ABOVE: *Frank Barson was one of the game's best-known characters. He played 353 league games for five clubs, most notably for Aston Villa and Manchester United. He was considered one of the first "hard" men in football and was often sent off and suspended. As a commanding centre-half who liked to go forward he was powerful in the air. On Boxing Day in 1921 he scored with a header from almost 30 yards to give Aston Villa victory over Sheffield United.*

New offside law brings goal avalanche

Newcastle's record of 96 goals scored and 58 conceded in 1926-7 made for an interesting comparison with Huddersfield's performance two years earlier. In their second championship-winning season the Yorkshire club's goals column read 69-28, their defence proving even meaner than Liverpool's. For Newcastle to have scored 27 more goals but let in 30 more suggests a cavalier approach. But the chief reason for the surge in goalscoring was a change in the offside law which had been brought in in 1925.

Since the 1870s three players were required between the attacker and the goal for him to be onside. Over that 50-year period defences had got the offside trap down to a fine art. Newcastle themselves were arch-exponents. It is said that when one visiting team pulled into the city's train station and heard a guard's whistle, a wag chimed: "Blimey! Offside already!"

Under the new law only two players were now required between the attacking player and the goal for him to be onside. As most teams played the traditional 2-3-5 formation, forwards could now be onside with just the two full-backs to beat. There was a goal avalanche, which was exactly what the FA had wanted. On 29 August 1925 the first matches took place under the new system and the effect was immediate and dramatic. Villa beat Burnley 10-0, and in the following weeks there was a plethora of high-scoring games. 1703 goals were scored in Division One in 1925-26, an increase of over 500 on the previous season. Sterile, negative play might have been eliminated but not everyone was thrilled by the goal-fest. Some felt that goalscoring had become devalued and that the ingenuity and skill required to find the back of the net before the rule change was somewhat lacking under the revised system.

BOTTOM: *The 1923 Cup Final, played at the new Empire Stadium at Wembley between West Ham United and Bolton Wanderers, attracted the largest crowd ever seen at a football match in the country. The King was present and was one of the most keenly interested spectators. Here the nearest fans are seen cheering as the National Anthem is played.*

BELOW: *'The Cup Draw' was already part of tradition by the 1920s.*

Dixie Dean 1907-80

Middlesbrough's George Camsell is unfortunate that his name is not better known in footballing circles. Camsell scored 59 goals for Boro in 1926-27 as they won the Division Two title. His record lasted just one year. William "Dixie" Dean hit 60 for Everton the following season, a record which stands to this day.

Dean moved to Goodison Park for £3000 in 1925, having scored 27 goals in as many games for Tranmere Rovers. Everton were languishing in mid-table at the time, but Dean's phenomenal strike rate soon changed all that. Everton already had the championship sewn up when Arsenal came to Goodison on the last day of the 1927-28 season. 48,000 turned up to see if their 21-year-old goal machine, who had netted 57 times, could beat Camsell's record. Dean scored a hat-trick, the third goal, fittingly, coming from a towering far-post header eight minutes from time. He was imperious in the air, despite the fact that he stood just 5ft 10in tall.

Dean also hit 44 goals as Everton won the league title in 1931-32. He ended his career with 473 goals from 502 appearances in all competitive matches. 379 of those came in the league, putting him second to Arthur Rowley on the all-time list.

His 18 games for England yielded 16 goals. He ended his career at Notts County, then went to play in Ireland, but Everton was his greatest love. Dean died after watching his beloved team play Liverpool at Goodison Park on 1 March 1980.

60-goal Dean fires Everton to title

Everton rattled in 102 goals on their way to the 1927-28 championship. They weren't the first team to hit the magic ton mark, but it was a record-breaking campaign for one man: Dixie Dean. When Everton went into their final league fixture, a home clash with Arsenal, they were already confirmed as champions. Nevertheless, a vast crowd turned up to see if Dean, who had hit 57 goals, could break the individual scoring record. That was held by George Camsell, who had hit 59 for Second Division champions Middlesbrough a year earlier. Dean got the hat-trick he needed, ending the campaign with a phenomenal 60 goals to his name. Herbert Chapman wanted Dean to spearhead the Arsenal side he was building and asked Everton to name their price. Unsurprisingly, the Merseyside club was in no hurry to part with its prized asset.

Everton slipped to 18th the following season, and the decade ended with Wednesday on top of the pile. Having finished 16th and 14th in the two previous campaigns, Wednesday edged out Leicester and Villa to claim their third championship. It was to be their last appearance under the Wednesday banner; by the time they began the defence of their title in the summer of 1929 the club had officially been renamed Sheffield Wednesday.

Dixie Dean playing record

International Caps	16
International Goals	18
Total appearances	502
Total Goals	473

1922-23 DIVISION ONE

1	Liverpool	60
2	Sunderland	54
3	Huddersfield	53
4	Newcastle United	48
5	Everton	47
6	Aston Villa	46
7	West Bromwich Albion	45
8	Manchester City	45
9	Cardiff	43
10	Sheffield United	42
11	The Arsenal	42
12	Tottenham Hotspur	41
13	Bolton Wanderers	40
14	Blackburn Rovers	40
15	Burnley	38
16	Preston	37
17	Birmingham City	37
18	Middlesbrough	36
19	Chelsea	36
20	Nottingham Forest	34
21	Stoke	30
22	Oldham	30

ABOVE LEFT: *Dixie Dean, his record 60 goals in a season still stands today.*

ABOVE: *Arthur Grimsdell picture in 1923 during a cup tie match. Initially a centre-half, Spurs manager Peter McWilliam converted Grimsdell to a wing half, the position he would excel in for 18 years at the club.*

F A Cup moves to Wembley

The first three postwar FA Cup competitions were staged at Stamford Bridge. This was not a popular venue and in 1919-20 nearly proved embarrassing for the FA as Chelsea won through to the semi-finals. Villa saved the authorities from the headache of having one of the finalists playing at home. They beat Chelsea and went on to score a 1-0 win over Huddersfield in the Final. It was the Midland club's 6th win, a record for the competition. The next two Finals, won by Spurs and Huddersfield respectively, were uninspiring affairs which were also decided by a single goal. By the time Bolton met West Ham on 28 April 1923 the new Wembley Stadium was ready.

1923-24 DIVISION ONE	
1 Huddersfield	57
2 Cardiff	57
3 Sunderland	53
4 Bolton Wanderers	50
5 Sheffield United	50
6 Aston Villa	49
7 Everton	49
8 Blackburn Rovers	45
9 Newcastle United	44
10 Notts County	42
11 Manchester City	42
12 Liverpool	41
13 West Ham United	41
14 Birmingham City	39
15 Tottenham Hotspur	38
16 West Bromwich Albion	38
17 Burnley	36
18 Preston	34
19 The Arsenal	33
20 Nottingham Forest	32
21 Chelsea	32
22 Middlesbrough	22

BELOW: *A crowded street scene in Wembley which was to host the F A Cup Final for the rest of the century.*
LEFT: *The West Ham United team who lost to Bolton Wanderers in the 1923 cup final. (L-R: Richards, Ruffell, Brown, Tresadern, Moors, Watson, Young, Henderson, Kay, Bishop, Huffton).*

200,000 see first Wembley final

With a capacity of 127,000, Wembley was capable of holding 70,000 more fans than had turned up to watch the previous year's showpiece. Few thought there would be a problem. But West Ham were a popular Second Division side and the occasion captured the public's imagination. Estimates vary as to how many flooded into Wembley that day, the figure put anywhere from 150,000 to 200,000-plus. The official gate of 126,047 didn't take into account the thousands who poured into the stadium by climbing walls and shinning up drainpipes. The game was held up for 45 minutes as fans spilled onto the pitch. PC George Scorey and his white horse Billy were in the thick of things trying to restore order and duly took their place in the annals of the sport. A grateful FA gifted the officer complimentary tickets for subsequent finals but Scorey, who was not a football fan, never took up the offer.

ABOVE RIGHT: *A spectacular aerial view of PC George Scorey and his white horse, Billy, trying to restore order. Admission by ticket was not even considered because it was thought there was room for all. Ever since the showpiece game has been an all-ticket affair. With the postwar expansion of the leagues and the ever-increasing popularity of the game, the FA wanted a prestigious stadium to host national and Cup games. After rejecting the idea of developing Crystal Palace the decision was made to move to Wembley. Work didn't commence until January 1922 but the stadium was ready for the legendary 1923 Final.*

RIGHT: *Storming the turnstiles - a vivid glimpse of the invasion in progress. The crowd is seen clambering over the turnstiles and 'making tracks' for the arena, while a solitary policeman looks on helplessly.*

BELOW RIGHT: *Bolton's David Jack and Pym the goalkeeper (facing the camera) are among the players waiting on the pitch while the police push the people back. Officially the gate was 126,000 but the actual number was closer to 200,000. Police reinforcements were sent for and the game kicked off 45 minutes late.*

Hughie Gallacher

Hughie Gallacher stood barely 5ft. 6in. tall, yet he is rated as one of the best centre-forwards of all time. He played for Queen of the South and Airdrie before heading south to join Newcastle for £5500 in 1926. He quickly established himself as an idol on Tyneside after firing Newcastle to the championship in 1926-27, his first full season with the club. He hit 36 goals in 38 games during the campaign, which remains a club record. Gallacher was a complete striker and amazingly powerful in the air considering his lack of inches. He was capped 23 times for Scotland, scoring 22 goals. Gallacher's private life was more turbulent. He ended his days in straitened circumstances and threw himself under a train in 1957.

1923: The White Horse Final

Bolton Wanderers 2 - West Ham United 0

West Ham, in contention for promotion to Division One, played exciting, fast-moving football and their 5-2 defeat of Derby in the Cup semi-final enhanced this reputation. However, once the match got underway, it was only two minutes before Bolton's Jack opened the scoring and from then on West Ham never regained their stride. The game was disrupted after 11 minutes when the crowd surged back onto the pitch and after order was restored, the police rode along the touchline to prevent a recurrence. Just minutes after half-time, during which the teams were unable to leave the field, Bolton's J.R. Smith headed the ball, hitting the underside of the West Ham crossbar. The ball bounced inside the goal then back onto the field and although West Ham protested, the goal was given. The match ended in a 2-0 victory for Bolton whose keeper, Pym, was scarcely tested during the contest. Smith, scorer of the second goal, completed a personal 'double' having already won a Scottish Cup medal. Jack's contribution to his club's Cup run had been crucial to their success; he was the only man to score

in four of their matches leading up to the Final and his early goal at Wembley set Bolton on their way.

BELOW LEFT: *Seymour setting the seal on Newcastle United's victory in the 1924 Cup Final just before the final whistle. Although the Cup Final was between Newcastle and Aston Villa, the most successful club of the middle part of the decade was Herbert Chapman's Huddersfield Town who topped the league in 1924, 1925 and 1926. Huddersfield had been on the verge of bankruptcy after the war and narrowly escaped a forced merger with Leeds United.*

BELOW: *A Bolton player heads the ball at a critical moment following a corner forced by West Ham. Within two minutes of the late kick-off David Jack put Bolton ahead and Smith scored their second early in the second half. Bolton went on to win the Cup twice more before the end of the decade - in 1926 and 1929.*

Future Cup Finals to be all-ticket

The West Ham camp were rather less enamoured with Billy and the other police horses on duty that day in 1923. The Hammers claimed the pitch was badly churned up as a result, something which didn't suit their nimble forwards. Bolton's attackers seemed to cope well enough, however. David Jack scored Wembley's first-ever goal and Bolton ran out 2-0 winners. After the game the FA quickly realised that only good fortune had prevented a catastrophe. Cup Finals thereafter became all-ticket affairs to prevent a recurrence of the 1923 situation.

Bolton went on to lift the Cup in 1926 and 1929. Amazingly, in those three triumphs over a seven-year spell only 17 players were used. In 1926 Manchester City were the beaten side. City went on to lose their last league match at Newcastle the following week and were relegated. It was the first time that a club had had that particular double disappointment.

1924-25 DIVISION ONE	
1 Huddersfield	58
2 West Bromwich Albion	56
3 Bolton Wanderers	55
4 Liverpool	50
5 Bury	49
6 Newcastle United	48
7 Sunderland	48
8 Birmingham City	46
9 Notts County	45
10 Manchester City	43
11 Cardiff	43
12 Tottenham Hotspur	42
13 West Ham United	42
14 Sheffield United	39
15 Aston Villa	39
16 Blackburn Rovers	35
17 Everton	35
18 Leeds United	34
19 Burnley	34
20 The Arsenal	33
21 Preston	26
22 Nottingham Forest	24

RIGHT: *Sheffield United's goalkeeper, Sutcliffe, punches clear.*

BELOW: *Cardiff's goal under siege. Thousands of Welsh fans flocked to London in 1925 to support Cardiff City's bid to bring the FA trophy back with them to Wales. Strong defences on both sides meant that the final score was 1-0 and Sheffield United won the cup for the fourth time in their history.*

1925-26 DIVISION ONE

1	Huddersfield	57
2	The Arsenal	52
3	Sunderland	48
4	Bury	47
5	Sheffield United	46
6	Aston Villa	44
7	Liverpool	44
8	Bolton Wanderers	44
9	Manchester United	44
10	Newcastle United	42
11	Everton	42
12	Blackburn Rovers	41
13	West Bromwich Albion	40
14	Birmingham City	40
15	Tottenham Hotspur	39
16	Cardiff	39
17	Leicester City	38
18	West Ham United	37
19	Leeds United	36
20	Burnley	36
21	Manchester City	35
22	Notts County	33

ABOVE: *A sea of umbrellas as a shower of rain falls during the opening ceremony of the 1925 Cup Final.*

ABOVE RIGHT: *Joe Smith, Bolton Wanderers' captain, showing the FA cup to a cheering crowd from the window of a 'motor-coach' while leaving Wembley after Bolton's 2-0 victory over West Ham.*

RIGHT: *Joe Smith flanked by David Jack and Goalkeeper Pym. Bolton won the FA Cup again just three years after the victory over West Ham when they defeated Manchester City by a single goal scored by Jack in 1926.*

David Jack

David Jack was 29 years old when Herbert Chapman targeted him as the man to replace Charlie Buchan after the latter retired at the end of the 1927-28 season. Jack had already had a glittering career at Bolton, with whom he won two FA Cup winners' medals. An inside-forward with terrific ball skills and a keen eye for goal, Jack scored the first-ever goal in a Wembley showpiece, the famous "White Horse Final" in which Bolton beat West Ham 2-0.

Chapman caused a stir when he paid £10,890 to bring Jack to Highbury, doubling the previous transfer record. It proved an astute move, however, as Jack was a key figure in the all-conquering Arsenal side of the 1930s. He picked up three championship medals and also made it a hat-trick of Cup successes when Arsenal beat Huddersfield in the 1930 final.

ABOVE: *David Jack watches the ball soar into the net as he scores the goal that won the Cup for Bolton Wanderers in 1926.*

BELOW: *England's Billy Walker scores against Scotland in the last international match of the 1924 season played at Wembley before 65,000 spectators. Harper, Scotland's goalkeeper rushes out in an attempt to save. The game finished all square at 1-1. Scotland's next visit to Wembley 4 years later ended in a famous 5-1 victory.*

Football takes to the airwaves

The excitement of domestic football continued to draw huge crowds. The minimum entrance fee had been raised from sixpence to one shilling, but football remained cheap entertainment for the masses. Inevitably, it also attracted the new broadcast media. 22 January 1927 saw the first radio commentary of a football match, a clash between Arsenal and Sheffield United. To enable the listeners to visualise proceedings, a pitch divided into numbered squares was published in Radio Times. As the commentators described the play they also reported in which square the action was taking place.

ABOVE: *An aerial photograph of the crowded Wembley Stadium during the Cup Final in which Bolton defeated Manchester City by 1-0 watched by 92,000 people. Despite reaching the Cup Final and scoring 89 goals in the 1925-6 season, Manchester City were relegated to the Second Division along with Notts County and Leeds.*

A change in the offside rule came into effect in the 1925-6 season. Three defenders between the attacker and the goal were no longer necessary to remain onside, two would suffice. The tally of goals scored soared at the beginning of the season until defenders learned to cope with the change.

BELOW: *Everton, the Football League first division champions, with the trophy after their match against Arsenal in 1928. (L-R: Cook (trainer) Critchley, Martin, Kelly, Cresswell, Virr, Mr. W.C. Cuff, Hart, Dean, Davies, Weldon, O'Donnell, Troup).*

Bolton and Jack again

The 1926 Cup Final between Lancashire sides Bolton and Manchester City kept the crowds on tenterhooks right until the last minutes of the game. Bolton had the better of the match and the Manchester side seemed to be nervous at the outset. But Pym, the Bolton keeper was called upon to make many saves during the afternoon, most spectacularly when he stopped a dangerous header from Manchester's Johnson in the second half. With just minutes to go, David Jack, standing in front of the Manchester goal, received the ball from Vizard. Jack grasped the opportunity and launched the ball into the back of the net, scoring his second goal in an FA Cup Final and winning the trophy for Bolton.

BELOW: *Goalmouth action. A late goal gave Bolton the Cup for the second time in three years.*
RIGHT: *The heroes of the day receive boisterous congratulations as they leave the Wembley grandstand with the FA Cup.*

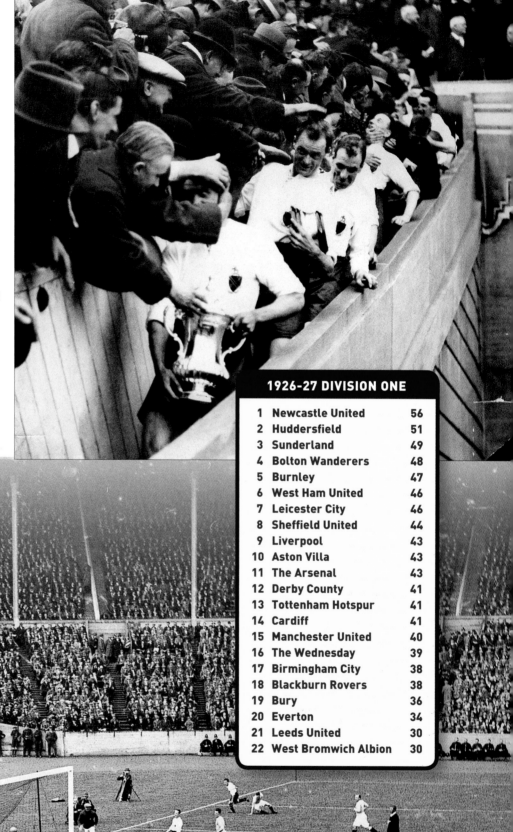

1926-27 DIVISION ONE	
1 Newcastle United	56
2 Huddersfield	51
3 Sunderland	49
4 Bolton Wanderers	48
5 Burnley	47
6 West Ham United	46
7 Leicester City	46
8 Sheffield United	44
9 Liverpool	43
10 Aston Villa	43
11 The Arsenal	43
12 Derby County	41
13 Tottenham Hotspur	41
14 Cardiff	41
15 Manchester United	40
16 The Wednesday	39
17 Birmingham City	38
18 Blackburn Rovers	38
19 Bury	36
20 Everton	34
21 Leeds United	30
22 West Bromwich Albion	30

"Wembley Wizards" thrash England

International football in the 1920s began on a sour note. The FA withdrew from FIFA over the question of rejoining competition with the defeated Axis powers, a rift that rumbled on until 1924. The late 1920s saw the England team suffer two reverses which became milestones in the record books. The first came on 31 March 1928, when Scotland came to Wembley and handed England a 5-1 thrashing. Alex Jackson, Alex James and Hughie Gallacher were among the stars who would go down in history as the "Wembley Wizards".

Continental football on the rise

Perhaps an even more significant defeat came on 15 May the following year. England went to Madrid and lost 4-3 to Spain, their first-ever defeat at the hands of a foreign side. This didn't surprise everyone. There were already rumblings from some commentators, who argued that English teams would do well to look to their continental cousins, who put greater emphasis on coaching and training. This was an era in which many English coaches were adherents of the "ball starvation" philosophy, denying players too much ball-work during the week so that they would be hungry for it on match days.

ABOVE: *England's goalkeeper, Brown, clearing from a corner kick in the international match with Wales at Wrexham in 1927. The game finished in a 3-3 draw.*

BELOW: *1928: Blackburn's Roscamp charges towards Mercer, the Huddersfield keeper, and seconds later scored when Mercer lost the ball. The 1928 Cup Final brought fewer surprises and upsets than that held the previous year when Cardiff City defeated Arsenal and carried the cup to Wales, but Roscamp's first goal scored in the opening minutes of the match was an exciting start. Huddersfield were outplayed by the Blackburn team, losing the match by three goals to one.*

FA CUP FINALS

Year		v		Score
1920	Aston Villa	v	Hudderfield T.	1-0
1921	Tottenham H.	v	Wolverhampton W.	1-0
1922	Huddersfield T.	v	Preston N.E.	1-0
1923	Bolton Wanderers	v	West Ham United	2-0
1924	Newcastle United	v	Aston Villa	2-0
1925	Sheffield United	v	Cardiff City	1-0
1926	Bolton Wanderers	v	Manchester City	1-0
1927	Cardiff City	v	Arsenal	1-0
1928	Blackburn Rovers	v	Huddersfield T.	3-1
1929	Bolton Wanderers	v	Portsmouth	2-0

FA Cup leaves England

One of the big Cup stories of the decade came in 1926-27. Arsenal and Cardiff were both mid-table sides when they won through to the Wembley Final. Cardiff boasted eight internationals, all of whom were well known to Gunners' 'keeper Dan Lewis, who had also been capped by Wales. The game was settled when Lewis fumbled a speculative shot by Cardiff centre-forward Hugh Ferguson. It rolled agonisingly over the line and the FA Cup left England for the only time in its history. Lewis later blamed the slippery sheen on his new jersey for the blunder, and thereafter Arsenal always made sure that new kit was washed before it was worn.

ABOVE: *Portsmouth goalkeeper Gilfillan makes a good save under pressure from a Bolton attacker in the 1929 Cup Final. His outstanding performance, however, couldn't stop Bolton running out 2-0 winners.*
RIGHT: *Ours again. Blackburn players show off the Cup from a motor-coach as the team leave Wembley.*

BELOW RIGHT: *Part of the excited crowd at the 1929 Cup Final. Football remained cheap entertainment and now commentary could be followed on the radio.*

1927-28 DIVISION ONE	
1 Everton	53
2 Huddersfield	51
3 Leicester City	48
4 Derby County	44
5 Bury	44
6 Cardiff	44
7 Bolton Wanderers	44
8 Aston Villa	43
9 Newcastle United	43
10 Arsenal	41
11 Birmingham City	41
12 Blackburn Rovers	41
13 Sheffield United	40
14 The Wednesday	39
15 Sunderland	39
16 Liverpool	39
17 West Ham United	39
18 Manchester United	39
19 Burnley	39
20 Portsmouth	39
21 Tottenham Hotspur	38
22 Middlesbrough	37

Bolton's third triumph in six years

1929 was a remarkable year for Bolton Wanderers who appeared in their third Cup Final since the fixture had first been staged at Wembley in 1923. The game, against Portsmouth, ended in 2-0 victory for the northern team and Pym, the Bolton keeper, kept a clean sheet for the third time in the final. This victory in 1929 brough Lancashire's tally of Cup wins to 17 since the competition was established in 1871.

However, the trophy didn't leave the capital straight away because the team, taking the Cup with it, attended a concert at the London Palladium before returning. In response to calls from the audience, Bolton's captain Seddon came up on to the stage so that the crowd would have a better view.

LEFT: *Thirteen minutes before the final whistle Gilfillan, the Portsmouth goalkeeper, stumbles when he rushes out to intercept a shot and the ball is deflected off his team-mate Mackie and crosses the line. Here, Mackie is trying to control the spinning ball but can't prevent the goal.*

BELOW: *The Prince of Wales presents the cup to Seddon, the captain of Bolton Wanderers in 1929.*

BOTTOM: *Bolton's goalkeeper Pym stops a shot by Weddle, the Portsmouth centre-forward.*

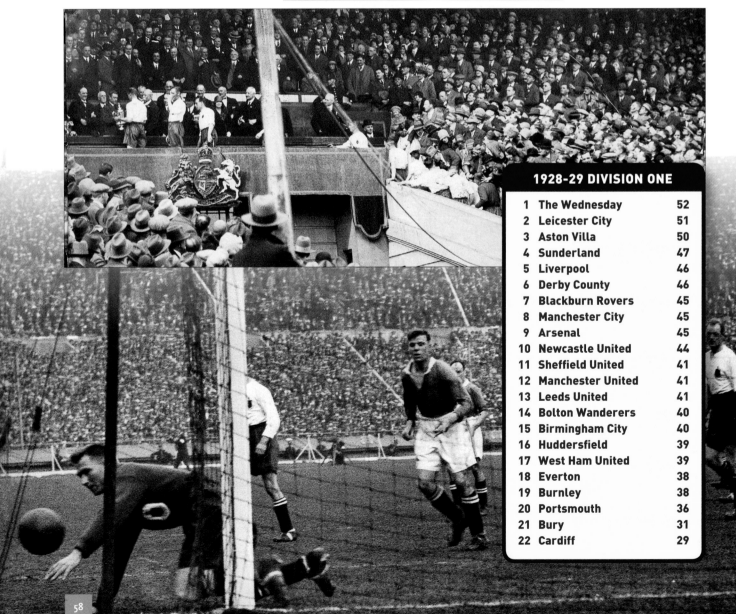

1928-29 DIVISION ONE	
1 The Wednesday	52
2 Leicester City	51
3 Aston Villa	50
4 Sunderland	47
5 Liverpool	46
6 Derby County	46
7 Blackburn Rovers	45
8 Manchester City	45
9 Arsenal	45
10 Newcastle United	44
11 Sheffield United	41
12 Manchester United	41
13 Leeds United	41
14 Bolton Wanderers	40
15 Birmingham City	40
16 Huddersfield	39
17 West Ham United	39
18 Everton	38
19 Burnley	38
20 Portsmouth	36
21 Bury	31
22 Cardiff	29

1929-30 DIVISION ONE

1	Sheffield Weds	60
2	Derby County	50
3	Manchester City	47
4	Aston Villa	47
5	Leeds United	46
6	Blackburn Rovers	45
7	West Ham United	43
8	Leicester City	43
9	Sunderland	43
10	Huddersfield Town	43
11	Birmingham City	41
12	Liverpool	41
13	Portsmouth	40
14	Arsenal	39
15	Bolton Wanderers	39
16	Middlesbrough	38
17	Manchester United	38
18	Grimsby Town	37
19	Newcastle United	37
20	Sheffield United	36
21	Burnley	36
22	Everton	35

Arsenal's first major honour

Fittingly, the 1930 FA Cup Final saw Huddersfield take on Arsenal, the team of the 1920s against the team which would dominate the 1930s. By now Herbert Chapman had forged a side capable of beating his former club. Arsenal won the match 2-0, Highbury's first major honour. Since Chapman's arrival five years earlier, Arsenal had spent much of the time in mid-table, saving their best form for the Cup. That was all about to change.

BELOW LEFT: *The Portsmouth team is introduced to the Prince of Wales before the start of the 1929 Cup Final. Bolton are without their 29-year-old star player David Jack on this occasion having agreed to sell him to Arsenal for the record sum of £10,890.*

BELOW: *Eddie Hapgood, a key defender in Herbert Chapman's Arsenal side who were to dominate the next decade.*

1930-1945
The Rise of Southern Clubs

English football in the 1930s was dominated by one club: Arsenal. The Gunners won the championship five times, and only once, in 1929-30, did they fail to finish in the top six. There were also three FA Cup Final appearances, two of them victorious, and five wins in the Charity Shield. Under Herbert Chapman Arsenal took professional football to a new level, and even after the legendary manager's death the Gunners continued to set the pace in the domestic game.

Cameras at Highbury

Fittingly, the team of the decade became the first to be filmed for television. In 1937, a decade after radio coverage of football had been established, the cameras rolled for a practice match at Highbury. With the age of television still in its infancy, and the ownership of a set a rarity, it is doubtful whether those present that day realised the role that televised football would come to play in the nation's cultural landscape.

LEFT: *Eddie Hapgood was Arsenal's powerful full-back who led his team to five championship medals and two F A cup victories. He also captained England 21 times in the thirties.*
BELOW RIGHT: *Arsenal manager Herbert Chapman chatting with Alex James. Chapman's mighty Arsenal team won the League five times during the 1930s.*
BOTTOM: *Goalmouth action in the England v Scotland international at Wembley in April 1930.*

OPPOSITE ABOVE: *Four of the Arsenal players named for the England team to meet world champions Italy at Highbury in November 1934. L-R; Copping, Hapgood, Moss and Bowden. The contest, later dubbed "The Battle of Highbury" ended in a 3-2 win for England but commentators were critical of the Italians' behaviour. Copping, Drake, Moss and Bastin all needed treatment for injuries incurred and Hapgood's nose was broken when he was hit in the face.*
OPPOSITE BELOW: *1931: West Bromwich Albion v Birmingham: Pearson, the Albion goalkeeper, dashes across to meet a shot that went past the post. West Brom had the better of the Final with Richardson scoring both goals. Despite a quick equaliser scored by Bradford and Gregg's early disallowed goal, Birmingham never looked in contention to win.*

Championship goes south for the first time

In 1930-31 Arsenal not only won the championship for the first time but also became the first southern club to do so since the inception of the league 43 years earlier. The team lost just four games and notched 66 points, a record that would stand for 38 years. In only one of their 42 league fixtures did they fail to score. Interestingly, the Gunners' home and away records were identical: Won 14, Drew 5, Lost 2. Jack Lambert top-scored with 38 goals, but all the forwards made handsome contributions. David Jack hit 31 goals, while the brilliant wingers Cliff Bastin and Joe Hulme scored 28 and 14 respectively.

An aggregate 127 goals was not quite enough to set a new record, however. That honour went to runners-up Aston Villa, for whom Tom "Pongo" Waring netted 49 times. Villa scored 128 goals in that campaign, which remains a record in English football's premier division.

1930-31 DIVISION ONE

1	Arsenal	66
2	Aston Villa	59
3	Sheffield Wednesday	52
4	Portsmouth	49
5	Huddersfield	48
6	Derby County	46
7	Middlesbrough	46
8	Manchester City	46
9	Liverpool	42
10	Blackburn Rovers	42
11	Sunderland	41
12	Chelsea	40
13	Grimsby	39
14	Bolton Wanderers	38
15	Sheffield United	38
16	Leicester City	36
17	Newcastle United	36
18	West Ham United	36
19	Birmingham City	36
20	Blackpool	32
21	Leeds United	31
22	Manchester United	22

Hard-fought Villa-Blues Derby

OPPOSITE: *Some of the large crowd that watched the hard-fought contest between Aston Villa and Birmingham at Villa Park in October 1930. The game provided an abundance of thrills and ended in a draw, each side scoring in the first half.*

ABOVE: *Huddersfield Town's forward line: Luke, Kelly, Mangnall, McLean and Smith training before their FA Cup final match with Arsenal in 1930.*

OPPOSITE ABOVE: *King George V shakes hands with the Huddersfield Town team before the Wembley showpiece.*

BELOW: *Victory – and the Cup. West Brom captain Glidden, surrounded by his elated team mates, carries the Cup after defeating their neighbours Birmingham 2-1. Second Division West Brom were the first team to win promotion and the FA Cup in the same year. Aston Villa also entered the record book in 1931, finishing the season with 128 goals, 49 of which were attributed to Pongo Waring, the season's top marksman.*

RIGHT: *Would-be referees take a practical examination using chess pawns to represent players before they appear in front of the Essex County FA Referees Committee.*

Promotion and Cup "double" for West Brom

LEFT: *Officials of the Football Association meet at their headquarters in Lancaster Gate to make the draw for the fourth round of the FA Cup.*
BELOW: *December 1932: Viennese goalkeeper Hiden stops an attack on the Austrian goal by England's Jimmy Hampson at Stamford Bridge. Austria, coached by ex–Bolton player Jimmy Hogan, and recognised as one of the most impressive teams in Europe, were defeated by 4 goals to 3 in an exciting contest. Had Herbert Chapman had his way, Austrian keeper Rudi Hiden would have joined Arsenal in 1930 but the Ministry of Labour refused to allow his transfer from Wiener Sportklub to protect the jobs of British goalkeepers.*

That season's Cup Final was an all-Midlands affair. Second Division side West Bromwich Albion came out on top against Division One strugglers Birmingham City, becoming the first club to win promotion and the Cup in the same season.

West Brom went up after finishing runners-up to Everton. The following season, 1931-32, the Liverpool club continued an extraordinary run of fluctuating fortunes. Champions in 1928, relegated in 1930, promoted in 1931, Everton lifted the title again in their first season back in the top flight. In winning the Second and First Division championships in successive seasons Everton emulated the achievement of their city rivals Liverpool between 1904 and 1906. Unsurprisingly, the key to Everton's revival was their goalscoring hero Dixie Dean, whom the club had managed to hold on to despite suffering the drop. Dean couldn't quite match his feat of 1927-28, but his 44 goals were enough to make him the number one marksman once again.

1931-32 DIVISION ONE

1	Everton	56
2	Arsenal	54
3	Sheffield Wednesday	50
4	Huddersfield	48
5	Aston Villa	46
6	West Bromwich Albion	46
7	Sheffield United	46
8	Portsmouth	45
9	Birmingham City	44
10	Liverpool	44
11	Newcastle United	42
12	Chelsea	40
13	Sunderland	40
14	Manchester City	38
15	Derby County	38
16	Blackburn Rovers	38
17	Bolton Wanderers	38
18	Middlesbrough	38
19	Leicester City	37
20	Blackpool	33
21	Grimsby	32
22	West Ham United	31

FIFA unveils World Cup

The main event in international football in the interwar period was the establishment of a World Cup competition. In 1930, when the inaugural tournament was staged in Uruguay, the prevailing attitude in England was that the country which had given football to the world remained its pre-eminent exponent. The defeat by Spain in 1929 was dismissed as an aberration, and a 7-1 win over the same opposition in 1931 seemed to confirm that view. A few lone voices suggested that English football could learn a thing or two from overseas opposition, but when FIFA unveiled its new tournament, none of the home countries was champing at the bit to be included.

ENGLAND BEAT THE SCOTS

TOP: *England's goalkeeper, Pearson, keeping out a determined attack from Scotland's forwards in the 1932 Wembley international. England won the game 3-0. Even though England had not competed in the inaugural World Cup, most spectators considered English football to be the best in the world.*

ABOVE LEFT: *50,000 fans packed into Highbury to watch the league champions.*

ABOVE: *Derby forwards: Crooks, Hutchinson, Bowers, Ramage and Duncan.*

England side run by committee

England certainly lagged behind some of the Continental sides regarding the employment of a manager for the national team. While other countries saw the value in having a single supremo responsible for international team affairs, the England side was still chosen by the International Selection Committee, which had been formed in 1888. The vagaries of this unwieldy system included political manoeuvrings. Committee members who favoured a particular player would try to garner support for their man, and some horse-trading undoubtedly went on. There was little consistency, and in the 1930s nearly a hundred players were capped, although many of these may have played just once or twice before being discarded.

Herbert Chapman was quick to recognise the shortcomings of this system and he persuaded the FA to allow him to take charge of the England side which toured Italy and Switzerland in May 1933. Chapman thus became the international side's only pre-war manager. England drew with Italy and beat Switzerland, but it would be another decade before the authorities took the idea on board seriously.

BELOW LEFT: *The 'over the line' Final: Jack, the Arsenal inside-right, gets his head to the ball in front of the Newcastle goal, but McInroy is ready to save the shot. The 1932 Cup Final was a battle between the North and the South remembered for Newcastle's equaliser which came in the 42nd minute after John had put Arsenal ahead. Arsenal defenders thought the ball had crossed the bye-line before Allen scored for Newcastle but referee Mr W.P. Harper thought otherwise and the goal was given. Allen scored again in the 71st minute and Newcastle took the Cup for the first time since 1924.*
BOTTOM: *Blackpool playing at home in 1933 - the year they finished bottom of the league.*

1932-33 DIVISION ONE	
1 Arsenal	58
2 Aston Villa	54
3 Sheffield Wednesday	51
4 West Bromwich Albion	49
5 Newcastle United	49
6 Huddersfield	47
7 Derby County	44
8 Leeds United	44
9 Portsmouth	43
10 Sheffield United	43
11 Everton	41
12 Sunderland	40
13 Birmingham City	39
14 Liverpool	39
15 Blackburn Rovers	38
16 Manchester City	37
17 Middlesbrough	37
18 Chelsea	35
19 Leicester City	35
20 Wolverhampton W.	35
21 Bolton Wanderers	33
22 Blackpool	33

Newcastle's controversial victory

At the end of the 1931-32 season Arsenal fans were left to reflect on what might have been. Having faded in the league and seen their crown pass to Everton, the Gunners also lost in the FA Cup Final, and in highly controversial circumstances. Bob John put Arsenal 1-0 up against Newcastle United but it was the equalising goal which provided the game's talking point. The Arsenal defenders momentarily stopped as Jimmy Richardson crossed from the right, the ball appearing to have gone well over the bye-line. Jack Allen pounced to score and the referee allowed the goal to stand. Allen went on to hit the winner 20 minutes from time.

Photographic evidence subsequently showed that Arsenal had been hard done by but that was scant consolation. At one point the Gunners looked like becoming the first twentieth-century team to achieve the coveted Double; in fact, Chapman's men ended the campaign empty-handed.

EVERTON BEAT NERVOUS MANCHESTER CITY

RIGHT: *Play around Manchester City's goal in the 1933 Cup Final. 93,000 people watched as Everton defeated a nervous-looking Manchester City by 3 goals to nil. The 1930s was a successful period in the history of Everton; having been promoted back into Division One in the 1931-2 season the Merseyside team finished the year at the top of the league pushing Arsenal into second place.*

BELOW: *Sagar, the Everton goalkeeper, makes a remarkable save in the 1933 Cup Final. Creswell, in white, is nearest the camera, behind him is White and on the left is Herd, Manchester City's centre-forward. This was the first Cup Final in which players wore numbers on the backs of their shirts. Everton was allocated numbers 1 – 11, printed in black on their white shirts, and Manchester City was given 12 – 22, written in white on red shirts.*

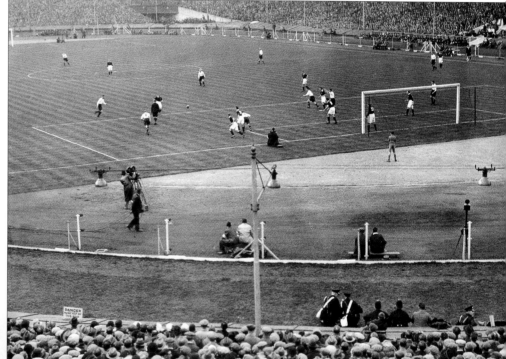

A spectacular view of Wembley just over ten years after it hosted the 1923 Cup Final. Gate receipts had now risen to £25,000. Of this, one third went to the Football Association and one third to each of the competing teams.

Arsenal follow Huddersfield into record books

The following three seasons saw Arsenal - and Chapman - equal Huddersfield's achievement of the previous decade. The Gunners' record over those three championship-winning campaigns was impressive: they won 73 of their 126 league matches, were beaten just 24 times and scored over 300 goals.

Chapman's sudden death in January 1934 meant that he did not see the triumphant completion of the hat-trick with either club. Yet no one was in any doubt as to who masterminded both achievements. Chapman was known for his attention to detail, and it was typical of the man that he insisted on watching his juniors play, despite the adverse conditions and the fact that he was already running a temperature. He contracted pneumonia and succumbed to the illness on 6 January. He was 62 years old.

Chapman the visionary manager

Chapman's legacy stretched far beyond another domestic championship for the Gunners. He was a prescient manager and many of the ideas he championed came to fruition long after his death. These included the advent of night matches under floodlights, the use of numbered shirts and even the Champions League!

In many ways Chapman's Arsenal side played in the modern style. The team was well schooled in the art of absorbing pressure, then quickly turning defence into attack. Swift counter-attacking football is one of the hallmarks of the modern era, yet to the fans in the 1930s it often seemed that the Gunners won matches when they appeared to be on the back foot. This gave rise to the "Lucky Arsenal" jibe which stuck for so long.

Chapman was also ahead of his time as far as transfer dealings were concerned. In 1930 he signed goalkeeper Rudi Hiden from Wiener Sportklub for £2600. International transfers of this type were almost unheard of, and this one sparked a row which is all too familiar more than 70 years later. The Ministry of Labour refused to sanction Hiden's entry into the country, on the grounds that he would put a British goalkeeper out of work.

City Swift to react

Below: *Frank Swift, Manchester City's 19-year-old goalkeeper clears from a corner kick in the 1934 Final at Wembley. After Cup Final nerves disrupted their performance in last year's tie, Manchester City defeated Portsmouth 2-1 in a*

dramatic game. Portsmouth led until almost the last 15 minutes of the match when Allen was knocked unconscious in the penalty area. While he recovered Tilson scored two goals in quick succession for City.

1933-34 DIVISION ONE	
1 Arsenal	59
2 Huddersfield	56
3 Tottenham Hotspur	49
4 Derby County	45
5 Manchester City	45
6 Sunderland	44
7 West Bromwich Albion	44
8 Blackburn Rovers	43
9 Leeds United	42
10 Portsmouth	42
11 Sheffield Wednesday	41
12 Stoke	41
13 Aston Villa	40
14 Everton	40
15 Wolverhampton W.	40
16 Middlesbrough	39
17 Leicester City	39
18 Liverpool	38
19 Chelsea	36
20 Birmingham City	36
21 Newcastle United	34
22 Sheffield United	31

Alex James

BELOW: *1934: Arsenal's first practice match of the season. Arsenal were the most successful team of the era. League champions in 1930-1 and 1932-33 and narrowly missing winning the Double in 1932 when they came second in the league and were runners-up in the Cup. However, disaster struck on 6 January when Herbert Chapman, manager and driving force behind their achievements, died suddenly. Director George Allison took on management duties and Arsenal finished the season on top of the First Division. Allison continued Chapman's work in strengthening the side, signing centre-forward Ted Drake and wing-halves Crayston and Copping.*

REFEREES UNDER FIRE

ABOVE: *During a game against Chelsea at Stamford Bridge in 1934, Blackburn players appeal to the referee after a goal was given against them - proving that some aspects of the game remain unchanged even 70 years later.*

Alex James was the outstanding player of Herbert Chapman's mighty Arsenal side of the 1930s. Probably the most complete player of his generation, James was equally adept in the scheming role or as a finisher. Chapman paid Preston £8750 for his services in 1929. It proved to be money well spent. Over the next eight years James was the orchestrator-in-chief in a phenomenally successful spell which included four championships and two FA Cup victories. James was a wayward star, however, and that contributed to the fact that he won a meagre eight caps for Scotland. One of those came in March 1928, when Scotland took on England at Wembley. James was outstanding, scoring twice in a 5-1 victory and cementing his place in the annals as one of the famous "Wembley Wizards".

Walsall in giant-killing act

Almost inevitably, fans of rival clubs envied and resented Arsenal's success in equal measure. Any ill-feeling was not simply down to the club's dominance on the pitch. This was a period of depression and high unemployment, and while the industrial heartlands of the Midlands and the North were hit hard, Highbury epitomised the affluence of a capital which seemed impervious to the economic climate.

Thus, in 1933 there was a widespread feeling of schadenfreude as Arsenal fell victim to one of the great giant-killing acts of all time. The team was weakened by the loss of several players through illness and injury, but no one expected an upset when mighty Arsenal went to Walsall for a third round FA Cup-tie. There were three new faces in the Gunners' line-up and each of them had a nightmare. One

of the trio, defender Tommy Black, gave away the penalty which resulted in the Third Division side going 2-0 up. That was how it finished. Black had no chance to make amends; he was transfer-listed immediately.

Chapman's successor was George Allison, a club director who was best known as a radio commentator. He had no playing experience, but the organisation at Highbury was so well established that this hardly proved a handicap, at least not in the short term. Allison had the benefit of inheriting Tom Whittaker as his right-hand man. Whittaker was an excellent coach and also a top physiotherapist. His methods meant that injured players were back in action in days rather than weeks, another factor in the club's success.

BOTTOM: *Arsenal stars (r-l) Alex James, goalkeeper Frank Moss and Eddie Hapgood admire the juvenile prowess of Hapgood's son, Tony. All three players had international experience: Hapgood and Moss with England and James representing Scotland. Of the three, Hapgood was most capped, making 30 appearances during 1933-9. Moss's recurring shoulder injury forced him to retire in 1937 to take up the post of manager of Heart of Midlothian in Edinburgh.*

BELOW: *A packed game at Preston North End. Preston finished third behind Arsenal and Wolves in the 1938-39 season*

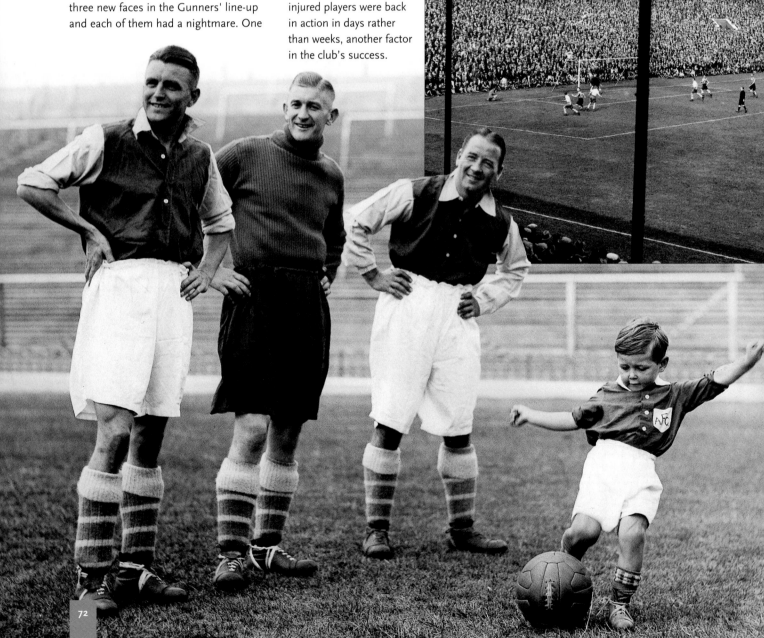

HIGHBURY LOCK-OUT

BELOW: *Amazing scenes were witnessed at Arsenal with huge numbers of people hoping to attend the clash between Spurs and Arsenal in January 1934. In the background is the vast crowd who were unable to get into the game. In 1936 a new East Stand was opened at Highbury which provided seating for a further 8000 spectators.*

RIGHT: *An aerial picture of Maine Road taken when Manchester City played Sheffield Wednesday in March 1934.*

PLAYING BY THE RULES

RIGHT: *Well-known referee J.M.Wiltshire from Dorset during the Brentford - Wolverhampton match in 1937.*

BOTTOM: *The scene at the Bristol City ground when spectators surged onto the pitch.*

BELOW: *An instructor takes a class with the aid of a miniature football field as the London Society of Referees commences courses for the training of new referees at the Feathers Hotel in Westminster.*

Pools disrupted

By the mid-1930s, fans were not only interested in their own team's performance; football was also hugely popular as a means of having a flutter. The Football Pools had been launched by Littlewoods in 1923, and in barely a decade filling in the coupon was for many a weekly ritual. There were those who were unhappy about the promotion of gambling on such a widespread scale, and in 1936 even the Football League itself began to have reservations. The memories of match-fixing were still relatively fresh, and the league took the draconian decision to withhold fixture lists to the last possible moment in order to disrupt the pools companies' operations. It was a short-lived experiment. There was an outcry as fans demanded to know who their team was playing against in good time. Normal service was quickly resumed and the public carried on checking their coupons to see if they'd hit the jackpot.

1934-35 DIVISION ONE	
1 Arsenal	58
2 Sunderland	54
3 Sheffield Wednesday	49
4 Manchester City	48
5 Grimsby	45
6 Derby County	45
7 Liverpool	45
8 Everton	44
9 West Bromwich Albion	44
10 Stoke	42
11 Preston	42
12 Chelsea	41
13 Aston Villa	41
14 Portsmouth	40
15 Blackburn Rovers	39
16 Huddersfield	38
17 Wolverhampton W.	38
18 Leeds United	38
19 Birmingham City	36
20 Middlesbrough	34
21 Leicester City	33
22 Tottenham Hotspur	30

LEFT: *Crowds look at the "Ground Full" notice outside the turnstiles at Stamford Bridge when Chelsea met Arsenal in 1934. Arsenal won their third league title in the 1934-5 season by a margin of four points over Sunderland and new signing Ted Drake was the season's top scorer with 42 goals.*

BELOW: *Even with Gallacher in the strike force Scotland couldn't score and went down 3-0 at Wembley in 1934.*

Drake keeps Gunners on top

Allison had mixed fortunes in the transfer market as he sought to keep Arsenal at the top of the pile. He told a young Len Shackleton that he wouldn't make the grade, and it was Sunderland and Newcastle who would benefit from the services of one of the great inside-forwards of the postwar era. If Allison made a long-term mistake with Shackleton, he certainly made an inspired signing shortly after Chapman's death. The acquisition of Ted Drake from Southampton undoubtedly helped maintain the club's supremacy. In 1934-35, his first full season at Highbury, Drake hit 42 league goals, making him the First Division's top marksman. In December 1935 Drake hit all seven of Arsenal's goals when they won 7-1 at Villa Park, and he also scored the goal which beat Sheffield United in the 1936 Cup Final.

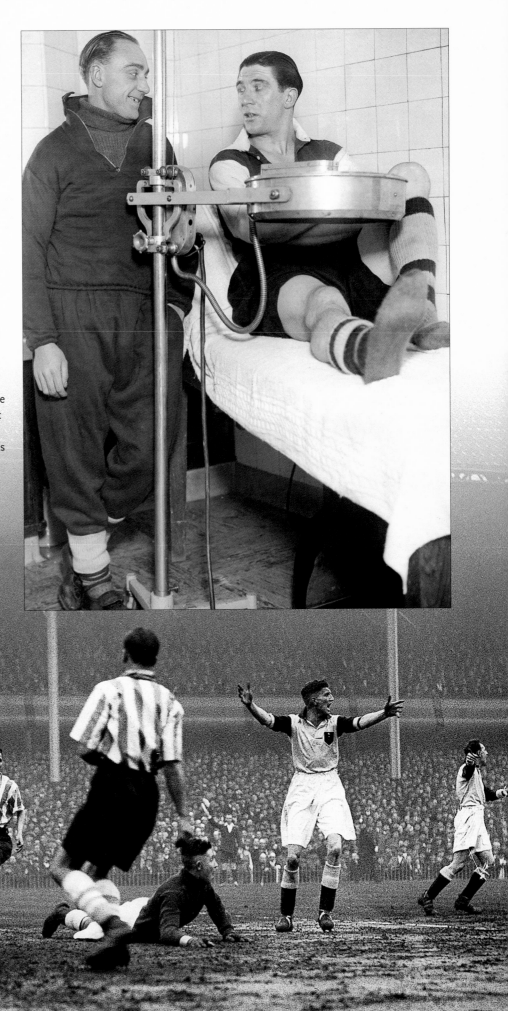

WEDNESDAY WIN GOAL FEAST

RIGHT: *Enthusiastic Sheffield Wednesday supporters trying to touch the Cup as the team coach drives away from the stadium.*

BELOW RIGHT: *Albion's Pearson punches clear a dangerous free kick. The scores were level at half-time, 2-2.*

BOTTOM: *West Brom attack the Sheffield Wednesday goal in the 1935 FA Cup Final. It was a six-goal thriller, the highest goal tally in the showpiece since Bury's 6–0 win over Derby County in 1903. The crowd had hardly settled after kick-off before Wednesday took the lead, while Rimmer's final goal for the Midlands team came in the last minute. Sheffield Wednesday won 4–2.*

OPPOSITE ABOVE: *While the other members of the team are in Brighton preparing for their FA Cup-tie with Bolton Wanderers, George Hunt (left) and Ted Drake remain at Highbury for treatment. They are seen in the electrical room where Drake is receiving infra-red rays. Hunt played with Arsenal for just one season, coming from Spurs in October 1937 for a fee of £7500 and transferring to Bolton for £4000 in March 1938.*

OPPOSITE BELOW: *A disputed goal at the Burnley end of the field when Sheffield Wednesday met Burnley in the semi-final of the FA Cup at Villa Park in 1935. Sheffield went on to win by 3 goals to nil having defeated Arsenal in the previous round.*

FA CUP FINALS

1930	Arsenal	v	Huddersfield Town	2-0
1931	West Bromwich A.	v	Birmingham	2-1
1932	Newcastle United	v	Arsenal	2-1
1933	Everton	v	Manchester City	3-0
1934	Manchester City	v	Portsmouth	2-1
1935	Sheffield Wed.	v	West Bromwich A.	4-2
1936	Arsenal	v	Sheffield United	1-0
1937	Sunderland	v	Preston North End	3-1
1938	Preston North End	v	Huddersfield	1-0
1939	Portsmouth	v	Wolverhampton W.	4-1
1940-45				No competition

ABOVE: *Cheering crowds lined the streets to greet the Sheffield Wednesday team on their arrival home with the Cup. Wednesday had last won the Cup in 1907 but the West Bromwich team had come to Wembley in 1935 with high hopes of repeating their success in the 1931 Final when they defeated their Birmingham neighbours.*

RIGHT: *A view from the stands: Preston North End football ground pictured during a game against Huddersfield.*

BELOW: *Action around the Spurs goal in the 1935 Cup tie between Spurs and Bolton Wanderers. Bolton narrowly missed out on a place in the final losing to West Brom in the replay of the semi-final. In the 1934-5 season there were still only 4 southern teams in Division One: Arsenal, Chelsea, Portsmouth and Spurs.*

MANCHESTER CITY ON THE RISE

BELOW: *Manchester City playing Portsmouth at Maine Road in January 1936. City finished ninth that season but went on to win the league the following year, losing only seven times.*

RIGHT: *Bags containing the numbered balls to be used in the draw for the FA Cup-ties which is to be broadcast live for the first time in 1935. Match commentaries had been broadcast since 1927, beginning with Arsenal v Sheffield United on 22 January of that year.*

1935-36 DIVISION ONE

#	Team	Pts
1	Sunderland	56
2	Derby County	48
3	Huddersfield	48
4	Stoke	47
5	Brentford	46
6	Arsenal	45
7	Preston	44
8	Chelsea	43
9	Manchester City	42
10	Portsmouth	42
11	Leeds United	41
12	Birmingham City	41
13	Bolton Wanderers	41
14	Middlesbrough	40
15	Wolverhampton W.	40
16	Everton	39
17	Grimsby	39
18	West Bromwich Albion	38
19	Liverpool	38
20	Sheffield Wednesday	38
21	Aston Villa	35
22	Blackburn Rovers	33

Sunderland hold off Gunners

It was Sunderland who halted Arsenal's run of championship successes. The Wearsiders' star was inside-forward Horatio "Raich" Carter, and he inspired the club's title-winning campaign of 1935-36, their first since 1913. Sunderland couldn't maintain their form, slipping to 8th the following season, but there was compensation in the form of a first FA Cup triumph. They came from a goal behind against Preston to win 3-1 in 1937. A Preston side including Bill Shankly made it to Wembley again the following year, with Huddersfield their opponents. A drab, goalless 90 minutes meant that this became the first Wembley final to go into extra time. It was also the first to be decided by a penalty, George Mutch scoring from the spot with the last kick of the match.

LEFT: *Alex James supported by his team-mates holds the 1936 FA Cup aloft, Arsenal having overcome Sheffield United in the Final by one goal to nil. The London club's goal was scored by Ted Drake who had recently rejoined the side after a knee operation. The victorious team returned to Islington Town Hall in North London driving through two miles of cheering crowds. In response to the demands of the fans, James and Drake stood on the roof of the motor vehicle holding the cup between them.*

BELOW: *Magnall heads Millwall's first goal in the 1937 Cup tie against Manchester City. Millwall became the first Third Division team to reach the semi-final of the Cup and were eventually eliminated by winners Sunderland.*

OPPOSITE BELOW: *Arsenal's Kirchen leaps to challenge Strong, the Portsmouth keeper at Highbury in April 1937. Television coverage of football began with a practice match transmitted from Highbury in 1937 but it wasn't until the 1940s that those with television sets could expect regular transmissions of games.*

OPPOSITE ABOVE: *Charlton v West Bromwich Albion in 1936. Charlton finished second in the League, just 3 points behind Manchester City in the 36-37 season.*

Swift is City star

Manchester City were another side that tasted both league and Cup success in the 1930s. In the 1933 FA Cup Final City were thumped 3-0 by Everton, who thus completed a remarkable treble, following their championship wins in the Second and First Divisions in the previous two seasons. The 1933 Final was unique in that the teams wore numbered shirts for the first time, but not in the familiar manner. The Everton shirts were numbered 1 to 11, City's 12 to 22.

City bounced back to reach the final the following year, and this time they got their hands on the Cup with a 2-1 win over Portsmouth. The City side boasted a fine wing-half called Matt Busby, but it was 19-year-old goalkeeper Frank Swift who made the headlines. Swift blamed himself for the goal which gave Portsmouth a half-time lead. Fred Tilson scored twice for City after the break, but when reporters behind Swift's goal began counting down the minutes, it all proved too much. At the final whistle he collapsed with nervous exhaustion. Three years later Swift helped

City to win their first championship, 44 years after the club entered the league. He went on to become one of the all-time great keepers, spending his entire playing

career at Maine Road. After retiring from the game he turned his hand to journalism and was among those killed in the Munich air crash in 1958.

SUNDERLAND WIN THEIR FIRST CUP

BELOW: *Cup Final 1937: O'Donnell, the Preston centre-forward and scorer of their first-half goal, receives attention after an injury. Despite holding 6 league titles, it was not until 1937 that Sunderland were successful in the Cup. After being 1-0 down through the whole of the first half, the team from the north-east came back to win the match 3-1 with goals from Gurney, Carter and Burbanks.*

ABOVE: *England v Czechoslovakia at White Hart Lane in December 1937.*

1936-37 DIVISION ONE	
1 Manchester City	57
2 Charlton Athletic	54
3 Arsenal	52
4 Derby County	49
5 Wolverhampton W.	47
6 Brentford	46
7 Middlesbrough	46
8 Sunderland	44
9 Portsmouth	44
10 Stoke	42
11 Birmingham City	41
12 Grimsby	41
13 Chelsea	41
14 Preston	41
15 Huddersfield	39
16 West Bromwich Albion	38
17 Everton	37
18 Liverpool	35
19 Leeds United	34
20 Bolton Wanderers	34
21 Manchester United	32
22 Sheffield Wednesday	30

BELOW: *Gurney, in stripes, scores Sunderland's equaliser.*

ABOVE: *Cup Final programmes from the late twenties and thirties. Most programmes gave very basic information until the 1950s.*

Tommy Lawton

Celebrated by Stanley Matthews as "a brilliant header of the ball", centre-forward Tommy Lawton also had two good feet and blistering pace. When he joined Third Division Notts County in 1947, attendances at Meadow Lane soared. The affection was mutual, with Bolton-born Lawton naming Nottingham his adopted city. He collected 103 goals in 166 run-outs for the club, and was also capped for England – one of the few lower division players ever to wear the national colours. In all his career, he was never booked or sent off.

A teenage sensation at Burnley, he was quickly signed up to a bigger club, Everton, for the then remarkable fee of £6500. As part of Everton's 1938-39 championship-winning side, he scored 35 goals and seemed set to be the next Dixie Dean. But the outbreak of war prevented Lawton from playing other than unofficial internationals, and he moved to Chelsea when he was demobbed. It was a golden time: in 1946–7 he broke the club's scoring record, with 26 goals in 34 matches.

Joining Brentford as player-manager in 1952, aged 33, he admitted to finding it a struggle, but he bowed out of the Football League in fine style with a spell in dangerously good form at Arsenal. He died of pneumonia in 1996.

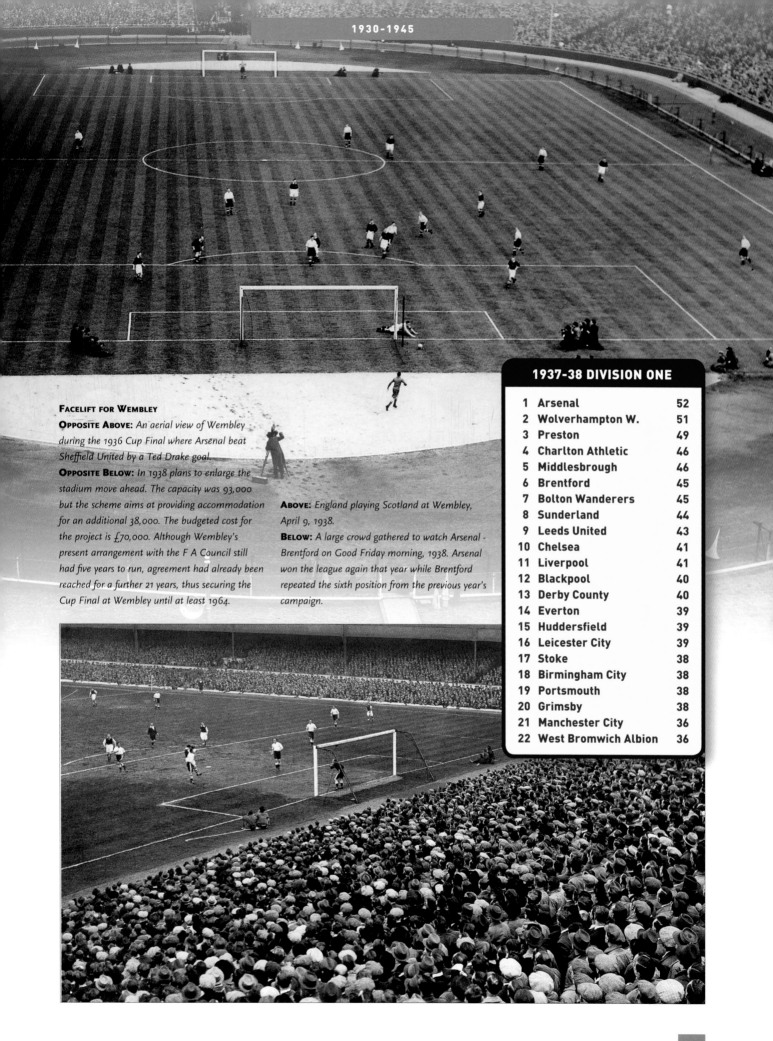

FACELIFT FOR WEMBLEY

OPPOSITE ABOVE: *An aerial view of Wembley during the 1936 Cup Final where Arsenal beat Sheffield United by a Ted Drake goal.*

OPPOSITE BELOW: *In 1938 plans to enlarge the stadium move ahead. The capacity was 93,000 but the scheme aims at providing accommodation for an additional 38,000. The budgeted cost for the project is £70,000. Although Wembley's present arrangement with the F A Council still had five years to run, agreement had already been reached for a further 21 years, thus securing the Cup Final at Wembley until at least 1964.*

ABOVE: *England playing Scotland at Wembley, April 9, 1938.*

BELOW: *A large crowd gathered to watch Arsenal - Brentford on Good Friday morning, 1938. Arsenal won the league again that year while Brentford repeated the sixth position from the previous year's campaign.*

1937-38 DIVISION ONE

1	Arsenal	52
2	Wolverhampton W.	51
3	Preston	49
4	Charlton Athletic	46
5	Middlesbrough	46
6	Brentford	45
7	Bolton Wanderers	45
8	Sunderland	44
9	Leeds United	43
10	Chelsea	41
11	Liverpool	41
12	Blackpool	40
13	Derby County	40
14	Everton	39
15	Huddersfield	39
16	Leicester City	39
17	Stoke	38
18	Birmingham City	38
19	Portsmouth	38
20	Grimsby	38
21	Manchester City	36
22	West Bromwich Albion	36

World football catches up

England's claim to footballing supremacy was dented in the early 1930s. There were defeats against France, Czechoslovakia and Hungary, albeit all away from home. In December 1933 Hugo Meisl's much-vaunted Austrian "Wunderteam" came to Stamford Bridge. England played to their strengths and won the match 4-3, but the Austrians had displayed some dazzling skills and were on top for long periods.

A year later, 14 November 1934, Vittorio Pozzo's Italy, the newly-crowned world champions, came to Highbury to try to become the first team to win on English soil. Pozzo, like Hugo Meisl, believed in meticulous preparation. In contrast, the England players all turned out for their clubs the previous Saturday, and there were several withdrawals before the team was announced, 24 hours before the game. There was hardly any time for practice, but England at least benefited from the fact that seven Arsenal players were in the line-up.

"Battle of Highbury"

It was an ugly game, one which would go down in the annals as the "Battle of Highbury". The scene was set in the opening moments when Ted Drake clashed with Italy's centre-half Luisito Monti. The latter came off worse, breaking a bone in his foot and eventually having to leave the field. His team-mates were bent on retribution for what they regarded as a blatant foul. As the world champions took their eye off the ball - quite literally - England eased into a 3-0 lead. In the second half the visitors regained their composure and began to play. They scored twice, both from the great Giuseppe Meazza, but couldn't complete the comeback. England's record remained intact, but at a cost. Eric Brook and Eddie Hapgood had to go to hospital and there was a queue of players for the treatment table.

No stroll for England in Vienna

Eighteen months later, 6 May 1936, England went to Vienna and lost to Austria in circumstances which showed up the international team's lack of an overseer. On the day of the match the players accepted Hugo Meisl's "generous" offer of a walking tour of the city, and it was only after they had pounded the streets for some miles that the players realised that the hospitality was perhaps not as gracious as it first appeared. England lost the game 2-1.

In May 1938 England went to Berlin to face Germany in the Olympic Stadium. The players reluctantly agreed to perform the Nazi salute prior to the game, and although they ran out convincing 6-3 winners, the occasion was overlaid with political rather than sporting significance.

VICTORY OVER WALES

BELOW: *England thwarted by the Wales goalkeeper in their international match at Middlesbrough in 1937. England went on to win the game 2-1. There were growing concerns that England needed a full-time manager in order to play a dominant role in world football.*

TOP: *Millwall scoring in the cup in 1937.*

ABOVE: *The game must go on: A groundsman uses braziers at Bolton in an attempt to beat the freeze in the winter of 1938.*

BELOW: *Thousands on the terraces watch as Wolverhampton's Dorsett scores in the 10th minute of the second half of the 1939 Cup Final.*
RIGHT: *A Wolves supporter gets that Cup Final feeling in Trafalgar Square. Wolverhampton Wanderers performed well in the league in the 1938-9 season finishing behind Arsenal and had high hopes of taking home the Cup.*

Pompey magic

Portsmouth beat the odds when they outplayed favourites Wolverhampton Wanderers to lift the F A Cup in 1939. Such was the quality of their play the 4-1 victory didn't flatter the victors.

RIGHT: *Jimmy Guthrie is chaired off the field carrying the Cup.*
BELOW: *The greatest moment of Cup Final day: Guthrie followed by his victorious team receives the coveted trophy from the King in the royal box at Wembley while the Queen looks on.*

Arsenal buy Wolves star

In 1937-38 Arsenal became champions for the fifth time in eight seasons. Even so, the Gunners' air of invincibility was beginning to fade. The great Alex James retired at the end of the 1936-37 campaign, and in August 1938 Allison splashed out £14,000 on a replacement.

The man with the new British record price tag on his head was Bryn Jones. No doubt Wolves were reluctant to sell their Welsh international, not least because they had a burgeoning side and had just finished runners-up to Arsenal by a single point. The depth of the Highbury coffers proved decisive, however, and Arsenal got their man. Whether the weight of expectation rested heavily on his shoulders, Jones was not at his best in 1938-39, which would be the last full season for seven years. Arsenal slipped to 5th in the league, Everton taking top honours, with Wolves once again having to settle for the runners-up spot.

Pompey hold the cup for seven years
The season turned into a double agony for Wolves as they went down in the Cup Final too. They faced Portsmouth, a team languishing in the bottom half of the table, and were red-hot favourites to lift

the trophy. Portsmouth used all manner of lucky omens and superstitions to aid their cause, as they had done in 1934. Bringing in comedian Bud Flanagan to relax the team hadn't worked back then, but manager Jack Tinn continued to put a lot of faith in his "lucky spats". There had been a lot of publicity surrounding Wolves' use of so-called "monkey gland" treatment to aid the performance of their players. It didn't help them on the big day. It is said that when the Pompey camp saw the spidery scrawl of their opponents in the official autograph book, they knew they had a golden opportunity. The hands that had signed the book had obviously been shaking, and those feelings of anxiety accompanied the Wolves players onto the pitch. Portsmouth ran out comfortable 4-1 winners and would remain Cup holders for seven years.

BELOW LEFT: Sheffield Wednesday playing Chelsea in the 5th round of the FA Cup at Hillsborough in 1939.
BELOW: A player appeals to the linesman in 1936.

1938-39 DIVISION ONE

1	Everton	59
2	Wolverhampton W.	55
3	Charlton Athletic	50
4	Middlesbrough	49
5	Arsenal	47
6	Derby County	46
7	Stoke	46
8	Bolton Wanderers	45
9	Preston	44
10	Grimsby	43
11	Liverpool	42
12	Aston Villa	41
13	Leeds United	41
14	Manchester United	38
15	Blackpool	38
16	Sunderland	38
17	Portsmouth	37
18	Brentford	36
19	Huddersfield	35
20	Chelsea	33
21	Birmingham City	32
22	Leicester City	29

ABOVE: *Now for the homecoming: Pompey captain, Guthrie, carries off the FA Cup under escort following his team's 4-1 victory over Wolves in 1939. With the outbreak of war just months away Portsmouth would remain Cup holders for seven years.*

LEFT: *'Play up Pompey'. The team certainly didn't let the fans down as Portsmouth overwhelmed Wolves at Wembley.*

Billy Liddell

Billy Liddell was as modest a man as his shots were explosive, and won the adulation of the Kop – who dubbed their club Liddellpool – as one of their most talented outside-lefts (and later, central striker) ever. His career was interrupted by service in the RAF, and in the post-war years Liverpool fell into a decline that not even Liddell's individual flashes of brilliance could stem.

Signing for the Reds in 1938 from Dunfermline, the "Flying Scot" scored in his league debut in 1946, in an FA Cup game against Chester City, and then put away a hat-trick in his next, a 7-3 win against Manchester City, helping Liverpool to the league title in his first full season. He played a record 537 games for the club and scored 229 goals. Liverpool's 2-0 defeat to Arsenal in the FA Cup Final of 1950 marked a turning point, and the club was relegated in 1954. Liddell did, however, win 28 caps for Scotland, and shared with Stanley Matthews the honour of playing twice for Great Britain, in 1947 and 1955, against Rest of the World sides.

Liddell retired in 1960. Sadly, he won few medals in his 22 years wearing the red shirt, but had he played in his prime under Bill Shankly, he would surely have had a cabinetful.

Winterbottom becomes first England manager

It was during the war years that FA Secretary Stanley Rous proposed that the England side should have a full-time manager. His idea was accepted, and Walter Winterbottom, a teacher who had played centre-half for Manchester

United, was given the job. Winterbottom's brief was purely team preparation; selection remained in the hands of the committee members.

RIGHT: *Walter Winterbottom, England manager from 1946 until after the 1962 World Cup.*

1939-40 DIVISION ONE

1	Liverpool	57
2	Manchester United	56
3	Wolverhampton W.	56
4	Stoke	55
5	Blackpool	50
6	Sheffield United	49
7	Preston	47
8	Aston Villa	45
9	Sunderland	44
10	Everton	43
11	Middlesbrough	42
12	Portsmouth	41
13	Arsenal	41
14	Derby County	41
15	Chelsea	39
16	Grimsby	38
17	Blackburn Rovers	36
18	Bolton Wanderers	34
19	Charlton Athletic	34
20	Huddersfield	33
21	Brentford	25
22	Leeds United	18

Wartime football boosts morale

The 1939-40 season was just three games old when it was aborted due to the outbreak of war. Initially all forms of football ceased, but Winston Churchill was among those who appreciated the morale-boosting role that the game could play. The Board of Trade even issued coupons to cover the purchase of football kit, effectively recognising that here was a commodity that had to be rationed, but not dispensed with entirely. Regional football was introduced, and although there were both league and cup competitions, the honours were hardly something to be coveted. Travel restrictions meant that clubs were allowed to field guest players, and those which had large numbers of soldiers stationed nearby reaped the benefit. Aldershot, for example, regularly fielded international players thanks to this highly flexible system.

Wartime internationals

After war was declared, in September of the following year, international football continued. But as with the revamped league competition, the matches were inevitably a victim of circumstance. In 1943, for example, Blackpool's young centre-forward Stan Mortensen made his debut - against England! Mortensen had been a substitute for the match against Wales and came on for the opposition after one of the Welsh players was injured.

30 games were played during the conflict, together with five "Victory" internationals between September 1945 and May 1946. These were not accorded official international status in the record books.

ABOVE: *All factories and institutions had their own roof spotters, usually members of staff who did an extra shift. The roof spotter's job was to act as an early warning to those inside the building of the approach of a raid. Here the roof spotter works on while West Ham play Chelsea in December 1940, at the height of the Blitz. The gate was less than 2000.*

BELOW: *A scene at Upton Park where West Ham United played Leicester City showing the usual football fans watching the game - in Army uniform. This picture was taken the day before war was declared and emphasises the degree to which the war was becoming inevitable.*

OPPOSITE ABOVE: *Manchester United's stadium after a bomb had dropped through the roof of the main stand.*

OPPOSITE BELOW: *Scotland's Baxter and Stephen try to prevent another England attack in the 1944 war-time international.*

Fans flock back to the game

As had happened in 1918, the end of the global conflict brought the fans flocking back to football. The clubs had to assess the state of their stadiums and check on their players. Inevitably, war had claimed the lives of some, and those who did return for duty were seven years older. It was a chaotic period, with many clubs forced to try out players who might otherwise never have been given an opportunity. There was no time to restart a league programme in 1945-46, but the FA Cup made a welcome return to the sporting calendar. Football was back.

OPPOSITE ABOVE: *A dramatic moment in the league Cup Final at Blackburn. Gallimore, Preston's right back, was trying to stop the ball but instead kicked it into his own goal. Despite this, Preston beat Arsenal 2-1.*

BELOW: *Part of the vast crowd of 133,000 spectators at Hampden Park who watched England play Scotland on April 22, 1944.*

OPPOSITE BELOW: *An England v Scotland game at Wembley in October 1941 gives fans some relief from the austerity and the trauma of the hostilities. Scotland's goalkeeper, Dawson, has a hard job to prevent England's forwards scoring from this clear-cut opportunity.*

1945-1959
Growing the Game

The early postwar years were a golden era for English
football. The global conflict might have been over but Britain
faced years of austerity and rationing. Ex-servicemen had
money burning a hole in the pockets of their demob suits
and precious little to spend it on. When it came to mass
entertainment and escapism, football had few rivals.
More than 35 million people crammed into football grounds
all around the country when the league programme was
relaunched in 1946-47. Within a couple of years the
40-million mark was surpassed.

League grows to 92 clubs

The huge wave of popularity led to many minor clubs seeking league status. In 1950 four applications were accepted. Colchester, Scunthorpe, Gillingham and Shrewsbury were added to the Division Three ranks, thereby increasing the league from 88 to 92 clubs.

The football that the fans flocked to see in those early postwar years was not always of the highest standard. The players that survived from the pre-war era were seven years older. Clubs were squeezed, since young talent could not be developed overnight. In an effort to steal a march on their rivals, many clubs tried out players on an unprecedented scale, giving opportunities to some who would scarcely have merited a look in days gone by. By the end of the 1946-47 campaign, a number of clubs had fielded more than thirty players in an effort to find a winning formula.

1946-47 DIVISION ONE	
1 Liverpool	57
2 Manchester United	56
3 Wolverhampton W.	56
4 Stoke	55
5 Blackpool	50
6 Sheffield United	49
7 Preston	47
8 Aston Villa	45
9 Sunderland	44
10 Everton	43
11 Middlesbrough	42
12 Portsmouth	41
13 Arsenal	41
14 Derby County	41
15 Chelsea	39
16 Grimsby	38
17 Blackburn Rovers	36
18 Bolton Wanderers	34
19 Charlton Athletic	34
20 Huddersfield	33
21 Brentford	25
22 Leeds United	18

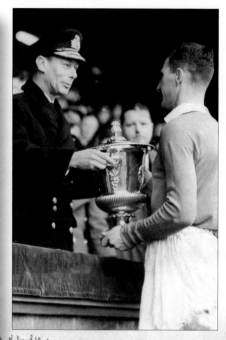

LEFT: *The King presents the Cup to Harris, the Chelsea captain after they defeated their London rivals Millwall in the 1945 Southern League Cup Final. Public demand for the resumption of fixtures was high, encouraging the FA to alter the rules for the 1946 FA Cup so that teams played 2 legs at each round until reaching the semi-finals.*

BELOW: *A capacity crowd watches Chelsea play Moscow Dynamo when the Russian team toured Britain in the winter of 1945. The match ended in a draw with three goals scored by each side. Dynamo went on to defeat Cardiff, draw with Rangers and, in a match full of controversies, defeated an Arsenal side con-taining many guest players, by 4 goals to 3.*

OPPOSITE: *Lawton scores the fourth goal for Britain when they faced the Rest of Europe at Hampden Park in May 1947. Britain defeated the Continental team comprising players from 9 countries by 6 goals to one; Mannion netting 3, Lawton 2 and Scotland's Billy Steel scoring one.*

ABOVE: *Clem Attlee shakes hands with Stanley Matthews as England line up to meet Belgium at Wembley in 1946. The postwar years brought greater interest in international football and England not only played abroad but entertained Continental teams more frequently. The national team travelled to Switzerland at the end of the 1946 season winning 1-0 but chalked up a remarkable victory in Portugal defeating their opponents by 10-0 with Lawton and Mortensen scoring 4 goals apiece.*

OPPOSITE BELOW: *On a blisteringly hot day, Charlton's Duffy scores the winning goal in the 1947 Cup Final against Burnley. The goal, scored in the last minutes of extra time, averted the threat of a replay which had last been necessary in 1912 when Barnsley drew with West Brom.*

BELOW: *Charlton face Bolton in the semi-final of the FA Cup at Villa Park in 1946.*

OPPOSITE ABOVE: *Arsenal begin their campaign at the start of the 1946-47 season at Highbury.*

Cullis and Busby turn to management

Of the 1930s stars, Tommy Lawton, Joe Mercer, Billy Liddell, Tom Finney and Bob Paisley were among those who successfully bridged the seven-year gap. And, of course, the incomparable Stanley Matthews, who had turned 30 but still had nearly twenty years of league football left in him. Wolves stalwart Stan Cullis managed just one more season before hanging up his boots. Former Manchester City and Liverpool half-back

Matt Busby was 36 when the war ended and his thoughts had already turned to management. Cullis and Busby would become two of the dominant figures in the 1950s, locking horns as bosses of Wolves and Manchester United respectively, as they had done in their pomp as players. Each would lead his side to three championships, though their footballing philosophies could hardly have been more different.

Tragedy at Burnden Park

1945-46 saw all the clubs take stock of their playing staffs and facilities. Many grounds had been damaged during the war, and while repairs were carried out some ground-sharing went on. Old Trafford was one of those affected, and for some time Manchester United played their home matches at Maine Road. Arsenal and Spurs also put aside their traditional rivalry to share facilities in the early peacetime months.

There may have been no league fixtures that year but the Cup returned to provide the players and fans with some competitive football. As this was the only competition of the season the FA decided to increase the number of matches by making each tie up to the semi-final a two-legged affair. It was in the second leg of a sixth-round tie between Bolton and Stoke at Burnden Park that football saw one of its worst-ever tragedies. The gates were closed on this eagerly-awaited match, but thousands forced their way in by every conceivable means. In the resulting crush some of the steel barriers gave way and there were 33 fatalities. There was little appetite for the game to go ahead, but after some delay the teams played out a goalless draw, Bolton going through thanks to their 2-0 win in the first leg.

Charlton lose a Cup match but make it to Wembley

Bolton were beaten by Charlton in the semi-final, and the London club faced Derby at Wembley. For both sides it had been a marathon campaign. Derby needed a semi-final replay to beat Birmingham, and so played ten matches to reach the final. Charlton's run was unique. Having been beaten by Fulham in the away leg of their third- round tie, Charlton thus became the first club to reach the Cup Final having lost a match. Derby had just splashed out to sign Raich Carter from Sunderland and he helped the Rams to their first major honour. Charlton's Bert Turner scored at both ends to take the game into extra time, when the classier Derby side scored three times without reply.

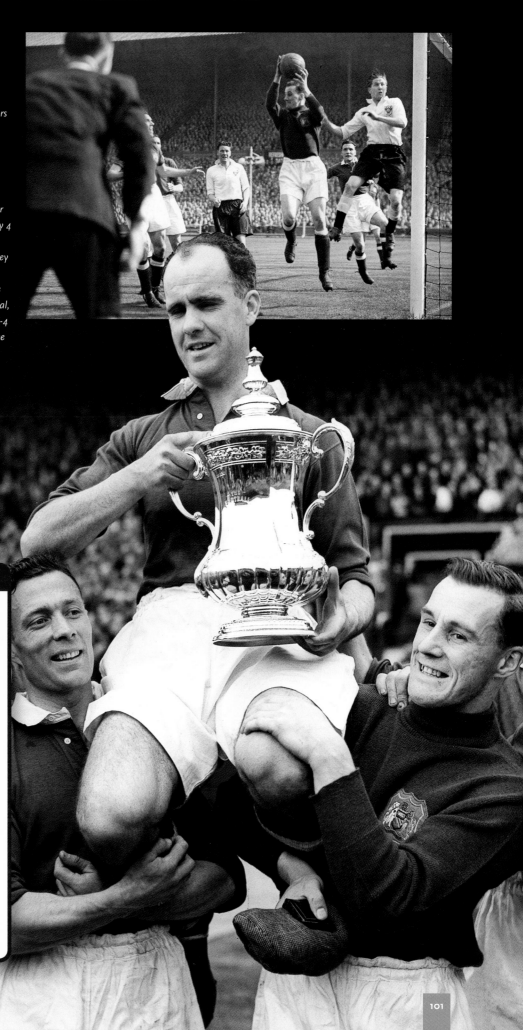

OPPOSITE ABOVE: *England manager Walter Winterbottom gives advice to his players during training before a match at Huddersfield against Holland in 1946.*

OPPOSITE BELOW: *Some of the 90,000 spectators at the Burnley v Charlton Cup Final in 1947.*

RIGHT: *Compton, the Manchester United goalkeeper, pressed by Blackpool's Mortensen makes a spectacular save in the 1948 Final. Mortensen and the newly-acquired Stanley Matthews presented a danger to the Manchester defence, but United were triumphant winning by 4 goals to 2 in a classic final.*

BELOW: *Manchester United captain Johnny Carey is carried on the shoulders of his enthusiastic team-mates after receiving the FA Cup from the King. Manchester had a difficult road to the Final, facing Division One teams in every round, the 6-4 defeat of Aston Villa in the third round being one of the highlights of the 1947-8 season.*

1947-48 DIVISION ONE

1	Arsenal	59
2	Manchester United	52
3	Burnley	52
4	Derby County	50
5	Wolverhampton W.	47
6	Aston Villa	47
7	Preston	47
8	Portsmouth	45
9	Blackpool	44
10	Manchester City	42
11	Liverpool	42
12	Sheffield United	42
13	Charlton Athletic	40
14	Everton	40
15	Stoke	38
16	Middlesbrough	37
17	Bolton Wanderers	37
18	Chelsea	37
19	Huddersfield	36
20	Sunderland	36
21	Blackburn Rovers	32
22	Grimsby	22

Agonising wait for Liverpool

The first postwar FA Cup whetted the appetite for the return of league action. The 1946-47 fixture list replicated that of the aborted 1939-40 season, trying to give a semblance of continuity. Liverpool became the first postwar champions, inheriting the title Everton had won eight years earlier. At the beginning of the season the two clubs had both vied for the signature of Newcastle hotshot Albert Stubbins. Both offered £12,500 and Stubbins is said to have opted for Anfield by tossing a coin. He proved his worth to the Reds, scoring 26 goals as Liverpool became involved in an exciting championship run-in.

The worst winter in living memory meant that the season ran into June. Liverpool went top after a 2-1 away win at Wolves, ending the latter's own title hopes. They then had an agonising two-week wait to see if Stoke could overhaul them by beating Sheffield United. The Potteries club lost and Liverpool were crowned champions for the fifth time.

ARSENAL LEAGUE CHAMPIONS
OPPOSITE ABOVE LEFT: *Arsenal fans stream into Highbury. The Gunners topped the league in the 1947-48 season for the sixth time equalling the record set by Sunderland and Aston Villa.*

OPPOSITE ABOVE RIGHT: *An enthusiastic Blackpool supporter gives vent to her feelings. Blackpool fans had much to be pleased about in the early 1950s having reached the FA Cup Final in 1948 and 1951 before winning in 1953. Both Mortensen and Matthews were stalwarts of the England team and Matthews was winner of the first Footballer of the Year award in 1948.*
OPPOSITE BELOW: *Middlesbrough gives Chelsea an anxious moment at Stamford Bridge in 1948.*
BOTTOM: *Players rush to the rescue as Arsenal team-mates Mercer and Leslie Compton collide during their match with Blackpool in 1949.*
BELOW: *Ben Fenton undergoes treatment by Charlton trainer Jimmy Trotter in 1949.*

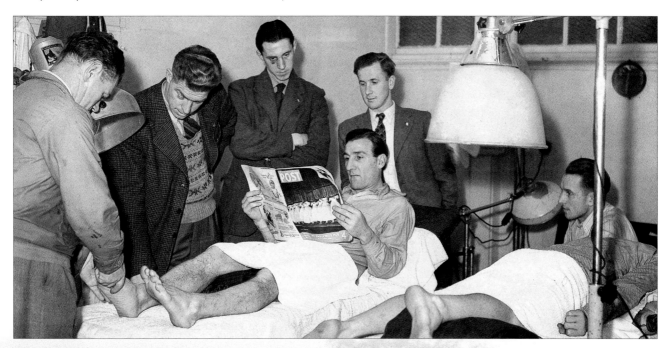

Jackie Milburn

Few Newcastle United players are held in greater affection by the fans than Jackie Milburn, or "Wor Jackie" as he was known. A gifted centre-forward, Milburn had a winger's pace, having played out on the flanks in his early days. This talent, combined with his great shooting power and brilliance in the air made him the foremost central striker in the country in the 1950s.

Milburn achieved a scoring rate of a goal every other game with 178 goals in 11 years at the Tyneside club. He led the attack as Newcastle won the FA Cup three times in five seasons, in1951, 1952 and 1955. He scored both goals in the team's 2-0 win over Blackpool in the 1951 FA Cup Final, and put away a classic header, rifled into the net just seconds into the game at Wembley to set up a 3-1 win over Manchester City four years later.

As the natural successor to Tommy Lawton in the England centre-forward position, Milburn scored 10 goals in his 13 international appearances. Part of a footballing family, with brothers who were also professionals; his nephews, Bobby and Jackie Charlton, were to follow him into the England team in the 1960s.

Third cup for Arsenal

BELOW: *Fans queue overnight for tickets to the Arsenal v Spurs local derby in 1949. Although intense rivals the teams had shared Spurs' ground at White Hart Lane during the war when Highbury was used as a first-aid post and ARP centre.*
OPPOSITE TOP: *Goring scores the first of Arsenal's goals against Manchester City in their 4-1 victory in April 1950.*
OPPOSITE MIDDLE: *The north London derby between Arsenal and Tottenham in 1950, the year Spurs won the league.*
OPPOSITE BELOW: *Arsenal, the 1950 Cup winners, parade the trophy in Islington after defeating Liverpool 2-0, both goals scored by Reg Lewis. The Gunners were the first club to reach Wembley without playing outside their own city and the first to allow their players to spend the night before the Final at home.*

1948-49 DIVISION ONE

1	Portsmouth	58
2	Manchester United	53
3	Derby County	53
4	Newcastle United	52
5	Arsenal	49
6	Wolverhampton W.	46
7	Manchester City	45
8	Sunderland	43
9	Charlton Athletic	42
10	Aston Villa	42
11	Stoke	41
12	Liverpool	40
13	Chelsea	38
14	Bolton Wanderers	38
15	Burnley	38
16	Blackpool	38
17	Birmingham City	37
18	Everton	37
19	Middlesbrough	34
20	Huddersfield	34
21	Preston	33
22	Sheffield United	33

"Stop-gap" Mercer captains Arsenal to Cup glory

Arsenal won the league in 1947-48, and did so again five years later. The FA Cup also went to Highbury in 1950, but this was not a period of dominance to match the 1930s. The team included Joe Mercer and the Compton brothers, Denis and Leslie. Mercer had played in Everton's championship-winning side of 1939, and Arsenal regarded him as a short-term acquisition after the war. The irrepressible Mercer played on for eight seasons and was named Footballer of the Year in 1950, when he lifted the Cup as the Gunners' captain.

The Compton brothers could not have been more different. The flamboyant Denis played on the wing with a devil-may-care style. In that 1950 Wembley Final, against Liverpool, Compton was looking weary when someone handed him a tot of brandy. He perked up immediately and provided the cross which led to the second goal in Arsenal's 2-0 win.

Elder brother Leslie, a rugged centre-half, carved his name in the record books by winning his first cap for England at the age of 38 years 2 months, the oldest player to make his England debut.

Nat Lofthouse

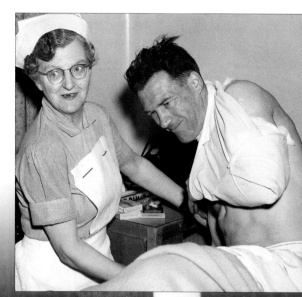

OPPOSITE: *Arsenal pictured with the Cup before their match with Portsmouth in 1950. The south-coast team were league champions in two consecutive seasons finishing five points ahead of their nearest rivals Manchester United in the 1948-9 season. The margin was much tighter the following year when Portsmouth finished above Wolves on goal difference.*

BELOW: *Cowell clears off the line for Newcastle in the 1951 FA Cup Final. The Magpies went on to beat Blackpool 2-0 with Jackie Milburn scoring bothgoals.*

RIGHT: *An injured Nat Lofthouse is helped by a nurse.*

Nat Lofthouse remains a living legend at Bolton Wanderers, the club where he spent his entire playing career between 1946 and 1960. With 255 goals scored during that period, he is still the club's highest league scorer. A powerful centre-forward, he scored in every round of the FA Cup in the 1952-53 season, and although he finished on the losing side in the "Matthews Final", he had the consolation of picking up the Footballer of the Year award. Five years later he was on the winning side at Wembley, scoring both goals in Bolton's 2-1 win over a Manchester United side devastated by the Munich air disaster.

Lofthouse made 33 appearances in an England shirt, scoring an astonishing 30 goals, placing him joint third on the all-time list of England scorers. He is best remembered for his heroic contribution to England's victory away to Austria in the 1951-52 season. Having already scored one goal against the team ranked the best in Europe, he hit a second-half winner but was knocked unconscious in the process. His bravery and commitment earned him the tag the "Lion of Vienna".

Courageous Arsenal defeated by Newcastle

BELOW: *Arsenal keeper George Swindin stretches to reach the ball with Milburn and Robledo nearby in the 1952 Cup Final. Newcastle had high hopes of repeating the previous season's success when they defeated Blackpool by 2-0 in the Cup Final but eleven minutes before the whistle there was still no score. Arsenal struggled on valiantly, playing with 10 men from the 20th minute when Barnes was injured and despite the handicap had their chances to score. But the game was over when Newcastle's Robledo put the ball in the net with only minutes to go.*

RIGHT: *After another Arsenal attack Lishman, the Gunners' centre forward, hooks a shot towards goal.*

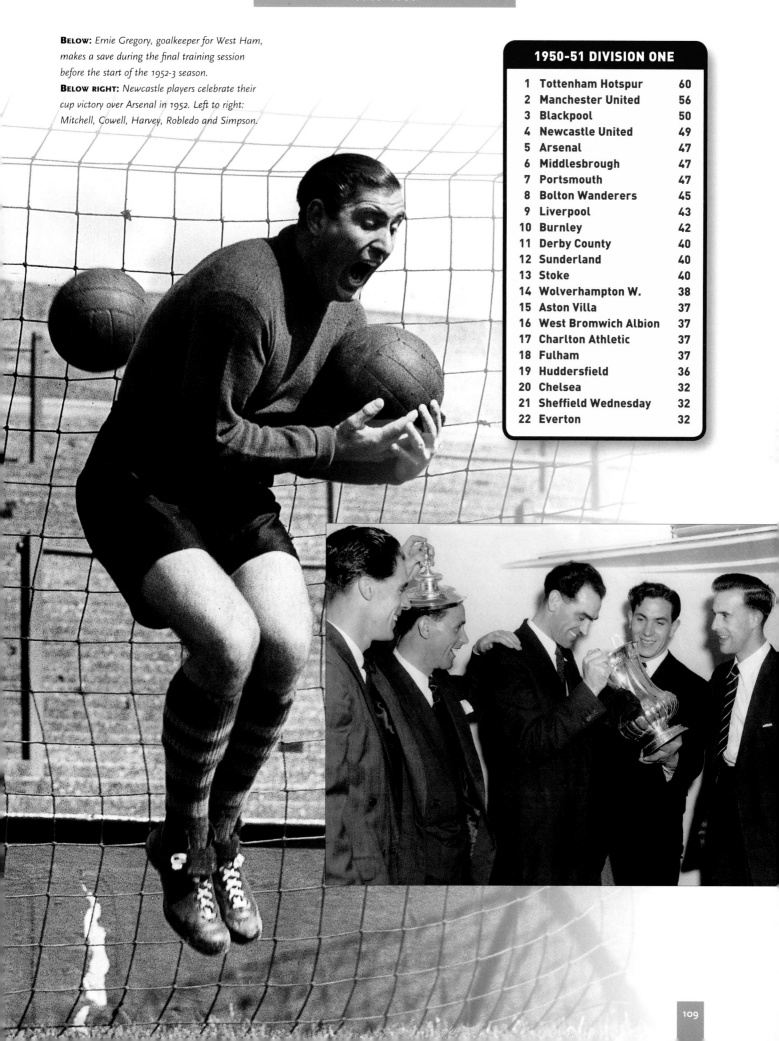

BELOW: *Ernie Gregory, goalkeeper for West Ham, makes a save during the final training session before the start of the 1952-3 season.*

BELOW RIGHT: *Newcastle players celebrate their cup victory over Arsenal in 1952. Left to right: Mitchell, Cowell, Harvey, Robledo and Simpson.*

1950-51 DIVISION ONE

1	Tottenham Hotspur	60
2	Manchester United	56
3	Blackpool	50
4	Newcastle United	49
5	Arsenal	47
6	Middlesbrough	47
7	Portsmouth	47
8	Bolton Wanderers	45
9	Liverpool	43
10	Burnley	42
11	Derby County	40
12	Sunderland	40
13	Stoke	40
14	Wolverhampton W.	38
15	Aston Villa	37
16	West Bromwich Albion	37
17	Charlton Athletic	37
18	Fulham	37
19	Huddersfield	36
20	Chelsea	32
21	Sheffield Wednesday	32
22	Everton	32

Tom Finney

Dubbed the "Preston Plumber", Tom Finney was a brilliant ball-playing winger. A contemporary of Stanley Matthews, he shared many of Matthews' creative and skilful qualities. However, he was a much more versatile player; Matthews concentrated on being simply the best outside-right of his era. Finney was two-footed and could operate on either wing, and he also played as a central striker.

He played throughout his career for Preston North End and his 187 goals in 24 seasons for the club remains a record at Deepdale – testimony to his clinical finishing; but Finney was also a provider for other strikers. His loyalty to his home-town club probably cost him in terms of silverware, for he ended his illustrious career with no major honours.

Nevertheless, his talents did not go unnoticed and he earned 76 England caps. During his service for the national side he bagged 30 goals, setting a new record. Even now, on the list of all time record England scorers he lies at joint fifth, alongside Nat Lofthouse and Alan Shearer.

He received a rare footballing accolade in being twice named Footballer of the Year, in 1954 and 1957. And Bill Shankly, a former team-mate, once famously said that Finney would have been brilliant in any era, 'even if he'd been wearing an overcoat'. Rewarded for his loyalty to Preston and his services to football, Tom Finney became club president at Deepdale, and was knighted in 1998.

RIGHT: *Tom Finney trains with the England team at Stamford Bridge.*

England back in FIFA fold

This period was also notable for England's return to the international fold. The hatchet was finally buried on the row with FIFA over payments to amateurs, a dispute going back to 1928. The reconciliation was celebrated with a match between a Great Britain XI and a side representing Europe. Wilf Mannion was the star of the show, hitting a hat-trick, with Tommy Lawton grabbing a brace. Great Britain won the match 6-1.

In May 1947 England went to Lisbon and thrashed Portugal 10-0, debutant Stan Mortensen hitting four goals. In the next 12 months there were wins over Belgium and Sweden, and a dazzling 4-0 victory over Italy in Turin. Such results no doubt suggested to some that England were ready to reassume their position as world-beaters. The 1950s would disabuse the optimists of any such feelings.

England make their World Cup debut

Throughout the 1950s, when he was well into his 30s, Stanley Matthews remained a regular in the international side. In 1950 he got his chance to grace a World Cup, along with stars such as Mannion, Mortensen, Milburn, Wright and Finney. FIFA declared that the home international championship would constitute a qualifying group for the tournament, which was staged in Brazil. England won, and Scotland also earned a place as runners-up. The Scots declined, however, one of a number of withdrawals. Other notable absentees included Hungary, Austria, Germany, France and Russia. Just 13 teams took part in the competition, and England were installed as joint-favourites.

1951-52 DIVISION ONE		
1	Manchester United	57
2	Tottenham Hotspur	53
3	Arsenal	53
4	Portsmouth	48
5	Bolton Wanderers	48
6	Aston Villa	47
7	Preston	46
8	Newcastle United	45
9	Blackpool	45
10	Charlton Athletic	44
11	Liverpool	43
12	Sunderland	42
13	West Bromwich Albion	41
14	Burnley	40
15	Manchester City	39
16	Wolverhampton W.	38
17	Derby County	37
18	Middlesbrough	36
19	Chelsea	36
20	Stoke	31
21	Huddersfield	28
22	Fulham	27

OPPOSITE BELOW LEFT: *Argentina score against England at Wembley when the teams meet for the first time in May 1951. Argentina's defence held on to their 1-0 lead until Mortensen equalised from a header and Milburn hit the back of the net 10 minutes before time.*

OPPOSITE BOTTOM LEFT: *1953 Cup Winners Blackpool appear on the popular TV show What's My Line?*

BELOW: *The championship-winning Manchester United team of 1952. L-R, Back row: Busby (manager), Blanchflower, Aston, Allen, Chilton, Gibson, Cockburn, Curry (trainer). Front row: Pearson, Rowley, Carey, Downie, McShane.*

Lawton signs for Third Division side

The shock of the 1947-48 season occurred off the pitch, when Chelsea and England centre-forward Tommy Lawton moved to Third Division Notts County in a record £20,000 deal. County quickly began recouping their huge investment with gates of 30,000, a three-fold increase on what they were used to. Lawton subsequently moved on to Brentford, and looked set for a career in management. But the man who had inherited Dixie Dean's mantle made a dramatic return to the top flight with Arsenal, and showed that even in his mid-30s he was still a fearsome competitor. His 231 league goals came in at well under a goal every other game, and he scored 23 goals for England in just 22 full internationals.

Busby's first trophy

In the first five postwar seasons Manchester United finished Division One runners-up four times, and fourth on the other occasion. The club finally got its hands on some silverware by winning the Cup in 1948. United twice came from behind against Blackpool to win 4-2, a match that was described as a classic for the purists. Blackpool's Stanley Matthews, who had been honoured with the inaugural Footballer of the Year award, was now 33 and all neutrals wanted to see him get a winners' medal. But two goals from Jack Rowley helped United to victory and ended the "Wizard of the Dribble" hopes for another year.

Matt Busby had inherited some good players when he took over as manager at Old Trafford in October 1945. He also bought wisely and moulded a side which was immediately challenging for top honours. The team was led by Johnny Carey, who played in every position except left-wing. Carey also had the unusual distinction of having played for both the Republic of Ireland and Northern Ireland, the latter thanks to his service in the British Army.

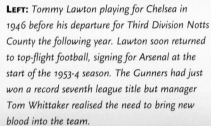

LEFT: *Tommy Lawton playing for Chelsea in 1946 before his departure for Third Division Notts County the following year. Lawton soon returned to top-flight football, signing for Arsenal at the start of the 1953-4 season. The Gunners had just won a record seventh league title but manager Tom Whittaker realised the need to bring new blood into the team.*

BELOW: *Arsenal threaten the Cardiff goal in a match at Highbury in 1953. Despite Cardiff's goalkeeper, Howells, being well out of position, Lishman's shot was stopped on the line.*

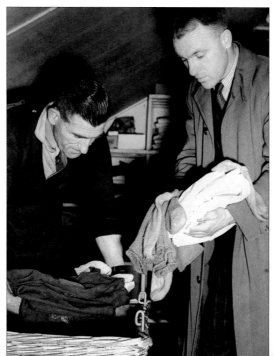

BELOW: *Stanley Matthews is presented to the Duke of Edinburgh before the 1953 Cup Final. It looked as though Matthews would be on the losing side for the third time when Blackpool was trailing 3-1 at the end of the first half. However, after the break Bolton faded and Blackpool's Mortensen scored 2 so that the teams were level at the start of injury time. In the final moments of the game Perry crashed the ball into the net and Blackpool won a thrilling 4-3 victory. A crowd of 200,000 lined the streets to welcome the team home.*

RIGHT: *Tommy McBain (left) and Bill Shankly pack the Carlisle team kit before setting off for a Cup-tie.*

1952-53 DIVISION ONE	
1 Arsenal	54
2 Preston	54
3 Wolverhampton W.	51
4 West Bromwich Albion	50
5 Charlton Athletic	49
6 Burnley	48
7 Blackpool	47
8 Manchester United	46
9 Sunderland	43
10 Tottenham Hotspur	41
11 Aston Villa	41
12 Cardiff	40
13 Middlesbrough	39
14 Bolton Wanderers	39
15 Portsmouth	38
16 Newcastle United	37
17 Liverpool	36
18 Sheffield Wednesday	35
19 Chelsea	35
20 Manchester City	35
21 Stoke	34
22 Derby County	32

"The Matthews Final"

If Manchester United and Wolves were the most consistent performers in the league during this period, Newcastle United were the most successful Cup side. Spearheaded by Jackie Milburn - "Wor Jackie" - and George Robledo, Newcastle won the Cup three times in five years. Blackpool were the first of their Wembley victims in 1951. Two goals from Milburn won the match, leaving Stanley Matthews to rue yet another missed opportunity.

Blackpool made it to Wembley again in 1953, their third appearance in six seasons. Trailing 3-1 to Bolton with 20 minutes left, it looked like a third agonising defeat. But in this most dramatic of all finals Blackpool drew level. Matthews crossed for Mortensen to score, and three minutes from time Mortensen crashed home a free-kick to level. With extra time looming, Matthews weaved yet another piece of magic on the right wing and crossed for Perry to rifle the ball into the net. The 38-year-old maestro finally got his hands on an FA Cup winners' medal, and the match would be forever known as the "Matthews Final".

ABOVE: *The Queen presents Matthews with his medal. One of the game's most gifted footballers, Matthews played professional football until he was 50 years of age.*

BELOW: *The winning goal: while the tremendous crowd urges him on, the "Wizard of the Dribble", Stanley Matthews, streaks down the wing to beat Bolton's Wheeler (4), and puts the ball across to Bill Perry who scored the fourth and winning goal giving Blackpool the FA Cup and Matthews his first winners' medal.*

Stanley Matthews

Stanley Matthews enjoyed a playing career spanning 32 years 10 months and was over 50 by the time he retired from top-class football. He is the oldest player ever to appear in English football's top flight. He is also the oldest England player, winning his last cap, at the age of 42, against Denmark in May 1957. He did not score in that match but his last goal in an international came against Northern Ireland in October 1956; he was 41 years 248 days, making him the oldest player to score for England. While it is conceivable that some of his records might be broken, it is inconceivable that Stanley Matthews' achievements will ever be eclipsed.

At the age of 15 Matthews joined his local side Stoke City and made his debut two years later. Matthews spent 17 years at the club, establishing himself as the best outside-right in world football and earning himself the tag "Wizard of the Dribble".

In his debut game for England in September 1934, he scored, helping the side to a 4-0 win over Wales. This was the start of a 20-year international career during which he won 84 caps, playing in the 1950 and 1954 World Cups. In the 1950 tournament in Brazil Matthews missed the humiliating 1-0 defeat at the hands of the USA; the selectors had decided to alternate Matthews and Tom Finney on the right wing and it was Finney who played that day in Belo Horizonte.

In 1947, Matthews joined Blackpool in a £11,500 transfer deal, but found himself on the losing side in the FA Cup Finals of 1948 and 1951. When Blackpool made it to Wembley again in 1953, all neutral supporters hoped he would finally get a winners' medal. Things looked bleak when opponents Bolton went 3-1 ahead, but 38-year-old Matthews inspired a terrific comeback, Blackpool triumphing as 4-3 winners. The match went down in footballing annals as "the Matthews Final".

Matthews was 46 when he left Blackpool, in October 1961, but incredibly he chose to return to Stoke as a player rather than retire. Four more years at the Potteries club saw Matthews play his last competitive match on 6 February 1965, five days after his 50th birthday. He had just received a knighthood in the New Year's Honours List and went out in style, with a 3-1 win over Fulham.

Matthews was twice Footballer of the Year, in 1948 and 1963, and was also the inaugural European Footballer of the Year in 1956. He died in February 2000, aged 85.

1953-54 DIVISION ONE		
1	Wolverhampton W.	57
2	West Bromwich Albion	53
3	Huddersfield	51
4	Manchester United	48
5	Bolton Wanderers	48
6	Blackpool	48
7	Burnley	46
8	Chelsea	44
9	Charlton Athletic	44
10	Cardiff	44
11	Preston	43
12	Arsenal	43
13	Aston Villa	41
14	Portsmouth	39
15	Newcastle United	38
16	Tottenham Hotspur	37
17	Manchester City	37
18	Sunderland	36
19	Sheffield Wednesday	36
20	Sheffield United	33
21	Middlesbrough	30
22	Liverpool	28

THE WINNING GOAL

BELOW: *Lofthouse opens the scoring for Bolton after 90 seconds as the ball flies past Farm and into the net.*

ABOVE: *Matthews pictured in 1952, 22 years after his debut for Stoke.*

Shock defeat by USA

After a 2-0 win over Chile, England took on the USA in Belo Horizonte. The Americans rode their luck and scored the only goal of the game, a header by Larry Gaetjens. Matthews didn't play in the game that would go down as the blackest moment in England's 80 years of international football. The selectors decided that he and Finney should alternate on the right wing, an extraordinary decision given the fact that Finney was equally potent on the left or through the middle. Matthews returned for the last group match, but even his magic couldn't save the day. A 1-0 defeat by Spain wrapped up a miserable World Cup debut, and England didn't even stay to watch the remaining matches.

Magyars teach England a lesson

Any doubts that England were no longer guaranteed a place at football's top table were ended three years later, when a brilliant Hungary side came to Wembley. The Mighty Magyars, including Puskas, Hidegkuti and Kocsis, taught England a painful lesson in a match that ended

6-3. It was the country's first defeat on home soil. A return match in Budapest six months later showed it was no fluke; Hungary won that encounter 7-1. England full-back Alf Ramsey had witnessed this 13-goal fusillade at close quarters. It was an experience which left an indelible memory on him and would inform his views when he turned his thoughts to management.

At the 1954 World Cup England went down 4-2 to reigning champions Uruguay at the quarter-final stage. In Sweden four years later, Walter Winterbottom was hampered by the loss of the Manchester United stars killed in the Munich disaster. England finished level on points with Russia and the two teams had to play off for the right to go through with Brazil. Russia won 1-0; England's third World Cup ended in disappointment once again.

BELOW: *England's goalkeeper lies prostrate as Johnston retrieves the ball from the net after Hungary scored for the fourth time.*

OPPOSITE: *Billy Wright and Hungarian captain Puskas exchange flags before the start of their Wembley clash in November 1953. England's record of never having been beaten at home by a Continental team was shattered when the Magyars scored six goals with only three in reply.*

1954-55 DIVISION ONE	
1 Chelsea	52
2 Wolverhampton W.	48
3 Portsmouth	48
4 Sunderland	48
5 Manchester United	47
6 Aston Villa	47
7 Manchester City	46
8 Newcastle United	43
9 Arsenal	43
10 Burnley	43
11 Everton	42
12 Huddersfield	41
13 Sheffield United	41
14 Preston	40
15 Charlton Athletic	40
16 Tottenham Hotspur	40
17 West Bromwich Albion	40
18 Bolton Wanderers	39
19 Blackpool	38
20 Cardiff	37
21 Leicester City	35
22 Sheffield Wednesday	26

ABOVE: *The England International football team as they appeared in a friendly match against the Rest of Europe at Wembley on October 21 1953, when they drew 4-4. Alf Ramsey is second from the left in the back row, and Stanley Matthews is on the far left of the front row.*

ABOVE RIGHT: *Captains peer into the pitch for the result of the toss prior to the kick-off of the match between Russian side Spartak and Arsenal. Contact between English and Continental clubs was growing but Chelsea, league champions in 1955, did not take part in the newly-established European Cup. Matt Busby's Manchester United was to enter the competition the following year.*

BELOW: *Allen scores for West Bromwich Albion in their 3-2 victory over Preston North End in the 1954 FA Cup final.*

FA CUP FINALS

Year		v		Score
1946	Derby County	v	Charlton Athletic	4-1
1947	Charlton Athletic	v	Burnley	1-0
1948	Manchester Utd	v	Blackpool	4-2
1949	Wolverhampton W	v	Leicester	3-1
1950	Arsenal	v	Liverpool	2-0
1951	Newcastle United	v	Blackpool	2-0
1952	Newcastle United	v	Arsenal	1-0
1953	Blackpool	v	Bolton W.	4-3
1954	West Bromwich A.	v	Preston N. E.	3-2
1955	Newcastle United	v	Manchester City	3-1
1956	Manchester City	v	Birmingham City	3-1
1957	Aston Villa	v	Manchester United	2-1
1958	Bolton Wanderers	v	Manchester United	2-0
1959	Nottingham Forest	v	Luton Town	2-1

LEFT: The captains lead out their teams at Wembley in 1955. In a repeat of the 1952 final Newcastle's opponents, this time Manchester City, were forced to play a man short for most of the 90 minutes. Newcastle won 3-1 and collected the trophy for the sixth time.

BELOW: Manchester United's Taylor jumps to convert a corner but is beaten by the Birmingham keeper in 1955.

LEFT AND BELOW: Bert Trautmann is assisted from the field in the 1956 FA Cup final. Manchester City's keeper played for 17 minutes in agony with a broken bone in his neck during the 3-1 victory over Birmingham City.

BOTTOM: Trautmann makes the spectacular save that led to his injury. Man of the match Don Revie controlled midfield while Hayes, Dyson and Johnstone scored City's three goals. Kinsey replied for Birmingham.

The "Babes" make their bow

By 1950 the Manchester United side was ageing. There was also disquiet in the ranks as some of the players wanted the club to break the wage cap so that they could cash in during the twilight of their careers. Busby refused, and had already set his sights on a major rebuilding job. He was nurturing a crop of excellent youngsters at the Old Trafford academy, and these represented the future. The old guard had one last moment of glory, finally taking the title in 1951-52. The championship was secured with a 6-1 win over Arsenal, who themselves had a mathematical chance of winning the league. Afterwards, the transition process gathered pace. 18-year-old Jackie Blanchflower and 21-year-old Roger Byrne were the first to make the breakthrough into the senior side, in November 1951. A local journalist commented that the "babes" had acquitted themselves well and, much to Busby's annoyance, this celebrated term soon became part of footballing folklore.

No stars proves no handicap for Pompey

While the Busby Babes were busy winning the FA Youth Cup five years in succession and slowly being incorporated into the first team, other sides were grabbing the headlines. Portsmouth peaked for two marvellous seasons, winning back-to-back championships in 1949 and 1950. The team had no real stars, not even an international in their line-up, showing that an outstanding unit could more than compensate for individual brilliance. The season in which they retained their crown, 1949-50, saw Pompey edge out Wolves on goal average. But as Portsmouth's bubble burst - they would be a Division Two side by the end of the decade - Wolves went on to rival Manchester United as the team of the era.

BELOW: *Brazil's number 8, Valente, walks away with the ball followed by his team-mates and the referee after a penalty was awarded against the South Americans when they played England in May 1956. The Brazilians entertained the crowd with their ball skills but England won by 4 goals to 2, scoring two within the first few minutes of the game.*

ABOVE RIGHT: *Luton play Leicester in particularly difficult conditions.*

1955-56 DIVISION ONE	
1 Manchester United	60
2 Blackpool	49
3 Wolverhampton W.	49
4 Manchester City	46
5 Arsenal	46
6 Birmingham City	45
7 Burnley	44
8 Bolton Wanderers	43
9 Sunderland	43
10 Luton	42
11 Newcastle United	41
12 Portsmouth	41
13 West Bromwich Albion	41
14 Charlton Athletic	40
15 Everton	40
16 Chelsea	39
17 Cardiff	39
18 Tottenham Hotspur	37
19 Preston	36
20 Aston Villa	35
21 Huddersfield	35
22 Sheffield United	33

Long-ball game reaps dividends for Wolves

Unlike Busby, who encouraged his talented players to express themselves, Wolves boss Stan Cullis favoured a much more regimented approach. He regarded over-elaboration as a sin. The emphasis was was on getting the ball as quickly and as often as possible into the opposition's box. Some denigrated this tactic as simply "kick and rush", yet it reaped considerable dividends. Anchoring the side was the redoubtable Billy Wright, who would go on to make nearly 500 appearances in the famous Old Gold shirt. Wright set a new world record by making 70 consecutive international appearances, and he went on to become the first England player to win one hundred caps.

Apart from the championships of 1954, 1958 and 1959, Wolves also enjoyed some sparkling triumphs over top European opposition. In two memorable floodlit matches during the 1954-55 season Wolves came out on top against Moscow Spartak and a Honved side that boasted Puskas, Kocsis and several other members of Hungary's all-star team. As Honved were regarded as the supreme club side of the day, Cullis was quick to acclaim his men as world champions. This piece of self-publicity is said to have prompted Gabriel Hanot, a sports reporter with *L'Equipe*, to seek support for his idea to stage a cup competition for Europe's leading clubs. UEFA quickly took the idea on board and in September 1955 the first European Cup matches were held.

Drake makes history at Chelsea

Wolves could only finish runners-up in 1954-55, and it was Chelsea who earned the right to play in the first Champions Cup. Under pressure from the Football League, who were concerned that the new competition would undermine the domestic programme, Chelsea declined to enter. The only league success in the club's history did earn a special place in the record books, however. Ted Drake had won the championship with Arsenal in the 1930s and had now repeated that success as a manager, the first man to do that particular double.

ABOVE: *Tom Finney negotiates a tackle and a flooded pitch in 1956.*
LEFT: *Tottenham v Burnley in 1956, the year Spurs finished second to Matt Busby's new young team.*
BELOW: *Jackie Henderson, signed twenty-four hours previously from Wolves for £18,000, paid dividends to his new club Arsenal when he scored a goal against West Bromwich Albion just ten minutes into the match.*

John Charles

One of the first British players to ply his trade on the Continent, John Charles was dubbed "The Gentle Giant" by Juventus fans, the club he joined in 1957. It was an affectionate and appropriate nickname, for Charles, with a magnificent physique, was a strong and powerful footballer. Yet, despite his strength and the many physical battles he fought in a 16-year career, both as a centre-half and centre-forward, he was never once booked.

Charles began his career at Leeds United as a central defender. It was in the 1953-54 season that he showed his credentials as a striker, hitting 42 league goals for Leeds, a record to this day.

When he joined Juventus for a record £67,000, he made an immediate impact, hitting 28 goals in 34 games in his first season in Italy. He became Serie A's top marksman and his goals helped Juve to win the Italian championship. By the time he left Italy in 1962, he had a tally of 93 goals in 155 games. During Charles's five years at the club Juventus won the league title three times and the cup twice.

He became the youngest player ever to be capped for Wales. Even though he had played only a few games for Leeds, he was picked to join the line-up for what turned out to be a goalless draw against Northern Ireland at Wrexham on 8 March 1950; he was just 18 years 71 days old. Although he missed Wales's greatest moment in international football, Charles was a key figure in his country's achievement in reaching the quarter-finals of the 1958 World Cup. An injury sustained during a tough play-off battle with Hungary meant that Wales had to face the competition's eventual winners, Brazil, without Charles, going down 1-0.

After a spell back at Elland Road, Charles wound down his career with Roma and Cardiff City.

ABOVE: *England and Russia line up at Wembley before the start of the international in October 1956, which the home team won by 5 goals to nil.*
BELOW: *John Charles trains with his brother Mel who also represented Wales.*

Duncan Edwards

Duncan Edwards was the jewel in the crown of the young and gifted Manchester United side that Matt Busby fashioned in the 1950s – the "Busby Babes" as they became known. Edwards came into the side as a half-back, but his athleticism and all-round ability meant that his influence spread all over the pitch. His tragic death from injuries sustained in the 1958 Munich air crash robbed football of what undoubtedly would have been one of the most outstanding players in the world game in the 1960s; he would probably have figured in the 1966 World Cup, when he would have been 29 years old.

Honours came early to Edwards. He made his debut for Manchester United at the age of 16, winning two championship medals, in 1956 and 1957 with Busby's talented team. When he won his first England cap in 1955 in a 7-2 victory over Scotland, he was just 18 years and 183 days old, a record which stood for more than 40 years until Michael Owen's England debut against Chile in February 1998. In his sadly short career, Edwards notched up 18 caps and scored five goals.

ABOVE LEFT: Duncan Edwards, one of the central figures in Matt Busby's new team. United won the league in 1952 but Busby looked towards the future, devoting attention to finding a new crop of juniors who could be moulded to make formidable unit. By 1956 this new team was ready to compete on the world stage, and Busby had bought just three players: Taylor, Berry and Ray Wood.

ABOVE: Manchester United players celebrate their second title in two years.

BELOW: Members of the Manchester United team travel from Blackpool to London in 1957 (L-R: McGuinness, Foulkes, Jones, Colman and Wood).

United romp to title by 11 points

Chelsea's decision to decline to enter the 1956 competition meant that Manchester United became the country's first champions to contest the European Cup. Busby's team earned the right by romping to the 1955-56 title by 11 points, equalling the biggest winning margin in the league's 68-year history. When Dennis Viollet scored the only goal of the match against Portsmouth on 21 April 1956, United were uncatchable.

By now the pieces of the jigsaw were all in place. Duncan Edwards had made his debut as a 16-year-old in 1953, with Tommy Taylor moving to Old Trafford from Barnsley in the same year for £29,999. Busby deliberately pitched the deal just short of £30,000 to try and ease the anxiety that might have accompanied a big-money move. Mark Jones, Eddie Colman, David Pegg and Bobby Charlton were others among the precociously talented crop of young players that Busby had assembled. In four years he had transformed a veteran side into one in which the average age was just 22.

"Push and run" brings success to Spurs

United retained their crown the following season, finishing eight points ahead of Tottenham. In style the Spurs side was closer to United than Wolves. Under Arthur Rowe the team had developed a marvellous "push and run" technique, which had brought the club the championship in 1951. Bill Nicholson and Alf Ramsey were members of that side, and the former joined the coaching staff at White Hart Lane when he finished playing. Spurs were also twice runners-up in the 1950s but their greatest moment, with Nicholson at the helm, still lay ahead.

United's European dream ended by Real Madrid

Meanwhile, United's first sortie into European competition ended at the semi-final stage, when they were beaten by holders Real Madrid. Tommy Taylor and Bobby Charlton earned United a 2-2 draw at Old Trafford, not enough to overturn a 3-1 defeat at the Bernebeu Stadium. Busby wasn't unduly worried. Earlier in the competition his team had beaten Anderlecht 12-0 on aggregate, and also put out Borussia Dortmund and Atletico Bilbao before going out to the best side in Europe. Youth was on United's side and they would be even stronger the following season.

LEFT: *The young Chelsea player, Jimmy Greaves, in training for his match against Wolverhampton in October 1957.*
BELOW: *1957: At Goodison Park engineers of the Merseyside and North Wales Electricity Board lay the first turf-warming system six inches below the surface of the pitch at a cost of £7000.*

1956-57 DIVISION ONE

1	Manchester United	64
2	Tottenham Hotspur	56
3	Preston	56
4	Blackpool	53
5	Arsenal	50
6	Wolverhampton W.	48
7	Burnley	46
8	Leeds United	44
9	Bolton Wanderers	44
10	Aston Villa	43
11	West Bromwich Albion	42
12	Birmingham City	39
13	Chelsea	39
14	Sheffield Wednesday	38
15	Everton	38
16	Luton	37
17	Newcastle United	36
18	Manchester City	35
19	Portsmouth	33
20	Sunderland	32
21	Cardiff	29
22	Charlton Athletic	22

"Villain" McParland makes it seven Cup wins

1957-58 DIVISION ONE	
1 Wolverhampton W.	64
2 Preston	59
3 Tottenham Hotspur	51
4 West Bromwich Albion	50
5 Manchester City	49
6 Burnley	47
7 Blackpool	44
8 Luton	44
9 Manchester United	43
10 Nottingham Forest	42
11 Chelsea	42
12 Arsenal	39
13 Birmingham City	39
14 Aston Villa	39
15 Bolton Wanderers	38
16 Everton	37
17 Leeds United	37
18 Leicester City	33
19 Newcastle United	32
20 Portsmouth	32
21 Sunderland	32
22 Sheffield Wednesday	31

Before then there was the prospect of the coveted Double. Having wrapped up the league, United faced Aston Villa in the FA Cup Final. The key moment came after just six minutes, when Villa's Peter McParland clattered into United keeper Ray Wood, breaking the latter's cheekbone. Jackie Blanchflower took over in goal, badly disrupting United's rhythm. McParland rubbed salt into United's wounds by scoring both Villa goals in a 2-1 win. It was Villa's seventh victory, a record for the competition.

The incident involving Wood was one of a succession of injuries which cast a shadow over Wembley Finals in the 1950s. In 1956 Manchester City keeper Bert Trautmann suffered a broken neck in the 3-1 win over Birmingham City. In 1959 Nottingham Forest winger Roy Dwight was carried off with a broken leg, and Blackburn full-back Dave Whelan suffered the same injury a year later. Some dubbed it the "Wembley hoodoo", while others put the number of injuries down to the fact that the turf was too soft.

ABOVE: *Villa captain Johnny Dixon holds the trophy aloft.*

BELOW: *Aston Villa goalkeeper Sims leaps but fails to stop Taylor's strike in the closing minutes of the 1957 Cup Final. A head-on charge by Villa's McParland on the Manchester goalkeeper left Wood unable to continue playing in goal. Despite the valiant efforts of Jackie Blanchflower who took his place, Manchester, playing with ten men, could not overcome the Villa defence.*

Eight United players killed in Munich tragedy

On 1 February 1958 United went to Highbury and won a sparkling match 5-4. The result kept them in second place in the league, looking ominously good to equal Huddersfield's and Arsenal's achievement of a hat-trick of championships. The team then headed to Belgrade to take on Red Star in the second leg of their European Cup-tie. Having won 2-1 at home, a 3-3 draw was enough to put United into the semis once again. On the return journey the plane stopped to refuel at Munich. In atrocious weather two attempted take-offs were aborted. The third attempt ended in disaster, the plane failing to get off the ground and slewing into the perimeter fence. There were 23 fatalities, including seven of the Babes. An eighth, Duncan Edwards, lost his battle for life two weeks later. Johnny Berry and Jackie Blanchflower survived but never played football again.

No sentiment as United go down fighting

The heart had been ripped out of United, yet amazingly, a side made up of reserve and youth team players, together with a couple of emergency signings, reached that year's FA Cup Final. There was no fairytale, however; two goals from Nat Lofthouse won the trophy for Bolton Wanderers.

Some suggested that the European Cup should be awarded to United as a mark of respect to the great players who had perished at Munich. But sentiment was not allowed to prevail and United's semi-final clash with AC Milan went ahead as scheduled. United lost 5-2 on aggregate. Having built two championship-winning sides, Busby immediately set about creating a third.

BELOW: *Manchester United's Cup finalists in 1957. Busby's team narrowly failed to win the trophy but had topped the league at the end of 1956 and 1957, qualifying for the embryonic European Cup. Playing against the wishes of the FA, United reached the semi-finals of the competition, eventually being knocked out by Real Madrid. (l-r, Inglis, Geoff Bent, Ray Wood, Mark Jones, Billy Foulkes, Dennis Viollet and Tom Curry. Front row: Jackie Blanchflower, Colin Webster, Wilf McGuinness, Tommy Taylor, Bill Whelan and David Pegg. With ball: Johnny Berry)*

BOTTOM: *Fans and players observe a one minute silence at the Tottenham v Manchester Ctiy game played on the Saturday after the tragedy in Munich.*

Structural problems highlighted

The experience of the 1950s showed that England would have to work hard to match the skills of the top Continental and South American sides. There were also structural and organisational problems. In 1950 Stanley Matthews was with an FA touring side in Canada when his team-mates arrived in Brazil. And when the food was discovered to be unpalatable, Winterbottom found himself in charge of the catering! In 1958 the team arrived in Sweden to find there were no training facilities, and Winterbottom had to chase round looking for a suitable venue. There was a minor step forward in that senior players were given a voice on selection matters, but overall the running of the international side left a lot to be desired. Success at international level could no longer be achieved with a part-time manager who had responsibility without power. It was not until the next decade that things changed dramatically for the better. A man of vision was brought in, and freed from the shackles of the Selection Committee he was able to put his ideas into practice.

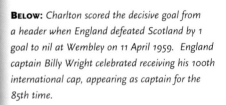

RIGHT: *Bobby Charlton on the training ground. Charlton, Viollet, Gregg and Foulkes were all fit to represent Manchester United in the 1958 FA Cup Final just months after the Munich disaster. Despite a spirited fight by United, Bolton won the match by 2 goals to nil.*

1958-59 DIVISION ONE	
1 Wolverhampton W.	61
2 Manchester United	55
3 Arsenal	50
4 Bolton Wanderers	50
5 West Bromwich Albion	49
6 West Ham United	48
7 Burnley	48
8 Blackpool	47
9 Birmingham City	46
10 Blackburn Rovers	44
11 Newcastle United	41
12 Preston	41
13 Nottingham Forest	40
14 Chelsea	40
15 Leeds United	39
16 Everton	38
17 Luton	37
18 Tottenham Hotspur	36
19 Leicester City	32
20 Manchester City	31
21 Aston Villa	30
22 Portsmouth	21

BELOW: *Charlton scored the decisive goal from a header when England defeated Scotland by 1 goal to nil at Wembley on 11 April 1959. England captain Billy Wright celebrated receiving his 100th international cap, appearing as captain for the 85th time.*

BOTTOM: *An incident at Stamford Bridge. Spectators ran on to the pitch after Everton inside-left Collins had brought down Chelsea's Blunstone in a tackle.*
BELOW: *England playing Sweden in 1959.*

RIGHT: *Billy Wright waves to the crowd as he leads out the England team. Wright's contribution to international football was matched by his dedication to his club, Wolves, who finished top of the league in 1954, 1958 and 1959.*

Billy Wright

Born in 1924, Billy Wright was one of Wolverhampton Wanderers' heroes in the 1950s. Short, tough, and a powerful header of the ball, he was the defensive backbone of the side. Having started out as a PT instructor, he made his debut for Wolves in 1941, took over the captaincy in 1947 and retained that role for 12 seasons. They were the glory days of the club, with Wright leading the team to F.A. Cup victory in 1949, followed in 1953/54 by the first of three League Championships in six years.

He began his international career in 1946, against Northern Ireland, and in 1959 he became the first player to reach 100 caps. Wright captained England in 90 of his 105 appearances, including three World Cups, in 1950, 1954 and 1958.

His last game for Wolves came in 1959, the year he married Joy Beverly of the Beverly Sisters and added a touch of glamour to what was already extraordinary popularity. After four years as manager of Arsenal, he became a sports journalist. He died in 1994.

1959-60 DIVISION ONE

1	Burnley	55
2	Wolverhampton W.	54
3	Tottenham Hotspur	53
4	West Bromwich Albion	49
5	Sheffield Wednesday	49
6	Bolton Wanderers	48
7	Manchester United	45
8	Newcastle United	44
9	Preston	44
10	Fulham	44
11	Blackpool	40
12	Leicester City	39
13	Arsenal	39
14	West Ham United	38
15	Everton	37
16	Manchester City	37
17	Blackburn Rovers	37
18	Chelsea	37
19	Birmingham City	36
20	Nottingham Forest	35
21	Leeds United	34
22	Luton	30

BELOW: *A brilliant save by Springett, the Sheffield Wednesday goalkeeper, who stops a shot by Clapton for Arsenal during the match at Highbury in August 1959. The new season got off to a bright start for the newly promoted Wednesday who defeated Arsenal by 1 goal to nil.*

RIGHT: *Skipper Burkitt of Nottingham Forest with the FA Cup after his team won the final against Luton 2-1 in 1959 – despite having a depleted team after Roy Dwight broke his leg.*

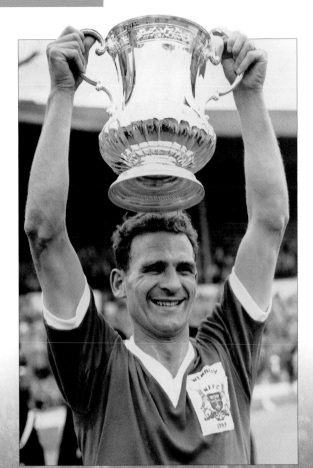

Sir Matt Busby

Matt Busby built three brilliant championship-winning sides in a glorious 26-year reign at Old Trafford. Busby spent his playing career at two of United's arch-rivals, neighbours Manchester City and Liverpool, winning an FA Cup winners medal with City in 1934.

He took over at Old Trafford after the Second World War and built a side which finished runners-up four times in five years. The title finally arrived in 1951-52, adding to an FA Cup victory over Blackpool in 1948.

As that ageing side was broken up, Busby scoured the country for the finest young players in the land. By the mid-1950s his outstanding young team, dubbed the "Busby Babes", looked as if it would dominate football for many years. There were successive league championships in 1956 and 1957. The team also twice made it to the sem-fiinals of the fledgling European Cup competition. It was on a return trip from a successful European quarter-final tie against Red Star Belgrade that the side was all but wiped out. Eight players lost their lives at Munich on 6 February 1958, and Busby himself was given last rites. He recovered to build yet another superb side in the 1960s. The likes of George Best and Denis Law were added to Munich survivors Bobby Charlton and Bill Foulkes. United lifted the FA Cup in 1963 and won the championship in 1965 and 1967. The latter success gave Busby yet another crack at the trophy he desperately wanted to win. The realisation of a long-held dream came at Wembley on 29 May 1968, when his side beat Benfica 4-1 in the European Cup Final. Busby became only the second British club manager to win the trophy. He was knighted for his achievements in the same year, retiring three years later. Busby died in 1994, an avid watcher of his beloved United right up to the end.

BELOW: *Quigley scores for Nottingham Forest to give the team a 1-0 victory over Aston Villa in the 1959 FA Cup semi-final at Hillsborough, Sheffield. (L-R: Sims (the Villa goalkeeper) Dwight, Dixon and Quigley).*

BOTTOM: *A goalmouth incident in the Tottenham v Burnley game at White Hart Lane. The Clarets won the League in the 1959-60 season finishing 2 points ahead of Spurs who were third. Wolves narrowly failed to win 3 consecutive titles when they were edged into second place.*

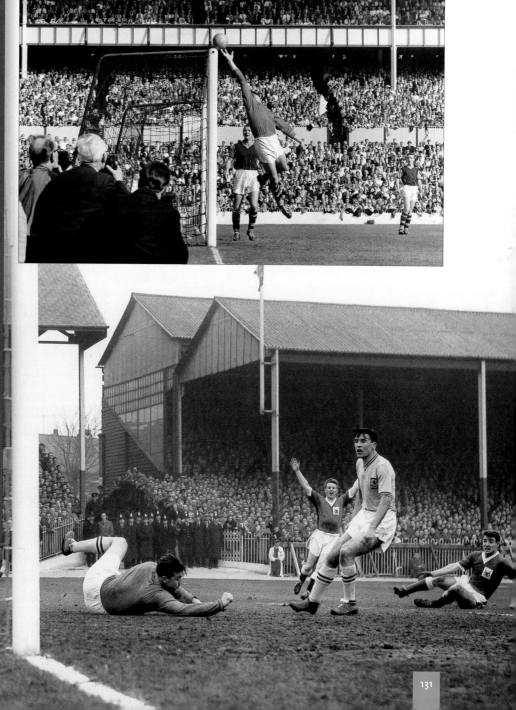

1960-1969
Champions of the World

As the new decade got into its stride football faced a number of problems. Hooliganism, corruption and falling gates all gave cause for concern. On the pitch there was a marked increase in foul play, and fewer goals were scored as defences got on top. On a brighter note, Matt Busby built his third great side, English clubs made the breakthrough in European competition and the national side were crowned world champions.

Changing attitudes

By the 1960s people were enjoying greater affluence and had many more options when it came to spending their "leisure pound". The demand for cars and foreign holidays went up, while every form of entertainment had to compete with television. In the Swinging Sixties England was at the cutting edge of the pop music and fashion industries, and these were yet more diversions as the Baby Boomers came of age. There was also a distinct change in attitude, women no longer being content with playing a domestic role while the menfolk went off to the match.

Fears over televised matches

The effect of all these factors was reflected in declining attendances, particularly for struggling clubs or those perceived as unglamorous. As the footballing authorities sought ways to encourage more people through the turnstiles, the one avenue they naturally fought shy of was the televising of matches. In 1960 negotiations between the Football League and the Independent Television Authority fell through over fears that broadcasting a live game might have an adverse effect on attendances. Concerns were not allayed by the proposal to schedule the matches so that they didn't clash with any other football taking place. Within a couple of years, however, the broadcasting companies persuaded the Football League that a highlights package would not be detrimental to the game, and indeed could help to generate more interest and a wider fan base.

When *Match of the Day* took to the airwaves in 1964, it quickly became an institution. Television turned the top players into celebrities as well as sportsmen. The authorities' fears that TV would lead to an army of armchair fans proved largely unfounded. However, seeing the likes of Greaves, Charlton and St John in action on the small screen did persuade a considerable number to switch their allegiance or to forge a new one. In short, the glamour clubs flourished at the expense of the rest.

ABOVE: *The score changes but the outcome is not in doubt at an exhibition match in May 1961. Commentators attributed England's recent run of victories to Walter Winterbottom's newly adopted 4-2-4 formation introduced in the face of current tactics.*

LEFT: *Forwards Johnny Haynes, Bobby Smith and Jimmy Greaves on England duty.*

BELOW: *Tottenham playing Manchester City in the 1960-61 season when the north London club won the double.*

OPPOSITE BELOW: *Jimmy Greaves scores his first league goal for Chelsea against Tottenham Hotspur.*

OPPOSITE ABOVE: *Ron Flowers (far right), beats Mexico's goalkeeper Mota to score England's fifth goal from the penalty spot in May 1961. England beat Mexico 8-1.*

Hill leads campaign to end wage cap

The cult of celebrity had another important knock-on effect: the rise of player power. In the early 1960s players became aware of their worth, and realised that they were being sorely undervalued. Before 1960 even the sport's greatest names reaped little financial reward for the pleasure they brought to millions of fans. After hanging up their boots there was no life of luxury. The lucky ones found alternative employment. Tommy Lawton and Hughie Gallacher both ended up on the dole, the latter committing suicide by throwing himself under a train in 1957. In that same year the Players Union got a new chairman, Fulham's Jimmy Hill. Hill led the campaign to end the wage cap which stood at £20 a week, £17 during the close season.

Haynes becomes first £100-a-week footballer

It took Hill four years to garner the support he needed to act. This was because the Players Union had been emasculated by mass resignations over the same issue more than 30 years earlier. In the depression of the 1920s the Union had been unable to prevent clubs from reducing the maximum wage to £8 a week. In the intervening years the Football League hardly condescended to meet with players' representatives. But in January 1961 the threat of strike action made the authorities sit up and take notice. In June of that year the maximum wage was abolished. England captain Johnny Haynes became the first £100-a-week footballer, his chairman Tommy Trinder declaring that he was delighted at finally being able to properly reward his star performer, who was worth every penny to the club.

BELOW: *The Blackburn goalkeeper fails to save and Deeley scores a second goal for Wolves in the 1960 Final. Blackburn fans were disappointed when left-back Wheelan broke his leg forcing their team to play more than half the match with only 10 men. The game ended in a 3-0 win for Wolves.*
LEFT: *Johnny Haynes takes a break from England training. The Fulham wing half, who was loyal to his club throughout his career, had just become the highest paid player in English football.*

Johnny Haynes

Johnny Haynes was ardently loyal to Fulham, his only club, and that loyalty cost him dearly in terms of honours. At the time – Haynes was at Craven Cottage from 1952 to 1969 – the club was either in the Second Division or struggling in the lower reaches of the First.

England captain

Despite playing for an unfashionable and relatively unsuccessful club, Haynes established himself in the England side in the mid-1950s. An inside-forward who was noted for his wonderful passing, Haynes was a regular on the scoresheet. In his 56 England appearances he bagged 18 goals and in 1959, took over the captaincy of the national side after Billy Wright's retirement. He was an essential player in both the 1958 and 1962 World Cups, helping England to the quarter-final in the latter tournament.

Soon after the World Cup in Chile, in 1962, a serious car crash ended his international career. But loyal to the end, he turned out for Fulham for another seven years. A reward for that loyalty and an indication of how valued Haynes was can be seen in the fact that he became the first £100-a-week footballer after the maximum wage was abolished in 1961. He ended his footballing days as player-manager of Durban City after emigrating to South Africa.

LEFT: *Tottenham stars Jimmy Greaves and Danny Blanchflower leave to play Benfica in the semi-final of the European Cup in March 1962. After losing 3-1 in Lisbon, Spurs played in a thrilling second leg and were narrowly defeated by 4 goals to 3.*

BELOW LEFT: *Fulham's Jimmy Hill and Parker of Everton find themselves in the net while the ball sails past in January 1960.*

1960-61 DIVISION ONE

1	Tottenham Hotspur	66
2	Sheffield Wednesday	58
3	Wolverhampton W.	57
4	Burnley	51
5	Everton	50
6	Leicester City	45
7	Manchester United	45
8	Blackburn Rovers	43
9	Aston Villa	43
10	West Bromwich Albion	41
11	Arsenal	41
12	Chelsea	37
13	Manchester City	37
14	Nottingham Forest	37
15	Cardiff	37
16	West Ham United	36
17	Fulham	36
18	Bolton Wanderers	35
19	Birmingham City	34
20	Blackpool	33
21	Newcastle United	32
22	Preston	30

England 9
Scotland 3

The early form of the international side in the 1960s was encouraging. After defeats in Spain and Hungary, England went on a fine run in the next six games. They rattled in 40 goals, including an 8-0 home win over Mexico and a 9-0 victory in Luxembourg. But the outstanding result was undoubtedly the 9-3 demolition of Scotland on 15 April 1961. It was a strong Scotland side - including Law, Mackay and St John - which came to Wembley for what was the decider in the home international championship. A Greaves hat-trick, together with two goals each from Johnny Haynes and Bobby Smith, contributed towards the Scots' worst- ever result in international football.

BELOW: *England 9 - Scotland 3: Haffey, Scotland's goalkeeper, is beaten by Bobby Smith's shot, England's fifth goal.*
RIGHT: *The victorious England team's celebration gets into full swing after the final whistle.*

Ramsey takes over from Winterbottom

Performances such as these boded well for the 1962 World Cup in Chile, but the tournament proved to be something of a disappointment. England did reach the last eight, squeezing through their group after a win, a draw and a defeat, but they were unconvincing. After a 3-1 defeat against holders Brazil they were on their way home.

The tournament marked the end of Walter Winterbottom's 16-year reign as England manager. In came Alf Ramsey, who had worked wonders at Ipswich,

although he was said to be only third choice for the job.

Defeats against France and Scotland got the new regime off to an inauspicious start. Even so, Ramsey was soon predicting victory in the 1966 World Cup. Despite home advantage, England were not fancied to do well. The international side had lost just four times on home soil against overseas opposition, but as the optimists rested their hopes on fortress Wembley, the doom-mongers pointed to England's World Cup record since 1950.

OPPOSITE TOP: *Prolific scorer Jimmy Greaves lashes the ball into the net when England met Spain in October 1960.*

ABOVE: *Despite a run of successes, England's lacklustre performance in the 1962 World Cup spelled the end of Winterbottom's tenure as manager. Mindful of the need to make a good showing in the next World Cup to be staged in England, the FA employed new manager Alf Ramsey and granted him autonomy in team selection.*

ABOVE LEFT: *Haffey falls to the ground in despair as England scores their seventh.*

LEFT: *The rewards of success. Fans queue for tickets at Ipswich's Portman Road ground. Alf Ramsey took the unfashionable club to the summit of division one in the 1961-62 season.*

Transfer court challenge

Clubs might have had to pay their top players more but they still had the whip hand by dint of the "retain-and-transfer" system that was in place. Under this arrangement players were bound to their clubs even at the end of their contracts. In 1963 England international George Eastham was seeking a move away from Newcastle United and challenged this restriction of his freedom in the courts. The ruling went in his favour, with the prevailing system condemned as an "unreasonable restraint of trade".

BELOW: *Ipswich playing West Ham in the club's championship year. The East Anglia club had risen from the Third Division (South) to English champions in just five years.*

TOP: *23 November 1963: Arsenal players wear black armbands and stand in silent tribute to the late President Kennedy before the start of their match against Blackpool. (l-r) Eastham, Barnwell, McCullogh, Anderson, Clarke, MacLeod, Strong, Brown, Baker, Ure and Furnell.*

ABOVE RIGHT: *Aston Villa, became the first winners of the Football League Cup after defeating Rotherham United at Villa park in September 1961. Villa won on 3-2 on aggregate. Villa's captain, Vic Crowe (centre) is surrounded by his winning team (L-R: Sidebottom, Burrows, Lee, Neal, Thomson, Dugdale, McEwan, O'Neill, Deakin).*

Bill Nicholson

Bill Nicholson spent his entire career at Tottenham, joining the club as a 16-year-old. When his playing days were over, Nicholson became a coach under Arthur Rowe, the architect of the "push and run" side that had won the title in 1951. He took over as manager in 1959, and assembled a team which took Rowe's ideas to dazzling new heights. His team combined superb ball skills with steely resolve, featuring players of the stature of Blanchflower and Mackay. In 1960-61 he guided Spurs through a glorious campaign which saw the team win 31 of their 42 league games, scoring 115 goals in the process. They secured the championship by an eight-point margin, then beat Leicester City 2-0 in the FA Cup Final, despite going into the game with an injury-ravaged squad. No twentieth-century team had won the Double, and many thought the demands of the modern game meant that it was unachievable. Nicholson proved the doubters wrong.

Spurs retained the Cup the following season, and in 1963 Nicholson became the first manager of a British club to win a European trophy. Spurs beat holders Atletico Madrid 5-1 in the Cup Winners' Cup Final in Rotterdam. Victory over Chelsea in the 1967 FA Cup Final meant that Nicholson had brought the trophy to White Hart Lane three times in seven years.

Nicholson stepped down during the 1974-75 season but remained associated with the club into his 80s.

Spurs become the century's first Double winners

On the pitch the decade got off to a sparkling start as Bill Nicholson's Spurs side became the first of the century to achieve the Double. The strength of the side was epitomised by the two wing-halves: granite-hard Dave Mackay and the cultured, cerebral Danny Blanchflower. Spurs began with a record run of 11 straight wins, and their 31 victories in all was another league best. 66 points equalled Arsenal's total of 1931. The team banged in 115 goals, a postwar record, and that was before the incomparable Jimmy Greaves had joined the club. Nicholson thus became only the second man to win the championship as both player and manager. The season took its toll in the latter stages of the Cup. Spurs needed a replay to beat Division Two side Sunderland in the 6th round, and they were below par when they took on Leicester City at Wembley. But top scorer Bobby Smith and Terry Dyson both beat City keeper Gordon Banks and history was made. Following the Cup successes of 1901 and 1921, and the championship in 1951, fans were already noting the club's peculiar affinity with the second year of the decade.

FAR RIGHT: *Blanchflower lifts the Cup. Following in the footsteps of Preston and Aston Villa, Spurs win the Double, for the first time since 1897. Nicholson's team had secured the league title in mid-April but had to wait three weeks before meeting Leicester in the Cup Final. Spurs won 2-0.*
RIGHT: *Leaving the pitch at Portman Road after a top-of-the-table clash between Ipswich and Tottenham.*

Cup Winners Cup takes off

Spurs kept the Cup the following year, beating Burnley 3-1 in the final, but slipped to third in the league. Their European Cup campaign ended at the semi-final stage, when they went down 4-3 on aggregate to holders Benfica. Retaining the Cup in 1962 gave Spurs entry into the following season's Cup Winners' Cup competition. This had been launched in 1960, the brainchild of a group of European Football Federations. In just two seasons it had made more impact than the third European trophy up for grabs, the Inter-Cities Fairs Cup. Under the rules of the Fairs Cup, which had been launched in the mid-1950s, industrial towns and cities competed with each other, matches arranged to coincide with trade fairs. This meant that the first two tournaments took five years to complete! Moreover, a city could enter a club side or a representative XI. Between 1955 and 1958 Barcelona beat a London side including Kelsey (Arsenal), Blanchflower (Spurs), Greaves (Chelsea) and Haynes (Fulham). By the mid-1960s the competition had severed its connections with trade fairs and become a sought-after trophy for the top European clubs who failed to win their domestic league or cup.

ABOVE LEFT: *Adamson of Burnley and Fulham's Cook and O'Donnell go for the ball as the teams fight for a place in the 1962 Cup Final. Burnley finishes as runners-up, losing in the Final to Spurs.*

ABOVE: *Leicester's Gordon Banks in training.*

LEFT: *When Bill Shankly arrived at Anfield in 1959 his first task was to help Liverpool regain its place in the First Division, and this was achieved by the beginning of the 1962-3 season.*

OPPOSITE ABOVE LEFT: *After 10 years with Spurs, Danny Blanchflower retired in 1964. Alan Mullery, bought from Fulham, was Nicholson's choice to fill the gap left by Blanchflower.*

OPPOSITE ABOVE RIGHT: *Dave Mckay and his fellow Spurs can't hide their astonishment as White's corner swings in without anyone touching it.*

OPPOSITE BELOW RIGHT: *Fulham's Johnny Haynes in action.*

Danny Blanchflower

Danny Blanchflower joined Tottenham Hotspur from Aston Villa for £30,000 in 1954. Over the next ten years Blanchflower, an intelligent wing-half with a sharp tactical brain, became a legend at White Hart Lane. He was the brains and the driving force of the side which, in the 1960-61 season, won the much sought-after Double; he was the first captain of the century to lift both trophies in one season. Following on from that unparalleled success it was fitting that Blanchflower won his second Footballer of the Year award – only Tom Finney had managed that achievement at the time.

Blanchflower steered Spurs to FA Cup victory the following season, even getting on the scoresheet himself in the team's 3-1 win over Burnley in the Final at Wembley. In what was to be his last but one season before retirement, Blanchflower inspired Tottenham to a 5-1 win over Atletico Madrid in the European Cup Winners' Cup Final, becoming the first captain of a British side to lift a European trophy.

Blanchflower was born in Belfast and played 56 times for Northern Ireland, where he also took on the captain's role. His most memorable moment with the national side was probably in the 1958 World Cup, when he led the side to the quarter-finals. He died in 1993, aged 67.

First British side to win European trophy

In 1962-63 Spurs became the first British side to win a European trophy when they lifted the Cup Winners' Cup. They put out Rangers, Slovan Bratislava and OFK Belgrade en route to the final, where they faced holders Atletico Madrid. Despite missing Mackay through injury, Spurs ran out 5-1 winners. The key moment came in the second half when Spurs were 2-1 up. Terry Dyson floated a cross into the box and it swirled over keeper Madinabeytia into the net.

Nicholson ends Greaves' Italian nightmare
Jimmy Greaves scored two of the goals that night in Rotterdam. Greaves had been one of a number of high-profile players lured to the Continent by a bigger wage-packet and better lifestyle. His time

at AC Milan following an £80,000 move from Chelsea had not been a happy one and he was only too pleased when Bill Nicholson paid £99,999 to bring him back to the First Division. It was a British transfer record, although Nicholson kept it below the six-figure mark so that Greaves wouldn't be burdened with the

tag of the first £100,000 player. Denis Law had an equally unhappy time after leaving Manchester City to join Torino. The one outstanding success story in this regard was John Charles, the Leeds United and Wales star who was lionised by Turin fans after his move to Juventus in 1957.

LEFT: *Scenes of jubilation in Tottenham as Spurs rack up another first when they bring home Britain's first European trophy in May 1963.*
ABOVE: *Danny Blanchflower and Bill Nicholosn celebrate at a civic reception.*

BELOW: *Players parade the Cup Winners' Cup through the streets of Tottenham (L-R: Cliff Jones (rear), Bill Brown (front), Ron Henry, Jimmy Greaves (holding cup) and Terry Dyson).*

Jimmy Greaves

Jimmy Greaves was a slightly built inside-forward with lightning-fast feet, a razor-sharp brain and a killer instinct in front of goal. Throughout the 1960s Greaves was the foremost goal-poacher in English football. Although closely associated with Tottenham Hotspur, he started his career at Chelsea where he became a teenage prodigy before joining AC Milan in 1961. His failure to settle in Italy, where he played just 15 games, enabled Spurs' boss Bill Nicholson to bring him to White Hart Lane for what was then the hefty price tag of £99,999.

Record goalscorer

During the following nine years Greaves hit 220 league goals for Spurs, including 37 in the 1962-63 season, both of which are still club records. He was the First Division's top scorer six times in that nine-year period. Despite a much-publicised, and ultimately victorious, battle with alcoholism, his goalscoring talents were evident throughout his career. By the time he retired, after playing for a number of seasons for another London club, West Ham, he had scored a total of 357 league goals, all in the First Division.

44 goals for England

Unfortunately for Greaves, in a decade which witnessed many of his most incredible achievements, he chose the worst possible moment to suffer a drop in form. He was Alf Ramsey's first-choice striker as the England team went into the 1966 World Cup, but was replaced by Geoff Hurst in the latter stages of the tournament. Despite missing several of the 1966 World Cup games, including the Final, he scored 44 times for England, putting him third behind Bobby Charlton and Gary Lineker in the all-time list of England strikers. But Greaves' haul came from just 57 international appearances, far fewer than either Lineker or Charlton, who won 80 and 106 caps respectively – testament to his magnificent goal-scoring talents.

Dave Mackay

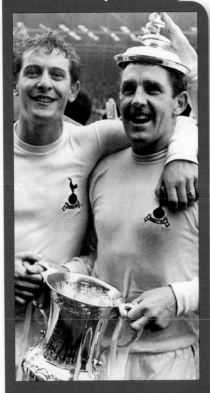

Mackay suffers two broken legs in a year

After 1963 the great Spurs side broke up very quickly. It was a new-look team which brought the club its only other piece of silverware of the decade, a third FA Cup win in 1967. Of the eleven who had won the Cup Winners' Cup only Greaves was on the pitch when Spurs beat Chelsea 2-1. Most of the changes had been organic but one was the result of a tragedy: John White, the 27-year-old Scottish international inside-forward, was killed by lightning on a London golf course in July 1964. In the same year Dave Mackay broke his left leg twice within ten months, something which would have ended the career of a player with less resolve. But having missed out on that European glory night, Mackay battled back to play on for eight more years, including the Wembley Final of 1967.

After starting his career with Heart of Midlothian, Dave Mackay joined Tottenham Hotspur in 1959. As a dynamic and inspirational half-back he provided the steel and drive in the great Spurs side of the early 1960s. Although he was already an established Scotland international before he joined Tottenham, it was at club level that Mackay enjoyed his greatest successes. Spurs celebrated Double was achieved in the 1960-61 season, and the team retained the FA Cup the following year. Injury forced him to miss the final of the European Cup Winners' Cup in 1963, when Spurs beat holders Atletico Madrid 5-1.

Footballer of the Year

His career looked in serious doubt as a result of two broken legs, sustained within a nine-month period in 1964, but the indomitable Mackay fought back to captain Spurs to another FA Cup triumph in 1967. The following season he transferred to Derby County where he led the team to the Division Two championship in 1968-69, an achievement which earned him the Footballer of the Year award, an honour he shared with Manchester City's Tony Book.

BELOW: *Spurs' John White in action. Nicknamed 'The Ghost' after his ability to pop up from nowhere to make key contributions in matches, White was ever-present in the double-winning side of 1960-61. His life was cut short when a tree he was sheltering under during a thunderstorm was struck by lightning. He was just 27.*

ABOVE: *Bobby Charlton and his manager Matt Busby talk with a young fan.*
LEFT: *Alan Mullery and captain Dave Mackay (right) hold the FA Cup after a 2-1 win over Chelsea in the 1967 Cup Final.*
Mackay and Greaves were the only representatives of the Tottenham side that won the Cup in 1962.

Ramsey's Ipswich take First Division by storm

The team that took the title from Spurs in 1962 was Alf Ramsey's unheralded Ipswich Town. The East Anglia club had risen from the Third Division (South) to English champions in just five years. Ramsey's men won the Division Two and Division One titles in successive seasons, the fourth club to record that particular achievement. Ramsey the player had been schooled in Spurs' great "push and run" side of the previous decade, and it was outstanding team play rather than brilliant individuals that carried Ipswich to the title.

It would put Ramsey's name in the frame when the England job became vacant following the 1962 World Cup.

Exit Accrington Stanley

While Ipswich were riding high, one of the famous names in the English game was making a sad exit. Accrington Stanley, one of the League's founder members, had mounting debts and was forced to resign from the Fourth Division. This was yet another sign of the polarisation between the haves and have-nots, a trend that was set to continue.

BELOW: *Accrington Stanley skipper Bob Wilson reads the bill for a match that was never to take place, the club being forced to resign from the league because of financial difficulties. Ironically, Exeter too was suffering from crippling debts.*
BOTTOM: *Spectators and staff show their feelings, as Ramsey's Ispwich are one goal away from winning the league title in 1962. Ramsey's side, recently languishing in the Third Division and with its absence of star players, were unlikely champions, tipped by pundits for relegation rather than triumph.*

1961-62 DIVISION ONE	
1 Ipswich	56
2 Burnley	53
3 Tottenham Hotspur	52
4 Everton	51
5 Sheffield United	47
6 Sheffield Wednesday	46
7 Aston Villa	44
8 West Ham United	44
9 West Bromwich Albion	43
10 Arsenal	43
11 Bolton Wanderers	42
12 Manchester City	41
13 Blackpool	41
14 Leicester City	40
15 Manchester United	39
16 Blackburn Rovers	39
17 Birmingham City	38
18 Wolverhampton W.	36
19 Nottingham Forest	36
20 Fulham	33
21 Cardiff	32
22 Chelsea	28

Everton champions in year of the big freeze

Accrington's demise was in sharp contrast to Everton, whose boss Harry Catterick had been on a spending spree in a bid to bring the glory days back to Goodison. The spine of the side was strong: keeper Gordon West, centre-half Brian Labone and centre-forward Alex Young. Everton didn't secure the title until 11 May 1963, when it became mathematically impossible for Spurs to catch them. The late finish to the season had been caused by a three-month winter freeze which had played havoc with the fixture lists. Over 400 games had to be postponed, disrupting the season even more than the big freeze of 1946-47. The Pools companies initially suffered like everyone else, before coming up with a novel solution to the problem. A Pools Panel made up of pundits decided the outcome of postponed matches. Punters were thus still able to have a flutter, although some of the experts' decisions were as controversial as any dubious offside. Everton would remain top-six contenders for the remainder of the decade but would not clinch the title again until the start of the next. Meanwhile, there were two FA Cup appearances, against Sheffield Wednesday in 1966 and West Bromwich Albion two years later. Everton were favourites to win both. They had to come back from 2-0 down to beat Wednesday, Mike Trebilcock hitting two and Derek Temple grabbing the winner. In 1968 they went down to an extra-time goal from Albion's Jeff Astle.

Match-fixing scandal

By that time one of Catterick's early acquisitions had left the game in disgrace. Wing-half Tony Kay, who was capped once for England, was one of a number of players implicated in a match-rigging scandal, a story which broke in The People in April 1964. Kay, along with former Sheffield Wednesday team-mate Peter Swan was found guilty of conspiring to throw a match against Ipswich in 1962. Swan was also an England player, and went to Chile as part of the 1962 World Cup squad. Investigations revealed that the problem was even more widespread than at first thought, with an ex-player named Jimmy Gauld the chief orchestrator of the scam. Gauld received a four-year prison sentence and ten players were given life bans.

BELOW: *17-year-old Manchester United player, David Sadler, scores the third goal in United's 5-1 victory over Everton in 1963.*

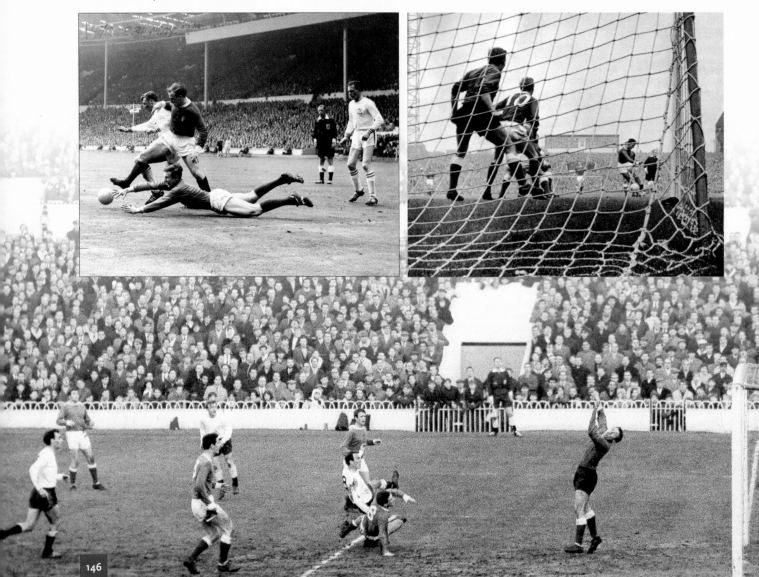

Bobby Charlton

Bobby Charlton won just about every honour in the game, at both club and international level. Football was in his blood; his brother Jack also became a professional footballer and his uncle was Jackie Milburn, a legend on Tyneside in the 1950s. A true gentleman of football, he was famed for playing the game in the spirit of genuine sportsmanship. Indeed in a sparkling 20-year career he was booked just once - for time-wasting when his side was losing!

Charlton was signed to Manchester United in 1955 as part of Matt Busby's grand scheme to comb the country for the best young talent in the land. In a wonderfully ironic turn, he scored twice against Charlton Athletic on his debut in 1956. He and the other "Busby Babes", as Busby's young team became known, looked set to dominate football for many years but on 6 February 1958 the team was all but wiped out in the Munich air crash. Charlton survived and recovered sufficiently to receive the first of his 106 England caps just a few weeks after the tragedy.

Deep-lying centre-forward

Originally a winger or inside-forward, Charlton developed into a deep-lying centre-forward and during the 1960s He was a key player in Busby's exciting new United side, and was equally influential for England. He distributed passes with pinpoint accuracy or burst forward to unleash thunderous shots with either foot. He helped England to World Cup glory in 1966; during the campaign, Mexico and Portugal both found themselves on the receiving end of his scoring power. His performances in that season won him the European Footballer of the Year award.

Triumph for Charlton

Two years later, in 1968, Charlton captained the United side which lifted the European Cup, scoring two goals in a 4-1 victory over Benfica at Wembley. It was an emotional and powerful triumph for Charlton, the team, and Busby, as it was during a campaign to win in Europe that so many of the "Busby Babes" had lost their lives in the Munich air crash, ten years earlier. Charlton played his 606th and final league game for United at Stamford Bridge in 1973.

During the 1970 World Cup in Mexico he played his final game for England in the quarter-final against West Germany. Many believe that England manager Alf Ramsey's decision to substitute Charlton in the second half, when England were 2-1 ahead, was a crucial factor in the team's defeat. His record 106 caps was subsequently overhauled, but his 49 goals has yet to be beaten. In 1994 he was honoured for his services to football – Sir Bobby Charlton.

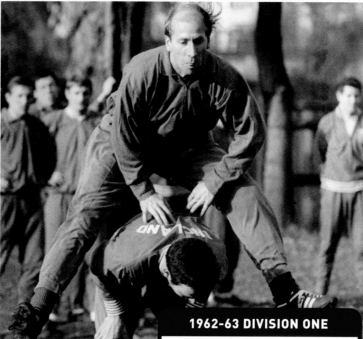

ABOVE: Bobby Charlton and Manchester United team-mate David Sadler try leap frog in a final toning up for their England international match against Russia in December 1967.

OPPOSITE ABOVE LEFT: Manchester United 'keeper Gaskell goes to full stretch to snatch the ball from Leicester's Cross in the 1963 Cup Final. David Herd and later Denis Law, back from Turin, had reinforced Busby's side at the start of the '61-2 season. Both players paid dividends in the 1963 Final - Herd chalking up two goals and Law the third.

OPPOSITE BOTTOM: Jimmy Greaves scores against Everton at White Hart Lane. Harry Catterick's Everton team beat Spurs to the title in the 62-63 season by six points.

1962-63 DIVISION ONE

1	Everton	61
2	Tottenham Hotspur	55
3	Burnley	54
4	Leicester City	52
5	Wolverhampton W.	50
6	Sheffield Wednesday	48
7	Arsenal	46
8	Liverpool	44
9	Nottingham Forest	44
10	Sheffield United	44
11	Blackburn Rovers	42
12	West Ham United	40
13	Blackpool	40
14	West Bromwich Albion	39
15	Aston Villa	38
16	Fulham	38
17	Ipswich	35
18	Bolton Wanderers	35
19	Manchester United	34
20	Birmingham City	33
21	Manchester City	31
22	Leyton Orient	21

THE ILLUSTRATED HISTORY OF ENGLISH FOOTBALL

Bobby Moore

An Essex boy, Bobby Moore was West Ham's, and England's, gentleman-footballer. His modesty belied the inspirational leadership he showed when captaining club and country. Famed for his incisive tackling, timing and sureness in defence, he was also one of the most accurate passers of the ball the English game has ever seen.

Moore joined the Hammers in 1958 at the age of 17 and showed tenacious loyalty, playing 545 games for the club. He led them to their first-ever FA Cup Final win, over Preston North End in 1964, and the European Cup Winners' Cup the following year, in a 2-0 victory over Munich 1860.

England's youngest-ever captain

His international career was stellar. After a record 18 outings for England's youth team, Moore joined the senior side in 1962. He played in that year's World Cup in Chile, when England lost to Brazil in the quarter-finals. A year later, with Alf Ramsey in charge, Moore became England's youngest-ever captain, and in 1966 led his team out at Wembley to their historic 4-2 World Cup win against West Germany. Four years later, he captained the defending champions in Mexico, where in the group-stage game against Brazil he had one of his most memorable games. Moore and Pele's embrace at the end of the match, which Brazil won 1-0, was eloquent - full as it was of genuine mutual respect.

Classically skilful

In the 70s, after a series of disagreements with manager Ron Greenwood, Moore left West Ham to join Fulham and helped the team to reach the 1975 FA Cup Final – ironically, against 2-0 winners West Ham. He ended his playing days in the United States, then went into management, but with little success, first at Oxford City and then Southend.

Moore had seemed to have it all in the optimistic era of the 1960s – he was blond, handsome, gracious and classically skilful, with an uncanny ability to read the game. Tragically, he died at the age of 51, in 1993, from bowel cancer.

BELOW: *Alf Ramsey confers with England skipper, Bobby Moore. Ramsey's experience in building Ipswich was used to good effect as he worked to mould an England side that would play as a team, rather than give individual performances. In 1966 Ramsey called Moore 'my right-hand man, my lieutenant in the field'*
OPPOSITE: *West Ham players celebrate their 3-2 victory over Preston North End in the 1964 FA Cup final.*

The Shankly era

After Everton's 1963 championship, three clubs dominated the domestic game: Liverpool, Leeds and Manchester United. Liverpool had had a miserable time of things in the 1950s, much of it spent in the Second Division. Manager Phil Taylor was sacked in November 1959 and a month later a new messiah arrived. 46-year-old Bill Shankly was persuaded to leave Huddersfield and take over the reins at Anfield on a £2500 salary. Over the next three years he let some players go, revitalised the careers of others and made some key signings. These included Ron Yeats from Dundee United, Ian St John from Motherwell and Gordon Milne from Preston. The Reds stormed to the Second Division championship in 1961-62 and after just one year of consolidation in the top flight became champions in 1964. After a slow start that season, Liverpool took 47 points from 30 games to secure their 6th championship. Defensive football was on the way, yet Liverpool were in irresistible goalscoring form, particularly at Anfield. They banged in 60 goals in front of their home fans, an average of nearly three per game. Roger Hunt was again the goalscoring hero, hitting 31 of the team's 92 league goals.

First FA Cup win for Liverpool

The following season Liverpool suffered a reaction in their league form, slipping to 7th, but the club had two memorable Cup runs. They finally got their name on the FA Cup, thanks to a 2-1 win over a Leeds side which had just finished as runners-up in the league. After a cagey 90 minutes in which defences were on top, Liverpool scored through Hunt. Bremner hit an equaliser, then St John confirmed his status as an Anfield legend by heading in an Ian Callaghan cross. However, the hero of the hour was Gerry Byrne, who played for most of the match with a broken collarbone following an early clash with Bobby Collins. The use of substitutes was finally allowed the following season, initially just for injuries and then for tactical purposes too. After all the debilitating injuries that had dogged Wembley finals in recent years it was a decision that was long overdue.

ABOVE: The Cup is held aloft by Liverpool skipper Ron Yeats and Gordon Milne, who had to stand down from the team because of injury, in the lap of honour at Wembley in 1965. Others are (L-R) Hunt who scored Liverpool's first goal, Smith and Stevenson. Shankly's team triumphed over Leeds by 2-1, all three goals being scored in extra-time.

ABOVE: Liverpool players celebrate with champagne in their dressing-room at Anfield in 1964. They defeated Arsenal 5-0 to win the League championship.

RIGHT: Ron Yeats and Ian St John at Euston Station, taking the Cup back to Anfield for the first time in Liverpool's 73-year history.

OPPOSITE ABOVE: Liverpool pose in 1965 with the FA Cup and the Charity Shield. However, having started the 1964-5 season as reigning champions, the club's performance in the league was less impressive. Liverpool finished in 7th place and Manchester United, the previous year's runners-up took the title, with Leeds hot on their heels.

OPPOSITE BELOW: Liverpool forward Roger Hunt in action against West Ham at Anfield in the championship-winning year.

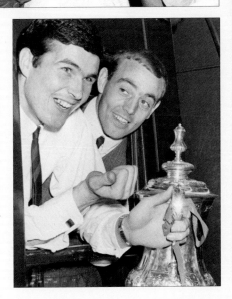

1963-64 DIVISION ONE	
1 Liverpool	57
2 Manchester United	53
3 Everton	52
4 Tottenham Hotspur	51
5 Chelsea	50
6 Sheffield Wednesday	49
7 Blackburn Rovers	46
8 Arsenal	45
9 Burnley	44
10 West Bromwich Albion	43
11 Leicester City	43
12 Sheffield United	43
13 Nottingham Forest	41
14 West Ham United	40
15 Fulham	39
16 Wolverhampton W.	39
17 Stoke	38
18 Blackpool	35
19 Aston Villa	34
20 Birmingham City	29
21 Bolton Wanderers	28
22 Ipswich	25

Reds lose two finals

New Cup-holders Liverpool barely had time to draw breath before facing World Club champions Inter Milan in the semi-final of the European Cup. Liverpool pulled off a sensational 3-1 win over Helenio Herrera's much-vaunted side at home, but three controversial goals by the Italians at the San Siro turned the tie on its head. The ball was kicked out of keeper Tommy Lawrence's hands for one of Inter's goals, and the fact that such

incidents went unpunished led Shankly and others to suspect that the officials had been bribed.

Liverpool recovered to lift the title again the following season. They also made it to the final of the Cup Winners Cup, following a titanic struggle with Celtic in the semis. They faced Borussia Dortmund at Hampden Park in the final, the German side winning 2-1 in extra-time.

ABOVE RIGHT: *Denis Law signing autographs*
ABOVE LEFT: *George Best and Manchester City's Mike Summerbee pose for photographers outside their boutique, Edwardia. Busby gave Best his first game for United on 14 September 1963 against West Bromwich Albion. It was not until December that Best was offered another opportunity to play and the famous line up of Charlton, Law and Best was born.*
LEFT: *Busby tops up Denis Law's glass with champagne as United celebrate their championship victory in 1965.*
OPPOSITE BELOW: *A Best, Law combination in the league game with Arsenal at Highbury.*

Denis Law

Playing alongside George Best and Bobby Charlton at Manchester United in the 1960s, Denis Law was the King of the Stretford End, an unstoppable firebrand, exciting and unpredictable going forward, a showman with one arm raised exultantly when he found the net, which he did so often – 236 goals in 399 appearances for the club. He scored the first, and created the other two, in United's 3-1 FA Cup Final victory over Leicester City in 1963, and his skill and infectious enthusiasm for winning helped the club to the league title in both 1964-65 and 1966-67. He was named European Footballer of the Year in 1964. In United's European campaigns, he scored four hat-tricks, but missed the 1968 European Cup-winning final with an injured knee.

30 goals for Scotland

Born in Aberdeen in 1940, he'd turned professional at Huddersfield Town in 1957, only to be poached by Manchester City in 1960, for a then record fee of £55,000. Another record fee, £100,000, took him to Torino the next year, but by 1962 he had joined United. On his international debut in 1958 aged 18, he was the youngest Scot to be capped since 1899, and his tally of 30 goals for Scotland (in 55 outings) was equalled only by Dalglish. The characteristic impish grin was broadly on display when he played in the Scottish side that beat England 3-2 at Wembley.

A passionate United man, Law found himself out of favour with manager Tommy Docherty in the declining side of the early 1970s, and in 1973 went back to rivals Manchester City, on a free transfer. There was to be no cockiness, pleasure or one-armed saluting when his backheeled goal against United sent his old club down to the Second Division in 1974. He called it a day at the end of that season, going out of the game he loved while he was still at the top of his form.

1964-65 DIVISION ONE		
1	Manchester United	61
2	Leeds United	61
3	Chelsea	56
4	Everton	49
5	Nottingham Forest	47
6	Tottenham Hotspur	45
7	Liverpool	44
8	Sheffield Wednesday	43
9	West Ham United	42
10	Blackburn Rovers	42
11	Stoke	42
12	Burnley	42
13	Arsenal	41
14	West Bromwich Albion	39
15	Sunderland	37
16	Aston Villa	37
17	Blackpool	35
18	Leicester City	35
19	Sheffield United	35
20	Fulham	34
21	Wolverhampton W.	30
22	Birmingham City	27

England's finest hour

England dispense with wingers

The ex-defender Ramsey brought a solid look to the England side. Nobby Stiles was the defensive anchor in front of a solid back four. Ramsey had wingers Ian Callaghan, John Connelly and Terry Paine in his squad but as the tournament progressed he decided to dispense with wide players altogether. That added to the defensive solidity of the team; the question now was whether they would be able to break the opposition down and score themselves.

Progress to the knockout stage was unspectacular. A dull, goalless draw against Uruguay was followed by 2-0 wins over Mexico and France. The quarter-final clash with Argentina was an explosive affair. The turning point came when Argentine captain Antonio Rattin was ordered off for verbally abusing the

German referee after he had already been booked. There was a long delay as Rattin refused to leave the field. Geoff Hurst scored the game's only goal, a glancing header 13 minutes from time. The Hurst-Hunt strike partnership would continue for the rest of the tournament. Jimmy Greaves, the most prolific striker in the squad with 43 goals in just 51

appearances, had chosen the worst possible moment to suffer a loss of form.

BELOW: *Greaves runs towards goal pursued by Uruguay's Ubinas in an inglorious beginning to England's World Cup campaign. Despite winning 16 corners and making 15 shots on goal, England did not score and the match ended in a draw.*

BOTTOM: *England beat Argentina 1-0 in the World Cup quarter-final. Ramsey branded the Argentine players "animals" and refused to let his players swap shirts at the final whistle.*

Geoff Hurst

West Ham striker Geoff Hurst, knighted in 1998, has the proud distinction of being the only man ever to score a hat-trick in a World Cup Final – and the only first-class cricketer to win a World Cup medal at football. He batted for Essex against Lancashire in 1962, and, of course, played for England in their 1966 victory over West Germany.

Over 400 games for the Hammers

The 24-year-old Hurst had come into form at exactly the right time – even if many Germans still believe his second goal, which came off the underside of the bar, never crossed the line. He hadn't even played in England's opening game of the tournament, but having taken the place of the injured Jimmy Greaves and scored the winner against Argentina in the quarter-final, he kept his place.

Between 1959 and 1972, Hurst made over 400 League appearances for the Hammers, helping them to win the FA Cup in 1964 and the European Cup Winners' Cup the following year. In 1972 he moved to Stoke City, then after a period at West Bromwich Albion, went into management and helped with the national squad.

RIGHT: *A clash of headgear as an England supporter reaches to shake hands with a Mexican supporter wearing a giant sombrero before the opening match of the World Cup tournament between England and Uruguay on 11 July 1966.*

The sporting semi-final

Ramsey branded the Argentine players "animals" and refused to let his players swap shirts at the final whistle. This was just one of many ill-tempered encounters. Pele had come in for very rough treatment as Brazil failed to make it beyond the group stages. By contrast, England's semi-final against Portugal was an oasis of sportsmanship. In a fast, free-flowing game Bobby Charlton scored twice, but England had to live on their nerves in the last few minutes as Eusebio pulled one back from the penalty spot.

Weber forces extra time

England's opponents in the final were West Germany. They had beaten a Uruguay side reduced to nine men in the quarter-finals, and in the semis Russia had also had a man sent off. Helmut Haller opened the scoring in the final, capitalising on a weak clearance from Ray Wilson after 13 minutes. Within minutes the teams were level as Bobby Moore flighted a free-kick onto the head of his West Ham team-mate Hurst, who powered the ball past Tilkowski. The third of the Hammers' contingent, Martin Peters, put England ahead with less than 15 minutes to go. The man whom Ramsey had described as "10 years ahead of his time" scored from close range after a Hurst shot was blocked. A West Germany free-kick in the last minute somehow found its way through a crowded box and

Wolfgang Weber squeezed the ball in at the far post. It meant that extra time would be played for the first time since 1934, which was also the last occasion that the host nation had won the tournament.

Hurst's controversial goal

20-year-old Alan Ball was still full of running, and it was his right-wing cross 10 minutes into extra time that led to the most controversial moment in World Cup history. Hurst controlled the ball, turned and let fly, only to see his shot hit the underside of the bar. It bounced down and was cleared, but had the ball crossed the line? The referee consulted his Russian linesman who was in no doubt that it had. Hurst sealed victory by hammering in a fourth for England in

the last minute. It also made him the only man to score a hat-trick in a World Cup final. Technology later suggested that he was fortunate not have his second goal ruled out, but that didn't detract from the jubilant scenes at Wembley on 30 July 1966. England were world champions. For Bobby Moore it was the completion of a memorable hat-trick of his own. He had captained the West Ham side which won the FA Cup in 1964 and the Cup Winners' Cup the following year. It was thus the third time in as many years that Moore had raised a trophy aloft at Wembley.

BELOW: *Helmut Haller scores the first goal for West Germany in the World Cup final at Wembley, 1966.*
BOTTOM: *Gordon Banks takes control in the World Cup Final. Banks did not concede a goal in the competition until the semi-final against Portugal.*

LEFT: *Jimmy Greaves puts an arm around the exhausted Alan Ball as the victorious England team leave the pitch. Greaves had played in the opening round of the competition but was replaced by Hurst when Greaves' form dipped.*

ABOVE: *The German goalkeeper, Tilkowski, and teammate, Schnellinger fail to stop England's second goal by Martin Peters.*

TOP: *England Centre half Jack Charlton can hardly believe that Germany have taken the lead.*

Sir Alf Ramsey

Alf Ramsey was a cultured full-back in the famous Spurs "push and run" side which won the championship in 1951. He was capped 32 times for England between 1949 and 1954. After his playing days were over, Ramsey took over as manager of Ipswich Town. In seven years Ramsey took the unfashionable East Anglia club from the Third Division to the top flight, culminating in the league championship in 1961-62. It was on the strength of this achievement that he was offered the England manager's job in 1963. Ramsey was the first full-time incumbent and he insisted on being given sole responsibility for selection, a freedom that his predecessor had not enjoyed.

Early in his tenure as national team boss he predicted that England would win the 1966 World Cup. That looked a long way off when his side was hammered 5-2 by France in his first game in charge. Three years later, Ramsey fulfilled his promise as his "wingless wonders" triumphed, beating West Germany in the final.

After going out at the semi-final stage of the 1968 European Championship, England went to Mexico to defend their world crown. Many thought that Ramsey's squad in 1970 was even stronger than that which had won the tournament four years earlier. West Germany ended England's hopes at the quarter-final stage, coming back from 2-0 down to win 3-2. Some thought Ramsey's decision to take off both Charlton and Peters was instrumental in the defeat.

He survived that disappointment, and another quarter-final exit in the 1972 European Championship, when the Germans again proved to be the stumbling-block. He was finally dismissed after England drew with Poland at Wembley in 1973, a result which meant that England failed to qualify for the 1974 World Cup. Ramsey was knighted in the 1967 New Year's Honours list. He died in 1999.

World Cup 1966 Results

GROUP 1

England	0	Uruguay	0
France	1	Mexico	1
Uruguay	2	France	1
England	2	Mexico	0
Uruguay	0	Mexico	0
England	2	France	0

	P	W	D	L	F	A	Pts
England	3	2	1	0	4	0	5
Uruguay	3	1	2	0	2	1	4
Mexico	3	0	2	1	1	3	2
France	3	0	1	2	2	5	1

GROUP 2

W.Germany	5	Switzerland	0
Argentina	2	Spain	1
Spain	2	Switzerland	1
Argentina	2	Switzerland	0
W.Germany	2	Spain	1
W.Germany	1	Argentina	1

	P	W	D	L	F	A	Pts
W.Germany	3	2	1	0	8	2	5
Argentina	3	2	1	0	4	1	5
Spain	3	1	1	1	2	3	3
Switzerland	3	0	1	2	1	7	1

GROUP 3

Brazil	2	Bulgaria	0
Portugal	3	Hungary	1
Hungary	3	Brazil	1
Portugal	3	Bulgaria	0
Portugal	3	Brazil	1
Hungary	3	Bulgaria	1

	P	W	D	L	F	A	Pts
Portugal	3	3	0	0	9	2	6
Hungary	3	2	0	1	7	5	4
Brazil	3	1	0	2	4	6	2
Bulgaria	3	0	0	3	1	8	0

GROUP 4

Sov.Union	3	N.Korea	0
Italy	2	Chile	0
Chile	1	N.Korea	1
Sov.Union	1	Italy	0
N.Korea	1	Italy	0
Sov.Union	2	Chile	1

	P	W	D	L	F	A	Pts
Sov.Union	3	3	0	0	6	1	6
N.Korea	3	1	1	1	2	4	3
Italy	3	1	0	2	2	2	2
Chile	3	0	1	2	2	5	1

QUARTER-FINALS

England	1	Argentina	0
W. Germany	4	Uruguay	0
Portugal	5	N.Korea	3
Sov. Union	2	Hungary	1

SEMI-FINALS

W. Germany	2	Sov. Union	1
England	2	Portugal	1

3RD PLACE PLAY-OFF

Portugal	2	Sov. Union	1

FINAL July 30 – Wembley Stadium

England	4	W. Germany	2

(Hurst 19, 100, 119, Peters 77) (Haller 13, Weber 89)

Aet ht: 1-1 90min 2-2. Ref: Dienst (Swi)
Att: 96,924.

England: Banks, Cohen, Wilson, Stiles, J Charlton, Moore, Ball, Hunt, R Charlton, Hurst, Peters

West Germany: Tilkowski, Höttges, Schnellinger, Beckenbauer, Schülz, Weber, Haller, Overath, Seeler, Held, Emmerich.

Rise of Leeds

Don Revie's transformation of Leeds United was if anything even more dramatic than Shankly's at Liverpool. The Yorkshire club was flirting with relegation to the Third Division in 1962, yet by the middle of the decade they were a formidable footballing machine. Revie had been a deep-lying centre-forward in the Manchester City side of the mid-1950s, and Footballer of the Year in 1955. Ten years later he was the architect behind a powerhouse Leeds side that was universally respected if not always admired. Players of the stature of Billy Bremner, Bobby Collins, Jack Charlton and Norman Hunter took Leeds to the top - or, more often, second place. 1964-65 was to prove all too typical: runners-up in the league and beaten finalists in the Cup.

New points record as defences get on top

After three more seasons of finishing in the top four, and defeat in 1966 Fairs Cup Final, Leeds finally won the title in 1968-69. And they did it in fine style, losing just twice in the League. 67 points set a new record, eclipsing Arsenal's 1931 tally by one. Leeds' goals column that season made interesting reading: 66 scored, just 26 conceded. At the beginning of the decade Spurs Double-winning side had scored 115 and let in 55. In that year even relegated Newcastle scored 86! English teams were now regularly coming up against Continental opposition, and in particular the miserly "catenaccio" system operated by Italian sides. Tight defence was seen as the key to success.

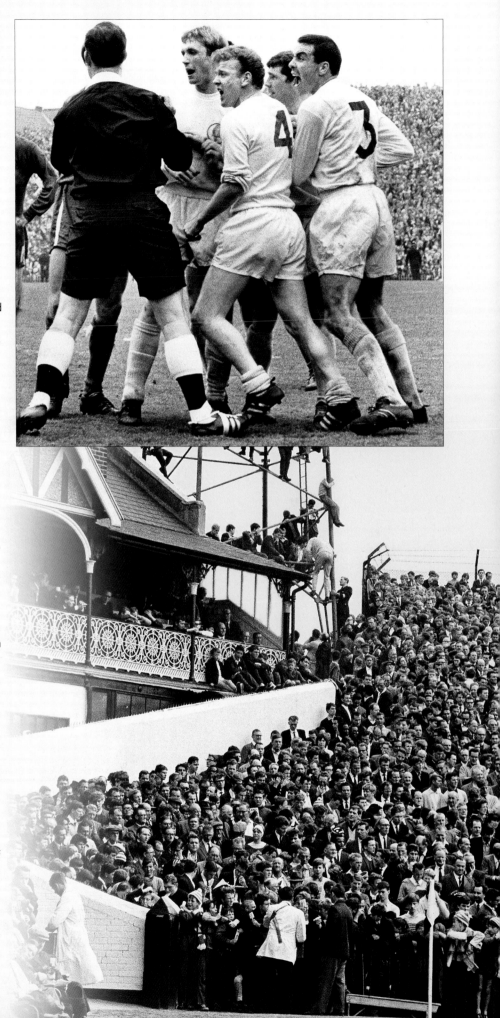

ABOVE RIGHT: *Referee Ken Burns hears the views of the disgruntled Leeds players (L-R: Greenhoff, Bremner, Giles and Bell) after he disallows Leeds' equaliser in the semi-final of the 1967 FA Cup. Their opponents, Chelsea, reached the Final defeating, Leeds by 1 goal to nil. But Don Revie's team were to take the league in the following season, losing only twice. Revie's contribution was recognised: he was awarded Manager of the Year in both 1969 and 1970, the preceding recipients being Matt Busby and Jock Stein.*

BELOW RIGHT: *Crowds at Craven Cottage cause officials to order the gates to be closed before the start of Fulham's derby with Chelsea.*

RIGHT: *North London rivalries are put aside for a moment when Spurs' Terry Venables (left) acts as best man for Arsenal centre-forward George Graham.*

BELOW RIGHT: *England and Tottenham Hotspur player Jimmy Greaves takes to a pipe at London airport before he and his England teammates leave for a tour of Yugoslavia, West Germany and Sweden.*

BELOW: *West Ham and England World Cup heroes Geoff Hurst, Bobby Moore and Martin Peters.*

1965-66 DIVISION ONE	
1 Liverpool	61
2 Leeds United	55
3 Burnley	55
4 Manchester United	51
5 Chelsea	51
6 West Bromwich Albion	50
7 Leicester City	49
8 Tottenham Hotspur	44
9 Sheffield United	43
10 Stoke	42
11 Everton	41
12 West Ham United	39
13 Blackpool	37
14 Arsenal	37
15 Newcastle United	37
16 Aston Villa	36
17 Sheffield Wednesday	36
18 Nottingham Forest	36
19 Sunderland	36
20 Fulham	35
21 Northampton	33
22 Blackburn Rovers	20

Faltering start for League Cup

Despite their reputation as "nearly men", Leeds did pick up two other trophies in the 1960s, a Fairs Cup and League Cup double in 1968. The latter competition had had a chequered history since Football League Secretary Alan Hardaker had championed it at the beginning of the decade. In the early years the top clubs boycotted the League Cup, feeling that it was an unwelcome addition to the fixture list. With three European trophies to aim for a second domestic cup competition hardly set the pulse racing. When Second Division Norwich City beat Fourth Division Rochdale over two legs in the 1962 final, the competition was in danger of withering on the vine.

Cup honours for Third Division sides

The turning point came in 1967, when the final became a one-legged affair at Wembley. The status was further enhanced with the award of a Fairs Cup place to the winners, provided they were in the First Division. That stipulation meant that Queen's Park Rangers and Swindon, winners in 1967 and 1969 respectively, weren't able to embark on a European adventure. Both were Third Division sides when they lifted the trophy and both came out on top against Division One opposition. Rodney Marsh

inspired QPR to come back from a 2-0 deficit to win 3-2 against West Brom. In 1969 two extra-time goals from Swindon winger Don Rogers ended the hopes of an Arsenal side that had finished fourth in the championship. By the end of the decade, the League Cup had become firmly established, although critics pointed out that it remained a poor relation to the premier knockout competition. Certainly no Third Division side had come close to lifting the FA Cup in the 50 years that those leagues had been in existence.

BELOW: *Jimmy Greaves (left) and Alan Gilzean in action for Spurs against Liverpool during a match at White Hart Lane in April 1967.*
BOTTOM: *Spurs players celebrate their second goal, scored by Saul, in the 1967 Cup Final, an all-London affair. Tommy Docherty's Chelsea side were overwhelmed by Spurs' skill and tactics and even a late Chelsea goal, bringing the score to 2-1, didn't loosen Spurs' hold on the game.*
OPPOSITE BELOW: *England World Cup hero Gordon Banks in action against Scotland in 1967.*

Gordon Banks

Gordon Banks earned his first cap in 1963 and, following that debut, was a fixture in the England side for nearly a decade, including the glorious 1966 World Cup campaign. But perhaps his most memorable moment came on 7 June 1970 when, as the finest goalkeeper of his age, he thwarted the world's greatest player with probably the best save ever seen. Pele's crashing downward header was miraculously scooped off the line by Banks ten minutes into the England v Brazil World Cup group match at Guadalajara, Mexico. England lost that game but made it through to the quarter-final, where Banks' late withdrawal through illness was widely seen as a key factor in the team's defeat in the match against West Germany.

Career was cut short

Banks began his career at Chesterfield and established his reputation after a move to Leicester City, who he joined in 1959. In the 1961 FA Cup Final he was on the losing side when his team went down 0-2 to Tottenham Hotspur; he picked up another losers' medal two years later. Banks moved to another unfashionable club, Stoke City, in 1967. Five years later in 1972, soon after he had signed a long-term contract with the Potteries side, his career was cut short by a car accident in which he lost an eye.

Busby rebuilds again

Many would agree that the accolade of team of the decade belonged to Manchester United. Following the Munich disaster, Busby embarked on yet another rebuilding process. It proved to be a long journey. In the four seasons from 1959-60 United finished 7th twice, 15th and 19th. Ironically, it was in the season that they flirted with relegation that the new-look side won its first silverware. Opponents Leicester City had finished 4th that year, but two goals from David Herd and one from Denis Law made a mockery of the clubs' respective positions. Four months later 17-year-old George best made his debut for the club. Pat Crerand also joined United in 1963, while players such as David Sadler and John Aston were showing promise in the youth ranks. And of course, Busby also had Munich survivors Bobby Charlton and Bill Foulkes at his disposal.

European Cup goes to Old Trafford

After finishing runners-up to Liverpool in 1963-64, United won the title twice in three seasons. In 1967-68 United had to be content with the runners-up spot again, this time to neighbours Manchester City. Yet this was to bring the club the proudest moment in its history. In the semi-final of the European Cup United took a slender 1-0 lead to the Bernebeu Stadium. Real Madrid went 3-1 ahead but two unlikely goals from Sadler and Foulkes put United into the final. Ten years on from Munich United went to Wembley to face a Benfica side which boasted the great Eusebio. He almost won the game for the Portuguese side with a thunderous shot in the dying minutes when the score stood at 1-1. But Alex Stepney made a great save and the game went into extra-time. United hit three in those 30 minutes. The first was a typical piece of virtuoso skill from Best;

Brian Kidd, celebrating his 19th birthday, headed United into a 3-1 lead; and Bobby Charlton swept home his second of the match to make the final score 4-1. After the events of 1958 there was an element of natural justice as United became the first English club to win European football's premier trophy.

BELOW LEFT: *Matt Busby presents the 1966-67 League championship trophy at Old Trafford.*
BOTTOM: *Best displays perfect balance and control.*

1966-67 DIVISION ONE		
1	Manchester United	60
2	Nottingham Forest	56
3	Tottenham Hotspur	56
4	Leeds United	55
5	Liverpool	51
6	Everton	48
7	Arsenal	46
8	Leicester City	44
9	Chelsea	44
10	Sheffield United	42
11	Sheffield Wednesday	41
12	Stoke	41
13	West Bromwich Albion	39
14	Burnley	39
15	Manchester City	39
16	West Ham United	36
17	Sunderland	36
18	Fulham	34
19	Southampton	34
20	Newcastle United	33
21	Aston Villa	29
22	Blackpool	21

ABOVE: *Pat Crerand (left) shares the moment of glory with Matt Busby. Ten years after the Munich disaster, Busby's dream is realised and a rebuilt Manchester United defeated Benfica by 4 goals to 1 to win the European Cup. Charlton and Foulkes, survivors of the crash, played at Wembley and Charlton had the satisfaction of scoring 2 of United's goals. In the following season, Busby announced his intention to step down as manager of the team to take on the role of general manager of the club.*

RIGHT: *United team-mates Law and Kidd celebrate after Best scored in the first leg of the semi-final of the 1968 European Cup against Real Madrid.*

BELOW: *Players and staff of Manchester United on the pitch at Wembley on 29 May 1968, the day of the European Cup Final.*

BELOW: *George Best plays against Wolves at Molineux in 1966 and (opposite below) in action in the 1968-9 season. United were riding high on their European success and Best was at the peak of his form; top scorer for United in both 1967- 8 and the following season and voted European Footballer of the Year in 1969. But at the end of the 1968-9 season, Busby's team had slipped to 11th place in the league and Best was in conflict with the management.*

1967-68 DIVISION ONE

1	Manchester City	58
2	Manchester United	56
3	Liverpool	55
4	Leeds United	53
5	Everton	52
6	Chelsea	48
7	Tottenham Hotspur	47
8	West Bromwich Albion	46
9	Arsenal	44
10	Newcastle United	41
11	Nottingham Forest	39
12	West Ham United	38
13	Leicester City	38
14	Burnley	38
15	Sunderland	37
16	Southampton	37
17	Wolverhampton W.	36
18	Stoke	35
19	Sheffield Wednesday	34
20	Coventry	33
21	Sheffield United	32
22	Fulham	27

FA CUP FINALS

1960	Wolverhampton W.	v	Blackburn Rovers	3-0
1961	Tottenham H.	v	Leicester City	2-0
1962	Tottenham H.	v	Burnley	3-1
1963	Manchester Utd	v	Leicester City	3-1
1964	West Ham Utd	v	Preston N.E.	3-2
1965	Liverpool	v	Leeds United	2-1
1966	Everton	v	Sheffield W.	3-2
1967	Tottenham H.	v	Chelsea	2-1
1968	West Bromwich A.	v	Everton	1-0
1969	Manchester City	v	Leicester City	1-0

George Best

George Best had everything: speed, strength, poise, creativity and incredible ball skills. A two-footed player, he was excellent in the air and fearless in the tackle and a lethal finisher. A team-mate in the Manchester United side of the 1960s once said that Best could have played in any outfield position - and outperformed the man who usually played there. By the time he was 22 he had won a European Footballer of the Year award and had a European Cup winners' medal. He looked set to win many more honours, yet the pressures of celebrity, combined with a tendency to press the self-destruct button all too often, meant that by his late 20s, his career in the top flight was virtually over.

Belfast Boy

Best was brought to Old Trafford from his home in Belfast in August 1961, when he was 15. Just two years later he made his debut for United and was soon a fixture in an exciting new side that Matt Busby was building. Busby recognised Best's natural talent and reasoned that it was best left alone. Consequently he had told the coaching staff not to try and teach the youngster anything. Later, despite all the headaches Best gave him, Busby never wavered in his view of the Irishman's ability on the field, claiming that he had never seen any other player who had so many different ways of beating an opponent.

After a stunning individual display in a 5-1 away victory over Benfica in the 1965-66 European Cup, he became the first pop star footballer and soon came under the most intense media scrutiny. Good-looking and fashionable, he was dubbed 'El Beatle' and for a time he managed to combine the life of a high-profile celebrity with outstanding performances on the pitch. But, inevitably, the revelling began to take its toll.

Best leaves United at 25

After United won the European Cup victory in 1968 it became necessary for Busby to reinforce the ageing team and Best felt that he should be more central to the make-up of the team. Unsurprisingly, this put pressure on relations between him, his team-mates and the club, which were already strained as a result of his high living and media profile. He walked out of Old Trafford in 1972, two days before his 26th birthday. The following decade saw him join a succession of clubs, both in Britain and America, but he would never reproduce the kind of dazzling displays which were a trademark of his younger days.

On the international front, Best was picked for Northern Ireland when he was 17, after just 15 appearances for United. Although he won 37 caps, he never really had the opportunity to show his skills on the world stage.

Long after he had hung up his boots, Best continued to find himself in demand as a football pundit and on the after-dinner circuit. However, his years of alcohol abuse finally caught up with him and in the summer of 2002 he underwent a liver transplant operation.

LEFT: *Neil Young scores the only goal of the match for Manchester City in the 1969 FA Cup final against Leicester City.*

BELOW LEFT: *Ecstatic QPR fans celebrate promotion to the first division in 1968.*

BOTTOM: *Manchester City players train before the Final of the 1969 FA Cup in the red and black striped shirt they will wear on the day. City won the Cup, for the fourth time in their history, Young scoring the only goal of the match against Leicester. Mercer and Allison's new signings of Mike Summerbee (second from the left), Francis Lee (third from the left) and Colin Bell (fourth from the left) played a crucial role in City's league and Cup success in the late 1960s.*

1968-69 DIVISION ONE

1	Leeds United	67
2	Liverpool	61
3	Everton	57
4	Arsenal	56
5	Chelsea	50
6	Tottenham Hotspur	45
7	Southampton	45
8	West Ham United	44
9	Newcastle United	44
10	West Bromwich Albion	43
11	Manchester United	42
12	Ipswich	41
13	Manchester City	40
14	Burnley	39
15	Sheffield Wednesday	36
16	Wolverhampton W.	35
17	Sunderland	34
18	Nottingham Forest	33
19	Stoke	33
20	Coventry	31
21	Leicester City	30
22	Queen's Park Rangers	18

English clubs make their mark

The year after winning the World Cup England came back to earth with a bump as Scotland came to Wembley and won 3-2, a game in which Jim Baxter was at his mercurial best. The Scots lost little time in claiming to be unofficial world champions.

England went into the 1968 European Championship as favourites. After beating Spain in the quarter-final, it all went wrong against Yugoslavia. Alan Mullery was sent off for retaliation, the first England player to receive his marching orders, and the team went down 1-0.

At the end of a turbulent decade, English clubs had made their mark in Europe, winning five trophies in all. And the national side was once again on top of the world. The next decade would see continued success at club level, while the national side would find it hard to reach a World Cup, let alone win it.

TOP: *Allan Clarke shows his delight after scoring for Leicester in the semi-final of the Cup in 1969. Clarke's goal took Leicester to Wembley, going some way to justify the new record-breaking transfer fee of £150,000 paid to Fulham.*
MIDDLE: *Manchester United display the European Cup.*
LEFT: *The 1968-9 Spurs team: back row Pearce, Beal, Collins, England, Jennings, Chivers, Knowles, Gilzean and Kinnear. Front Row: Bond, Robertson, Greaves, Mullery, Venables, Jones and Want. Martin Chivers had recently joined the side from Southampton commanding a record transfer fee of £125,000.*

1970-1979
Conquering Europe

English clubs had won five European trophies in the 1960s. In the next decade Liverpool alone almost managed that. The Reds embarked on a period of domination the like of which the game had never seen. As their traditional rivals found it hard to maintain the pace, two new contenders emerged. Derby County and Nottingham Forest won the title three times between them, a remarkable achievement by the controversial manager who took both clubs from the Second Division to the top of the pile: Brian Clough.

Division Two teams get to Wembley

If Derby County and Nottingham Forest were the surprise packages in the league, there were several in the cup competitions. Between 1970 and 1980 seven Division Two sides made it to Wembley, while Division One strugglers Stoke and Ipswich also struck a blow for the underdog.

Ironically, as English sides prospered in Europe, the fortunes of the national team declined. After going to Mexico as holders in 1970, England suffered successive failures in the next two World Cup qualification campaigns.

Fences go up to counter hooligan threat

The 1970s also saw the introduction of a three-up, three-down system, and red and yellow cards for onfield misdemeanours. From 1974 the players also got to choose their own Player of the Year. It wasn't until the seventh vote took place, in 1980, that their choice, Terry McDermott, coincided with that of the Football Writers Association. On a more worrying note, the twin problems of indebtedness and hooliganism continued to cast a shadow over the game. Fences started to go up to try and counter the threat of pitch invasions, which became an increasingly common occurrence. The fact that few clubs were operating in the black didn't stop transfers from continuing their upward spiral, and before the end of the decade the English game had seen its first million-pound transfer.

OPPOSITE BELOW: *Leeds celebrate Mick Jones' goal in the 1970 FA Cup Final, believing that the Cup was theirs. But the celebrations were short-lived. Two minutes later Hutchinson scored to make it 2-2. Extra time at Wembley was followed by extra time in the replay at Old Trafford, where Chelsea ended victorious against a Leeds side recognised as one of the English league's greatest teams.*

OPPOSITE ABOVE: *Alan Gilzean scores his team's winning goal against Manchester United in 1970. After robbing Best of the ball, Gilzean evaded Ure to make the score 2-1.*

BELOW: *Harris and Hollins parade the FA Cup after Chelsea's 2-1 win in the replay against Leeds United.*

LEFT: *New Year, 1971, the terraces at Ibrox Park where 66 fans died as a result of a crush when departing spectators tried to make their way back to the stand after Rangers scored a late goal in the derby match against Celtic. It raised questions about ground safety in British football stadiums which were not fully addressed until the end of the next decade.*

Mexico 1970

Wonder save by Banks denies Pelé

The decade began with a footballing jamboree in Mexico. Many thought the squad Sir Alf Ramsey took to defend England's world crown was stronger than that which had won the Jules Rimet trophy four years earlier. Things got off to a bad start in Bogota, where England were acclimatising to the kind of temperatures they would face in Mexico. Bobby Moore was accused of stealing a bracelet and taken into custody. Although the charge was soon dropped, the incident overshadowed the squad's pre-tournament preparations.

England and Brazil were the joint favourites, and they were drawn in the same group. After each side had recorded a victory, the two teams met in Guadalajara. After a bright start by England, Jairzinho beat Cooper on the right wing and picked out Pelé with his cross. Pelé powered a downward header just inside the far post, but somehow Banks managed to scoop it up and over the bar. It was hailed as one of the greatest saves of all time. Pelé set up Jairzinho for the only goal of the match 14 minutes into the second half, but England had reason to be optimistic. Peters and Lee had missed chances, and Astle missed a golden opportunity when he came on as substitute. There was every indication that the two teams would meet again in the final.

England throw away 2-0 lead

That hope disappeared in Leon, where England faced West Germany in the quarter-final. 2-0 up through goals from Mullery and Peters, England looked odds-on to go through. In the second half Beckenbauer beat Peter Bonetti to pull one back for the Germans. The Chelsea keeper had been a late replacement for Banks, who had gone down with stomach cramps before the game. Suddenly it was the German side which had the momentum. Ramsey took off Bobby Charlton and Peters, replacing them with Colin Bell and Norman Hunter. A back header from Uwe Seeler looped agonisingly over Bonetti's head, forcing extra time. England's misery was complete when Gerd Muller, who would go on to be the tournament's top scorer, volleyed the winner from close range.

Two years later, West Germany again proved to be the stumbling-block in the quarter-final of the European Championship. Helmut Schoen's side was at its peak, and England had no answer as the Germans cruised to a 3-1 victory at Wembley. Ramsey's men earned a goalless draw in Berlin a fortnight later, but the damage had been done. Worse was to come the following year, and it would be a disappointment too many for the England manager.

BOTTOM: *Members of the England team training at the Atlas Club in Guadalajara as they prepare for their match against Brazil in the 1970 World Cup in Mexico.*

OPPOSITE BELOW: *As they receive cars and membership of the RAC, some of the England World Cup squad pose for photographs. The 1970s saw the beginnings of sponsorship which was to develop as a major feature in the 1980s.*

BELOW: *West Germany's Muller scores the winning goal in the quarter-final of the 1970 World Cup. England were defeated 3-2 after extra time by the team they beat to win the World Cup four years before.*

1969-70 DIVISION ONE

1	Everton	66
2	Leeds United	57
3	Chelsea	55
4	Derby County	53
5	Liverpool	51
6	Coventry	49
7	Newcastle United	47
8	Manchester United	45
9	Stoke	45
10	Manchester City	43
11	Tottenham Hotspur	43
12	Arsenal	42
13	Wolverhampton W.	40
14	Burnley	39
15	Nottingham Forest	38
16	West Bromwich Albion	37
17	West Ham United	36
18	Ipswich	31
19	Southampton	29
20	Crystal Palace	27
21	Sunderland	26
22	Sheffield Wednesday	25

ABOVE LEFT: *Footballers on fashion parade – Bob McNab, Geoff Hurst and Peter Marinello show that they can impress off the pitch as much as on it!*

ABOVE RIGHT: *Martin Chivers scores for Tottenham Hotspur. Spurs had paid £125,000 for Chivers in 1968 and throughout the early 1970s continued to pay big money in transfer deals. However, the decade was not particularly successful for the London club and they spent the 1977-78 season in Division Two.*

Double for Arsenal

Domestic football in the new decade got off to a dramatic start, Arsenal coming through with a late burst to record a famous Double in 1970-71. It was ten years on from Spurs' achievement, and fate decreed that the Gunners had to win their last match at White Hart Lane to secure the title. A Ray Kennedy goal settled the issue. Arsenal had been six points off the pace with six weeks to go, but 27 points from the last 16 games was unstoppable championship form. Almost inevitably it was Leeds who missed out, pipped by a single point.

Arsenal also left it late in the Cup. They needed a last-minute penalty to salvage a draw against Stoke in the semi-final before winning the replay 2-0. Five days after the Spurs match Arsenal went to Wembley for the 64th and final match of the campaign.

They were up against a Liverpool side that was in a state of flux. The likes of Tommy Lawrence, Ron Yeats, Peter Thompson, Roger Hunt and Ian St John had all disappeared as Shankly overhauled the squad completely. Teenager Emlyn Hughes had arrived from Blackpool

in 1967. He had been joined by John Toshack, Larry Lloyd, Steve Heighway and Brian Hall in a new-look side. There were also two youngsters who would enjoy very different fortunes at the club. Shankly paid Wolves £100,000 for striker Alun Evans. He would show flashes of what he could do at Anfield but overall the verdict was one of disappointment. The same could hardly be said of Shankly's £35,000 buy from Scunthorpe, who sat in the stands to watch his new team-mates take on Arsenal. His name was Kevin Keegan.

LEFT: *In extra time, Charlie George slams the ball into the net past Liverpool's keeper Ray Clemence to provide the goal that won Arsenal the FA Cup and the Double in the 1970-71 season; they had won the league with just one point to spare over Leeds United.*

BELOW: *The Double-winning Arsenal team arrive aboard an open-top bus at Islington Town Hall for a civic reception.*

1970-71 DIVISION ONE

1	Arsenal	65
2	Leeds United	64
3	Tottenham Hotspur	52
4	Wolverhampton W.	52
5	Liverpool	51
6	Chelsea	51
7	Southampton	46
8	Manchester United	43
9	Derby County	42
10	Coventry	42
11	Manchester City	41
12	Newcastle United	41
13	Stoke	37
14	Everton	37
15	Huddersfield	36
16	Nottingham Forest	36
17	West Bromwich Albion	35
18	Crystal Palace	35
19	Ipswich	34
20	West Ham United	34
21	Burnley	27
22	Blackpool	23

George hits Wembley winner

When Steve Heighway opened the scoring in extra time, it seemed that Keegan was about to take his place in a Cup-winning team. But Eddie Kelly poked in a scrappy equaliser, and Charlie George rifled in a 25-yard winner. It was a special day for Frank McClintock, who had suffered a string of Wembley disappointments. He was named Footballer of the Year for leading Arsenal to the fourth Double in history. Gunners' boss Bertie Mee received many plaudits, although credit was also due to the groundwork laid down by his predecessor, Billy Wright.

ABOVE RIGHT: *Goal-scorer Martin Peters is lifted in celebration by Martin Chivers as Geoff Hurst rushes to congratulate and Scotland's Frank McLintock shouts in dismay in England's 3-1 win at Wembley in the Home Championships of 1971.*

RIGHT: *Members of the Arsenal team that had won the 1970 Fairs Cup (from 1972, the UEFA Cup), set off for the airport for a flight to Rome where they were to play Lazio at the start of their defence of the title.*

BELOW RIGHT: *Charlie George, Ray Kennedy and Frank McClintock celebrate after the final whistle of the FA Cup.*

Derby take title in sunny Spain

Derby County finished a respectable 9th that year. Brian Clough had been at the Baseball Ground for four years, taking the club up as Division Two champions in 1968-69. 4th place in their first year back in the top flight was an excellent effort by the Rams. 9th this time round was still respectable. But to a perfectionist such as Clough that was never good enough. In 1972 his side won the title, albeit by the narrowest of margins and in the most dramatic circumstances. Derby beat Liverpool in their last game of the season to go one point clear at the top. Clough and his men then promptly decamped to Majorca, leaving Liverpool and Leeds - who both had one remaining fixture - to do their worst. Leeds needed just a point at mid-table Wolves. If they failed, Liverpool could go top with a win at Arsenal. In the event neither club could meet its target. Leeds went down 2-1, while Liverpool were held to a goalless draw. Liverpool thought they'd won it with a last-minute goal from Toshack, but it

was disallowed. Derby were champions for the first time in their history.

Hereford humble Newcastle

Leeds had the consolation of winning the centenary FA Cup Final, Allan Clarke scoring the only goal of the match against holders Arsenal. The highlight of the 1972 FA Cup came in the third round, when Hereford took on Newcastle United. The Southern League side seemed to have had their moment of glory with a 2-2 draw

at St James's Park. In the replay at Edgar Street Hereford rode their luck until ten minutes from the end, when Malcolm Macdonald finally found the back of the net. Ronnie Radford sent the 15,000 crowd delirious with a 30-yard screamer, and Ricky George slotted home the winner in extra time. Hereford went on to draw 0-0 with West Ham before going down 3-1 at Upton Park in a replay. The club's Cup heroics helped to earn them election to the Football League the following season.

RIGHT: *Derby's John Robson receives medical attention on the pitch during their match against Arsenal in 1972.*

BELOW: *The Leeds squad at the beginning of the 1972-73 season. The early 1970s were a part of the golden age for the club. They won the league in 1974 and were runners-up three years in succession between 1970 and 1972, and also had a series of good Cup runs.*

Billy Bremner

Despite beginning his career as a winger, it was at the heart of the brilliant Leeds United side of the late 1960s and early 1970s that Billy Bremner made his name and where he enjoyed a phenomenal run of success. He forged a formidable midfield partnership with Johnny Giles and, although Giles was regarded as the skilful artist and canny ball-player, Bremner's superb passing and incisive forward runs made him a vital cog in the Elland Road machine.

54 caps for Scotland

As captain, Bremner led the side to two league championships, in 1968-69 and 1973-74, and to FA Cup victory over Arsenal in 1972. Leeds United also had two successful Inter-Cities Fairs Cup campaigns, in 1968 and 1971. Regrettably, Bremner's haul of runners-up medals was even bigger: Leeds finished runners-up in the league on five occasions during Bremner's era, and were beaten FA Cup finalists three times. After the team's defeat at the hands of Bayern Munich in the 1975 European Cup Final, Bremner moved to Hull City, and then finished his playing career at Doncaster.

Capped 54 times for Scotland, Bremner's appearances for his national side fell one short of Dennis Law's all-time record. His greatest triumph on the international stage was when he led the Scots in the 1974 World Cup Finals in West Germany, where they were unbeaten and unlucky to be eliminated on goal difference.

No stranger to controversy, he and Liverpool's Kevin Keegan became the first British players to be sent off at Wembley when they exchanged blows during the 1974-75 Charity Shield match. This was followed shortly afterwards by the decision to award a life ban from the Scottish FA following a misconduct charge during a trip to Copenhagen for a European Championship match. He died in 1997.

ABOVE LEFT: George Best in happier days. By the early 1970s, his career in the top flight was almost over. In December 1972 he was transfer-listed by the club after a series of failures to turn up for training and matches, as well as disagreements with United's new manager, Frank O'Farrell, who was sacked by the board at the same time as Best was given his marching orders. Ironically on the same day as United told him they no longer wanted him as a player, Best had written to the club saying he no longer wished to play for them.

ABOVE RIGHT: Liverpool's Kevin Keegan races for the ball in his team's match against Birmingham City in 1973. Keegan won European Footballer of the Year twice in the 1970s.

LEFT: Smiles on the faces of Leeds manager Don Revie and club captain, Billy Bremner as they hold the FA Cup which the club won in 1972, the competition's centenary year when they beat Arsenal 1-0.

Stoke win League Cup after 7-hour marathon

The 1971-72 League Cup matched the FA Cup for drama. Entry to the League Cup was now compulsory and competition was fierce. Stoke and West Ham fought out a seven-hour semi-final marathon, a Terry Conroy goal settling the tie after two legs and two replays. Stoke beat Chelsea 2-1 in the final, and had thus played twelve games to get their hands on their first piece of silverware in their 109-year history. 35-year-old George Eastham hit the winner, his first goal for nearly two years. It was also a first medal at club level for 34-year-old Gordon Banks.

BELOW: *'The Charlton Brothers'. During the 1970s Jackie (left) and Bobby Charlton continued to be successful at both club and national level. Jackie was an important member of the great Leeds team of the early years of the decade while Bobby remained loyal to Manchester United, despite the club's struggle to remain mid-table. At the end of the 1972-73 season Bobby retired, having played 751 games and scored 247 goals for the club.*

Clough quits Derby

Clough and his assistant, Peter Taylor, were the toast of Derby after winning the championship in 1972, yet barely a year later they and the club had parted company. The outspoken and abrasive Clough had not always endeared himself to the directors at the Baseball Ground, who feared that his controversial outbursts might land the club in hot water. In the autumn of 1973 relations worsened and Clough and Taylor resigned. Derby initially fared better than Clough. Former player Dave Mackay took over and he would lead the Rams to another championship in 1975. But by the end of the decade Derby would be back in Division Two, while Clough and Taylor would be managing the European champions.

ABOVE: *Archie Gemmill playing for Derby against Spurs in 1972 , the year the Rams won the title. Gemmill had been considering signing for the reigning champions Everton until Clough lured him to the Baseball ground.*

First European trophy for Liverpool

By the 1972-73 season Shankly had completed his rebuilding process. Liverpool stormed to a record 8th championship, using just 16 players all season. They made it a domestic and European double by winning the UEFA Cup, which had replaced the Fairs Cup the previous year. The fact that UEFA wanted to take the competition under its umbrella, as it had the Cup Winners' Cup a decade earlier, made no difference to English clubs' domination. Arsenal, Leeds and Spurs had won the last three finals, adding to Leeds' and Newcastle's victories at the end of the 1960s. Liverpool were thus bidding to bring the trophy back to England for the sixth successive year.

They faced holders Spurs in the semi-final and took a narrow 1-0 lead to White Hart Lane for the second leg. Martin Peters, who had moved to Spurs for a record £200,000 after the 1970 World Cup, scored twice in a

2-1 win, but Heighway's away goal put Liverpool through.

In the final they faced a highly rated Borussia Moenchengladbach side that included Netzer, Bonhof, Heynckes and Vogts. The first leg at Anfield showed Shankly at his cunning best. He played Brian Hall instead of John Toshack, feeling that the smaller, quicker man might get more joy against the German defence. Torrential rain forced an abandonment after 30 minutes, but in that time the Liverpool boss had seen that Moenchengladbach were susceptible to the high ball. 24 hours later Toshack was in the side champing at the bit after being left out of the original line-up. His flicks created two goals for Keegan and the Reds won 3-0. The German side nearly turned it round, winning the return leg 2-0, but Liverpool had their hands on their first European trophy.

1971-72 DIVISION ONE	
1 Derby County	58
2 Leeds United	57
3 Liverpool	57
4 Manchester City	57
5 Arsenal	52
6 Tottenham Hotspur	51
7 Chelsea	48
8 Manchester United	48
9 Wolverhampton W.	47
10 Sheffield United	46
11 Newcastle United	41
12 Leicester City	39
13 Ipswich	38
14 West Ham United	36
15 Everton	36
16 West Bromwich Albion	35
17 Stoke	35
18 Coventry	33
19 Southampton	31
20 Crystal Palace	29
21 Nottingham Forest	25
22 Huddersfield	25

Manchester United relegated

In 1973-74 Southampton finished 20th in the league and became the first Division One side to suffer from the new three-up, three-down system. Manchester United, European champions just six years earlier, finished one place below the Saints and found themselves in Division Two for the first time since 1938. The Manchester derby at Old Trafford has gone down in folklore as the game in which Denis Law, who had returned to his former club, backheeled the goal which put United down. Law, playing his last game before hanging up his boots, did put City one up, and after a pitch invasion that was the score when the game was halted four minutes from time. Several days later, the Football League decided to allow the result to stand. However, in the final table United finished four points behind Southampton and five adrift of Birmingham, the team which just avoided the drop. Manager Tommy Docherty would bring a new young side back to the top flight as Division Two champions the following year.

ABOVE RIGHT: *A delighted Sunderland manager, Bob Stokoe, hugs Porterfield after the team's stunning win*

ABOVE LEFT: *Sunderland's captain Bobby Kerr proudly shows supporters the cup. On his right is Sunderland goalkeeper, Jim Montgomery.*

ABOVE: *Leeds' unbeaten record is maintained when Billy Bremner (right) stops a Southampton shot on the line. Leeds won the match 2-1.*

BELOW: *Ian Porterfield's (right) shot flies over Leeds goalkeeper, Harvey, to score the goal that gave Second Division Sunderland a miraculous FA Cup victory against the favourites.*

Ramsey sacked after "clown" denies England

The 1973-74 season saw a number of managerial bombshells. Hard on the heels of Clough's acrimonious departure from the Baseball Ground, Sir Alf Ramsey finally paid the price for failure. On 17 October 1973 a 1-1 draw against Poland ended England's hopes of qualifying for the 1974 World Cup. Poland keeper Jan Tomaszewski had been dubbed a "clown" but he was in inspired form on that night at Wembley. England peppered his goal for 90 minutes, but it took an Allan Clarke penalty to beat him. By then Poland were one up, Domarski's shot squeezing under Shilton's body. The fact that Poland went on to be one of the teams of the tournament in Germany, playing some delightful football on their way to finishing third, was of little consolation. Nor could it save Ramsey, who had been sacked a month earlier.

Revie takes England job

Joe Mercer was given temporary charge of the England team, and in July the FA announced that Don Revie would take over. Leeds had just won the title, five points ahead of arch-rivals Liverpool. Revie's men had been under threat from the FA following their appalling disciplinary record in previous seasons. In this campaign it was their footballing qualities which took the eye. Leeds went on a 29-match unbeaten run to win their second championship in style. Revie's decision to take the England job may have had something to do with the fact that he now had an ageing side that would need a major overhaul sooner rather than later. The man who stepped into Revie's shoes was Brian Clough, but he was barely there long enough to claim a car-parking space, let alone put his stamp on the team. Amid rumours of a dressing-room bust-ups between manager and players, Clough departed after just 44 days in charge.

1972-73 DIVISION ONE	
1 Liverpool	60
2 Arsenal	57
3 Leeds United	53
4 Ipswich	48
5 Wolverhampton W.	47
6 West Ham United	46
7 Derby County	46
8 Tottenham Hotspur	45
9 Newcastle United	45
10 Birmingham City	42
11 Manchester City	41
12 Chelsea	40
13 Southampton	40
14 Sheffield United	40
15 Stoke	38
16 Leicester City	37
17 Everton	37
18 Manchester United	37
19 Coventry	35
20 Norwich City	32
21 Crystal Palace	30
22 West Bromwich Albion	28

BELOW: *Allan Clarke scores from a penalty to put England level at one goal apiece with Poland. The draw in this game was not sufficient to take England through to the 1974 World Cup Finals in West Germany.*

Johnny Giles

When Johnny Giles joined Leeds United from Manchester United in 1963 they were a Division Two side. Even in those days, at a cost of £35,000, Leeds got a bargain, for over the next 12 years Giles was a major influence in helping turn Don Revie's side into a force to rival Manchester United and Liverpool.

Leeds playmaker

Giles was originally a winger but at Leeds he became a superbly skilled and creative midfield playmaker, forming an almost telepathic partnership with the fiery Billy Bremner. In his first season at the club, 1963-64, Leeds won promotion to the First Division. During the following 10 years Leeds were never out of the top flight – never finishing lower than fourth in the table and twice taking the championship. Giles went on to win the FA Cup with Leeds in 1972, adding to the winners' medal he gained when he was part of Manchester United's victory over Leicester City nine years earlier. He also won two winners' medals in the Fairs Cup, but missed out on a European Cup victory when Leeds lost 2-0 to Bayern Munich in Paris in 1975. Soon after that defeat Giles left Elland Road for West Bromwich Albion. As a Republic of Ireland international for nearly two decades, playing his 59th and last game in 1979, it was fitting that he ended his playing career with Shamrock Rovers.

Leeds fans riot as Bayern are crowned European champions

Jimmy Armfield took up the reins and although Leeds slipped to 9th in the league, they did make it to the 1975 European Cup Final. Leeds dominated in the early stages against holders Bayern Munich. They were unlucky not to be awarded a penalty and also had a Lorimer strike ruled out. Bayern weathered the storm and won the match with late goals from Roth and Muller. Leeds fans went on the rampage after the game and the club received a three-year ban from European competition. It hardly mattered as it was the end of a glorious era. Leeds were more commonly to be found in mid-table for the rest of the decade and were relegated early in the next.

BELOW: *Peter Osgood shows his delight as he scores Chelsea's equaliser in the 1-1 draw at Elland Road in the 1973 season. The vanquished Leeds men are Trevor Cherry, Paul Madeley and Norman Hunter.*
BOTTOM: *QPR's Stan Bowles strides confidently away from the goalmouth after scoring against Manchester United; Martin Buchan looks on disconsolately. That season, 1973-74, saw Manchester United relegated to Division Two when they scored only 32 points from 42 games.*

Another World Cup exit for England

If Revie had timed his Elland Road exit well, his decision to take on the England job was to prove no great boost to his managerial career. He failed to establish a settled side, and although the usual club versus country wrangle didn't help matters, Revie himself contributed to the problem with constant changes in personnel. England failed to reach the last eight of the 1976 European Championship, and in July the following year he handed in his resignation. England were on the brink of yet another World Cup exit and Revie headed off to the Middle East with comments that he jumped before he was pushed ringing in his ears.

Ron Greenwood stepped into the breach and that autumn guided England to victories in their last two World Cup qualifying matches. A 2-0 win over Italy merely reversed the result in Rome. It was the victory over Luxembourg by the same score that settled England's fate, the Italians going through on goal difference. As in 1974, England lost out to a side that went on to do well in the tournament - Italy would finish fourth - but after the heady days of 1966, and to a lesser extent 1970, it was a bitter pill to swallow.

The gruelling nature of the domestic season was highlighted as a contributory factor in the national team's fortunes. Grudgingly, the Football League finally accepted the postponement of fixtures prior to key international matches.

LEFT: *Villain – Keegan lands a right to the jaw of Leeds captain Billy Bremner when the pair got into a brawl during the 1974 Charity Shield match.*
BELOW LEFT: *Hero – Kevin Keegan soars in the air to score England's second goal in their 2-0 win over Wales at Cardiff in 1974.*
BOTTOM: *The 1974 FA Cup Final saw Liverpool win 3-0 against Newcastle United. Here Keegan powers home the opening goal; he would later score the third.*

1973-74 DIVISION ONE	
1 Leeds United	62
2 Liverpool	57
3 Derby County	48
4 Ipswich	47
5 Stoke	46
6 Burnley	46
7 Everton	44
8 Queen's Park Rangers	43
9 Leicester City	42
10 Arsenal	42
11 Tottenham Hotspur	42
12 Wolverhampton W.	41
13 Sheffield United	40
14 Manchester City	40
15 Newcastle United	38
16 Coventry	38
17 Chelsea	37
18 West Ham United	37
19 Birmingham City	37
20 Southampton	36
21 Manchester United	32
22 Norwich City	29

End of an era as Shanks steps down

When Ron Greenwood picked his first England side, he named seven Liverpool players. By the middle of the decade they were the team everyone had to beat. In 1973-74, having finished runners-up to Leeds and beaten Newcastle Utd in the FA Cup Final, Liverpool were the latest club to experience a shock managerial resignation. Bill Shankly announced his retirement, ending his 15-year reign at

Anfield. After Liverpool's 3-0 demolition of Newcastle at Wembley, Liverpool fans had prostrated themselves at Shankly's feet on the pitch. Two months later he was gone. His final act was a typically shrewd move. The Liverpool way was to strengthen well before it was necessary. Competition was so fierce that players dreaded being sidelined through injury for fear that they might not get back in the

team. It was after Shankly unveiled his last signing, Arsenal's Ray Kennedy, that he shuffled off the stage. The Liverpool board may have been worried that the Shankly aura might continue to pervade Anfield in the way that Busby's had at Old Trafford. In the event the break was swift and final, something Shankly was said to have found surprising and hurtful.

Bill Shankly

When Bill Shankly left Anfield for the last time after winning the 1974 FA Cup, it brought down the curtain on a glorious 15-year reign. In that time Shankly had turned Liverpool from a struggling, unambitious club into one of the most formidable sides in world football.

Waking the sleeping giant
Shankly had had success with the other clubs he had managed - Carlisle, Grimsby, Workington and Huddersfield - but was hampered by their lack of vision and unwillingness to invest. Liverpool, on the other hand, was a true sleeping giant, and it was Shankly who woke it up and unleashed it on the world. Promotion to the top flight came in 1961-62, his second full season at the club. After just one season of consolidation Liverpool won the championship. Over the next 10 years he steered the club to two more league titles and two FA Cup victories. He also lifted the UEFA Cup in 1973, Liverpool beating Borussia Moenchengladbach in the final. The man from Glenbuck, Ayrshire was revered by fans and players alike, who loved his dry wit. He certainly laid the foundations for the side which dominated the English game in the 1970s and 1980s. Shankly died in 1981. His name adorns a pair of gates at the entrance to his beloved Anfield and his spirit pervades the club to this day.

LEFT: *Bill Shankly offers a prayer of thanks as Liverpool win the League Championship by three points from rivals Arsenal in the 1972-73 season. The following year, Shankly's last at the helm, Liverpool were beaten into second place by Leeds.*

Another League and European double for the Reds

In 1975-76 Queen's Park Rangers were the surprise package. Led by England captain Gerry Francis, QPR were top of the league when they'd completed their fixtures. But Liverpool could pip them by winning their last game, at Molineux. Wolves had to win to have any chance of avoiding relegation and they scored first. The Reds came back to win 3-1, however. Wolves were down and Paisley had his first championship under his belt. He also matched Shankly's feat of three years earlier by capturing the UEFA Cup in the same season. Liverpool put out a Barcelona side that boasted Johan Cruyff in the semis, then faced FC Bruges in the final. The Belgians rocked Liverpool by taking a 2-0 lead at Anfield, but the Reds staged a magnificent fightback to win 3-2. Bruges also scored first in the second leg, but a Keegan strike won the trophy for Liverpool.

1974-75 DIVISION ONE		
1	Derby County	53
2	Liverpool	51
3	Ipswich	51
4	Everton	50
5	Stoke	49
6	Sheffield United	49
7	Middlesbrough	48
8	Manchester City	46
9	Leeds United	45
10	Burnley	45
11	Queen's Park Rangers	42
12	Wolverhampton W.	39
13	West Ham United	39
14	Coventry	39
15	Newcastle United	39
16	Arsenal	37
17	Birmingham City	37
18	Leicester City	36
19	Tottenham Hotspur	34
20	Luton	33
21	Chelsea	33
22	Carlisle	29

OPPOSITE TOP: *A fan adorns Bill Shankly with a scarf as he bids farewell to Anfield after fifteen years as Liverpool's manager.*

OPPOSITE MIDDLE: *The Aston Villa team, with manager Ron Saunders (pointing), inspect the Wembley pitch before their League Cup Final match against Norwich in 1975. Villa won the tie 1-0.*

ABOVE: *Alan Taylor scores the second of his two goals which clinched the FA Cup for West Ham against London rivals Fulham in the 1975 Final.*

LEFT: *West Ham's Trevor Brooking is mobbed by fans after the team's defeat of their Second Division rivals.*

Strikes bring Sunday football

1974 saw Sunday football played for the first time. This was a tentative move and by no means uncontroversial. A combination of rail and power strikes persuaded the authorities to sanction these matches. Sunday trading laws meant that grounds could not simply open for business as they would on any other day. There were legal restrictions on charging at the gate and clubs circumvented these by selling programmes at the turnstiles for the normal entrance price. These games proved to be very popular with the fans and Sunday soccer would eventually become a way of life.

BELOW LEFT: *Southampton goalkeeper Ian Turner saves a header from Manchester United's Gordon Hill. Southampton unexpectedly won the FA Cup in 1976 with a Bobby Stokes strike in the 83rd minute.*

BELOW: *The Manchester United squad, with manager, Tommy 'The Doc' Docherty (far right), at the end of the 1975-76 season. Although the club lost the 1976 FA Cup Final to Southampton, they won the following year and were back on track after their spell in Division Two during 1974-75.*

Paisley emerges from "boot room" to take over at Anfield

The famous Anfield "boot room" had been established during the Shankly years. Bob Paisley, Joe Fagan, Ronnie Moran and Reuben Bennett were the key men in the backroom team. Paisley was given the top job, everyone took a step up in the pecking order and a seamless transition was effected.

In Paisley's first season in charge Liverpool finished runners-up to Derby. It was notable for two inspired purchases as Paisley showed he had Shankly's golden touch in the transfer market. Northampton's Phil Neal joined the Reds in a £60,000 deal in October 1974. A month later Terry McDermott, who had played against Liverpool in that year's Cup Final, arrived from Newcastle for £170,000.

United reach successive Cup Finals

1975-76 marked Manchester United's return to the First Division, and Tommy Docherty's young side was immediately chasing the double. They eventually finished third in the league, but in the FA Cup Final they were hot favourites to beat Lawrie McMenemy's Southampton, who had finished only sixth in the Second Division. Mick Channon and Peter Osgood led the line for Southampton but it was a solitary goal from Bobby Stokes seven minutes from time that brought the club its first major honour.

United returned to Wembley the following year and this time they faced a Liverpool side which was seeking an unprecedented treble. Having secured a 10th league title, Liverpool had to play two Cup Finals in quick succession. The dream was ended at Wembley, where Docherty's burgeoning young side came out on top. Only Alex Stepney remained from the glory team of the 1960s. Stepney saw a Jimmy Case thunderbolt fly past him, cancelling out a Stuart Pearson shot which had squeezed under Clemence's body. A Lou Macari effort deflected off Jimmy Greenhoff for United's winner. It was an outrageous fluke but after the previous year's disappointment neither United nor the Doc were worried about that.

BOTTOM: *United's Alex Stepney watches the ball go into the net as Bobby Stokes' goal, the only goal of the match, secures the 1976 FA Cup for Southampton.*

BELOW: *West Ham's Frank Lampard and Manchester City's Rodney Marsh race for the ball during a league game at the beginning of the 1975-76 season. Despite West Ham's Cup win in 1975, they struggled to avoid relegation at he end of the 1975-76 season.*

BOTTOM RIGHT: *The 'Saints come rolling home' – the Southampton players who won the 1976 FA Cup travel through the streets of their home city, lined by 175,000 people, to attend a civic reception.*

1975-76 DIVISION ONE

1	Liverpool	60
2	Queen's Park Rangers	59
3	Manchester United	56
4	Derby County	53
5	Leeds United	51
6	Ipswich	46
7	Leicester City	45
8	Manchester City	43
9	Tottenham Hotspur	43
10	Norwich City	42
11	Everton	42
12	Stoke	41
13	Middlesbrough	40
14	Coventry	40
15	Newcastle United	39
16	Aston Villa	39
17	Arsenal	36
18	West Ham United	36
19	Birmingham City	33
20	Wolverhampton W.	30
21	Burnley	28
22	Sheffield United	22

Keegan bows out as Liverpool become champions of Europe

Five days later Liverpool had to pick themselves up as they made their bid to become only the second English side to win the European Cup. Their quarter-final clash with St Etienne had been the key match in their run to the final. St Etienne, the previous year's beaten finalists, had scored a 1-0 win at home, and were outstanding at Anfield. The French side scored to cancel out a Keegan goal, and even after Ray Kennedy restored Liverpool's lead on the night, the Reds still trailed on away goals. Enter David Fairclough, who came on with 20 minutes to go and scored the winner after a breathtaking solo run. "Supersub" had done it again.

Liverpool eased into the final with a win over FC Zurich. They travelled to Rome to face a Borussia Moenchengladbach side for the second time in a major final. The players shrugged off their FA Cup disappointment with an excellent 3-1 victory. It was a great day for two veterans. Tommy Smith, who had made his debut in 1963, headed in a Heighway corner to make it 2-1. Smith was a relative newcomer compared to Ian Callaghan, who had been at Anfield when the club was fighting for promotion to the top flight in the late 1950s.

It was also a special day for Kevin Keegan, playing his last game in the famous No. 7 shirt. His £500,000 move to SV Hamburg had already been agreed. Keegan didn't manage to get on the scoresheet in his final appearance but he gave Berti Vogts a torrid time. The ace German marker finally made a rash challenge, bringing Keegan down inside the box. Penalty king Phil Neal fired in the team's third goal, and Liverpool had equalled Manchester United's achievement of 1968.

BELOW: *After Liverpool's European Cup victory in 1977, Kevin Keegan signed for SV Hamburg.*
RIGHT: *Emlyn Hughes, Liverpool captain, holds the European Cup aloft, after the club's 3-1 win over Borussia Moenchengladbach.*

Kevin Keegan

For a player who knew he wasn't the most naturally gifted in the game, Kevin Keegan demonstrated that a football career can be built as much on hard work, commitment and self-belief as on virtuoso skills. Surprisingly powerful in the air for a small man, he had a rocketing shot that made him a notable goal-scorer, and was always looking to create opportunities for others during six glorious years at Liverpool FC, after Bill Shankly brought him to Merseyside in 1971 from Scunthorpe United, paying just £35,000.

European Footballer of the Year

Keegan scored in his very first game, and he soon made himself vital at the heart of the team. The very next season he netted 22 goals, helping Liverpool to win both the League Championship and the UEFA Cup. He scored twice in Liverpool's 3-0 victory over Newcastle in the 1974 FA Cup Final, and was named the Footballer of the Year in 1976 after the Reds again took the league title and he scored in both legs of the final of the UEFA Cup when they beat Bruges.

The Anfield faithful paid handsome tribute when Keegan was lured to Hamburg in a record £500,000 deal, for he had played 230 games and scored 68 goals in the famous red shirt. Playing in the Bundesliga, he twice won European Footballer of the Year, in 1978 and 1979, the only British player ever to do so.

63 England caps

First appearing for England (against Wales) in 1972, his international career spanned 10 years, during which he won 63 caps (31 of them as captain) and scored 21 goals. The end came when he missed a vital chance in a second-round match against Spain in the 1982 World Cup, and was then dropped for a European Championship qualifying game by Bobby Robson. Keegan soon quit international football.

But his return to the English league provided a happier swansong. At Southampton and finally at Newcastle, he came right back into form and helped the Geordie side to win promotion to the First Division at the end of the 1983-84 season.

Returning to Tyneside as manager in 1992, he took the Magpies back to the top flight in short order, then made a surprise move to Fulham. Though he confessed to feelings of inadequacy at the end of his tenure as England manager, he showed he could still work his magic at club level, establishing Manchester City as a Premiership force once again before stepping down during the 2004-05 season.

ABOVE: *Arsenal's Liam Brady leaps over a tackle from David Geddis of Ipswich in the 1978 FA Cup Final. Despite Brady's athleticism, he was on the losing side as Ipswich won with a single goal from Roger Osborne.*

LEFT: *Arsenal's Malcolm MacDonald leaves the pitch at Wembley after his team's defeat in the FA Cup Final. His dejection can be understood – he had been on the losing side in a Wembley Final twice before, with Newcastle United, in the FA Cup in 1974 and the League Cup in 1976.*

TOP: *Scotland beat England 1-0 at Wembley in the 1977 international match.*

Dalglish the new No.7 hero

Keegan went on to win the European Footballer of the Year award twice while at Hamburg. The blow of losing a player who had become a legend in his six years at Anfield was softened as Paisley went north of the border for a big-name replacement. 26-year-old Kenny Dalglish arrived in Liverpool a month after Keegan's departure. He had scored over a hundred goals for Celtic, the club he had joined at the age of 16. By the end of his first season at Liverpool he had notched 30, putting him well on the way to becoming a double centurion. The Kop had a new idol in the famous number 7 shirt.

ABOVE RIGHT: *Chelsea's Gary Stanley comes out top in a duel with Gerry Francis in the 1-1 draw of 1977.*

RIGHT: *A champion welcome for Liverpool when they returned to Merseyside after their 1-0 victory over Bruges in the European Cup final at Wembley in 1978. Thousands took to the streets during a 14-mile lap of honour around the city. (L-R: Alan Hansen, David Fairclough, Emlyn Hughes, Kenny Dalglish and Ray Clemence).*

BELOW: *A Dalglish diving header beats Chelsea's Micky Droy but hits the woodwork in a league game in March during the 1977-78 season when Liverpool turned out runners-up to Nottingham Forest in the championship.*

Kenny Dalglish

Already established as a legend at Celtic after a decade of service to the club he joined straight from school, Kenny Dalglish transferred to Liverpool in 1977. A month after Kevin Keegan had left Anfield for SV Hamburg, Liverpool boss Bob Paisley swooped to buy the most feared striker in the Scottish League.

Hundred league goals for Liverpool

Dalglish proved his worth to the club over the next 14 years, both as a player and as a manager; he became the idol of the Kop. In November 1983, he scored his hundredth league goal for Liverpool, the first player to reach that landmark both north and south of the border. He won five championship medals and three European Cups before taking over the reins from Joe Fagan in May 1985, in the wake of the Heysel Stadium disaster. With Dalglish as player-manager, Liverpool won the coveted Double in the 1985-86 season.

On the international stage, the player widely considered to be the greatest ever to wear the red of Liverpool also won a record 102 caps for Scotland, scoring 30 goals at international level to match Denis Law's record.

Forest storm to the championship

Kenny Dalglish had arrived at Anfield in a blaze of publicity. There had been less of a fanfare when Paisley signed centre-back Alan Hansen from Partick Thistle for £100,000 a couple of months earlier. The 1977-78 season also saw the arrival of a third Scot who would become an Anfield legend. Paisley paid Middlesbrough £350,000 for midfielder Graeme Souness, who provided skill and steel in the heart of the midfield.

Three quality additions to a European Cup-winning side wasn't enough for Liverpool to retain the title in 1977-78. The Reds trailed in seven points behind Brian Clough's newly-promoted Nottingham Forest. Following the Leeds debacle, Clough had been reunited with Peter Taylor and taken over at Forest. The team only went up in third place behind Wolves and Chelsea and were tipped to make a rapid return to Division Two. Instead, Forest made it a Championship and League Cup double, with mighty Liverpool having to settle for second-best in both cases.

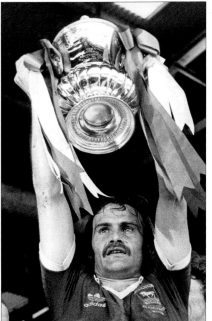

ABOVE LEFT: *Kenny Dalglish moves in to score the goal that put the holders of the title, Ipswich, out of the 1978-79 FA Cup competition. It was Dalglish's second season at Liverpool and he had proved worthy of the record £440,000 paid to bring the Celtic striker to Anfield as a replacement for Kevin Keegan. In his first season, Dalglish scored 31 goals in 62 appearances for the club.*

LEFT: *Ipswich's Mick Mills holds up the Cup for the fans after the team's 1-0 win over Arsenal in the 1978 FA Cup Final.*

ABOVE: *Just one year later and Arsenal reverse their fortunes to take the Cup to Highbury in a 3-2 win over Manchester United.*

Clough matches Chapman's record

Clough's side included ex-Derby players John McGovern, John O'Hare and Archie Gemmill, together with former Liverpool stopper Larry Lloyd. Clough added Kenny Burns, turning the former Birmingham City bad boy into the Footballer of the Year. There was also Viv Anderson, a young attacking full-back who became England's first black player when he took the field against Czechoslovakia on 29 November 1978. But the key acquisition was probably Peter Shilton, bought from Stoke for £270,000, the highest amount ever paid for a goalkeeper. Forest lost just three games all season, conceding only 24 league goals, and took the title with four games to spare. Clough followed in the illustrious footsteps of Herbert Chapman in taking two clubs to the championship.

Liverpool retain European Cup

Forest also got the better of Liverpool in the 1978 League Cup Final, a John Robertson penalty settling the issue at Old Trafford after a goalless draw at Wembley. Having been pipped for domestic honours twice, Liverpool made sure they didn't finish the season empty-handed by retaining their European

crown. FC Bruges were their Wembley opponents. The Belgians set their stall out defensively, inviting Liverpool to try and break them down. The Reds managed to do so just once, Dalglish chipping the keeper delightfully for his 30th goal of the season.

Osborne overcome as Ipswich lift FA Cup

Between 19 November 1977 and 9 December 1978 Forest were unbeaten in the league. Their only defeat in any competition was an FA Cup quarter-final tie with West Bromwich Albion, who won 2-0. Having beaten the country's form team, West Brom went down to Ipswich in the semis, and it was the East Anglian club who were the surprise winners of the trophy. That game will be remembered for the Roger Osborne goal which beat favourites Arsenal in the final. Osborne was so overwrought with the occasion that he was substituted, apparently through sheer nervous exhaustion. His goal took the Cup to Portman Road for the only time in the club's history.

1977-78 DIVISION ONE	
1 Nottingham Forest	64
2 Liverpool	57
3 Everton	55
4 Manchester City	52
5 Arsenal	52
6 West Bromwich Albion	50
7 Coventry	48
8 Aston Villa	46
9 Leeds United	46
10 Manchester United	42
11 Birmingham City	41
12 Derby County	41
13 Norwich City	40
14 Middlesbrough	39
15 Wolverhampton W.	36
16 Chelsea	36
17 Bristol City	35
18 Ipswich	35
19 Queen's Park Rangers	33
20 West Ham United	32
21 Newcastle United	22
22 Leicester City	22

BELOW: *Nottingham Forest goalkeeper, Peter Shilton, and team-mate, Tony Woodcock hold the League Cup after the team's 3-2 win against Southampton in 1979. The late 1970s were a golden time for Nottingham Forest. Under manager Brian Clough, they won the league in 1978, the European Cup in 1979 and the League Cup in 1978 and 1979.*

BELOW: *Arsenal's goalkeeper, Pat Jennings, tries to thwart a Liverpool attack as Graeme Souness looks on during a league match in the 1978-79 season when honours were shared - Liverpool won the league and Arsenal the FA Cup.*

LEFT: *Aston Villa keeper Jimmy Rimmer punches clear from the heads of Spurs' attackers Ian Moores and Gerry Armstrong.*

BOTTOM: *League champions Liverpool beat FA Cup holders Arsenal 3-1 in the Charity Shield curtain raiser to the 1979-80 season. Terry McDermott scored two of the Liverpool goals.*

FA CUP FINALS

Year				Score
1970	Chelsea	v	Leeds United	2-1
1971	Arsenal	v	Liverpool	2-1
1972	Leeds United	v	Arsenal	1-0
1973	Sunderland	v	Leeds United	1-0
1974	Liverpool	v	Newcastle United	3-0
1975	West Ham United	v	Fulham	2-0
1976	Southampton	v	Manchester United	1-0
1977	Manchester United	v	Liverpool	2-1
1978	Ipswich Town	v	Arsenal	1-0
1979	Arsenal	v	Manchester United	3-2

Reds set defensive record

1978-79 saw Liverpool and Forest dominant once again, although this time their roles were reversed. On 9 December 1978 Liverpool ended Forest's year-long unbeaten run in the league. The Forest bubble didn't burst, however, and they again lost just three times in the league. Incredibly, that was only good enough to earn them second place behind a Liverpool side that was in record-breaking mood. Forest's 60 points would have won the championship on numerous postwar occasions. Liverpool themselves had won with that same points tally in 1973 and 1976, and Derby's two titles had been won with a lesser total. Liverpool lost one more game than Forest but 30 wins and eight draws gave them 68 points, one better than the record set by Leeds in 1968-69. The Reds' defence was phenomenal conceding just 16 goals all season.

Million-pound Francis wins European Cup for Forest

If Liverpool had reclaimed their domestic crown from Forest, it was Clough's men who took Liverpool's mantle as champions of Europe. The two sides were unlucky to be drawn together in the first round of the European Cup, a game that would have graced the final. New young striking sensation Garry Birtles scored one of the goals as Forest took a 2-0 lead to Anfield. There they fought out a goalless draw and it was Forest who went forward to try and bring Europe's premier cup back to England for the third successive year. They did so, but not without a scare or two. In their semi-final against Cologne Forest could only draw 3-3 at home. But Clough masterminded a 1-0 win in Germany, Ian Bowyer scoring the goal which put Forest into the final.

They faced Swedish champions Malmo in the Olympic Stadium, Munich. The hero of the hour was Trevor Francis, who headed the only goal of the game just before the break. Francis had become Britain's first million-pound footballer earlier in the season, Birmingham City finally being forced to part with their prize asset. Francis had not been eligible to play in the earlier European ties. His first taste of European football had won the premier trophy and paid off a large chunk of that record fee.

Brian Clough

Brian Clough was the fans' choice to be given the England manager's job in the 1970s and early 1980s. The accepted wisdom was that it was his outspoken, abrasive style that cost him a chance of getting the top job rather than his footballing credentials, which were of the highest order.

Clough had been a prolific goalscorer with Middlesbrough and Sunderland, and was capped for England before his playing career was cut short through injury. In 1965 30-year-old Clough became the youngest manager in the league when he took over at Hartlepool, but it was when he moved to Derby County that he established his reputation. He led the Rams to the Division Two championship in 1969, and after two years of consolidation in the top flight, his side won the league title in 1972. The team reached the semi-final of the European Cup the following year, losing 3-1 on aggregate to Juventus. Derby fans were up in arms when Clough left the Baseball Ground following a disagreement with the board. After an infamous 44-day reign at Leeds United at the beginning of the 1974-75 season, Clough embarked on a glorious 18-year association with another unfashionable club, Nottingham Forest. He won the championship in 1977-78, relegating Liverpool to second place for once. In doing so he became only the third manager in history to win the title with two different clubs. In 1979 he won the European Cup with a 1-0 win over Malmo. The goal was scored by Trevor Francis, whom Clough had made the first £1million player. Forest retained the trophy the following year, a John Robertson penalty giving the team victory over Hamburg. Clough also won the League Cup four times during his reign at the City Ground. He retired after the team was relegated in 1993. Brian Clough died on 20 September 2004.

BELOW: *The joy on Arsenal's Alan Sunderland's face says it all, after he snatches a last-gasp winner in the 1979 FA Cup Final to beat Manchester United 3-2.*

1978-79 DIVISION ONE	
1 Liverpool	68
2 Nottingham Forest	60
3 West Bromwich Albion	59
4 Everton	51
5 Leeds United	50
6 Ipswich	49
7 Arsenal	48
8 Aston Villa	46
9 Manchester United	45
10 Coventry	44
11 Tottenham Hotspur	41
12 Middlesbrough	40
13 Bristol City	40
14 Southampton	40
15 Manchester City	39
16 Norwich City	37
17 Bolton Wanderers	35
18 Wolverhampton W.	34
19 Derby County	31
20 Queen's Park Rangers	25
21 Birmingham City	22
22 Chelsea	20

Brady stars in five-goal Wembley thriller

The last FA Cup Final of the decade provided a goal flurry in the dying minutes. Arsenal, with Liam Brady in imperious form, took a 2-0 lead over Manchester United and seemed to be coasting to victory. Some United fans were already making their way to the exits when goals from McQueen and McIlroy, in the 86th and 88th minutes, levelled the match. Man-of-the-match Brady had the final word, setting up the move which

ended with Alan Sunderland scoring from a Graham Rix cross.

Liverpool domination set to continue

The 1979 FA Cup Final was refreshing in that it was untypical of the trend, which was for scoring fewer goals and conceding fewer. The decade's champions had, on average, scored 69.9 goals and let in 32.2. In the 1960s the average had been 87.3 and 45.7; in the 1950s it was 92.4 and 51.2. In 1961-62 Ipswich conceded 67 goals on their way to the title, which compared favourably with the number of goals scored by championship-winning sides of the 1970s. The new orthodoxy was getting men behind the ball, denying the opposition space and protecting leads.

15 of the 60 teams that had made it to the finals of the three European competitions over the decade were English, and ten of those had been successful. Liverpool had led the charge, and the Anfield juggernaut showed every sign of rolling on into the 1980s.

1980-1992
The Global Game

In the 1980s Liverpool continued their stranglehold on the English game, their level of performance and trophy haul enduring a number of personnel changes, including two at managerial level. By the middle of the decade it was Everton who posed the greatest threat, and their two championships meant that only twice in the decade did the title leave Merseyside.

Heysel, Hillsborough and Bradford

If the city of Liverpool basked in the glory of being footballing top dogs, it also suffered two horrific tragedies. A total of 135 people lost their lives in the Heysel and Hillsborough disasters. On 11 May 1985, less than three weeks before the Heysel tragedy, Bradford entertained Lincoln City in their last match of the season. It should have been a joyous occasion, Bradford celebrating promotion to Division Two as champions. A discarded cigarette set the wooden stand ablaze and 56 died in the inferno. These three events put the game into its proper perspective. Liverpool boss Kenny Dalglish declared that football was "irrelevant" as the city struggled to come to terms with the tragic events at Hillsborough. These disasters also led the game's administrators to realise that fencing in spectators may have prevented pitch invasions, but it also prevented fans from escaping life-threatening situations.

European victory for Forest

The decade began much as the last one had ended, with Liverpool and Nottingham Forest vying for supremacy at home and in Europe. In 1980 the Reds took the championship but crashed out of the European Cup at the first hurdle to Dinamo Tbilisi. Forest came through some tough matches, even surviving a home defeat against Dynamo Berlin. A Trevor Francis double helped Forest turn that tie around and they marched on to meet Kevin Keegan's SV Hamburg in the Final. The showcase events were becoming worryingly sterile affairs and this was no great advertisement for the game. John Robertson scored the only goal, cutting in from the left and firing home from 20 yards. Francis had been sidelined through injury and the team was content to sit back and play on the break. When Hamburg did manage to carve an opening, they found Shilton in prime form.

Brooking sets up Hammers

Forest also made it to the League Cup Final, for the third year running. There was no hat-trick of wins, though. A catastrophic mix-up between Shilton and Dave Needham allowed Wolves' Andy Gray to score the game's only goal. Also playing in the famous Old Gold shirt that day was Emlyn Hughes, recently arrived from Liverpool. In his 13 years at Anfield he had won just about every honour in the game - except the League Cup.

The 1980 FA Cup Final was also settled by a solitary goal. Arsenal must have thought their name was on the Cup after coming through a mammoth semi-final against Liverpool which went to three replays, seven hours of football in total. A Brian Talbot goal finally broke the deadlock and put the Gunners into the Final for the third year running. They faced a West Ham side that had finished 7th in Division Two but a rare header from midfield maestro Trevor Brooking was enough to give the Hammers victory. It was a red-letter day for 17-year-old Paul Allen, the youngest player ever to appear in an FA Cup Final.

OPPOSITE ABOVE:
Liverpool's Alan Hansen, flanked by Terry McDermott (left) and Kenny Dalglish, show off the FA Charity Shield. Liverpool won 1-0 against West Ham in the season curtain raiser at Wembley, 1980.

OPPOSITE BELOW:
Arsenal's Liam Brady shoots at goal while West Ham's Trevor Brooking can only watch, in the 1980 FA Cup final at Wembley. Arsenal won the match 1-0.

LEFT: *Goalkeeper Peter Shilton of Nottingham Forest punches the ball clear of the goal as Arsenal attack. Arsenal won the match 1-0, but Forest were in fine form in 1980 and were to beat SV Hamburg in the European Cup Final.*

1979-80 DIVISION ONE

1	Liverpool	60
2	Manchester United	58
3	Ipswich	53
4	Arsenal	52
5	Nottingham Forest	48
6	Wolverhampton W.	47
7	Aston Villa	46
8	Southampton	45
9	Middlesbrough	44
10	West Bromwich Albion	41
11	Leeds United	40
12	Norwich City	40
13	Crystal Palace	40
14	Tottenham Hotspur	40
15	Coventry	39
16	Brighton	37
17	Manchester City	37
18	Stoke	36
19	Everton	35
20	Bristol City	31
21	Derby County	30
22	Bolton Wanderers	25

Arsenal miss out in Cup Winners Cup

Arsenal's dramatic win over Manchester United the previous year had put them through to the Cup Winners' Cup competition and the Gunners made it through to the Final. Valencia provided the glamorous opposition, but 120 minutes of football produced no goals and this became the first major Final to be decided on penalties. Argentine World Cup hero Mario Kempes missed, but parity was restored when Liam Brady also failed with his spot-kick. Graham Rix was the unlucky man to miss the vital kick and the trophy went to Spain. Arsenal were left with the unique distinction of returning to Highbury empty-handed despite having gone through the tournament unbeaten.

England's Euro failure

In the European Championship England dropped just one point in their eight qualifying matches to reach the finals, which were staged in Italy. A revised format saw the eight countries split into two groups with the winners of each contesting the Final. Tear gas had to be used to quell disturbances as England opened with a goalless draw against Belgium. Marco Tardelli scored the only goal of the game when England met the hosts in the second game. England were out without registering a single goal, although they did manage a 2-1 win against Spain in a meaningless final group match.

Three points for a win

By 1981 concern over the state of the game was being expressed in high places. A lot of the fare on offer was of indifferent quality; hooliganism was a cancer that was proving difficult to excise; and with the country in the grip of recession a match-day ticket became a luxury some fans could ill afford. Liverpool's dominance didn't help matters. Gates were barely above the 20 million mark, half what they had been in the golden postwar years. Several clubs were teetering on the edge of bankruptcy, Wolves among them.

The Football League announced that from 1981-82, there would be three points for a win. The message was clear: football was entertainment as well as sport, and the carrot of three points would surely make teams think twice about putting up the defensive drawbridge.

Villa take the championship

The intervening season brought plenty of drama, not least of which was the sight of Liverpool languishing in 5th place in the league. The Reds lost just eight games, which was as good as anyone, but had drawn as many as they'd won. It was Ron Saunders' Aston Villa who took the title, for the first time in 71 years. Villa used just 14 players all season and seven of them were ever-present. Ex-Coventry player Dennis Mortimer captained the side, forming an impressive midfield axis with Gordon Cowans and Des Bremner, who provided skill and steel respectively. Up front Peter Withe and Gary Shaw made up a potent little-and-large strike force. Flying winger Tony Morley was responsible for many assists and was also a regular on the scoresheet himself.

Ardiles and Villa in Cup classic

1981 saw Spurs continue their love affair with years ending in one. In the FA Cup Final Manchester City's Tommy Hutchinson scored twice, the second of which he would rather not have claimed. A Glenn Hoddle free-kick deflected off him and earned Spurs a replay. Keith Burkinshaw had pulled off the transfer coup of the year when he brought Ricardo Villa and Osvaldo Ardiles to White Hart Lane after Argentina's World Cup victory in 1978. In 1981 the two shared in a spectacular triumph. The teams put on a terrific display when they returned to Wembley for the replay. With minutes to go and the score 2-2, Villa danced his way through the City defence to score what many regard as the best individual goal ever in a Cup final.

OPPOSITE ABOVE LEFT: *Referee Clive Thomas is mobbed by West Ham players as he overrules the linesman's offside flag in the 1981 League Cup Final.*
OPPOSITE ABOVE RIGHT: *Ricky Villa holds aloft the FA Cup for the crowds of admiring fans gathered in the streets outside Tottenham Town Hall in 1981. Following a 1-1 draw against Manchester City, Tottenham went on to win the replay at Wembley 3-2.*
OPPOSITE BELOW: *Wolverhampton Wanderers attack the Tottenham goal in the FA Cup semi-final in 1981.*
ABOVE: *Aston Villa's Peter Withe scores against Stoke in a 1-1 draw, gaining an important point for the team which ended the 1980-81 season at the top of the First Division for the first time in 71 years.*
RIGHT: *Ipswich Town manager Bobby Robson brings back the UEFA Cup having defeated Dutch side AZ 67 Alkmaar 5-4 on aggregate.*

1980-81 DIVISION ONE

1	Aston Villa	60
2	Ipswich	56
3	Arsenal	53
4	West Bromwich Albion	52
5	Liverpool	51
6	Southampton	50
7	Nottingham Forest	50
8	Manchester United	48
9	Leeds United	44
10	Tottenham Hotspur	43
11	Stoke	42
12	Manchester City	39
13	Birmingham City	38
14	Middlesbrough	37
15	Everton	36
16	Coventry	36
17	Sunderland	35
18	Wolverhampton W.	35
19	Brighton	35
20	Norwich City	33
21	Leicester City	32
22	Crystal Palace	19

Bob Paisley

Although people often speak of Shankly and Ferguson as the greatest managers to grace the English game, in terms of honours won nobody can match the achievements of Bob Paisley. He took over from Shankly after the FA Cup victory over Newcastle in 1974, 35 years after joining the club. Paisley had been a member of Liverpool's title-winning side of 1947, joining the coaching staff on his retirement seven years later. But it was for his nine years at the helm that he will be best remembered. He led the club to six championships and three League Cups, but it was his four European trophies that set him apart from his peers. His team lifted the UEFA Cup in 1976 with a victory over FC Bruges. The following year he made Liverpool the third British side to win the European Cup when Liverpool beat Borussia Moenchengladbach 3-1 at the Olympic Stadium in Rome. Liverpool retained the trophy the following year, beating Bruges once again in a major Final. The hat-trick was completed in 1981, Alan Kennedy scoring the goal which beat Real Madrid. The affable Geordie stepped down in 1983, signing off with a championship and League Cup double. On the latter occasion, Graeme Souness took the unprecedented step of ushering the manager up the 39 Wembley steps to collect the trophy. Paisley died in February 1996.

Rush signs from Chester

Although the two major domestic honours had escaped them, Liverpool did add two more trophies to the cabinet. The Reds finally added the League Cup to their tally, though they needed a replay to beat West Ham. An Alan Hansen header gave Liverpool a 2-1 victory. Making only his second full appearance that night at Villa Park was young striker Ian Rush, who had signed from Chester City for £300,000 having played just 33 games in Division Four.

Having broken their League Cup duck, Liverpool proceeded to form a firm attachment to it. Victories over Spurs, Manchester United and Everton in the next three Finals set a new record and gave the club outright ownership of the trophy.

Liverpool's third Euro success
1981 also brought Liverpool a third European Cup success. Alex Ferguson's Aberdeen and Bayern Munich were among their scalps en route to the final. There they met six-time winners Real Madrid, whose side included ex-West Brom star winger Laurie Cunningham. It was a cagey contest, Alan Kennedy breaking the deadlock with a shot from an acute angle nine minutes from time. The victory meant that Liverpool joined Bayern and Ajax as three-time winners of European club football's most prestigious trophy.

LEFT: The 1981 Charity Shield is shared by Aston Villa and Spurs, following a 2-2 draw. Goalscorers Peter Withe of Villa (left) and Mark Falco of Tottenham pose with the trophy.
BELOW: Trevor Francis, the league's first million-pound footballer, is on target for Forest in the 1981 European campaign.

Muhren and Butcher lift Robson's Ipswich

Bobby Robson's Ipswich Town made it a European double by lifting the UEFA Cup. Ipswich had finished runners-up in the league, their formidable line-up including Terry Butcher, Paul Mariner, Alan Brazil and John Wark. Like Spurs, the team had two outstanding overseas players, the Dutch midfield duo Frans Thijssen and Arnold Muhren. Ipswich overcame Dutch champions AZ 67 Alkmaar 5-4 on aggregate in the Final. Wark scored a record-equalling 14 goals during the campaign. Wark, Thijssen and Mariner made it an Ipswich clean sweep in the PFA awards, with Thijssen topping the Football Writers poll.

Robson's careful housekeeping at Ipswich showed that success could be had for a modest outlay. Many clubs wielded the chequebook all too readily and huge amounts were changing hands. Some players would prove to be worth every penny. In October 1981 Ron Atkinson paid his former club West Bromwich Albion £1.5 million to bring Bryan Robson to Old Trafford. A decade later that would look a knockdown price. Steve Daley, Kevin

Reeves, Justin Fashanu and Gary Birtles were among those whose form - and value - slumped dramatically after high-profile moves.

In one remarkable move Clive Allen joined Arsenal from Queen's Park Rangers, and was sold on to Crystal Palace two months later without having kicked a ball. Allen's cut of the two million-pound deals was around £100,000, players receiving 5% of the fee provided they didn't seek a move.

Swansea's rollercoaster

While Robson was signing for United, an unfamiliar name sat on top of Division One. John Toshack's Swansea had leapt from the Fourth Division to the top flight in just four seasons. They won seven and drew one of their first 10 games and went on to finish 6th in the championship. Relegation came the following year, however, and by 1986 they were back in the basement, a repeat of the rollercoaster ride Northampton Town had taken in the 1960s.

BELOW: *Steve Perryman and John Gregory clash during the 1982 FA Cup Final between Spurs and QPR.*
RIGHT: *England's Trevor Francis in action against Scotland at Wembley.*

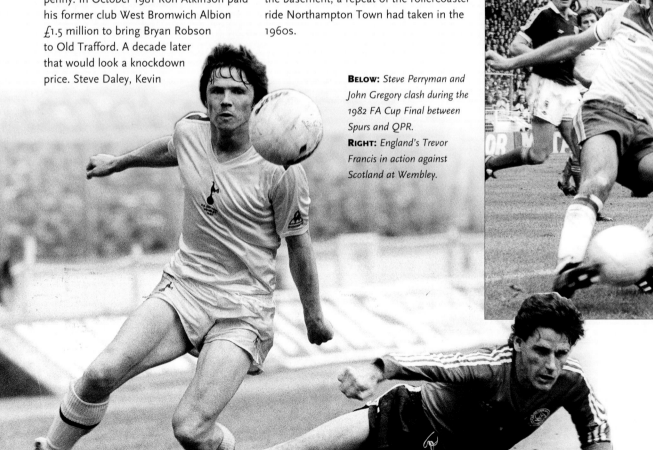

Spurs bounce back

Spurs were battling on four fronts in 1981-82. They went down to Barcelona in the Cup Winners' Cup Final and lost to Liverpool in the Final of the League Cup, renamed the Milk Cup after its new sponsor. A late equaliser by Ronnie Whelan took the game into extra time. The Spurs players were visibly deflated. Paisley told his men to look raring to go for another 30 minutes. Whelan and Rush scored to make the final score 3-1 to the holders.

In goal for Spurs that day was Ray Clemence, who had moved to White Hart Lane the previous summer for £300,000. His old team had come back to haunt him, and his new club had tasted Wembley defeat for the first time.

Hoddle's decisive penalty

Spurs finished 4th in the league, 16 points behind champions Liverpool. A possible "quadruple" had been reduced to a single battlefront: the FA Cup. Glenn Hoddle scored the two goals which salvaged Spurs' season. It was his deflected shot which earned Spurs a 1-1 draw against Second Division QPR. He then struck a 6th-minute penalty in the replay to bring the Cup back to White Hart Lane for the second year running.

It was a day of mixed emotions for Ardiles and Villa. Since their semi-final victory over Leicester, Britain had gone to war with Argentina over the Falkland Islands. Under the circumstances it would have been impossible for the two to play in the Final. Both were diplomatically moved on, though Ardiles would return to White Hart Lane when hostilities ended.

BELOW: *Watford's John Barnes, and Arsenal's Kenny Sansom struggle for a high-ball in a match that Watford went on to win 2-1.*

BOTTOM: *Hoddle scores the penalty in the replay that would win Tottenham the FA Cup in 1982.*

1982-83 DIVISION ONE	
1 Liverpool	82
2 Watford	71
3 Manchester United	70
4 Tottenham Hotspur	69
5 Nottingham Forest	69
6 Aston Villa	68
7 Everton	64
8 West Ham United	64
9 Ipswich	58
10 Arsenal	58
11 West Bromwich Albion	57
12 Southampton	57
13 Stoke	57
14 Norwich City	54
15 Notts County	52
16 Sunderland	50
17 Birmingham City	50
18 Luton	49
19 Coventry	48
20 Manchester City	47
21 Swansea	41
22 Brighton	40

FA CUP FINALS

1980	West Ham United	v	Arsenal	1-0
1981	Tottenham Hotspur	v	Manchester City	1-1 (3-2)
1982	Tottenham Hotspur	v	Queens Park Rangers	1-1 (1-0)
1983	Manchester United	v	Brighton H.A.	2-2 (4-0)
1984	Everton	v	Watford	2-0
1985	Manchester United	v	Everton	1-0
1986	Liverpool	v	Everton	3-1
1987	Coventry City	v	Tottenham Hotspur	3-2
1988	Wimbledon	v	Liverpool	1-0
1989	Liverpool	v	Everton	3-2

ABOVE: *QPR's Tony Currie avoids a tackle from Spurs' Paul Miller during the 1982 FA Cup final.*
Below: *The Tottenham squad included two Argentinian players, Ossie Ardiles (third from right) and Ricardo Villa (far right) who were unable to play in the FA Cup Final as Britain was at war with Argentina.*

Aston Villa make it six in a row

The domestic season ended with Aston Villa bringing the European Cup back to England for the 6th year running. Ron Saunders had departed and it was coach Tony Barton who found himself in the hot seat as Villa battled through to play Bayern Munich in the Final. Villa, with just two modest UEFA Cup campaigns in the 1970s behind them, had put out Dynamo Berlin, Dynamo Kiev and Anderlecht along the way. Bayern was the last club to hold the trophy before English sides took over and they were favourites to end that period of domination. It looked even more likely when Villa lost keeper Jimmy Rimmer 10 minutes into the game. 19-year-old rookie Nigel Spink took over and proceeded to have a storming match. A mishit shot by Peter Withe from a Tony Morley cross won the game. It meant that Rimmer - on United's bench for their 1968 triumph - now had two European Cup winners' medals having played a total of 10 minutes in the two finals.

Ron Greenwood's England

30-year-old Peter Withe was the new European champions' only representative in Ron Greenwood's squad that went to Spain for the World Cup. The team's qualification had not been the smoothest. Defeats in Basel, Oslo and Bucharest left England needing Switzerland to win in Romania. They did, and Greenwood showed his appreciation by donning a Swiss FA tie at the World Cup draw.

England were seeded, somewhat surprisingly, and got off to a dream start. Bryan Robson made World Cup history by scoring after just 27 seconds against France. That set up a 3-1 win over a team that would go on to reach the semi-final. But while France got stronger, England fell away. Victories over Czechoslovakia and Kuwait had put England into the second phase with maximum points, a record matched only by Brazil. In the second round mini-league England found themselves up against West Germany and hosts Spain. They created the better chances against the Germans but also survived a scare when Rummenigge hit the bar from 25 yards. After Germany beat Spain 2-1, England took on the hosts needing to win by two goals to go through. Once again they failed to take their chances, against a team that had nothing to play for. The performance was summed up by a glaring miss from substitute Kevin Keegan. The game ended goalless and England were out.

Robson becomes new England boss

It marked the end of Greenwood's reign as national team boss. It was shades of 1962 as the FA named Bobby Robson as his successor. Ramsey had peaked at the right time, taking an unheralded side to the top of the league. Robson had spent relatively little in guiding his team to the runners-up spot in the past two seasons, together with a UEFA Cup victory.

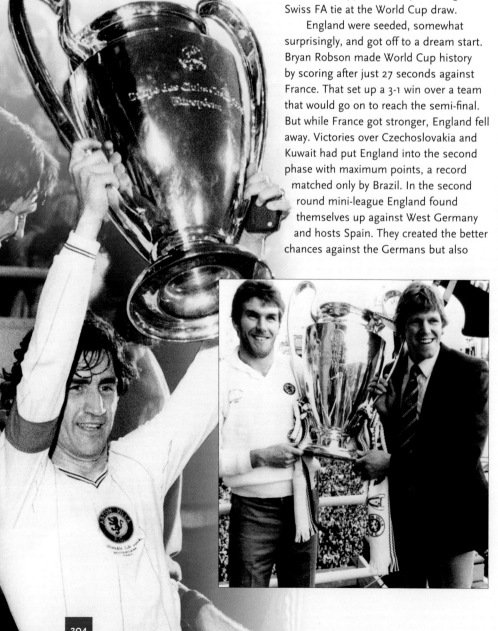

FAR LEFT: *Villa captain Dennis Mortimer holds the European Cup aloft. The Villains beat Bayern Munich with a Peter Withe goal following a Tony Morley cross.*
LEFT: *Peter Withe and Nigel Spink of Aston Villa with the European Cup.*
ABOVE: *Gary Lineker is among Leicester City players celebrating when Ian Wilson scores against Fulham, helping Leicester pursue promotion to the First Division.*

Graham Taylor's Watford finish second

Luton and Watford were promoted to Division One in 1981-82, and the following season were a breath of fresh air in the top flight. They decided that attack was the best form of defence. Only four teams scored more than David Pleat's Luton. Unfortunately, the worst defensive record in the division meant that they finished 18th, surviving with a win over Manchester City on the last day of the season.

Graham Taylor's Watford ended the season second to Liverpool, both in goals scored and league position. Watford had

taken five years to get from the basement to Division One, but made a better fist of it than Swansea once they got there. Elton John had taken over as chairman in 1976, when the team was a mid-table Division Four outfit. But it was the appointment of Taylor that was undoubtedly the key to Watford's meteoric rise. The team was always dangerous going forward, Luther Blissett and Ross Jenkins spearheading the attack. Blissett's performances earned him an England call-up, and he scored a hat-trick in his first full appearance, against Luxembourg in December 1982.

Refereeing inconsistencies

The resurgence of attacking football was partly down to the new three-points-for-a-win system. This term the authorities showed their determination to stamp out cynical play by making professional fouls a sending-off offence. This remained a grey area, however, with the seriousness of the misdemeanour left to the referee's discretion. The season was peppered with controversial incidents, some of which resulted in dismissal while others merely earned a caution.

FAR LEFT: *A scene at the opening ceremony of the 1982 World Cup held in Spain. England were to perform well in the initial stages but could not maintain the momentum.*
LEFT: *Liverpool goalkeeper Bruce Grobbelaar holds on to this Everton cross during the 1984 Charity Shield, but a later mistake would see Everton win the match 1-0.*

1983-84 DIVISION ONE

1	Liverpool	80
2	Southampton	77
3	Nottingham Forest	74
4	Manchester United	74
5	Queen's Park Rangers	73
6	Arsenal	63
7	Everton	62
8	Tottenham Hotspur	61
9	West Ham United	60
10	Aston Villa	60
11	Watford	57
12	Ipswich	53
13	Sunderland	52
14	Norwich City	51
15	Leicester City	51
16	Luton	51
17	West Bromwich Albion	51
18	Stoke	50
19	Coventry	50
20	Birmingham City	48
21	Notts County	41
22	Wolverhampton W.	29

Paisley leaves Anfield

1982-83 saw Bob Paisley end his 43-year association with Anfield. Paisley had won 13 major trophies in nine years, plus a string of Charity Shield successes. The FA Cup was missing from his haul, but he was still comfortably the most successful manager in history. He bowed out with two more trophies. By April Liverpool were 16 points clear and had the championship sewn up. After Ronnie Whelan's extra-time winner against Manchester United in the Milk Cup Graeme Souness pushed his manager up the Wembley steps to accept the trophy, something which had never happened before.

Brighton test United

In the 1983 FA Cup Final Brighton took on Manchester United. Brighton were propping up the league and on their way to Division Two. They had the chance of easing the pain of relegation by beating Ron Atkinson's attractive United side which had finished a point behind Watford in third place. They very nearly pulled it off. Gordon Smith headed Brighton into a first-half lead, but Stapleton and Wilkins put United in front after the break. A dramatic late equaliser took the game into extra-time, and in the dying seconds Smith fluffed his lines with only

Gary Bailey to beat. Brighton's chance evaporated in that moment; United cruised to a 4-0 win in the replay.

BELOW LEFT: *Liverpool celebrate their win the 1984 Milk Cup Final against Everton at Maine Road.*
BOTTOM LEFT: *Everton manager Howard Kendall leaves the pitch after his team's FA Cup Final win over Watford in 1984.*
BELOW: *The Everton scorers Andy Gray (left) and Graeme Sharp celebrate their Cup win.*
BOTTOM: *Watford players salute their fans after defeating Birmingham to enter the FA Cup semi-finals.*

Fagan sets up three in a row

Striker Michael Robinson had set up Smith for that golden chance to win the Cup Final for Brighton. He was soon a Liverpool player, one of the first pieces of business concluded by the new Anfield boss, 62-year-old Joe Fagan. Fagan, who had been at the club since the late 1950s, won three trophies in his first season, something that not even Paisley had achieved. Liverpool's 15th championship was also their third in a row, which meant that the club equalled the achievement of Huddersfield in the 1920s and Arsenal a decade later.

The Milk Cup Final pitted the Reds against Everton in the first ever Merseyside Final. It was scoreless after 120 minutes, and in the replay at Maine Road Graeme Souness scored the goal which gave Liverpool their fourth successive victory and won the trophy outright.

Fagan's hat-trick was completed at the Olympic Stadium in Rome, where Liverpool overcame a Roma side that enjoyed home advantage. Liverpool took the lead on the quarter-hour, Phil Neal pouncing on a defensive error. Roma equalised on the stroke of half-time and that's the way the scores stood after extra time. Steve Nicol's penalty miss was wiped out by Bruno Conti. Bruce Grobbelaar looked to be the calmest man in the stadium, causing much mirth as he pretended that his knees had turned to jelly. If his clowning was designed to put Graziani off, it worked. He blazed over, leaving Alan Kennedy to calmly slot home the crucial penalty. It was the second time that Kennedy had scored the decisive goal in a European Cup Final.

Kendall's Everton beat Watford

Everton made up for their unlucky defeat in the Milk Cup by beating Watford in the FA Cup Final. After a long time in the doldrums, former Goodison hero Howard Kendall was building a side capable of competing with their neighbours. Kendall had been a key member of the championship-winning side of 1970, the last major honour that the club had won. Graham Sharpe and Andy Gray scored the goals which left Watford fans in tears - quite literally in the chairman's case.

1984-85 DIVISION ONE	
1 Everton	90
2 Liverpool	77
3 Tottenham Hotspur	77
4 Manchester United	76
5 Southampton	68
6 Chelsea	66
7 Arsenal	66
8 Sheffield Wednesday	65
9 Nottingham Forest	64
10 Aston Villa	56
11 Watford	55
12 West Bromwich Albion	55
13 Luton	54
14 Newcastle	52
15 Leicester City	51
16 West Ham United	51
17 Ipswich	50
18 Coventry City	50
19 Queen's Park Rangers	50
20 Norwich City	49
21 Sunderland	40
22 Stoke	17

BELOW: *Liverpool, who topped the league in 1982, display the League Cup which they won in the same year.*

Ian Rush

The Welsh predator Ian Rush was a goal machine while he played for Liverpool FC, with a first touch and pace that gave him a phenomenal strike-rate. Born in 1961, he began his playing career at Chester, moving to Anfield in 1980 and acquiring legendary status with the Kop. In 658 games for Liverpool, he scored an incredible 346 goals.

Apart from the 1987-88 season when he made a brief, ill-fated move to Juventus, he remained at Liverpool for 16 years. With them he won the championship five times and the FA Cup on three occasions. He scored in each of those three Wembley finals, and his aggregate tally of five goals remains a Cup Final record. Rush won the European Cup with Liverpool in 1984, his 32 goals during that campaign earning him the golden boot award. That year was the highpoint of his career, as he was also named double Footballer of the Year. He also captained Wales, for whom he scored a record 28 goals in 73 games. He joined Leeds in 1996 and later played for Newcastle, Wrexham and Sydney Olympic.

Forest robbed of UEFA final place

Spurs made it another English double in Europe by beating holders Anderlecht in the UEFA Cup Final. Both legs ended 1-1 and Spurs came out on top in the first Final to be decided on penalties. This victory was to take a surprising twist 13 years later, when it was revealed that Anderlecht had bribed the referee who took charge of the second leg of their semi-final against Nottingham Forest. In that game Anderlecht overturned a 2-0 deficit to win the tie 3-2. The Belgian side was awarded a dubious penalty, and Forest also had a goal disallowed. These decisions led some in the Forest camp to believe they had been cheated but it was not until 1997 that their suspicions were confirmed. The referee in question had been killed in a car crash by then, but that didn't stop Forest instituting legal proceedings in pursuit of compensation. They came up against UEFA's 10-year statute of limitations regarding retrospective disciplinary action. Financial reparation would hardly have made up for a night of European glory, and to Forest fans 1984 will be remembered as the year they were robbed.

England fail again

The familiar pattern of success in Europe and failure at international level continued as England missed out on the 1984 European Championship. A penalty by former European Footballer of the Year Allan Simonsen gave Denmark a crucial 1-0 win at Wembley, and that country's first-ever victory over England. This result, together with a goalless home draw against Greece, put paid to England's chances and it was the Danes who went to France for the finals.

Barnes dazzles against Brazil

While that tournament was being played out, England went on a three-match tour of South America. There was a defeat by Uruguay and and a draw against Chile, but it was the 2-0 win over Brazil which grabbed the headlines. The first goal, a towering header from Mark Hateley, was typically English. The second, a dazzling solo effort by Watford's John Barnes, bore comparison with any Brazil had ever scored.

BELOW: *Kevin Ratcliffe is helpless when Ian Rush scores for Liverpool as the Reds beat rivals Everton 3-1 in the 1986 FA Cup final.*

Heysel tragedy rocks English football

1984-85 saw Liverpool fail to win a trophy for the first time in nine years. They lost the European Cup Final to a Michel Platini penalty but that was an irrelevance after it was clear that there had been fatalities at the Heysel Stadium. There had been fighting between Liverpool and Juventus fans before the match, and the collapse of a wall precipitated the tragedy. 39 supporters, mostly Italian, were killed. Liverpool fans were deemed to be primarily responsible and an indefinite ban was imposed on all English clubs competing in European competition.

Everton romp

The Heysel disaster and the Bradford fire, which occurred only weeks earlier, rocked football to the core. The season had also witnessed some of the worst acts of hooliganism ever seen, prompting

the government to set up a task force to address the issue.

These events overshadowed the achievements of an Everton side which won two trophies playing champagne football. Howard Kendall's men romped to the title with a record 90 points, 13 clear of their Liverpool rivals. Kendall joined the select group to have won the championship as both player and manager.

It was the first leg in a treble, Everton having reached both the Cup Winners' Cup and FA Cup Finals. Having taken the scalp of Bayern Munich 3-1 on aggregate in the semis, Everton faced Rapid Vienna in the Cup Winners' Cup Final. Austria's legendary striker Hans Krankl scored Rapid's consolation goal in a 3-1 defeat and was quick to sing Everton's praises for the quality of their performance. Andy Gray, Trevor Steven and Kevin Sheedy had all been on target.

ABOVE: *Chris Waddle of Tottenham rescues his side by scoring against up-and-coming Oxford United to send the game into extra time.*
BELOW LEFT: *The pairing of John Barnes and David Bardsley was to prove too much for the Arsenal defence as Watford defeated them 3-1.*
BELOW RIGHT: *Wimbledon, perhaps the most unconventional and unlikely team in the First Division at the time, celebrate a 3-0 win over Sheffield Wednesday. John Fashanu and Wally Downes embrace Vinny Jones (with his back to the camera), who only three weeks prior to this game had been employed as a hod-carrier.*

1985-86 DIVISION ONE	
1 Liverpool	88
2 Everton	86
3 West Ham United	84
4 Manchester United	76
5 Sheffield Wednesday	73
6 Chelsea	71
7 Arsenal	69
8 Nottingham Forest	68
9 Luton Town	66
10 Tottenham Hotspur	65
11 Newcastle United	63
12 Watford	59
13 Queen's Park Rangers	52
14 Southampton	46
15 Manchester City	45
16 Aston Villa	44
17 Coventry City	43
18 Oxford United	42
19 Leicester City	42
20 Ipswich Town	41
21 Birmingham City	29
22 West Bromwich Albion	24

First Cup Final dismissal halts Liverpool

The FA Cup proved to be a trophy too far. Everton went down 1-0 to Manchester United, Norman Whiteside curling in a beautiful winner in extra time. The first 90 minutes had been largely uneventful, until with 12 minutes to go Peter Reid pounced onto a loose ball and was upended by Kevin Moran. The referee deemed it a professional foul and sent the Irishman off, the first Cup Final dismissal. The incident served to galvanise the United side, and they carved out other scoring opportunities apart from the one delightfully taken by Whiteside. Two years earlier he had become the youngest-ever player to score in a Wembley Final - 17 years 324 days - when United lost to Liverpool in the Milk Cup. No doubt this strike gave the Irishman more satisfaction
.

Dalglish steps up as player-manager

Joe Fagan had already announced that the 1985 European Cup Final would be his last game in charge. Liverpool made yet another internal appointment, but surprised many by opting for a player-manager: Kenny Dalglish. With the Paul Walsh-Ian Rush strike partnership flourishing, Dalglish was content to spend time in the dugout. His team didn't have things all their own way, and at one point

they trailed champions Everton by 11 points. The Reds needed to win their last seven games, five of them away, and hope that others would slip up. On the last day of the season they needed to win at Stamford Bridge and it was Dalglish who scored the game's only goal.

A week later Everton again had to settle for second best in the first Merseyside FA Cup Final. Lineker escaped Hansen's clutches to open the scoring. When Rush equalised, the omens looked bad for Everton, as Liverpool had never lost a game when their Welsh striker was on target. So it proved again. Craig Johnston put the Reds into the lead and Rush rifled in a third six minutes from time. Liverpool thus joined the Spurs and Arsenal as the century's only Double winners.

Future stars

Two future Liverpool stars lined up in the Oxford United side which beat QPR in the Milk Cup Final. Ray Houghton and John Aldridge were in the side which had climbed from Division Three to Division One in successive seasons. It was an outstanding achievement for a club that had been on the verge of bankruptcy in 1982.

BELOW LEFT: *Glenn Hoddle of Spurs on the ball in an England World Cup qualifying game.*
BELOW: *Goal-scorer Norman Whiteside holds aloft the FA Cup after Manchester United defeat Everton by a goal to nil in extra time in the 1985 Cup Final.*

Kenny Dalglish

When Joe Fagan stepped down as Liverpool manager at the end of the 1984-85 season, the club surprised many by naming Kenny Dalglish as his successor. The Anfield trend of appointing from within was thus continued, but instead of a member of the backroom team it was someone who was still performing at the height of his powers. Fittingly, it was Dalglish who scored the goal at Stamford Bridge which secured the championship the following May. Victory over Everton in the FA Cup Final meant that Dalglish had achieved the Double in his debut season as a manager. He added two further championships before resigning in February 1991, citing the pressures of the job as the reason for his decision to stand down. He returned to the managerial fray with Blackburn Rovers. He had Jack Walker's millions at his disposal and used the money wisely. He steered Rovers to the Premiership title in 1995, the club's first championship since 1914. He thus became only the fourth manager in history to win the title with two different clubs. After another brief spell out of the game he took over at Newcastle. He led the club to the FA Cup Final in 1998 but couldn't prevent Arsenal from completing the Double.

Lineker fires England in Mexico

England were unbeaten in qualifying for the World Cup finals, although they had been held to a draw by Romania, Finland and Northern Ireland. Defeat by Portugal and a goalless draw against Morocco left Bobby Robson's men facing an early exit. He was hampered by a shoulder injury to his inspirational captain, Bryan Robson, whose tournament was over. Vice-captain Ray Wilkins was sent off against Morocco, the first England player to be given his marching orders in a major tournament. Star striker Gary Lineker, who had topped the scoring chart with 30 goals for Everton, was playing with his arm in plaster. England needed to beat Poland in the final group match and did so in style. Hodge, Reid, Steven and Beardsley came in for Robson, Waddle, Wilkins and Hateley, and the team put on a show guaranteed to wake up the supporters

who had dubbed this "the group of sleep". Lineker grabbed the headlines with a hat-trick in a 3-0 win.

Maradona's "Hand of God"
Another brace by Lineker helped England to a 3-0 victory over Paraguay, setting up a quarter-final clash with Argentina. The best and worst of Diego Maradona caused England's downfall. He picked up the ball on the halfway line and beat half the team to score the goal of the tournament and one of the greatest of all time. But before then he had punched the ball into the net when challenging for a high ball with Peter Shilton. Lineker made it 2-1, heading in his sixth goal of the tournament. He would be the tournament's hotshot, but the "hand of God" along with the genius of Maradona had put paid to England's hopes.

LEFT: *Gary Lineker, by now Everton's star striker, celebrates scoring for England against Northern Ireland in 1986.*

1986-87 DIVISION ONE	
1 Everton	86
2 Liverpool	77
3 Tottenham Hotspur	71
4 Arsenal	70
5 Norwich City	68
6 Wimbledon	66
7 Luton Town	66
8 Nottingham Forest	65
9 Watford	63
10 Coventry City	63
11 Manchester United	56
12 Southampton	52
13 Sheffield Wednesday	52
14 Chelsea	52
15 West Ham United	52
16 Queen's Park Rangers	50
17 Newcastle United	47
18 Oxford United	46
19 Charlton Athletic	44
20 Leicester City	42
21 Manchester City	39
22 Aston Villa	36

Moves abroad

Lineker's World Cup form caught the eye of many big Continental sides, and in the summer of 1986 Barcelona coach Terry Venables paid £4.25 million to see if he could reproduce his scoring form in La Liga. Although Everton no doubt would have preferred to keep Lineker, the fee represented a healthy profit on the £800,000 they had paid Leicester in July 1985.

Venables had already added Mark Hughes to his squad, and Juventus had agreed a £3.2 million deal to take Ian Rush to Turin, although the latter move would not take place until the end of the 1986-87 season.

According to the established principle, Rush should have signed off from Liverpool with a victory in the Littlewoods Cup, which was the League Cup's latest incarnation. Rush put the Reds in front against Arsenal at Wembley in the knowledge that in the previous 143 matches in which he'd got on the scoresheet the team had never lost. The run came to an end in the 144th match. Charlie Nicholas had never recaptured his Celtic form since moving to Highbury but he hit two goals to bring Arsenal their first silverware for eight years.

BELOW LEFT: *A jubilant Alan Hansen raises the FA Cup. In Dalglish's first season as player-manager, Liverpool defeated Everton 3-1 in the 1986 Final to achieve the rare feat of winning the Double. Rush, netting two, and Johnston a third, were responsible for the Reds' Cup glory but Dalglish himself scored the goal against Chelsea that secured the 1985-6 league title for Liverpool.*
RIGHT: *Arsenal captain Kenny Sansom holds aloft the Littlewoods Cup after two goals from Charlie Nicholas saw Liverpool defeated 2-1.*

Ferguson replaces Atkinson at Old Trafford

Liverpool were also knocked off top spot in the league. Everton took their second title in three years, this time by a nine-point margin. The big managerial story of the season came in November, when Ron Atkinson's five-year reign at Old Trafford came to an end. United had won the FA Cup twice and never finished lower than 4th in the league. But with the championship going to Merseyside with monotonous regularity and a Cup Winners' Cup semi-final their best effort in Europe, it simply wasn't good enough. Aberdeen boss Alex Ferguson was appointed. Ferguson had broken the Celtic-Rangers duopoly, winning the Scottish title on three occasions. He had also led the Dons to Cup Winners' Cup glory in 1983 when they overcame Real Madrid. Ferguson's first major signings were

Viv Anderson and Brian McClair, in the summer of 1987. United had just ended the season in 11th place, their worst finish since returning to the top flight in 1975.

Wimbledon's meteoric rise
Five places above United at the end of the 1986-87 season was Wimbledon. Dave Bassett's side had gone from non-league to Division One in nine years, and 6th place in their first season represented a phenomenal achievement. Swansea had done exactly the same five years earlier, but the Dons would prove to have much more resilience as a top-division side.

For Coventry and Scarborough 1986-87 was a memorable season, albeit at different ends of the footballing scale. Coventry met Spurs in the FA Cup Final. Spurs had never finished on the losing side in their seven previous appearances. Coventry ended that run and in the process picked up the club's first major honour. Coventry twice came from behind, their second equaliser a spectacular flying header from Keith Houchen. The winner came in extra-time, when Gary Mabbutt deflected a McGrath cross into his net. Coventry coach John Sillett did a Wembley jig to rival Nobby Stiles' effort in 1966.

Play-offs introduced

Neil Warnock's Scarborough became the first club to win automatic promotion to the Football League. The system of applying for re-election was scrapped; the 4th Division's bottom club would change places with the winners of the Vauxhall Conference.

Play-off matches were also introduced in all divisions. The team which finished just above the automatic relegation spot entered into a play-off with the three clubs that had just missed promotion from the division below. Charlton finished in that precarious position in Division One but survived the two-match ordeal.

The play-offs were introduced to make the run-in more exciting, with fewer "dead" matches. It was also designed over two seasons to decrease the size of

Division One from 22 clubs to 20.

In the second year Chelsea finished fourth from bottom and lost their Division One status at the expense of Middlesbrough.

Liverpool back on top

Liverpool, meanwhile, were back on top. After three seasons in which the Merseyside clubs had taken the top two spots, in 1987-88 Everton slipped to 4th and Manchester United were the closest challengers. Even then, Ferguson's men finished nine points behind a team that looked stronger than ever. John Barnes, Ray Houghton and Peter Beardsley - bought from Newcastle for a record £1.9 million - all added even more flair to the Anfield machine.

Liverpool went 29 matches unbeaten, equalling Leeds' 1974 record. Everton's Wayne Clark scored the goal which prevented Liverpool from taking the record outright, but the Reds lost just once more in the campaign to match Everton's record points tally. Both finished on 90, although Liverpool had played two games fewer. Their 17th championship was secured with four matches to spare.

1987-88 DIVISION ONE		
1	Liverpool	90
2	Manchester United	81
3	Nottingham Forest	73
4	Everton	70
5	Queen's Park Rangers	67
6	Arsenal	66
7	Wimbledon	57
8	Newcastle United	56
9	Luton Town	53
10	Coventry City	53
11	Sheffield Wednesday	53
12	Southampton	50
13	Tottenham Hotspur	47
14	Norwich City	45
15	Derby County	43
16	West Ham United	42
17	Charlton Athletic	42
18	Chelsea	42
19	Portsmouth	35
20	Watford	32
21	Oxford United	31

BELOW: *Arsenal's Niall Quinn lines up a volley that narrowly misses its target and is just tipped wide by Spurs and former England keeper Ray Clemence.*

LEFT: *Everton's Gary Stevens and Manchester United's Arthur Albiston bear down on the ball in a Charity Shield match.*

Gary Lineker

Sports broadcaster Gary Lineker's role in the consortium that rescued Leicester City was fitting, for it was where, in 1978, his playing career began. Known for lightning acceleration, he scored 26 goals in 1983, helping Leicester back into the First Division. Two years later, he signed for Everton and scored 30 goals in his first season, winning him the PFA and Football Writers' Player of the Year.

He did well initially at Barcelona under Terry Venables, but was later less consistent. Though he contributed to Barca's Cup Winners' Cup victory in 1989, he came back to England that summer to join Venables at White Hart Lane. In 1991 Spurs won the F.A. Cup, beating Nottingham Forest, and in his final season at the club put away a relegation-saving 28 League goals.

It is as a marksman for England, however, that he's most celebrated, with 80 caps and 48 goals – only one fewer than Bobby Charlton. Six of those, including a hat-trick against Poland, came in the 1986 World Cup in Mexico, winning him the Golden Boot. Four years later at Italia 90, it was Lineker's 80th-minute equaliser that kept England in the semi-final against West Germany, though the side went out on penalties. The 1992 European Championships made a frustrating end to Lineker's England career, as he was substituted by Graham Taylor in the final game, against Sweden. He ended his playing days with two seasons in the Japanese League, at Grampus Eight.

Wimbledon's FA Cup glory

A second double looked a foregone conclusion as Liverpool faced Wimbledon in the FA Cup Final. The Dons had finished a commendable 7th this term but surely they couldn't overturn the mighty Reds. The bookies didn't think so, making Liverpool 1-4 favourites. Wimbledon were fearless, committed and no respecters of reputations. They had already gone to Anfield and won.

Peter Beardsley had the ball in the net, only for the referee to disallow it - for a foul on Beardsley! Laurie Sanchez's glancing header from a Dennis Wise free-kick gave the Dons a 36th-minute lead. After 61 minutes John Aldridge was brought down in the box. Aldridge had a perfect record from his previous 11 spot-kicks that season. The 12th was saved by Dave Beasant. It was the first penalty save in an FA Cup Final and it helped carry the Dons to an unlikely victory.

ABOVE: *Gary Lineker takes a tumble whilst playing for England, having been fouled by Scotland's Richard Gough in 1988. After a spell at Barcelona, Lineker returned to England to join Spurs in the summer of 1989.*

England eclipsed by Charlton's Ireland

Houghton and Aldridge lined up in the Republic of Ireland side which qualified for the 1988 European championships. England made it to Germany too, and the two countries met in the opening match of the group stage. Houghton gave the Republic a 1-0 win and although both went out of the competition it was Jack Charlton's men who emerged with more credit. England also lost to eventual finalists the USSR and Holland to finish as wooden spoonists.

A chink of light in a gloomy season for England came in April, when 17-year-old Alan Shearer hit a hat-trick for Southampton against Arsenal, the youngest player ever to do so in the First Division.

BELOW: *Bobby Gould with his victorious Wimbledon players after winning the FA Cup in 1988. Laurie Sanchez's glancing header from a Dennis Wise free-kick secured the Dons a 1-0 win over hot favourites Liverpool.*

Arsenal's last gasp championship

BELOW RIGHT: *Peter Beardsley of Liverpool battles with Arsenal's Tony Adams in a title showdown which saw the Gunners come out on top.*
BELOW: *Floral tributes in the Anfield goalmouth commemorating those killed at Hillsborough on April 15 1989.*

Liverpool had Ian Rush back in their ranks in 1988-89. Rush scored 14 goals in his season at Juve but failed to settle. He returned for a season which saw the Reds engaged in a terrific championship battle with Arsenal. At the end of February Liverpool were 8th, 19 points behind the table-topping Gunners. On 26 May Arsenal came to Anfield for the title showdown. Liverpool had eaten away at Arsenal's lead and it was they who held the advantage. Arsenal, who had not won at Anfield for 15 years, needed a victory by two goals to take the title. After a goalless first half, Nigel Winterburn struck an indirect free-kick which Liverpool protested had gone straight into the net. The referee judged that it brushed Alan Smith's head and the goal was given. With seconds to go Michael Thomas burst into the box and flicked the ball past Grobbelaar to give Arsenal the 2-goal margin they needed.

Hillsborough

Second in the league and a 3-2 extra-time win over Everton in the second Merseyside FA Cup Final represented another fine season for Liverpool. But footballing matters had become irrelevant after the events at Hillsborough on 15 April. The eagerly awaited FA Cup semi-final clash with Nottingham Forest was six minutes old and it became clear that there was a tragedy unfolding in the Leppings Lane end. Gates were opened to prevent a crush outside and a mass of fans surged into a part of the ground that was already packed. Perimeter fencing meant that there was no easy outlet. 94 supporters were killed, and the toll rose to 95 a few days later. Tony Bland remained in a coma for four years before his life-support machine was switched off. Lord Justice Taylor was commissioned to head an inquiry into the worst tragedy in British sporting history.

The Taylor Report

In the wake of the tragedy there had been no appetite to complete the competition and an abandonment was considered. But both Liverpool and the bereaved families came to regard the winning of the trophy as a tribute to those who had lost their lives.

In the 1980s the game had been tarnished by hooliganism and touched by tragedy, yet it ended on a note of dignity. The sportsmanship shown in both the FA Cup Final and the championship decider gave rise to cautious optimism. The game would endure; but as football moved into a new decade the Taylor Report would be a damning indictment of the conditions in which the fans were expected to watch their heroes perform.

The Taylor Report

First and Second Division clubs were required to have all-seater stadia by the start of the 1994-95 season, with lower league clubs following suit by the end of the decade. The cost of improved facilities would be high - running into hundreds of millions - but the cost of doing nothing would be infinitely higher.

The Taylor Report also addressed the hooligan problem and the part played by alcohol in the appalling scenes that had blighted the game. A compulsory ID scheme was considered but rejected. Policing and ticket arrangements needed reviewing. While perimeter fencing which represented a threat to safety ought to be removed, harsh penalties were recommended for unwarranted pitch invasions.

The changing face of football

The construction of fabulous new grounds such as the Reebok, the Stadium of Light and Pride Park took football into a new era. New facilities such as these would show Wembley in a poor light. By the end

of the decade plans would be under way for a new flagship stadium in the capital.

If the face of football was changed with the redevelopment and upgrading of grounds, a shift of equally seismic proportions occurred with the establishment of a Premier League. This coincided with the arrival of satellite broadcasters, who saw football as the main driver for their fledgling business. The game became polarised as never before. At the top level inflation in transfer fees, wages and ticket prices was rampant; meanwhile, the demise of Aldershot, the first league club to go out of business for thirty years, showed that the vast sums of money in the game were not filtering down to the basement.

Merchandise and brand

There was a price to be paid for improved facilities and multi-million-pound TV rights deals, and in the end it was the fans who had to put their hands in their pockets. There were fears that die-hard fans would be priced out of the game

1989-90 DIVISION ONE

1	Liverpool	79
2	Aston Villa	70
3	Tottenham Hotspur	63
4	Arsenal	62
5	Chelsea	60
6	Everton	59
7	Southampton	55
8	Wimbledon	55
9	Nottingham Forest	54
10	Norwich City	53
11	Queen's Park Rangers	50
12	Coventry City	49
13	Manchester United	48
14	Manchester City	48
15	Crystal Palace	48
16	Derby County	46
17	Luton Town	43
18	Sheffield Wednesday	43
19	Charlton Athletic	30
20	Millwall	26

BELOW: *Paul Gascoigne in full flight in the World Cup quarter final between England and Cameroon in 1990.*

and that the sport was undergoing a gentrification process, a return to the kind of constituency it had had in the nineteenth century. Perhaps more worryingly, the clubs did not seem to mind. Middle-class supporters with large disposable incomes were highly desirable to clubs which had a product to sell. Nor was the product simply football. Replica strips and all manner of domestic goods bearing the club brand went on sale. Fans could even get financial services from their clubs as football exploited every possible income stream.

A glorious era coming to an end

On the pitch the decade began with yet another league triumph for the team of the 80s. Liverpool rounded off their season with a 6-1 win at Coventry, though the club's eighteenth championship had already been secured by then.

The team that had suffered most heavily at hands of the Red machine was Crystal Palace, who were on the receiving end of a 9-0 mauling in the early part of the season. There must have been trepidation among Palace fans as the team faced Liverpool again in the

FA Cup semi-final at Villa Park. It was a remarkable game and a turning point for Liverpool. Andy Gray equalised to make it 3-3 in the 90th minute, and Alan Pardew headed Palace into the Final in extra time. A glorious era was coming to an end. Over the next few seasons Liverpool would show flashes of their brilliant best, but these would be punctuated by many inept performances. The strong defence of days gone by would become quite porous and Liverpool would be relegated to the role of just another member of the chasing pack.

LEFT: *England on the pitch ready to play Germany in the 1990 World Cup semi-final. With the score at 1-1 after extra time, England lost the game on penalties.*
BELOW: *Stuart Pearce, who famously missed his penalty against Germany in the World Cup scores from this free kick to give Nottingham Forest the lead in the 1991 Cup Final against Spurs.*

Ferguson's job on the line

After beating Liverpool, Palace went on to face the team which was to assume the mantle that had been worn by the Reds for so long. Manchester United had finished 11th and 13th in the past two seasons, and it was said that after four years in charge Alex Ferguson's job was on the line. A Mark Hughes' goal salvaged a replay for United, and Lee Martin scored the goal which brought Ferguson his first piece of silverware.

Italia '90

Before England went to the World Cup in Italy, manager Bobby Robson announced that he would be quitting to return to club management with PSV Eindhoven. Robson's team topped their group, albeit with a one-goal win over Egypt and draws against the Republic of Ireland and Holland. A superb David Platt volley late in extra time accounted for Belgium in the second round. By then it was clear that the team's precocious young midfielder, Paul Gascoigne, was the star turn. "Gazza" had become the country's first £2 million footballer when he moved from Newcastle to Spurs in 1988. At Italia '90 the raw talent blossomed and he proved that he was a great showman as well as a great player.

England beaten on penalties

Against Cameroon in the quarter-final England were trailing 2-1 with time running out. Lineker was brought down in the box and converted the penalty to take the match into extra time. It was a case of deja-vu, and Lineker's second spot-kick set up a semi-final clash with West Germany. That match will long be remembered for the tears Gascoigne shed after a rash tackle earned him a booking which would have kept him out of the final. In the end that was academic. An Andreas Brehme free-kick took a wicked deflection and looped over Shilton to put the Germans ahead. Lineker equalised and the game went to penalties. Pearce and Waddle both missed and England were out. There was the consolation of the Fair Play award and the fact that the team had provided rich entertainment and no small amount of drama.

RIGHT: *Spurs' Eric Thorsvedt punches clear in the hard-fought contest that went into extra time.*
BELOW RIGHT: *Paul Gascoigne with Steve Sedgeley and Gary Mabbutt celebrating Spurs 3-1 victory over Arsenal in the semi-final of the FA Cup in 1991 played at Wembley. The following month Tottenham secured the Cup with a 2-1 win over Nottingham Forest.*
BELOW: *Gary Mabbutt holds the trophy aloft.*

Power Struggle

1990-91 saw the beginnings of a power struggle at the top of the game. Relations between the FA and Football League had never been particularly warm, and when the League suggested that the game should be unified under a single umbrella, the response amounted to exactly the opposite. The FA's blueprint for the future was the establishment of a premier division. This would be the game's gold standard, and would help to improve the fortunes of the national team. Unsurprisingly, the Football League was horrified at the prospect of the glamour clubs seceding in this way. They went to court to challenge the legality of the FA's proposals but found they had no case.

The end of the UEFA ban
This season marked the end of the UEFA ban on English clubs, although Liverpool received a further year's penalty. The 6-year ban was said to have put English football down the pecking order in relation to the other traditional powerhouses on the Continent. That didn't stop Manchester United from lifting the Cup Winners' Cup. The 2-1 victory over Barcelona in Rotterdam must have been particularly pleasing for Mark Hughes. His brief spell at the Nou Camp had been a nightmare, and a superb winning goal from a narrow angle showed Barca what an in-form "Sparky" could do. This victory meant that Alex Ferguson joined a select group of managers to have won a European trophy with two different clubs.

Arsenal's title
United had been deducted a point in the league following a brawl in their clash with Arsenal at Old Trafford in October. The Gunners were docked two points, but neither penalty proved costly in the shake-up. United finished 6th, while Arsenal still ended the campaign seven points clear of Liverpool at the top.

Liverpool had started the season the stronger, recording ten straight wins. The turning point came in a 5th round FA Cup-tie against Everton. After a goalless draw at Anfield, the two teams met at Goodison. The game ended 4-4, highlighting the fact that Liverpool were still potent up front but far from secure at the back. The following day Kenny Dalglish announced his resignation, citing the strain of the job. The man appointed in his place was an Anfield thoroughbred but he didn't come from within. Graeme Souness was persuaded to leave Rangers and take over the reins at the club he had captained with such distinction

BELOW: *Steve Nicol, Bruce Grobbelaar and Ian Rush with the FA Cup in 1992.*

1990-91 DIVISION ONE	
1 Arsenal	83
2 Liverpool	76
3 Crystal Palace	69
4 Leeds United	64
5 Manchester City	62
6 Manchester United	59
7 Wimbledon	56
8 Nottingham Forest	54
9 Everton	51
10 Tottenham Hotspur	49
11 Chelsea	49
12 Queen's Park Rangers	46
13 Sheffield United	46
14 Southampton	45
15 Norwich City	45
16 Coventry City	44
17 Aston Villa	41
18 Luton Town	37
19 Sunderland	34
20 Derby County	24

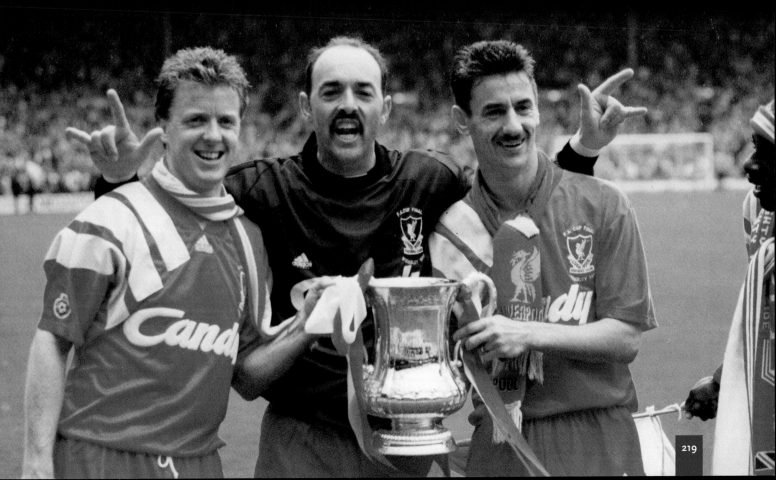

Arsenal set defensive standard

Alan Shearer

In November 2002, Alan Shearer scored his 100th Premiership goal for his home city club, Newcastle United, and became the first player to achieve this landmark at two clubs, the other being Blackburn Rovers. No wonder that after the 2002-3 season, he was named Player of the Decade - a sweet moment for a striker who had retired from international football after Euro 2000 to make way for younger blood, but can still produce magic in the box.

His career began as a teenager in 1988 with Southampton. Blackburn secured him in the summer of 1992 for a British record transfer of £3.6 million, and Shearer's deadly finishing helped the club to win the Championship three years later.

He returned to Newcastle in 1996 for a £15 million fee. Shearer won the first of his 63 caps in February 1990, coming off the bench to score against France. It was the first of a 30-goal haul, putting him joint-fifth in the all-time list. Before the end of the 2004-05 season the Toon Army received the welcome news that their talisman had agreed to stay on for one more campaign. It represented a final opportunity for Shearer to bring silverware to St James' Park and he had Jackie Milburn's record 178 league goals within his sights.

Shearer embarked on a career as a media pundit but answered a call to arms when Newcastle's Premiership status hung in the balance in the run-in to the 2008-09 season. He couldn't save the club from the drop, but that didn't stop the Toon Army clamouring for his appointment as Newcastle's permanent manager.

Although Liverpool maintained their position as league runners-up in 1992, the writing was on the wall. The Reds conceded 40 goals and lost eight games; Arsenal were defeated only once and let in just 18 goals. George Graham had paid QPR £1.3 million for David Seaman the previous summer, a record for a goalkeeper. He took his place behind Adams, Bould, Dixon and Winterburn to form a defensive unit that would set the standard for defensive meanness.

Arsenal faced Spurs in the FA Cup semi-final, the first to be staged at Wembley. Gascoigne stole the show with a stunning 35-yard free-kick, setting up a marvellous 3-1 win. Gazza was again centre stage in the final, against Nottingham Forest, but this time for the wrong reasons. He had already put in a couple of rash tackles when he challenged Gary Charles on the edge of the Spurs area. Gascoigne conceded the free-kick but it was he who came off worse. He suffered knee ligament damage which was to put him out of action for months. Stuart Pearce rubbed salt into Spurs' wounds by scoring from the free-kick after Gazza was stretchered off. Paul Stewart hit an equaliser and although Spurs' winner came via a deflection off Des Walker in extra-time, the better team won.

ABOVE: *Alan Smith celebrates after scoring Arsenal's first goal in their match against Sunderland in the year they beat Liverpool in the title race.*

BELOW: *Manchester United players following their championship in the 1993-94 season. It was the end of the first full season at the club for Eric Cantona (third from the left).*

Gazza to Lazio

Lazio had already been chasing Gascoigne's signature, and the deal was finally done in June 1992. It would be six years before Gazza would return to the domestic game. His time in Italy, and subsequently with Glasgow Rangers, would show him in every possible light: flashes of genius one minute, pressing the self-destruct button the next and everything done in his inimitably impish way. Injuries didn't help, but for a player of his gifts there should have been a greater return than his 1992 FA Cup winners' medal with Spurs. That would remain his only honour in the English game.

ABOVE: *Eric Cantona in an aerial duel against Chelsea in the 1994 Cup Final. His two spot kicks helped win the trophy, to make Manchester United only the fourth team to do the Double in the twentieth century.*
LEFT: *Paul Merson (right) celebrating an Arsenal goal. The Gunners won the championship in the 1990-91 season by seven points. Liverpool were second and United a distant sixth.*
BELOW: *The Arsenal faithful trudge through the rain on the way to the towering new stand at Highbury, in December 1993.*

Eric Cantona

Of all the brilliant players from overseas that found their way into the English game in the1990s Eric Cantona stands alone as the player who has had the most influence on the teams he played for. Having just helped Marseille to win the French Championship, he joined Leeds halfway through the 1991-92 season. Cantona's success continued as the Yorkshire club went on to win their first championship since the heady days of the 1970s, in what was the final year of the League system before the introduction of the Premier League. Leeds fans were shocked when Howard Wilkinson sold the 26-year-old to rivals Manchester United in November 1992.

Four championships and two Doubles

With his incredible vision and majestic touch, and his trademark upturned collar, Cantona performed complex skills with apparent ease. The Old Trafford faithful took him to their hearts and chanting 'Oo-ah-Cantona' in praise of their hero became a trademark of the fans. Cantona went on to win four championships with United, including the Double on two occasions. The second of those came in 1996, when he scored the goal that beat Liverpool in an exciting FA Cup Final. At the end of the 1995-96 season Cantona was named Footballer of the Year for his superb performances during that campaign.

Unfortunately, in the 1994-95 season, Cantona showed the other side to his character. His kung fu-style kick at a fan after being sent off at Crystal Palace in January 1995 earned him an eight-month ban. It was not the first time Cantona had run into disciplinary problems. His career was punctuated with arguments with players and managers alike, including run-ins with national team coaches, without which he would certainly have won more than 44 caps for France. To the dismay of United fans Cantona announced his retirement from football at the end of the 1996-97 season, when he was just 30 years old.

Ryan Giggs

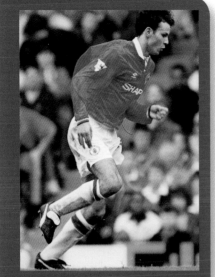

Ryan Giggs burst onto the footballing stage just as the Premiership was coming into being. On his debut in 1991, he was the first of Manchester United's brilliant youth side to become a regular in the first team. His amazing speed, superb control and awe-inspiring dribbling immediately invited comparisons with the great George Best. But Giggs has managed to avoid many of the pitfalls and temptations that lured Best. Instead he has preferred to impress on the pitch, and in the past decade has helped United to dominate the domestic scene, including winning the Double on three occasions. One of those occasions came in 1999, when United also lifted the European Cup, more than thirty years after their first win in the prestigious competition.

Nine years later, Giggs became a Champions League winner for a second time when United overcame Chelsea on penalties on a dramatic night in Moscow. The day had added significance for Giggs as he passed Bobby Charlton's appearance record of 758 games for United.

Giggs won his fist cap at 17 years 322 days, becoming Wales's youngest-ever international. He played for his country 64 times before retiring in 2007, and although there were no honours at international level, he more than made up for it with his club. In 2008-09 Giggs won his 11th championship medal, the most decorated footballer in the game's history. He was also named PFA Player of the Year, 17 years after winning the first of his two Young Player of the Year awards.

Wilkinson's Leeds win the championship

Leeds were the last winners before the new Premiership era got under way. Howard Wilkinson's side had won promotion in 1990 and finished 4th in their first season back in the top flight. In 1991-92 Leeds held off the challenge of Manchester United to bring the club their first championship since 1974. Gordon Strachan, who had joined the club from Manchester United in 1989 for just £300,000, had been in sparkling form, despite turning 35 during the season. Alongside him in midfield were Batty, McAllister and Speed, giving a blend of youth and experience, finesse and steel. Midway through the season Wilkinson added more flair by bringing in the controversial French star Eric Cantona. 25-year-old Cantona had had a string of clubs and several run-ins with the authorities in France. He briefly turned his back on the game but decided to start afresh on the other side of the Channel. Sheffield Wednesday boss Trevor Francis had a look at him, but as he vacillated, Howard Wilkinson stepped in to offer terms.

Cantona's Gallic flair

The honeymoon would not last much beyond securing the championship as far as the club was concerned. For the fans it was a different matter. They warmed to the Gallic flair and air of arrogance Cantona showed on the field. The chant

"Oo-ah-Cantona" rang round the Elland Road terraces, but not for long. By the end of the year Cantona had moved to Old Trafford for just £1 million. Over the next five years the Frenchman would become the pivotal player in Ferguson's dream team.

BOTTOM: *Terry Venables demonstrating his craft as a master coach with his Tottenham players in 1992.*
BELOW: *Tottenham's Gary Lineker escapes Coventry defenders in the 1992 league campaign.*

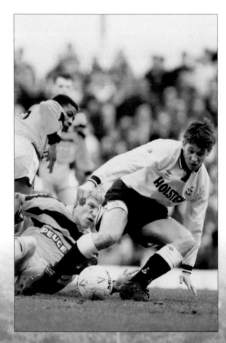

Roy Keane

It is Roy Keane that Sir Alex Ferguson points to as the most influential of all the superstars that have made Manchester United the dominant force in English football during the first ten years of the Premiership.

But it was Brian Clough who spotted Keane's potential when he was playing for Cobh Ramblers in the Irish League. Clough paid just £10,000 to take the Irishman to Nottingham Forest in what must rank as one of the bargains of all time. In 1993 Keane moved to Old Trafford from Forest and, at United, his fierce competitiveness, tireless running and great technical ability enabled him to develop into one of the most complete midfielders in world football. In the six seasons between 1996 and 2001 United conceded the title just once, to Arsenal in 1997-98. Many thought it was no coincidence that Keane was sidelined through injury for most of that campaign.

World Cup 1994

On the international front, Keane excelled as part of the Republic of Ireland team in the 1994 World Cup in the USA, where the team progressed respectably before being knocked out by Holland. Although the team failed to qualify for France in 1998, Keane was regarded as a key figure for the Republic's chances in Japan and Korea, 2002. The infamous bust-up between Keane and manager Mick McCarthy meant that Keane was back home before the tournament even started.

Despite the fracas of the World Cup in the summer, 2002-03 saw Keane at his best, driving United on towards yet another title when it looked certain to go to Arsenal for the second successive season. Meanwhile, the arrival of Brian Kerr as the new Republic of Ireland manager prompted Keane to change his mind and return to the international stage.

After a swansong season as a player at Celtic Park, Keane launched into management with Sunderland, steering the side to the Championship title at the first attempt. Sunderland survived their first season back in the Premiership, but Keane quit midway through the 2008-09 campaign after a poor run had left them in the relegation zone. In April 2009 Keane took over the reins at Championship side Ipswich Town.

Souness makes changes

The 1992 FA Cup went to Liverpool, who beat Sunderland 2-0 in the final. Souness had been busy in the transfer market, not all of his deals finding favour with the fans. Beardsley and Staunton left for Everton and Villa respectively. In came Mark Walters from Rangers and the Derby pair, Mark Wright and Dean Saunders. Michael Thomas, the man who had broken Liverpool fans' hearts in 1989,

arrived from Arsenal. Thomas hit one of the goals that beat Sunderland. The other came from Rush, a record fifth goal for the Welshman in FA Cup finals.

For Souness, who had suffered a mild heart attack and was recovering from a bypass operation, FA Cup victory in 1992 would be a false dawn; it would be Liverpool's only trophy in his three-year reign.

LEFT: *Republic of Ireland's Roy Keane brings down Holland's Marc Overmars during a World Cup qualifying game.*
BELOW: *Ian Rush replaces Stan Collymore for Liverpool in the 1996 Cup Final against Manchester United.*

1991-92 DIVISION ONE	
1 Leeds United	82
2 Manchester United	78
3 Sheffield Wednesday	75
4 Arsenal	72
5 Manchester City	70
6 Liverpool	64
7 Aston Villa	60
8 Nottingham Forest	59
9 Sheffield United	57
10 Crystal Palace	57
11 Queen's Park Rangers	54
12 Everton	53
13 Wimbledon	53
14 Chelsea	53
15 Tottenham Hotspur	52
16 Southampton	52
17 Oldham Athletic	51
18 Norwich City	45
19 Coventry City	44
20 Luton Town	42
21 Notts County	40
22 West Ham United	38

1992-2009
A Premier League

1992-93 ushered in the new era of the Premier League. Squad numbers were introduced and players' shirts sported their names. Sponsorship was now big business, and Carling put their name - and money - into the new venture. Only nine fixtures on the opening Saturday showed that one of the game's great traditions was no longer set in stone. BskyB wanted football to fit in with its schedule, rather than the other way round. It was a case of he who pays the piper calls the tune.

United first Premier champions

Manchester United were the inaugural Premiership champions. Ferguson's side romped home 10 points clear of the pack to bring the league crown to Old Trafford for the first time since 1967. Arsenal were left languishing in mid-table, while Liverpool could finish only 6th, failing to qualify for Europe for the first time in 30 years. The Gunners did have the consolation of winning both cups, beating Sheffield Wednesday in each of the finals. Bit-part player Steve Morrow scored the winner in the League Cup final, and suffered a broken arm after Tony Adams hoisted him aloft and then dropped him. It was another fringe player, Andy Linighan, who headed a dramatic winner in the FA Cup final, which went to a replay.

Keane joins United

United added Roy Keane to their ranks for the defence of their title. His arrival from Nottingham Forest for a British record

£3.75 million made the United side even more formidable. This time they went one better, finishing eight points clear of Blackburn in the title race, and completing the double with an FA Cup victory over Chelsea.

The national team's fortunes went from bad to worse. Defeats against Norway and Holland left England needing to beat minnows San Marino by seven goals and hope that Holland lost in Poland. England started disastrously, conceding a goal in under ten seconds, which was believed to be an international record. The team recovered to win 7-1 but that was of little consequence as Holland got the win they needed. England had failed to qualify for the World Cup for the first time since 1978. Taylor, who had come in for some vitriolic criticism in the press, fell on his sword.

Venables replaces Taylor

Terry Venables was named as his successor. Venables had been ousted from White Hart Lane in a power struggle with chairman Alan Sugar, a dispute that was being played out in the High Court. With England hosting Euro '96, Venables had no immediate concerns of getting his England side through a competitive series. Graeme Souness's immediate concern was in finding another job as the Liverpool board finally lost patience. He became the first Liverpool manager to be shown the door since the 1950s. The club reverted to their tried and trusted system of appointing from within, Roy Evans being given the task of bringing back the glory days.

George Graham's record

Manchester United's first European Cup

campaign since 1967-68 came to an abrupt end as they were beaten by Galatasaray in the Second Round. It was left to Arsenal to fly the flag for England in the 1993-94 European Cup Winners' Cup, and they did so in fine style. An Alan Smith goal was enough to beat Parma in the final, and although George Graham's side wasn't known for champagne football, six trophies in eight years told its own story.

The following season Graham nearly made it seven when they reached the final again. A freak 50-yard lob by ex-Spurs player Nayim won the match for Real Zaragoza seconds before the end of extra time.

Taylor's England reign

Graham Taylor had been appointed England manager after the 1990 World Cup. His achievements at Watford and Aston Villa had been considerable. He had taken Villa from 17th in 1989 to runners-up the following year. Qualification for the 1992 European Championship was secured, although not without the odd moment of disquiet. A late Gary Lineker goal in Poland gave England the point they needed to edge out the Republic of Ireland. That strike was Lineker's 48th for England, one short of Bobby Charlton's record. After goalless draws against Denmark and France, Lineker's third chance to equal the record came against hosts Sweden, a game which England needed to win to progress. David Platt volleyed England into an early lead but Sweden hit back to win 2-1. Taylor substituted Lineker with half an hour to go, a decision which mystified many onlookers. It was to be his last game in an England shirt. Taylor came in for fierce criticism for his team selection and tactics. A country which had reached the last four at Italia '90 had finished bottom of their group in the European Championship two years later.

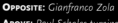

OPPOSITE: *Gianfranco Zola*

ABOVE: *Paul Scholes turning away from Van Bommel in a friendly international against Holland.*

LEFT: *England players Alan Shearer and David Platt make a point to the referee in an international match against Norway. England lost 2-0 in a qualifying game in Oslo and failed to make the 1994 tournament.*

BELOW: *Manchester United celebrate after beating Liverpool in the 1996 Cup Final. Eric Cantona's stunning strike was the difference between the teams.*

F.A. CUP
LITTLEWOODS
F.A. CUP WINNERS 1996
SPONSORED BY
LITTLEWOODS
F.A. CUP
LITTLEWOODS

Sutton and Shearer lead Blackburn to the title

The 1994-95 championship went to the wire. Kenny Dalglish's Blackburn, spearheaded by the SAS - Sutton and Shearer - went to Anfield on the last day of the season needing a victory to be sure of the title. Anything less could let in United, who were at West Ham. A last-minute goal by Jamie Redknapp looked to have spoiled Blackburn's party, until news came through that United had been held to a goalless draw. Blackburn thus claimed their first championship since 1914.

Newcastle go close

United reclaimed top spot in 1995-96, reeling in Kevin Keegan's Newcastle side, who had held a 12-point advantage early in the New Year. The two clubs would finish in the same positions the following season, Alex Ferguson having a distinct edge in the battle of wits that accompanied the onfield skirmishes.

In February 1995 it was revealed that George Graham had received illegal payments in transfer deals brokered by the agent Rune Hauge. Graham's track record couldn't help him; he was sacked by Arsenal and given a one-year ban by the FA. Allegations that Bruce Grobbelaar was involved in match-fixing at the behest of a Far East betting syndicate also hit the headlines. As recently as 1990, Swindon Town had been denied promotion to Division One after being found guilty of betting on the outcome of matches they were involved in.

In January 1995 the game was further tarnished when Eric Cantona lashed out at a fan with a kung fu-style kick after being red carded at Crystal Palace. He received an eight-month ban and a community service order. Arsenal's Paul Merson revealed that he had a drug problem, while team-mate Tony Adams had already served a prison sentence for drink-driving. All three players showed that rehabilitation was possible. In Cantona's case he returned to hit the goal which beat Liverpool in the 1996 FA Cup final. United had won the double again and the Frenchman was named Footballer of the Year.

RIGHT: *Alan Shearer celebrates his goal against Switzerland in Euro '96.*
BELOW RIGHT AND FAR RIGHT: *One of the most dramatic moments of Euro '96 when Stuart Pearce scored against Spain. After blasting the kick into the corner, he roared with delight. Pearce had missed from the spot when England were knocked out of the 1990 World Cup semi-finals by West Germany.*
OPPOSITE RIGHT: *Teddy Sheringham shares the moment with an emotional Pearce.*
OPPOSITE TOP: *Sheringham and Gascoigne celebrate after the midfielder's stunning goal clinched England's victory over Scotland in Euro '96.*

Paul Gascoigne

Problems with alcohol, injuries and his weight jinxed one of the most dazzling midfield players England has ever seen. "Gazza" grabbed the headlines for both self-destructive behaviour and brilliance. It was a tragedy for him, and for England, that he lacked the mental strength to match his mazy dribbling and slide-rule passes – a great footballing talent was squandered.

A Geordie full of laddish humour, he quickly made an impact at Newcastle United, which he joined in 1985 at 17. Terry Venables paid a record £2 million to bring the prodigious talent to Tottenham Hotspur in 1988. But in the 1991 FA Cup Final, having scored some fabulous goals on the road there, including a blinding 35-yard free-kick against the Gunners in the semi-final, Gascoigne recklessly fouled Forest's Gary Charles and injured his own cruciate ligament, which put him out of the game for a season.

National hero

Italia 90 had seen him emerge as a national hero, with the fans loving his heartfelt emotion when England went out to West Germany on penalties in the semi-final as much as they'd admired his moments of inspirational genius. He returned to Italy in 1992 for three difficult and injury-beset years at Lazio, but came back to Britain in 1995 for a renaissance at Glasgow Rangers, helping them to the Scottish title with 14 league goals in his first season and becoming Scotland's Footballer of the Year.

Euro 96, held in Britain, was a stage on which Gascoigne shone, and he scored a memorable goal against Scotland – one of the best of the championship. It was to be his high-water mark, for Glenn Hoddle left him out of the England squad for France 98, and he would never play for his country again.

Erratic in fitness and performance, Gazza's subsequent career, via Middlesbrough in 1998 and briefly Everton, has seen him unsigned at home and desperately trying to keep his place in China. It would be wonderful if he made a spectacular comeback, but sadly it now seems beyond him.

Football's Coming Home

Euro 96 provided welcome relief from a lot of unseemly publicity. The fans sang "Football's Coming Home" and England gave the country something to smile about. A piece of Gascoigne magic helped the team to a 2-0 win over Scotland, and a 4-1 demolition job on the Dutch masters sent the country into a fever of anticipation. David Seaman was the hero in the penalty shoot-out victory over Spain in the quarter-final. When Alan Shearer scored after two minutes against Germany in the semis it looked as if England might go all the way. But the Germans levelled and the two countries went into a shoot-out for the second time in a major tournament. Gareth Southgate had been immaculate in central defence but his spot-kick was saved, leaving Moller to score the goal which put England out.

1994-95 PREMIER LEAGUE

1	Blackburn Rovers	89
2	Manchester United	88
3	Nottingham Forest	77
4	Liverpool	74
5	Leeds United	73
6	Newcastle United	72
7	Tottenham Hotspur	62
8	Queen's Park Rangers	60
9	Wimbledon	56
10	Southampton	54
11	Chelsea	54
12	Arsenal	51
13	Sheffield Wednesday	51
14	West Ham United	50
15	Everton	50
16	Coventry City	50
17	Manchester City	49
18	Aston Villa	48
19	Crystal Palace	45
20	Norwich City	43
21	Leicester City	29
22	Ipswich	27

FA CUP FINALS

1990	Manchester United	v	Crystal Palace	3-3 (1-0)
1991	Tottenham Hotspur	v	Nottingham Forest	2-1
1992	Liverpool	v	Sunderland	2-0
1993	Arsenal	v	Sheffield Wednesday	1-1 (2-1)
1994	Manchester United	v	Chelsea	4-0
1995	Everton	v	Manchester United	1-0
1996	Manchester United	v	Liverpool	1-0
1997	Chelsea	v	Middlesbrough	2-0
1998	Arsenal	v	Newcastle United	2-0
1999	Manchester United	v	Newcastle United	2-0

Arsene Wenger

The choice of this quietly spoken, cerebral polyglot raised a few eyebrows among Arsenal fans when he was named as the man to take over from Bruce Rioch in September 1996. But Wenger was a very experienced coach, well known and respected within footballing circles. In 1981 he became youth coach at Strasbourg, the club he had played for. He then had spells at Cannes and Nancy, but it was when he joined Monaco that he started to make a name for himself. He won the French league with Monaco in 1988, his attractive side including the mercurial talents of Glenn Hoddle and Chris Waddle. In 1997-98, less than two years after arriving at Highbury, Wenger masterminded a famous League and Cup Double. He repeated the feat in 2001-02, and it looked as if his outstanding team had taken Manchester United's mantle as the best in the Premiership. Arsenal looked on course for a third Double in five years in 2002-03, but the team faltered after a blistering start. The Gunners had to be content with runners-up to United, though they retained the FA Cup with a victory over Southampton. In 2003-04 Wenger's side completed its league programme unbeaten as the Gunners claimed their third Premiership crown of his reign. A year later, he brought the FA Cup to Highbury for the fourth time in eight years, Arsenal beating Manchester Utd on penalties in the final. A rebuilt side packed with exciting young talent showed erratic league form in 2005-06 but reached the Champions League final, going down to favourites Barcelona 2-1 in Paris.

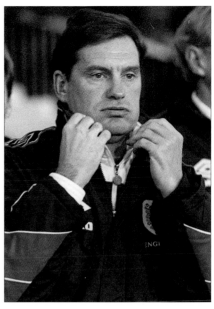

ABOVE: Two England managers show the strains of the job. Glen Hoddle (right) who took England to the World Cup finals in France 1998 only to see his team bow out following another penalty shoot-out and Kevin Keegan (left) who replaced him for the unsuccessful campaign of Euro 2000. England had let a vital two-goal lead slip in their opening match against Portugal, losing 3-2.

BELOW: David Beckham sets a fashion trend in boots that were to become his hallmark.
ABOVE LEFT: Arsene Wenger achieved the Double with Arsenal in only his second season in charge of the team. David Seaman (below) was England's first choice keeper and fundamental to the Gunners' success.

The Bosman ruling

Jean-Marc Bosman had never set Belgian football alight, let alone the world. But when he took his club Liege to the European Court of Justice on the issue of freedom of contract, he secured a ruling that was to have profound implications for all clubs. From now on contract negotiations - and an eye on the clock - would become of paramount importance when it came to a club's balance sheet. Few businesses had to contend with multi-million pound assets disappearing overnight, but that wasn't far from the case post-Bosman.

Wenger joins Arsenal

Many Arsenal fans scratched their heads when Arsene Wenger was named as the man to take over at Highbury in 1996, following Bruce Rioch's brief tenure. Wenger couldn't prevent United from taking the title again in his first season, but in 1997-98 he led the Gunners to the Double. It was to be the start of a long battle for supremacy in the domestic game, one involving psychological warfare as well as battles on the field.

Hoddle at the England helm

Terry Venables had announced before Euro 96 that he would be standing down to devote his energies to sorting out his legal and business affairs. Chelsea's

Glenn Hoddle was installed as the new supremo; at 38 he became the youngest ever England manager. Hoddle's first test came at France '98. England scraped into the finals, looking far from impressive. A defeat against Romania at the group stage didn't prove costly as it was sandwiched between victories over Tunisia and Colombia. Michael Owen had come off the bench to score against Romania and the clamour among fans for him to start in the second-round match against Argentina was deafening. Hoddle had taken the brave decision to leave Gascoigne out of his final 22; the decision to play Owen was far easier. The 17-year-old Liverpool prodigy scored the goal of the tournament to put England 2-1 ahead. Argentina levelled, and after David Beckham was red-carded for a petulant kick at Diego Simeone it looked to be slipping away from England's grasp. Sol Campbell thought he'd given 10-man England a 'golden goal' winner with a towering header in extra time. It was ruled out for an infringement and England suffered yet another penalty shoot-out exit. Paul Ince and David Batty were the unlucky men to miss from the spot on this occasion.

BELOW: *Chelsea celebrating after beating Middlesbrough 2-0 in the 1997 Cup Final.*

1995-96 PREMIER LEAGUE	
1 Manchester United	82
2 Newcastle United	78
3 Liverpool	71
4 Aston Villa	63
5 Arsenal	63
6 Everton	61
7 Blackburn Rovers	61
8 Tottenham Hotspur	61
9 Nottingham Forest	58
10 West Ham United	51
11 Chelsea	50
12 Middlesbrough	43
13 Leeds United	43
14 Wimbledon	41
15 Sheffield Wednesday	40
16 Coventry City	38
17 Southampton	38
18 Manchester City	38
19 Queen's Park Rangers	33
20 Bolton Wanderers	29

1996-97 PREMIER LEAGUE	
1 Manchester United	75
2 Newcastle United	68
3 Arsenal	68
4 Liverpool	68
5 Aston Villa	61
6 Chelsea	59
7 Sheffield Wednesday	57
8 Wimbledon	56
9 Leicester City	47
10 Tottenham Hotspur	46
11 Leeds United	46
12 Derby County	46
13 Blackburn Rovers	42
14 West Ham United	42
15 Everton	42
16 Southampton	41
17 Coventry City	41
18 Sunderland	40
19 Middlesbrough	39
20 Nottingham Forest	34

Alex Ferguson

Alex Ferguson arrived at Old Trafford in 1986 with an impressive record from his eight years at Aberdeen. He succeeded in breaking the Celtic-Rangers stranglehold on Scottish football, winning the championship three times and the Scottish Cup on four occasions. He also guided the Dons to a famous European Cup Winners' Cup victory over Real Madrid, beating the mighty Spanish side 2-1 in the Final in Gothenburg. He had a brief spell as caretaker manager of Scotland following the death of Jock Stein.

Youth system bears fruit

Ferguson then turned his attention to making Manchester United a powerhouse in England's top flight at a time when Liverpool were the undisputed top dogs. Fortunes in the early days were mixed. His team lifted the FA Cup in 1990 and followed it up with a victory over Barcelona in the European Cup Winners' Cup Final the following year. Shortly afterwards the youth system in which Ferguson had invested so heavily began to bear fruit. Players of the stature of Giggs, Beckham, Scholes and the Neville brothers progressed to the senior side. Ferguson also made some astute signings, notably Peter Schmeichel and Eric Cantona, who together cost just £1.5 million. Ferguson's side proved irresistible, winning the inaugural Premiership title in 1993. A league and Cup Double followed in 1994, and again in 1996. But the crowning moment came in 1999, when Ferguson added the European Cup to his sizeable haul of domestic trophies. He announced that 2002 would be his final season, but had a change of heart and took United to yet another championship in 2002-03. Victory over Millwall in the 2004 FA Cup final gave United their fifth win in the competition in the Ferguson era. A year later it should have been six, but while United dominated the final, Arsenal left with the silverware. In 2006-07 United embarked on yet another hat-trick of championship wins – no manager had ever achieved that feat – and Sir Alex added a second Champions League success to his cv when the Red Devils beat Chelsea in a dramatic shoot-out in Moscow in 2007-08. A championship and League Cup double in 2008-09 brought Ferguson's tally to 31 major trophies in his managerial career, comprising 14 league titles, 13 domestic cup wins and four European successes.

United crowned champions of Europe

In the domestic game the United bandwagon rolled on. Ferguson's men reclaimed the title in 1999, the first in a hat-trick of championships that would equal Liverpool's feat of the 1980s. European Cup success was still proving elusive, however, a 1997 semi-final defeat by Borussia Dortmund being the nearest United had come to repeating the club's achievement under Busby. In May 1999 the coveted trophy was finally claimed, and in dramatic fashion. United entered the tournament as runners-up, but while Arsenal faltered in their group matches, United emerged to dispose of Inter Milan and Juventus at the knockout stage. A 32-match unbeaten run had carried the club to yet another domestic double and to the Champions' League final, against Bayern Munich in Barcelona. Trailing 1-0 with a minute to go, Sheringham scored to give United a lifeline. Seconds later Sheringham flicked on a Beckham corner and Solskjaer stabbed the ball into the roof of the net.

1997-98 PREMIER LEAGUE

1	Arsenal	78
2	Manchester United	77
3	Liverpool	65
4	Chelsea	63
5	Leeds United	59
6	Blackburn Rovers	58
7	Aston Villa	57
8	West Ham United	56
9	Derby County	55
10	Leicester City	53
11	Coventry City	52
12	Southampton	48
13	Newcastle United	44
14	Tottenham Hotspur	44
15	Wimbledon	44
16	Sheffield Wednesday	44
17	Everton	40
18	Bolton Wanderers	40
19	Barnsley	35
20	Crystal Palace	33

A FAMOUS TREBLE

RIGHT: *United fans swarm the streets of Manchester in celebration of their team's victory, after beating Bayern Munich 2-1 in the European Cup Final in Barcelona.*

ABOVE: *Alex Ferguson proudly parades the European Cup at Manchester Airport.*

OPPOSITE ABOVE: *Sven-Goran Eriksson*

OPPOSITE BELOW: *The scoreboard records the moment - England's great victory over rivals Germany after having lost the home game of the World Cup qualifying group at Wembley 1-0.*

Eriksson silences his critics

Sven-Goran Eriksson

After Terry Venables, Glenn Hoddle and Kevin Keegan had come and gone in a relatively short space of time, FA administrators took the unprecedented step of appointing Sven-Goran Eriksson as national team boss, the first overseas incumbent. The decision angered some, while others praised the farsightedness of bringing in a man with an excellent record as a coach. Eriksson hit the headlines in 1982, when he took IFK Gothenburg to the UEFA Cup Final. His team beat Valencia and Kaiserslautern along the way and Hamburg in the Final, becoming the first Swedish side to lift a European trophy. Eriksson was back there again in 1983, this time with Benfica. On this occasion he finished on the losing side, Anderlecht coming out on top over the two legs.

Lazio's first title for 26 years

Eriksson won three championships with Benfica and made it to the 1990 European Cup final, where his team lost 1-0 to the all-conquering AC Milan. Serie A beckoned next and Eriksson had spells at Roma, Fiorentina and Sampdoria before joining Lazio in 1997. His first season with the Rome club was a rollercoaster. The team won the Italian Cup, fell away in the league and went down 3-0 to Inter in the UEFA Cup final. In 2000 he delivered the Serie A title, Lazio's first championship for 26 years. He was appointed England manager the following year, when the team was in a precarious position in the World Cup qualifying campaign. He galvanised the team, taking England to the top of their group with results including a memorable 5-1 win in Germany. He got England out of the "Group of Death" in Japan and Korea and the team beat a good Danish side before going out to eventual winners Brazil. Eriksson's men also fell at the quarter-final hurdle at Euro 2004, going out on penalties to hosts Portugal. The same opposition provided the stumbling block at the same stage at Germany 2006, Eriksson's swansong with the England side. Sven's verdict on his five-year reign was that reaching the last eight in 2002 and 2004 had been acceptable; with the talent at his disposal this time round it was an underachievement.
After a season in charge at Manchester City, Eriksson returned to international management with Mexico, but was sacked midway through the World Cup 2010 qualifying campaign.

There was another England-Germany clash at Euro 2000 as the countries were drawn together at the group stage. A Shearer goal gave England victory, but both countries made an early exit. England had let a two-goal lead slip in their opening match against Portugal, losing 3-2. They also led Romania 2-1 in their final match but again failed to press home the advantage and were on the receiving end of another 3-2 defeat.

Failure to qualify for the latter stages led Kevin Keegan to question his ability at the highest level. He stood down with qualification for the 2002 World Cup in Japan and Korea hanging in the balance. The FA looked further afield for their next appointment. Sven-Goran Eriksson was not a universally popular choice, despite his excellent credentials. He silenced many of his critics with a stunning 5-1 win in Germany in September 2001, a result which got England's World Cup campaign back on track.

"Group of Death"

Eriksson succeeded in getting the country out of the "Group of Death", a Beckham penalty against Argentina exorcising the ghost of France '98. A comfortable win over Denmark followed, but England went down to favourites Brazil in the quarter-final. England went ahead through Owen, Rivaldo and Ronaldinho replied for Brazil and Eriksson's men couldn't get back on terms, even when the favourites were reduced to ten men.

1998-99 PREMIER LEAGUE

1	Manchester United	79
2	Arsenal	78
3	Chelsea	75
4	Leeds United	67
5	West Ham United	57
6	Aston Villa	55
7	Liverpool	54
8	Derby County	52
9	Middlesbrough	52
10	Leicester City	49
11	Tottenham Hotspur	47
12	Sheffield Wednesday	46
13	Newcastle United	46
14	Everton	43
15	Coventry City	42
16	Wimbledon	42
17	Southampton	41
18	Charlton Athletic	36
19	Blackburn Rovers	35
20	Nottingham Forest	30

Deutschland Olympi
England Mü
1 : 5

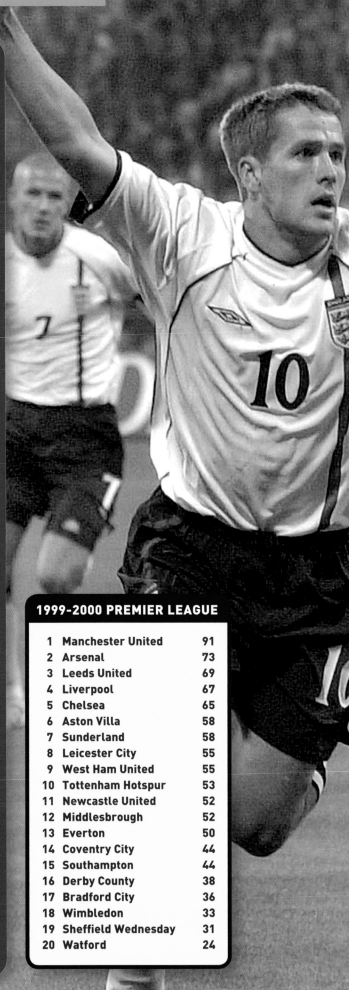

David Beckham

David Beckham has been a villain and he has been a hero. After a bad-tempered kick on Diego Simeone in England's 1998 World Cup clash with Argentina, he was cast as the villain of the piece. But, by the end of the 2002 World Cup, he was universally regarded as England's new hero. His artistry on the ball, superb distribution and the quality of his dead-ball kicks were always acknowledged – what he had gained in the intervening years was a greater maturity and outstanding leadership skills.

When he was still a youngster, Beckham won an award at a Bobby Charlton Soccer Skills school and had trials with his local club, Leyton Orient, but it was Manchester United who signed him just after his 16th birthday. Although he made his debut in a League Cup tie against Brighton in September 1992, Alex Ferguson nurtured his young star carefully and it wasn't until April 1995 that he gave Beckham his Premiership debut. The following season he established himself in United's midfield and in September 1996 Glenn Hoddle gave him a place in the England team.

Three successive Premiership titles

Beckham was a key figure in United's celebrated Treble-winning team of the1998-99 season. During the Champions League campaign, United played Inter Milan, a game that was billed as the return clash between Beckham and Simeone. It was less than a year since the infamous World Cup incident but Beckham gave a superb performance, the two players swapped shirts at the end of the game and the victory went to United. At the end of that season, Beckham was narrowly beaten by Rivaldo for the World Footballer of the Year award.

'Becks' was instrumental in helping United to their third successive Premiership title in 2001. In October of the same year it was his stunning free-kick in the closing seconds of the game against Greece which reserved England's place at the 2002 World Cup in Japan and Korea.

His service in that World Cup meant that Beckham had a virtually unassailable position as England captain during the 2002-03 season, yet he was unsure of a place in United's starting line-up. After much speculation on his future, in June 2003 Beckham signed a £25 million deal to take him to Real Madrid, the team that knocked United out of that season's Champions Cup.

He became a 'Galactico' at a time when Real's period of dominance was waning, the team failing to land any silverware in his first three seasons at the Bernebeu. There was more disappointment with the national side as Beckham led England to a quarter-final defeat at Germany 2006. He relinquished the captain's armband, but on the verge of becoming only the fifth player to break the 100-cap barrier, he stressed that he wanted to play on under the new Steve McClaren regime.

His chances appeared to diminish when he was dropped by the new England boss, then signed to play for MLS side LA Galaxy. But Beckham returned to the international fold in May 2007, just as he was signing off from Real Madrid with a La Liga winners' medal. He finally joined the 100 club when selected for a friendly against France in March 2008 by new coach Fabio Capello, under whom he had played at Madrid. A year later he made his 109th appearance, overtaking Bobby Moore as the most capped outfield player in history. By then Beckham was back playing top-level club football for AC Milan, who had taken him on loan. Galaxy and Milan couldn't agree terms for a permanent move, so a deal was cut in which Beckham would turn out for both clubs.

1999-2000 PREMIER LEAGUE

1	Manchester United	91
2	Arsenal	73
3	Leeds United	69
4	Liverpool	67
5	Chelsea	65
6	Aston Villa	58
7	Sunderland	58
8	Leicester City	55
9	West Ham United	55
10	Tottenham Hotspur	53
11	Newcastle United	52
12	Middlesbrough	52
13	Everton	50
14	Coventry City	44
15	Southampton	44
16	Derby County	38
17	Bradford City	36
18	Wimbledon	33
19	Sheffield Wednesday	31
20	Watford	24

Michael Owen

Since he electrified first the Premiership, then the world, in the 1997-98 season, Michael Owen has continued to rewrite the record books. By the end of the 2004-05 season Owen had notched 32 international goals, standing fourth in the all-time list of England marksmen. Averaging almost a goal every other game, he remains on course to achieve his aim of 50 goals in 100 appearances for his country. Owen was the star of Liverpool's Youth Cup-winning side in 1996. Roy Evans handed him his Premiership debut at Wimbledon at the end of the 1996-97 season, and the 17-year-old immediately notched his first senior goal. He scored 30 more in the 1997-98 season, earning him the PFA Young Player of the Year award, and more significantly an England call-up. When, in February 1998, he lined up against Chile, Owen became the youngest England player of the century; at 18 years 59 days he took the record previously held by Duncan Edwards. Shortly afterwards, he became the youngest player to score for England when he netted a goal against Morocco in a World Cup warm-up match.

England manager Glenn Hoddle took him to the World Cup in France 1998, but not as first-choice striker. Owen changed that after he came off the bench to score against Romania. In the second round clash with Argentina he won a penalty, then struck the goal of the tournament.

Owen's glittering career has presented numerous highlights, including a stunning two-goal tally to seize the FA Cup from Arsenal in 2001, and the marvellous hat-trick in the 5-1 demolition of Germany in a World Cup qualifier four months later. It was such performances which earned him the 2001 European Footballer of the Year award. He celebrated, in true Owen style, by striking his hundredth goal for Liverpool in the same month.

His second World Cup in Japan and Korea in 2002 brought him goals against Denmark and Brazil. And the penalty he won in the game against Argentina in the 'Group of Death' was instrumental in England's momentous defeat of their historic rivals.

In the summer of 2004 Owen left Anfield to join Beckham at Real Madrid. His season at the Bernebeu was a frustrating one. No one bettered his goal return in relation to minutes on the pitch, but fierce competition restricted his opportunities and Newcastle Utd paid a club record £17 million to bring him back to the Premiership. He recovered from an injury-hit domestic season in time for Germany 2006, but was left facing another long lay-off after suffering cruciate ligament damage in the group decider against Sweden.

Owen's brace against Russia in the Euro 2008 qualifiers took his international tally to 40 but his chances of breaking Bobby Charlton's record faded as he became a peripheral figure under Fabio Capello. His surprised move to Old Trafford for the 2009-10 season could reignite his international career in time for the World Cup finals.

Gunners Double Up

In 2001-02 Arsenal won their second Double under Wenger and the third in the club's history. The Gunners began the 2002-03 season like an express train and Wenger tentatively suggested that his side was capable of going through the season unbeaten. Clubs in the chasing pack, looking to strengthen, had the new transfer arrangements to contend with. After the start of the season the 'window' would not be open to further deals until January. Arsenal faltered in the second half of the season and in the end they had to settle for retaining the FA Cup and the runners-up spot in the league. United, by contrast, went on a blistering run in the new year to claim their 8th Premiership title in 11 seasons. There was also the prospect of a second European Cup Final appearance, this time at Old Trafford. United managed to beat holders Real Madrid in the home leg of their quarter-final clash, but the damage had already been done at the Bernebeu.

The season ended with the England captain departing to join the team that had knocked United out of the European Cup. David Beckham's name had been linked with several clubs when it became clear that United were prepared to let him go. Real Madrid were one of the few clubs who could afford the £25 million fee as the inflationary bubble had undoubtedly burst. A significant part of Beckham's fee was for the acquisition of a unique brand; Real would expect to recoup the outlay in the sales of merchandise as well as in his contribution on the pitch.

Football's finances

The financial correction that had occurred since the heady days of the 1990s was stark. The collapse of On Digital showed that football was not a cash cow that could be milked at all levels. Leeds fans watched their Champions League semi-final side of 2001 disintegrate before their eyes, hard proof that gambling on a seat at European football's top table was a high-risk strategy.

The parlous state of football's finances meant that even Champions League qualification was not necessarily a passport to a land of milk and honey. On the final day of the 2002-03 season Chelsea beat Liverpool to secure the fourth Champions League spot. Less than two months later chairman Ken Bates sold his majority shareholding to Russian oil billionaire Roman Abramovich. In seven seasons Chelsea had never finished out of the top six in the Premiership, had twice lifted the FA Cup and also won the Cup Winners' Cup. And yet the club was £80 million in debt and Bates admitted that pockets deeper than his were needed to take Chelsea forward.

2000-01 PREMIER LEAGUE		
1	Manchester United	80
2	Arsenal	70
3	Liverpool	69
4	Leeds United	68
5	Ipswich Town	66
6	Chelsea	61
7	Sunderland	57
8	Aston Villa	54
9	Charlton Athletic	52
10	Southampton	52
11	Newcastle United	51
12	Tottenham Hotspur	49
13	Leicester City	48
14	Middlesbrough	42
15	West Ham United	42
16	Everton	42
17	Derby County	42
18	Manchester City	34
19	Coventry City	34
20	Bradford City	26

Thierry Henry

Thierry Henry has won just about every honour in the game. In a glittering career he has picked up championship medals in France, England and Spain, winning the domestic double in the latter two countries. He has hoisted aloft the Champions League trophy, and joined the select group who have won both the World Cup and European Championship.

Henry burst onto the scene with Monaco but after a high-profile move to Juventus in 1999 his form hit the buffers. He was neither assured of a first-team place, nor enjoying his football. Arsene Wenger made the inspired decision to play him in a central role after his move to Arsenal, a decision about which even the player himself had his doubts. Those disappeared as the goals started raining in, and Henry developed into one of the most feared central strikers in world football.

Henry was the Premiership's hotshot in 2001-02, and topped the scoring charts in three of the next four seasons. He picked up the PFA Player of the Year award in 2003 and 2004, the first person to be honoured thus in consecutive years. In 2007 he joined Barcelona's stellar line-up in a £16 million move. The first season at the Nou Camp was a blank, but in 2008-09 Henry's goals helped fire Barca to a magnificent Treble, victory over Manchester United in the Champions League final coming on top of the domestic double.

On the international stage in 2007 Henry passed Michel Platini's record of 41 international goals, which had stood for 20 years. By the end of the 2008-09 season he had moved on to 48 goals and clocked up 111 appearances, putting him third behind Lilian Thuram and Marcel Desailly in the all-time list.

Arsenal match Invincibles

Even established Premiership sides now had to strike a balance between sound investment and over-commitment. For Leeds it was all too late; a string of stars had been sold at knockdown prices and the team propped up the division in 2003-04.

Chelsea, backed by Abramovich's personal fortune, was the one club able to buck the trend. Coach Claudio Ranieri spent over £100 million on a crop of international stars, players of the stature of Makelele, Duff, Crespo and Mutu. Inevitably there were accusations of trying to buy success, and for most of the 2003-04 season it looked as if the strategy was going to bear fruit. Chelsea stayed with the scorching pace set by Arsenal longest, but in the end not even Ranieri's all-stars could match the brilliance of Arsene Wenger's team. The Gunners completed their league programme unbeaten, a feat not achieved in English football's top flight since 1888-89, when Preston's Invincibles won the inaugural League Championship.

Chelsea took revenge over their London rivals with a quarter-final victory in the Champions League, but went down to Monaco in the semis. By most standards Chelsea had had a successful season, but the lack of silverware meant that football's worst-kept secret was finally revealed: out went Ranieri and in came Jose Mourinho, who had just steered Porto to Champions League victory, following a UEFA Cup triumph over Celtic in 2003.

Manchester United was among Porto's scalps in the latter's Champions League campaign. United also trailed in a distant third in the Premiership, 15 points behind Arsenal. Ferguson's side did win the FA Cup semi-final clash between the two giants, and a comfortable 3-0 victory over Millwall in the final gave United their 11th victory in the competition, stretching the club's lead at the top of the all-time list.

Changes at Anfield

The fact that Chelsea had managed to break the Manchester United-Arsenal duopoly in 2003-04 undoubtedly helped to bring down the curtain on Gerard Houllier's reign at Anfield. Liverpool fans saw their team secure Champions League football by finishing fourth in the Premiership, but with a 28-point gulf separating the Reds from Arsenal. In terms of points Liverpool were closer to the relegated clubs, having finished just 26 points ahead of Leeds, Wolves and Leicester. The man charged with bringing the glory days back to Anfield was Rafael Benitez, who had just completed a Primera Liga-UEFA Cup double with Valencia.

2001-02 PREMIER LEAGUE

1	Arsenal	87
2	Liverpool	80
3	Manchester United	77
4	Newcastle United	71
5	Leeds United	66
6	Chelsea	64
7	West Ham United	53
8	Aston Villa	50
9	Tottenham Hotspur	50
10	Blackburn Rovers	46
11	Southampton	45
12	Middlesbrough	45
13	Fulham	44
14	Charlton Athletic	44
15	Everton	43
16	Bolton Wanderers	40
17	Sunderland	40
18	Ipswich Town	36
19	Derby County	30
20	Leicester City	28

Euro 2004

With domestic matters settled, there was the usual pre-tournament mood of buoyant optimism as England departed for Portugal. There was almost a dream start as Sven Goran Eriksson's men led holders and favourites France through a Frank Lampard header in their opening group fixture. Two injury-time goals from Zidane meant that England emerged with considerable credit but no points.

A comfortable 3-0 win over Switzerland followed, Wayne Rooney grabbing a brace and becoming the youngest scorer in the competition's history. That record was taken a few days later by Switzerland's Johan Vonlanthen, but with two more goals in the 4-2 victory over Croatia, it was Rooney's name that was on everyone's lips. He headed the list of the tournament's marksmen and the impact he had made was compared with Pele's debut on the world stage at the 1958 World Cup.

England qualified for the quarter-finals behind France, the first time that the country had reached the knockout stage of the competition on foreign soil.

The team got off to a dream start against hosts Portugal, Michael Owen silencing his critics with a brilliant strike after three minutes. It was his 26th goal in his 60th appearance in an England shirt. Rooney limped out with a broken metatarsal midway through the first half, and as the game wore on England fought an increasingly rearguard action. With seven minutes to go the hosts equalised through substitute Helder Postiga, who had all too rarely found the back of the net when turning out for Spurs. There were shades of France '98 as Sol Campbell thought he'd headed England into the semis in the dying seconds, but the Swiss referee spotted an infringement and the game went to extra-time.

Rui Costa's ferocious strike in the second period was cancelled out when Lampard pounced on a knockdown to score his third goal of the tournament. After 120 minutes the teams were locked at 2-2.

Beckham capped a hugely disappointing tournament by blazing over in the penalty shoot-out. Rui Costa did the same to level matters and it went to sudden death. Portuguese 'keeper Ricardo saved from Darius Vassell and then slotted home the decisive spot-kick. In reaching the last eight, and thus only matching the performance at the 2002 World Cup, Euro 2004 was widely regarded as a missed opportunity for England.

BELOW: *Frank Lampard celebrates his goal against France with Wayne Rooney.*

2002-03 PREMIER LEAGUE		
1	Manchester United	83
2	Arsenal	78
3	Newcastle United	69
4	Chelsea	67
5	Liverpool	64
6	Blackburn Rovers	60
7	Everton	59
8	Southampton	52
9	Manchester City	51
10	Tottenham Hotspur	50
11	Middlesbrough	49
12	Charlton Athletic	49
13	Birmingham City	48
14	Fulham	48
15	Leeds United	47
16	Aston Villa	45
17	Bolton Wanderers	44
18	West Ham United	42
19	West Bromwich Albion	26
20	Sunderland	19

Triumphs for Chelsea and Liverpool

2004-05 will be remembered as the season when Manchester United and Arsenal, between them winners of the Premiership title in 11 of the previous 12 years, could do nothing to stop the Chelsea juggernaut. Jose Mourinho's men didn't quite manage to emulate Arsenal's achievement of the previous campaign – defeat at Manchester City prevented that - but it was still a record-breaking season. 29 wins and 95 points eclipsed the previous marks, while Petr Cech's 1025 minutes without conceding broke Peter Schmeichel's record for shut-outs. Chelsea shipped just 15 goals, two fewer than Arsenal in 1998-99. The meanest defence in the land was marshalled by the outstanding John Terry, who edged Frank Lampard for the PFA Player of the Year award, the first defender to be thus honoured since Paul McGrath in 1993. The title came in Chelsea's centenary, and exactly 50 years after Ted Drake delivered Chelsea's only other championship.

The Carling Cup also went to Stamford Bridge, Chelsea beating Liverpool in the final. Rafael Benitez's erratic side saved its best performances for Europe. With Utd and Arsenal both out of the Champions League at the last 16 stage, Liverpool scored excellent wins over Bayer Leverkusen and Juventus to set up a semi-final clash with Chelsea. It was billed as the biggest game in the history of English club football, and also saw the reigning Champions League and UEFA Cup-winning managers go head to head. A Luis Garcia goal at Anfield settled the issue. Liverpool, who would finish 37 points adrift of the champions, were through to their sixth European Cup final on the 20th anniversary of the Heysel tragedy.

Gerrard leads Reds' revival
Opponents AC Milan were favourites in Istanbul, and odds of 300-1 against the Reds were being quoted at half-time, by which time they were three goals down. Steven Gerrard led from the front as Liverpool fought back to take the game to penalties, and two Dudek saves in the shoot-out saw Liverpool complete the greatest ever comeback in a European final. Their fifth win in the competition meant that the cup would stay at Anfield.

Arsenal beat Man Utd in the Premiership runners-up race, Arsene Wenger maintaining his record of never finishing outside the top two. Third spot for the second year running represented Utd's 'worst' performance since the inception of Premiership, and came amid the uncertainties created by Malcolm Glazer's take-over of the club.

BELOW: *An elated Frank Lampard scores against Bolton Wanderers. The 2-0 victory makes Chelsea winners of the Barclays Premiership for 2004-05.*
ABOVE: *Jose Mourinho, winner of the Premiership at his first attempt.*
OPPOSITE BELOW: *Liverpool's captain, Steven Gerrard, holds the trophy as teammates celebrate after the UEFA Champions League Final at the Ataturk Olympic Stadium in Turkey.*
OPPOSITE ABOVE: *Arsenal's Freddie Ljungberg saves off the line from Manchester United centre forward Ruud van Nisterooy in the 2005 FA Cup final. The Gunners won 5-4 on penalties after extra time.*

Gunners win Cup Final shoot-out

Arsenal and Utd's only hope of silverware rested on the FA Cup, and they met in the final. Utd did everything but score, but after a goalless 120 minutes Lehmann's save from Scholes meant that the Gunners won the first Cup Final shoot-out.

Everton, widely tipped as relegation candidates, secured the fourth Champions League spot, earning David Moyes the Manager of the Year award. Everton lost Rooney just before start of season, and the influential Gravesen in January, but still secured the club's first European Cup campaign for 34 years. Fifth place Liverpool had to sweat on a dispensation to be allowed to defend their Champions League crown, while Bolton fans looked forward to European football for first time in the club's history.

On the final day of the season the relegation dogfight provided the greatest drama. It was perm three from four to go down, and at various times Norwich, Crystal Palace, Southampton and West Brom all occupied the vital 17th place. The Baggies were the only side to win, a 2-0 victory over Portsmouth guaranteeing Premiership football for Bryan Robson's men. Eight points adrift at the foot of the table at Christmas, West Brom made Premiership history by surviving the drop. For Southampton it was the end of a 27-year run in the top flight.

In the Championship, Wigan Athletic won automatic promotion as runners-up to Sunderland. Elected to the league at end of 77-78 season, Wigan had been bought in 1995 by Dave Whelan, 68-year old founder of the JJB sportswear empire. His money, together with Paul Jewell's shrewd management, had produced a fairytale rise to the top. Alan Pardew, much castigated by West Ham fans, answered his critics by taking the Hammers back to the Premiership via the play-offs.

2003-04 PREMIER LEAGUE	
1 Arsenal	90
2 Chelsea	79
3 Manchester United	75
4 Liverpool	60
5 Newcastle United	56
6 Aston Villa	56
7 Charlton Athletic	53
8 Bolton Wanderers	53
9 Fulham	52
10 Birmingham City	50
11 Middlesbrough	48
12 Southampton	47
13 Portsmouth	45
14 Tottenham Hotspur	45
15 Blackburn Rovers	44
16 Manchester City	41
17 Everton	39
18 Leicester City	33
19 Leeds United	33
20 Wolverhampton W	33

2004-05 PREMIER LEAGUE	
1 Chelsea	95
2 Arsenal	83
3 Manchester United	77
4 Everton	61
5 Liverpool	58
6 Bolton Wanderers	58
7 Middlesbrough	55
8 Manchester City	52
9 Tottenham Hotspur	52
10 Aston Villa	47
11 Charlton Athletic	46
12 Birmingham	45
13 Fulham	44
14 Newcastle United	44
15 Blackburn Rovers	42
16 Portsmouth	39
17 West Bromwich A	34
18 Crystal Palace	33
19 Norwich	33
20 Southampton	32

Chelsea retain Premiership crown

Even before a ball was kicked in the 2005-06 season, Chelsea Chief Executive Peter Kenyon predicted that the champions would come 'from a small group of one'. Jose Mourinho was singing from the same hymn sheet, insisting that 'one Premiership is not enough' as he revealed his aim was not simply to build one or two title-winning sides but to create a dynasty that would dominate English football for a generation. In their bid to emulate Manchester Utd and become only the second club to retain the Premiership crown, Chelsea splashed out over £50 million on Asier del Horno, Shaun Wright-Phillips and Michael Essien. With Hernan Crespo returning from his loan spell at AC Milan to add extra firepower, the Blues looked ominously strong as they embarked on a nine-month battle to land five trophies.

Lampard breaks record

A brace from Drogba meant that one piece of silverware was in the Stamford Bridge cabinet before August was out, Chelsea completing a 2-1 victory over Arsenal in the Community Shield curtain-raiser.

The team's league form was not always scintillating but it was mightily effective. 52 points from 19 games – just five points dropped in the first half of the season – set the standard for the chasing pack. During this run Frank Lampard added another stat to his impressive cv, breaking David James's Premiership record of 159 consecutive games. He clocked up 164 matches before a virus laid him low, an extraordinary achievement for any top-flight player, let alone a combative midfielder.

Liverpool initially looked best placed to run Chelsea close. Rafa Benitez's men also had a summer trophy under their belt, coming from behind to beat UEFA Cup holders CSKA Moscow in the European Super Cup. A brace from Djibril Cisse helped Liverpool to a 3-1 extra-time win, adding to the club's Super Cup victories of 1977 and 2001. The Reds couldn't break their duck in the World Club Championship, though. Liverpool hadn't won the play-off against South America's top dogs following their first four European Cup victories, and in the revamped tournament staged in Japan in December they went down to Sao Paulo in the final.

In the Premiership Liverpool went on an autumn run of nine straight wins, despite the fact that £7 million recruit Peter Crouch didn't find the net until December. It was title-winning form – in normal circumstances – but not with Chelsea setting such a scorching pace.

United lift Carling Cup

After Christmas it was Manchester Utd who took up the challenge. Alex Ferguson's side recovered from the acrimonious departure of talismanic captain Roy Keane, and some indifferent Champions League performances which saw the club fail to reach the competition's knockout stage for the first time in a decade. United hit top gear in the second half of the season. They beat Wigan 4-0 in the Carling Cup final, only the second time that trophy had gone to Old Trafford. That avoided a second barren season, but any hope of catching Chelsea and landing the top domestic prize disappeared with a 3-0 defeat at Stamford Bridge on 29 April. Chelsea retained the Premiership title with two games to spare, becoming the first London side to record back-to-back championships since Arsenal in the 1930s.

LEFT: *Ferreira, Terry and Robben celebrate Chelsea winning back-to-back Championships.*

They had suffered five defeats, though two of those were dead rubbers, coming after the title was secured. Only Manchester Utd matched Chelsea's attacking potency – both teams found the net 72 times – while John Terry once again marshalled the meanest defence in the division.

End of the road for Highbury

United pipped Liverpool for the runners-up spot and automatic Champions League qualification, while Thierry Henry brought down the curtain on Highbury after 93 years with a hat-trick against Wigan, helping the Gunners clinch fourth place at Spurs' expense.

The relegation issues were settled before the final day. Sunderland set a new Premiership record in notching just 15 points, four less than when the Black Cats suffered the drop in 2002-03. Portsmouth, eight points adrift at one stage, had looked nailed on to join them. But with Harry Redknapp back at the helm, Pompey staged a remarkable revival, taking 20 points from nine games in the run-in to ensure their survival. Jubilation on the south coast, contrasted with long faces in the Midlands as Birmingham and West Brom joined the Championship-bound Mackems.

Replacing them were Reading, who suffered just two league defeats all season and broke the 100-point barrier, with Sheffield Utd taking the other automatic spot and Watford, tipped by many as relegation candidates, coming through via the play-offs. Hornets manager Adrian Boothroyd was a former number two to Kevin Blackwell at Leeds, and he got the better of his old boss in a match worth around £40 million, in cash terms said to be the biggest game in world football.

Gerrard inspires FA Cup victory

Liverpool were worthy FA Cup winners. They came back from 3-1 down to beat Luton 5-3 in the tie of the Third Round, then put out both Manchester Utd and Chelsea en route to a Millennium Stadium showdown with promoted West Ham. In a pulsating final, the Hammers led 2-0, and 3-2 with seconds to go. But a year on from his inspired performance in Liverpool's dramatic Champions League victory, Steven Gerrard again led from the front. His stunning 90th-minute strike - his second of the match - took the game into extra-time, and he was also on target in the 3-1 shoot-out victory. The FA Cup was back in the Anfield trophy room for the seventh time, and Gerrard had turned in the kind of trademark performance which would see him named PFA Player of the Year.

Arsenal had a curate's egg of a season. They were beaten eleven times in the league, a far cry from the 'Invincibles' of 2003-04. The Gunners came within seconds of going out to Doncaster Rovers in the last eight of the Carling Cup, surviving a shoot-out at Belle Vue before going down to Wigan in the semis. Arsenal appeared to be a club in transition, with players and pundits alike suggesting that Patrick Vieira's departure to Juventus had left a large void.

ABOVE: *Liverpool's Mohamed Sissoko faces a challenge from Yossi Benayoun in the 2006 FA Cup Final. Final score: 3-3 after extra time, Liverpool won 3-1 on penalties.*

BELOW: *Rafa Benitez celebrates with his captain. The FA Cup was back in the Anfield trophy room for the seventh time, and Gerrard had turned in the kind of trademark performance which would see him named PFA Player of the Year.*

10-man Arsenal go down fighting

Arsene Wenger's men produced their most consistent form in the Champions League. Real Madrid and Juve were both swept aside in a sparkling run to the final in Paris. There they faced favourites Barcelona, who had just retained their Primera Liga title. Arsenal took a first-half lead through a bullet Sol Campbell header, despite having been reduced to ten men. Jens Lehmann, the hero of the semis after his last-minute penalty save from Villareal's magician Juan Riquelme, was red carded in the 20th minute for bringing down Eto'o. The Gunners fought bravely and had chances to put daylight between the sides, but conceded twice in the last fifteen minutes. They had set a new Champions League record

of ten games without conceding, but the fans were left to reflect on what might have been if the game had been played out eleven against eleven.

It was England v Spain in the UEFA Cup final too. Middlesbrough pulled off two of the greatest Houdini acts of the modern era against FC Basel and Steaua Bucharest, hitting four goals against each at the Riverside to snatch victory from the jaws of defeat. There was no glorious send-off for Steve McClaren, in his last game before taking over the reins of the national team. Boro fell behind to a classy Sevilla outfit, and were picked off in the final quarter as they chased an equaliser. The better team won, though 4-0 was a harsh scoreline.

Accrington Stanley's return

As the big boys shared the top domestic honours once again, football's basement threw up a heartwarming story: the return of Accrington Stanley. One of the founder members of the Football League, Accrington had disappeared off the footballing map after resigning from the League during the 1961-62 season. In an ironic twist, the team heading in the opposite direction was Oxford, the club that had taken Accrington's place in the old Fourth Division 44 years earlier.

BELOW LEFT: *Arsene Wenger and Thierry Henry following Arsenal's 2-1 defeat by Barcelona in the UEFA Champions League final.*
BELOW RIGHT: *Chelsea's John Terry and Manchester United's Wayne Rooney fight for the ball in the 2007 FA Cup final.*

World Cup 2006:
40 years of hurt – and counting

England fans are hardy perennials when it comes to pre-tournament optimism, but in the run-up to Germany 2006 the feeling abroad was even more hopeful than usual. The 'golden generation' had cruised through the qualifying campaign, a draw in Austria and shock defeat in Northern Ireland the only blemishes in the 10-match series. England were named as one of the eight seeded countries, and the draw could scarcely have been more favourable. Nine of the players who had gone to Japan and Korea were still there. Steven Gerrard and Gary Neville, who both missed out through injury in 2002, were naturally champing at the bit this time round. With John Terry, Frank Lampard and the mercurial Wayne Rooney added to the mix, Eriksson pronounced it the strongest squad he had led into battle. It was also better prepared than any before, the domestic season having been compressed to allow the players an extra week together prior to the big kick-off. It really did seem that '40 years of hurt' might finally be soothed away by the healing balm of World Cup victory.

Sven's strike force poser

The problems began as the clock ticked round to June 9, and revolved round the first-choice strike partnership. Michael Owen had had an injury-hit season at Newcastle, and Rooney was stretchered off with a broken metatarsal in United's championship showdown with Chelsea at Stamford Bridge. Both were included, but with only two other recognised strikers on the plane, Peter Crouch and surprise wildcard selection Theo Walcott, the firepower options looked thin. Sven hadn't seen Arsenal's 17-year-old whiz kid play, but picked him ahead of proven Premiership strikers Jermain Defoe and Darren Bent, a decision that left many pundits scratching their heads.

BELOW: *The England team training at Frankfurt Stadium on the eve of their opening World Cup 2006 group match against Paraguay.*

The campaign got off to a dream start against Paraguay, David Beckham's third-minute free kick skimming off the head of defender Carlos Gamarra for the only goal of the game. Next up were rank outsiders Trinidad and Tobago, who frustrated England until the 83rd minute, when Crouch rose to plant Beckham's cross past Shaka Hislop. Gerrard's left-foot screamer in injury-time sealed the win and confirmed England's place in the last 16 with a game to spare. The performances hadn't been scintillating, but it was the best start to a World Cup campaign since 1982, and better than Ramsey's men had managed in '66. More significantly, Rooney took his World Cup bow as a second-half substitute, well ahead of schedule.

Owen limps out

The 38-year winless streak against Sweden continued in the group decider. Joe Cole volleyed into the top corner from 35 yards and then turned provider when his cross was met perfectly by Gerrard. However, defensive lapses from set pieces allowed Sweden to level twice, and it could have been worse as the bar saved England on one occasion and Gerrard cleared off the line on another. It was a case of job done, topping the group and thereby avoiding Germany in the last 16, but England had again failed to press home their advantage after a promising start. Of even greater concern was the loss of Michael Owen, who fell awkwardly in the first minute, an innocuous incident later confirmed as a cruciate ligament injury.

David Beckham had come in for considerable criticism over his performances in the group matches, many commentators beginning to question his place in the side. The skipper issued the perfect riposte with a trademark free kick which beat Ecuador in the first knockout round. Beckham became the first English player to score in three World Cups, his 30-yard curler setting up a mouthwatering clash with Portugal, the team that had dumped England out of Euro 2004. It also meant Sven v Big Phil Take Three, for Portugal coach Luis Felipe Scolari had also masterminded Brazil's victory over England in Japan and Korea. The fact that the FA had courted Scolari as a possible successor to Eriksson added extra spice to the occasion.

Shades of '98

The game proved to be an eerie reworking of France '98: a hotheaded moment from the young golden boy resulting in a red card; 10-man England valiantly holding out for the remainder of the match and extra-time, only to suffer an agonising shoot-out defeat. Back then it was Beckham, this time it was Rooney, red-carded just after the hour mark for

FA CUP FINALS

Year				Score
2000	Chelsea	v	Aston Villa	1-0
2001	Liverpool	v	Arsenal	2-1
2002	Arsenal	v	Chelsea	2-0
2003	Arsenal	v	Southampton	1-0
2004	Manchester United	v	Millwall	3-0
2005	Arsenal	v	Manchester United	0-0 (5-4 pens.)
2006	Liverpool	v	West Ham United	3-3 (3-1 pens.)
2007	Chelsea	v	Manchester United	1-0
2008	Portsmouth	v	Cardiff	1-0
2009	Chelsea	v	Everton	2-1

a stamping incident involving Chelsea's Ricardo Carvalho. After a goalless 120 minutes, Portugal missed twice from the spot, but that open invitation to proceed to the semis was declined as Lampard, Gerrard and Carragher all fluffed their lines.

An emotional David Beckham relinquished the captaincy the following day, though he stressed that he wanted to extend his international career under new supremo Steve McClaren. Eriksson's verdict on his five-year reign as England boss was that a quarter-final exit in 2002 and 2004 was acceptable, but for the high-calibre class of 2006 reaching the last eight represented a disappointing underachievement.

OPPOSITE: *Steven Gerrard scores in England's group match against Sweden.*
RIGHT: *Sven-Goran Eriksson and Steve McClaren during England's opening group match against Paraguay.*
BELOW: *Wayne Rooney fights for the ball with Portugal's Ricardo Carvalho (left) and Petit (right).*

United Back on top

After ceding the Premiership title to rivals Arsenal and Chelsea for the past three seasons, Manchester United returned to the position of top dogs in 2006-07. Only Chelsea managed to hang on to United's coattails; Liverpool and Arsenal fought their own private battle for third place, 21 points adrift of the champions. Chelsea's faint hopes disappeared when they could manage only a 1-1 draw at the Emirates, while a Ronaldo penalty won the Manchester derby, results that left Mourinho's men with a seven-point deficit and just two games remaining. United were worthy champions, having won 28 games – four more than their nearest rivals – and found the net 83 times, 19 more than Chelsea. Their dominance was reflected in the fact that eight of the side featured in the PFA Team of the Year, including Edwin van der Sar and the entire back four. Another of that number, Cristiano Ronaldo, picked up both the PFA Player of the Year and Young Player of the Year awards, the first man to do that double since Aston Villa's Andy Gray in 1976-77.

Top flight first for Reading

Reading, tasting top-flight football for the first time in the club's 135-year history, finished a creditable eighth, just missing a Uefa Cup spot. For the other promoted sides, Watford and Sheffield United, it was a battle in the basement. The game was up for Watford long before the final day, while Charlton's hopes died with defeat at Spurs in the penultimate game of the season. It was the end of a seven-year run in the Premier League for the Addicks, who got through three managers during the course of the season.

BELOW: *Wayne Rooney celebrates scoring Manchester United's third goal in the club's 4-2 victory over Everton at Goodison Park.*

ABOVE RIGHT: *Manchester United players celebrate with the Barclays League trophy at the end of the 2006-07 season.*

BELOW RIGHT: *Michael Owen, playing for Newcastle, under pressure from Reading's Ivar Ingimarsson at the Madejski Stadium. Owen was playing his first game for the club since New Year's Eve 2005. Reading won the game 1-0.*

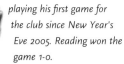

2006-07 PREMIER LEAGUE	
1 Man Utd	89
2 Chelsea	83
3 Liverpool	68
4 Arsenal	68
5 Tottenham	60
6 Everton	58
7 Bolton	56
8 Reading	55
9 Portsmouth	54
10 Blackburn	52
11 Aston Villa	50
12 Middlesbrough	46
13 Newcastle	43
14 Manchester City	42
15 West Ham United	41
16 Fulham	39
17 Wigan	38
18 Sheffield United	38
19 Charlton	34
20 Watford	28

Sheffield United relegation controversy

The last relegation spot went down to the wire, with Sheffield United, West Ham and Wigan all fighting to preserve their top-table status on the final day of the season. The Blades and the Hammers were on 38 points, Wigan on 35. West Ham faced a daunting trip to Old Trafford, while Wigan could stay up on goal difference if they could win at Bramall Lane. Sheffield United, who had been 10 points clear of the drop zone at one stage, had the most favourable position, needing only a point at home to Wigan. They went down 2-1, the winner coming from a penalty converted by former Blade David Unsworth. News came through that a Carlos Tevez goal had beaten a United side with half an eye on the Cup Final, confirming the worst for Blades fans. It couldn't have been closer between Sheffield and Wigan: the figures in the Wins, Draws and Losses columns were identical, but, crucially, Wigan had a one-goal superior goal difference.

7-goal Tevez sinks Blades

Sheffield United turned their fire on West Ham, whose survival, they argued, had in large part been down to the goalscoring efforts of Tevez. The Argentina star had arrived at Upton Park with his international team-mate Javier

Mascherano the previous August, one of the transfer coups of the summer. It emerged that the players were owned by a third-party consortium, a breach of Premier League rules. Mascherano moved to Liverpool in the January window, but Tevez remained for the relegation dogfight, firing seven goals in the last ten games. The Hammers won seven of their last nine matches; the team's hot streak mirrored that of their star striker.

West Ham were hit with a £5.5 million fine, but the fact that the club had new owners - the regime that had misinformed the Premier League over the deal had gone - appeared to have saved

them from a points deduction. That cut little ice with Blades boss Neil Warnock, who said that the club would seek legal redress. The matter would rumble on for two years before an out-of-court settlement was reached.

BELOW: *Carlos Tevez celebrates his first goal in West Ham's 3-1 victory over Bolton Wanderers. His goal-scoring achievements played a significant part in keeping United in the Premier League.*

BOTTOM: *A dejected Chris Morgan at the final whistle after Sheffield United were relegated to the Championship league when they lost 2-1 to Wigan.*

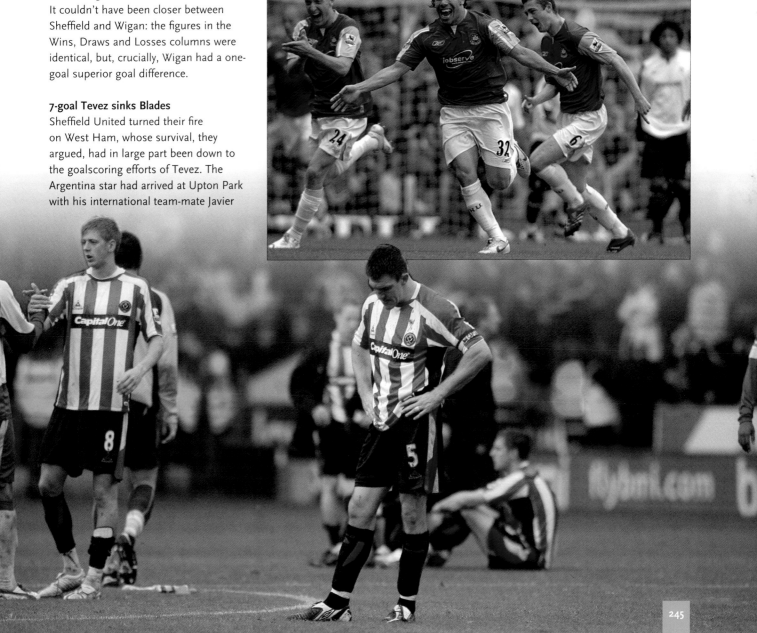

Keane leads Sunderland revival

Sunderland clinched the Championship title on the last day of the season, a remarkable reversal of fortune for a club that had been lying second bottom when Roy Keane took over. Birmingham City secured the other automatic promotion spot, leaving Billy Davies's Derby – top of the league in January – to enter the play-off lottery. The Rams beat West Brom 1-0, ending an unlucky streak for Davies, who had suffered play-off defeat with Preston two years running.

Leeds relegated

As the three promoted sides prepared for the challenge of Premier League football, and for the hike in income and expenditure that went with it, Leeds United stood as a stark warning to any club tempted to overstretch itself in the quest for glory. Leeds were relegated to football's third tier for the first time since it rose from the ashes of the defunct Leeds City in 1920. Just six years earlier the team had been Champions League semi-finalists.

Double consolation for Chelsea

Chelsea missed out in the title race but had the consolation of doing the domestic cup double. They didn't have to face Manchester United in the Carling Cup, for the holders were dumped out by a Freddie Eastwood goal at Roots Hall. Southend were unlucky to go down at Spurs in the quarters, but League Two side Wycombe Wanderers went a stage further, the first time since Chester City in 1974-75 that a team from the fourth tier of English football had made it through to a League Cup semi-final. But it was two big guns who battled it out at the Millennium Stadium, Chelsea taking on an Arsenal side packed with Arsene Wenger's whiz kids. 17-year-old Theo Walcott drew first blood, his first goal for the Gunners putting him in the record books as the second youngest player to score in a domestic cup final, behind Norman Whiteside. Two goals by the Premiership's hotshot Didier Drogba meant that the trophy went to Stamford Bridge for the second time in three years.

ABOVE RIGHT: *David Beckham, Steven Gerrard and Frank Lampard defend a Brazilian free kick in the first international match to be staged at the new Wembley.*

RIGHT: *John Terry and Frank Lampard celebrate Chelsea's 1-0 victory over Manchester United in the 2007 FA Cup.*

BELOW: *Didier Drogba scores the winning goal in the Cup Final past Manchester United keeper Edwin van der Sar.*

Drogba strikes for Mourinho's men

In the FA Cup Manchester United faced top-division opposition in each round, as they had done in the victorious 1947-48 run under Matt Busby. Chelsea had an easier ride to the final, though they had to come back from 3-1 down to Spurs in the Sixth Round to force a replay, where Mourinho's men prevailed. An extra-time semi-final win over Blackburn carried Chelsea into the first final at the new Wembley. It was another extra-time goal that decided the showpiece, Drogba prodding the ball past the advancing van der Sar after playing a deft one-two with Lampard.

Three english teams reach Champions League Semis

Chelsea and United also reached the semi-finals of the Champions League, along with Liverpool, who had put out holders Barcelona in the first knockout round. It was the first time that Premiership clubs had occupied three semi-final berths in the Champions League, and the bookies' odds suggested that the trophy was heading to England as the last off the quartet, AC Milan, were installed as outsiders.

Milan made a mockery of the betting with a crushing 5-3 aggregate victory over Manchester United. United took a narrow 3-2 lead to a rain-soaked San Siro, where they were comprehensively outplayed. Kaka added to the brace he bagged at Old Trafford after 11 minutes, and goals from Seedorf and Gilardino made it a forgettable evening for United fans. Liverpool heaped more semi-final misery on Chelsea, going through on penalties to set up a repeat of the extraordinary 2005 final, this time in Athens.

The Reds went behind on the stroke of half-time, Pippo Inzaghi deflecting a Pirlo free kick past Reina. Milan doubled their lead eight minutes from time when Inzaghi, played through by Kaka, rounded Reina to score from a narrow angle. Kuyt headed a late consolation but there was no repeat of the dramatic comeback in Istanbul.

BOTTOM: *Joe Cole scores past Jose Reina in the UEFA Champions League Semi-final between Chelsea and Liverpool at Stamford Bridge. Chelsea won the game 1-0.*
BELOW: *Dirk Kuyt scores Liverpool's only goal as they go down 2-1 in the final to AC Milan at the Olympic Stadium in Athens.*

United and Chelsea contest the major honors

Manchester United and Chelsea occupied the top two spots in the Premiership for the third year running in 2007-08, and continued their battle royal in Moscow, where the teams contested a dramatic Champions League final.

There was early-season turmoil in both camps. United dropped seven points in their first three games and found themselves at the wrong end of the table, the club's worst start to a Premiership campaign for a decade. It never looked to be anything other than a blip, however, and a run of 14 wins and a draw in their next 16 games put the reigning champions on course to defend their crown.

Mourinho exit

Chelsea's wobble – defeat at Villa, two points dropped at home to Blackburn and a tame draw against Rosenborg at the Bridge in the Champions League – had rather more significant fall-out. Barely a month into the season it was announced that Jose Mourinho, the man who had spoken of building an all-conquering dynasty at Chelsea, was leaving 'by mutual consent'. Despite guiding Chelsea to two championships and three domestic cups in just three years, the Special One paid the price for falling out of favour with his employers. Avram Grant, who had joined the club as director of football just two months earlier, was handed the top job and invited to follow an extremely tough act.

Chelsea's 2-1 defeat by Spurs in the Carling Cup final was to set an unfortunate pattern for Grant; two more runners-up spots awaited him, and he would find that second place wasn't good enough for a club that had grown accustomed to amassing silverware.

Records fall to Giggs

Arsenal and Liverpool both remained unbeaten in the league until December, but it was United and Chelsea who were battling for the Premiership crown at the business end of the season. The teams met at Stamford Bridge with three games to go, United holding a three-point advantage. A Michael Ballack double gave Chelsea a 2-1 win and brought them level, though United remained top on goal difference. Both won their next games to take the race to the final game of the season. United went to Wigan knowing that victory would secure the championship; anything less could allow Chelsea, who were playing host to Bolton, to snatch the crown. In the event, it was Chelsea who faltered, conceding a late equaliser, though it hardly mattered as United ran out 2-0 winners at the JJB.

Ronaldo bagged his 31st Premiership goal – he would find the net an astonishing 42 times in all competitions – while a Ryan Giggs strike ensured that the championship was on its way to Old Trafford yet again. It was Giggs's 758th outing in a United shirt, equalling Bobby Charlton's record. He would set a new mark in the Champions League final.

BOTTOM: *Chelsea's Frank Lampard equalises to make the score 1-1 in the all English Champions League final between Chesea and Manchester United at the Luzhniki Stadium in Moscow.*
BELOW: *Manchester United's Wayne Rooney and Chelsea's Ricardo Carvalho compete for the ball in the Champions League final.*

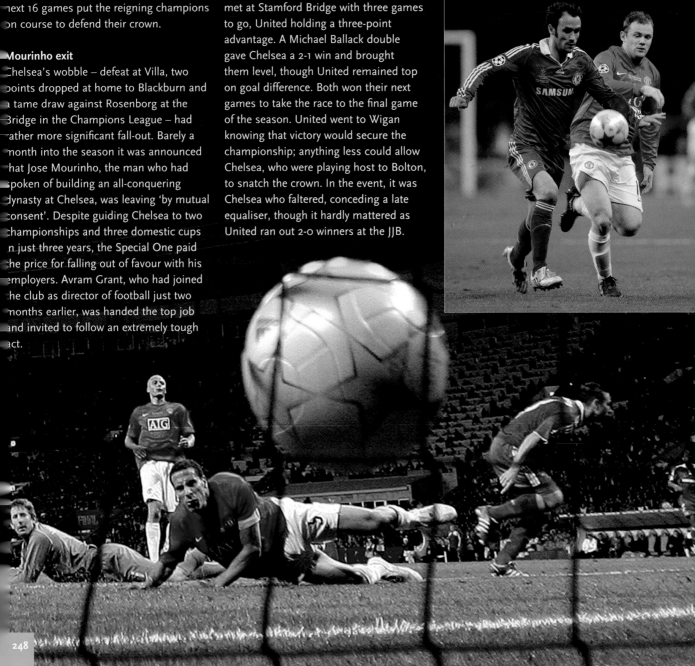

Living the dream

At the other end of the table, promoted Derby County set an unwanted Premier League record by confirming their return to the Championship before March was out, with six games still to play. The Rams ended the campaign with a solitary win and just 11 points to show for their efforts. Birmingham City and Reading joined them, Fulham finishing above Steve Coppell's side by virtue of a three-goal better goal difference.

The Championship provided a romantic counterpoint to the harsh realities of a results business. West Brom went up as champions, the Baggies' third promotion to the Premier League in seven years. Joining them were Stoke City, bringing top-flight football back to the Potteries for the first time since 1985. But it was Hull City's fans who had to pinch themselves to make sure they really were 'living the dream'. Victory over Bristol City in the play-off final meant the Tigers were in the elite division for the first time in their 104-year history.

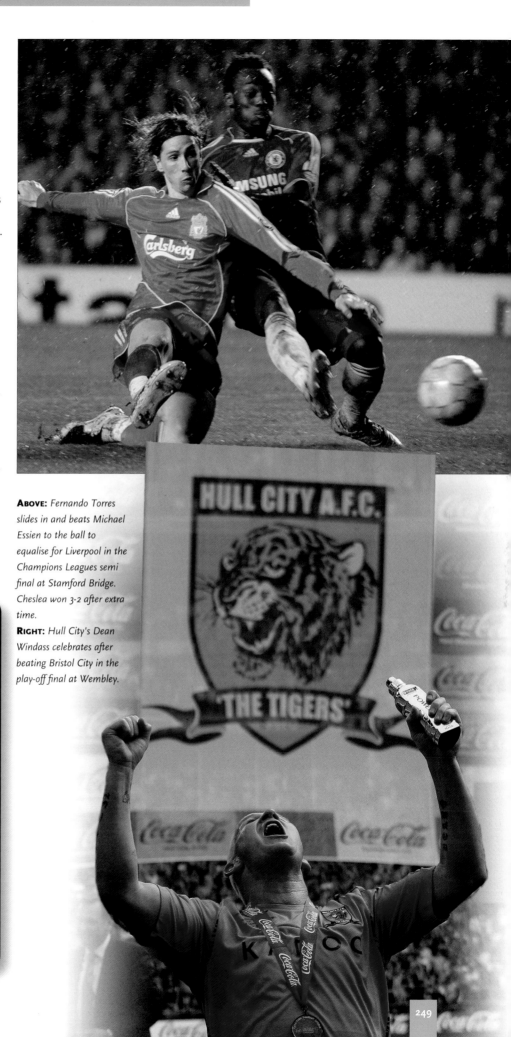

ABOVE: *Fernando Torres slides in and beats Michael Essien to the ball to equalise for Liverpool in the Champions Leagues semi final at Stamford Bridge. Cheslea won 3-2 after extra time.*

RIGHT: *Hull City's Dean Windass celebrates after beating Bristol City in the play-off final at Wembley.*

2007-08 PREMIER LEAGUE	
1 Man Utd	87
2 Chelsea	85
3 Arsenal	83
4 Liverpool	76
5 Everton	65
6 Aston Villa	60
7 Blackburn	58
8 Portsmouth	57
9 Manchester City	55
10 West Ham United	49
11 Tottenham	46
12 Newcastle	43
13 Middlesbrough	42
14 Wigan	40
15 Sunderland	39
16 Bolton	37
17 Fulham	36
18 Reading	36
19 Birmingham City	35
20 Derby County	11

Pompey play up

The 2008 FA Cup provided a breath of fresh air, ending a 12-year run in which the trophy had gone to one of the Big Four. Havant & Waterlooville of the Conference South encapsulated the giant-killing mood by twice taking the lead at Anfield before going down 5-2 in the Fourth Round. Championship strugglers Barnsley put the Reds out in the next round, and repeated the trick against Chelsea in the quarters. At the same stage a Sulley Muntari penalty gave Portsmouth victory over Manchester United, while Cardiff City's win at Boro meant that there was just one top-flight team in the last four, the first time that had happened in a hundred years. Not everyone put that down to the vagaries of cup football; Bobby Robson was among those who bemoaned the fact that some top teams appeared to be disrespecting the competition by fielding weakened sides.

A spectacular Joe Ledley volley settled the Cardiff-Barnsley semi, putting the Bluebirds into their first final since the historic win over Arsenal in 1927. They faced West Brom's conquerors Portsmouth, who prevailed in the showpiece courtesy of a Kanu goal. The Cup went to Fratton Park for only the second time in the club's history, the first having come 69 years earlier, on the eve of the Second World War.

England fail to qualify for Euro 2008

There was no little irony in the fact that while Premiership clubs dominated the Champions League, the national team failed to qualify for the finals of Euro 2008. Defeats in Croatia and Russia were setbacks, but being held to a goalless draw at home to Macedonia was a major body blow. Israel did England a huge favour by beating Russia in the final round of matches, which left Steve McClaren's men requiring just a point at home to a Croatia side that had already booked their place in Austria and Switzerland. England failed to grasp the lifeline. A 3-2 defeat meant that the team missed out on a major tournament for the first time since the 1994 World Cup. There was a small crumb of comfort as Russia went on to reach the semi-finals, and Croatia came within a whisker of joining them, though it was of little consequence to McClaren, who had long since been shown the door.

FA appoint Capello

The FA again looked overseas for a replacement, appointing Fabio Capello, a coach with impeccable credentials. In 16 seasons of club management Capello had won nine championships with four different clubs in two countries. The two Serie A successes with Juventus were revoked in the wake of the corruption scandal that rocked Italian football, but Capello's cv was still first rate.

BELOW: *Portsmouth's manager Harry Redknapp holds the FA Cup aloft following Portsmouth's 1-0 victory over Cardiff. It was Pompey's second FA Cup victory.*

BOTTOM: *The new England manager Fabio Capello watches his team against Trinidad at Port of Spain.*

Europe: big four make last eight

The Premiership's Big Four all made it through to the last eight of the Champions League, a record for the competition. Manchester United and Barcelona faced each other after comfortable wins over Roma and Schalke respectively. Chelsea overturned a 2-1 defeat at Fenerbahce to set up yet another semi-final clash with Liverpool, who overcame Arsenal 5-3 on aggregate. It was the third time in four years the clubs had met in the last four, the Reds running out winners on the two previous occasions. Chelsea had their revenge this time, Drogba grabbing a brace in the 3-2 extra-time victory at the Bridge, after the game at Anfield had finished level. In the final they faced Manchester United, who saw off Barcelona with a 25-yard Paul Scholes drive in the home leg. Sir

Alex Ferguson praised the pocket genius who had missed the 1999 final through suspension, confirming that he would be on the team-sheet for Moscow.

First all English Championship final

The first European Champions' Cup final to be contested by two English clubs was all square after 120 minutes, Lampard's goal on the stroke of half-time cancelling out a Ronaldo header. Drogba saw red during an extra-time fracas, but United had little time to capitalise on the man advantage. Ronaldo, the Premiership's top scorer, missed from the spot, a lapse that paved the way for John Terry to shoot for cup glory. He slipped at the crucial moment and saw his effort rebound off the post. Chelsea blinked first in the sudden-death exchange, van

der Sar saving from Anelka. Terry was inconsolable as United celebrated being crowned kings of Europe for the third time on the 50th anniversary of the Munich disaster.

BOTTOM: *Manchester United players pictured after winning the Champions League cup. United celebrated being crowned kings of Europe for the third time on the 50th anniversary of the Munich disaster.*

BELOW LEFT: *United's Christiano Ronaldo scores to put his team into the lead.*

BELOW: *John Terry shoots for cup glory but slips at the crucial moment and sees his effort rebound off the post. Terry was inconsolable as United went on to win after van der Sar saved Anelka's spot kick.*

United match Liverpool's league record

There was a time when talk of Doubles and Trebles was regarded as fantasy football. The elite clubs had shown that such giddy heights were indeed attainable, and the fans, with inflationary zeal, were already looking for the next target. Midway through the 2008-09 season, the buzz on the Old Trafford terraces was all about United's bid for an unprecedented Quintuple.

The reigning champions, bolstered by the arrival of £30 million striker Dimitar Berbatov, deposited one trophy in the cabinet before Christmas by winning the World Club Cup, beating LDU Quito in the

final. Next up was the Carling Cup final and a shoot-out victory over Spurs. United were in a rich vein of form, underpinned by a near-impregnable defence. When Roque Santa Cruz scored at Old Trafford on 21 February, it was the first goal United had conceded in the Premiership since the 2-1 defeat at Arsenal on 8 November. Edwin van der Sar's run of 1334 minutes without picking the ball out of the net smashed Petr Cech's record.

Liverpool's double consolation
Liverpool ran United close, and completed a league double over their arch-rivals with a stunning 4-1 win at Old Trafford in March. United then lost at Fulham, but steadied the ship by reeling off seven straight victories. The title was secured with a game to spare, United ending the campaign four points clear of the Reds, whose record of 18 championships they had now equalled. Benitez's side had undoubtedly closed the gap, losing just twice in the league. No team had ever failed to take the league crown with such a record, but a double-digit figure in the Draws column proved costly; United's 28 wins was the key statistic. It was the 11th title of the Ferguson era – Ryan Giggs playing a part in each of those glorious campaigns - and the second time that United had completed a hat-trick of championships.

RIGHT: *Sir Alex Ferguson celebrates another Premiership title following the game against Arsenal at Old Trafford. The title was secured with a game to spare, United ending the campaign four points clear of Liverpool, whose record of 18 championships they had now equalled.*

ABOVE: *Wayne Rooney and Dimitar Berbatov, who arrived from Spurs for £30 million at the start of the season, celebrate winning the Premier League title.*

ABOVE RIGHT: *Liverpool's Yossi Benayoun scores against Newcastle. At the end of the season The Magpies were relegated to the Championship after 16 years in the top flight.*

Aston Villa fall away

Aston Villa flirted with breaking the stranglehold the Big Four exerted on the division, but fell away at the business end of the campaign. Chelsea, revitalised by the arrival of Guus Hiddink after dispensing with 'Big Phil' Scolari's services in February, took third, while some Arsenal fans felt that mere Champions League qualification was insubstantial fare after four trophyless years.

Shearer can't save Newcastle

At the other end of the table, West Brom knew their fate before the final round of matches, relegated after just one season back in the top flight. That left two clubs from four to face the drop. Middlesbrough, in 19th place, needed a highly unlikely turn of events to avoid the trapdoor, while for the fans of the three teams immediately above them, Newcastle, Hull and Sunderland, it was a case of keeping an eye on the pitch and an ear to the radio. Hull and Sunderland faced Man U and Chelsea sides that had Champions League and FA Cup finals on their minds, while Newcastle had to go to Villa Park. In the event, calculators weren't needed; all four lost and the table remained unaltered. It was a black day in the north-east –Wearside apart – as Boro and Newcastle ended 13 and 16-year stays respectively in the top flight. For Alan Shearer, who steered his side to just one win in eight after taking the managerial hotseat, it was proof that Newcastle needed more than a messianic hand on the tiller.

2008-09 PREMIER LEAGUE	
1 Man Utd	90
2 Liverpool	86
3 Chelsea	83
4 Arsenal	72
5 Everton	63
6 Aston Villa	62
7 Fulham	53
8 Tottenham	51
9 West Ham United	51
10 Manchester City	50
11 Wigan	45
12 Stoke	45
13 Bolton	41
14 Portsmouth	41
15 Blackburn	41
16 Sunderland	36
17 Hull City	35
18 Newcastle	34
19 Middlesbrough	32
20 West Bromwich Albion	32

LEFT: Aston Villa's Ashley Young celebtates a goal. Villa spent much of the season in the top four but fell away towards the end of the campaign, as once again, United, Chelsea, Liverpool and Arsenal occupied the top 4 positions.

ABOVE: Alan Shearer steered his side to just one win in eight after taking the managerial hotseat but Newcastle were relegated to the championship on the last day of the season.

BELOW: Wayne Rooney scores England's opener in the World Cup qualifier against Andorra at Wembley. England went on to win the match 6-0.

Burnley back in the top tier

Wolves secured their place in the Premiership long before the end of the campaign, and Birmingham landed the other automatic promotion spot with a final-day victory at Reading. In the play-off final Burnley faced Sheffield United, who thought they had unfinished Premiership business after suffering relegation in 2006-07. The Blades had just won an out-of-court settlement in their suit against West Ham over the Carlos Tevez affair, but suffered their third play-off defeat as a Wade Elliott rocket won the most lucrative match in world football match for the Clarets. Burnley were back at the top table for the first time since 1976.

Saha's record strike fails to stop Chelsea

Manchester United's bid for a clean sweep ended with an FA Cup semi-final defeat at the hands of Everton. Sir Alex Ferguson had reached that stage eight times and never tasted defeat, but came unstuck as an under-strength side went down on penalties. Everton had put already put out Liverpool and Villa, and faced yet another top-six side in the final, Chelsea. Louis Saha gave the Merseysiders a dream start with a goal after 25 seconds, the fastest in the competition's history. Chelsea equalised through a Drogba header and Lampard's left-foot drive ensured that the

cup was going to Stamford Bridge for the fifth time. It was a red-letter day for Ashley Cole, who became the first player in over a century to pick up five winners' medals.

BOTTOM: *Didier Drogba scores Chelsea's first goal in their 2-1 victory over Everton in the 2009 FA Cup final. Saha had put the Merseyside club ahead after only 25 seconds.*

RIGHT: *Everton manager David Moyes tastes defeat at Wembley. In previous rounds Everton had knocked out Manchester United, Villa and Liverpool.*

BELOW: *John Terry lifts the FA Cup for Chelsea while Frank Lampard displays his delight.*

No Euro repeat for Ferguson

The Premiership's Big Four all reached the Champions League quarter-finals once again. Arsenal and United eased into the last four with wins over Villareal and Porto, but the tie of the round was a Liverpool-Chelsea clash that brought an avalanche of goals. Chelsea went through 7-5 on aggregate to book their fifth semi-final berth in six years.

United brushed Arsenal aside in the semis, and a repeat of the 2008 final looked to be on the cards when Chelsea returned from the Nou Camp with a 0-0 draw. Hiddink's men also nullified Barcelona's much-vaunted attack for 90 minutes in the home leg, and seemed to be heading for the final thanks to Essien's thunderous volley. The game was turned on its head deep into injury time when Chelsea's rock-solid defence opened up fleetingly, enough for Iniesta to find the

top corner from the edge of the box. There were unedifying scenes as Chelsea players berated the Norwegian referee, who had rejected several penalty claims.

Many thought a Barca team shorn of three first-choice defenders would struggle to contain Rooney, Ronaldo and Co., but it was La Liga's champions who played to their potential, while the United machine for once misfired. Xavi and

Iniesta were the orchestrators-in-chief, while Eto'o and Messi struck in each half to consign United to their first defeat in a major European final. United had to settle for three trophies, and their 67-year-old manager immediately began planning for the acquisition of further silverware with a squad he regarded as the best in his 23 years at Old Trafford.

LEFT: *John O'Shea celebrates his goal in the Champions League semi-final against Arsenal at Old Trafford.*
ABOVE RIGHT: *Man of the Match Lionel Messi takes on Wayne Rooney and Michael Carrick in the Champions League final at the Stadio Olympico, Rome. Barcelona went on to win the game 2-0.*
RIGHT: *Manchester United goalkeeper Ben Foster celebrates with his teammates following their victory over Spurs in the Carling Cup.*

Acknowledgements

The photographs in this book are from the archives of the *Daily Mail*.
Particular thanks to Alan Pinnock for his invaluable knowledge and research.

Thanks also to:
Steve Torrington, Dave Sheppard, Brian Jackson, Alan Pinnock, Richard Jones and all the staff at Associated Newspapers.

Cliff Salter, Richard Betts, Peter Wright, Trevor Bunting, Alice Hill, Simon Taylor,
Gareth Thomas, Jane Hill, Carol Salter, Corinne Hill, Jim Carpenter, Maureen Hill,
Harry Nettleton, Tom Nettleton, Matthew Nee, Barry Hoile and Duncan Hill
Design by John Dunne.

The following photographs are Copyright Topham Picturepoint:
Pages: 9T; 10T; 11B; 13M; 14B; 15T ;20T; 27B.

The Lakeland Fells

Only a hill: earth set a little higher
above the face of earth: a larger view
of little fields and roads: a little nigher
to clouds and silence: what is that to you?
Only a hill; but all of life to me,
up there, between the sunset and the sea.

from 'A Hill' by Geoffrey Winthrop Young
in *Wind and Hill*, Smith, Elder and Co, 1909

Jill M.Aldersley

The Lakeland Fells

The Fell and Rock Climbing Club's
complete illustrated guide for walkers

Edited by

June Parker and Tim Pickles

Fell and Rock Climbing Club
The Ernest Press

The Lakeland Fells
The Fell and Rock Climbing Club's complete illustrated guide for walkers

Edited by June Parker and Tim Pickles
Published by the Fell and Rock Climbing Club of the English Lake District and The Ernest Press

First published 1996.

A catalogue record for this book is available from the British Library.
ISBN 0-85028-039-7

Designed by Tim Pickles and Peter Hodgkiss
Typeset by Tim Pickles
Produced by Peter Hodgkiss
Graphic reproduction by Arneg, Glasgow
Printed by GNP–Booth, Glasgow
Bound by Hunter & Foulis, Edinburgh
Distributed by Cordee, 3a De Montfort Street, Leicester LE1 7HD

Front cover: Pillar Rock from Robinson's Cairn (Colin Fearnley)
End papers: The Langdale fells from Gummer's How (from an original watercolour by Jill Aldersley)
Frontispiece: Napes Needle (from an original watercolour by Jill Aldersley)
Rear Cover: The head of Wasdale (Peter Fleming)

The Fell and Rock Climbing Club will donate part of the profits from the sale of this book to wards the costs of fell conservation in the Lake District.

All enquiries regarding this book should be sent in the first instance to the editors at:
The Archway, 17 St John Street, Keswick, Cumbria CA12 5AE.

Disclaimer
The publishers, editors and contributors have taken all reasonable care to ensure that the information in this book is accurate at the time of publication. The routes described use definitive footpaths, bridleways and other commonly used routes across open land. It should be remembered that most land in the Lake District is privately owned. The description of a route in this book is not meant to signify a right of way. If in doubt about access, please ask the landowner first.
The publishers, editors and contributors are not responsible for the actions, behaviour and omissions of walkers using this book. Walkers must use their own judgement and assess local conditions before venturing onto the hills. If in doubt, please consult the appropriate authority.

Dedication

To those who first introduced us to these hills

Acknowledgements

Producing a guide of this complexity requires the collaborative efforts of many people. In addition to the contributors and sponsors identified elsewhere in these pages, we would particularly like to acknowledge:

The Ordnance Survey for their excellent maps of the area

The National Park wardens for their assistance with this project

The Lake District Mountain Rescue Teams for their unstinting work
(Please note that teams receive no subsidy and that members give their time voluntarily)

The National Trust for its sterling work as stewards of so much of this area

The earlier guidebook writers for showing us the way

Contributors and sponsors

The Fell and Rock Climbing Club thanks the following people for their help in creating this book:

Concept
Stephen Reid

Editors
June Parker
Tim Pickles

Writers
Richard Barnes
Clive Beveridge
Chris Bonington
Andy Coatsworth
Richard Coatsworth
Chris Craggs
Bill Comstive
Neil Dowie
Cath and Paul Exley
Irene Farrington
Don Greenop
Dave Gregory
Hatty Harris
Paul Hudson
Ron Kenyon
Maureen Linton
Sylvia Loxam
Chris and Ron Lyon
Lesley Marlow
John Moore
June Parker
Alasdair Pettifer
Tim Pickles
Roy and Norma Precious
Tom Price
Trevor Price
Bill Roberts
Les Shore
Alan Slater
John Slater
David Staton
Pauline Sweet
Iain and Brenda Whitmey
Adrian Wiszniewski

Cartographers
Clive Beveridge
Paul Hudson
Tim Pickles
Adrian Wiszniewski

Photographers
Jill Aldersley
Richard Barnes
Stella Berkeley
Clive Beveridge
Jack Carswell
Andy Coatsworth
Bill Comstive
Brian Cosby
Chris Craggs
Paul Exley
Irene Farrington
Colin Fearnley
Peter Fleming
Richard Gibbens
Don Greenop
Dave Gregory
Hatty Harris
Peter Hodgkiss
Ron Kenyon
Mike Margeson
David Miller
Peter Moffat
Graham Moss
June and Alan Parker
Al Phizacklea
Stephen Reid
Ken Richards
Bill Roberts
Mark Scott
Ernest Shepherd
Les Shore
David Staton
Stan Thompson
Colin Wells
Iain Whitmey
Adrian Wiszniewski
Alick Woods

Route checkers
The writers, plus
Donald Brumfitt
Irene Farrington
Hugh Mantle and Maggie Fulton
Ann McWatt
Audrey Plint
Alison and Richard Williams
George Wright

Proofreaders
Andy Coatsworth
Cath Exley
Maureen Linton

Administration
John Coates
Ron Kenyon

Sponsors
Michael Ackerley
Pat and Jack Baines
Richard Barnes
Clive Beveridge
Aubrey Brocklehurst
Peter Brunt
Margaret Chapman
Andy Coatsworth
Bill Comstive
John Dee
Cath and Paul Exley
Livia Gollancz
Jim Haggas
Andrew Hall
George Hall
AB Hargreaves
Margaret Harris
David Hill
Ruth and Harry Ironfield
Hatty Harris
Peter Hodgkiss
Ron Kenyon
Peter Ledeboer
Sylvia Loxam
Ron and Chris Lyon
Neville Morton
June and Alan Parker
Helen Pickles
May Pickles
Tim Pickles
Audrey Plint
Stephen Reid
Bill Roberts
Margaret Roberts
Nancy Smith
Iain and Brenda Whitmey
LS Wilson

The author and photographer of each contribution to this book are identified on page 210.

Contents

Blencathra from the NE ridge of Hindscarth

Foreword

by Chris Bonington

On coming back from a trip, I'm often asked "Isn't it an anti-climax when you get back?" The answer is an emphatic "No". It doesn't matter where I've been climbing. Each time I return to our Lakeland Fells my conviction that this tiny range of mountains is as varied and as beautiful as anything in the world is even more strongly reinforced.

There are so many different factors that contribute to this unique equation. It starts with the form of the hills and valleys, created by geological upheaval and then carved out by glaciers in the ice age. These yield the valleys and cirques, the lakes and tarns that give this mountain range its name. But there is more to it than that. There is a subtlety of tone and colour in the Lakes that I have seen nowhere else. It is a terrain crafted by man since ealiest times. Clearings were made in the dense oak forests that filled the valleys in Neolithic times, in man's first ventures into agriculture. Mining followed and with it charcoal burning. The forests contributed to the wooden hulls of the British Navy in the eighteenth century and the Lake District took on the form recognisable today with its patchwork of drystone walls in the valleys, snug farm houses and, up on the fell, a sward grazed by countless generations of sheep.

I have now climbed, wandered and lived around the Lake District for over thirty years and yet still find tops and valleys to which I have never been, or even on familiar hills, little folds and facets that give a fresh perspective to familiar and much loved views. There is the constant change of light and shade, at different times of day and year. On a wild winter's day, when the tops are clad in hard packed ice and snow, the mountains can feel as fierce as any in the world. On the other hand, on a summer's evening, the hills have a gentle beauty that is unsurpassed anywhere.

The Lakes became a tourist area as early as the eighteenth century, immortalised by the poetry of Wordsworth and Coleridge, both of whom walked so prodigiously. It was Coleridge who make one of the first rock climbs, admittedly in descent, on the way down Broad Stand in 1802. Once climbing began to develop as a sport in the mid-nineteenth century, initially as training for the Alps, but very quickly as a sport in its own right, the crags of the Lakes became a climbers' Mecca. The Fell and Rock Climbing Club, founded in 1906 is one of Britain's oldest clubs and its members have always had an appreciation for wandering the fells as well as cragging.

It is particularly appropriate therefore that the combined knowledge and experience of so many club members should be concentrated in this wonderfully full and comprehensive guide to the Lakes.

Small Water and High Street from Harter Fell

Langdale Pikes from near Elterwater

Introduction

Grasmoor group and Great Gable from Scafell Pike

Guides to the Lakes

The Lakeland Fells provides, in one volume, a complete walker's guide to all the hills and mountains within the Lake District National Park. It aims to be comprehensive with descriptions of every fell over 300 metres, informative in the detail and interest given for each entry, and authoritative in its accuracy.

Since Thomas West first published his 'Guide to the Lakes' in 1778, when the major influx of visitors to this area began, several hundred guidebooks have been written. Some of these have become classics, worthy of regular reprints. The guides by WG Collingwood and William Wordsworth are obvious examples. Others by Harriet Martineau, Jonathan Otley, and Henry Jenkinson are equally deserving of attention for their contemporary descriptions. All the early guides described the landscape of the Lakes. Although rock climbing guides to the area were written around the turn of the century by WP Haskett-Smith, OG Jones and George and Ashley Abraham, the first exclusively walking guide to the fells did not appear until 1933.

The preparation of this guide would have been a great deal harder without these forerunners. The first standard guide to the central fells, HH Symonds's 'Walking in the Lake District' was followed by WG Poucher's 'The Lakeland Peaks' which uses extensive photographs to illustrate his selected ascents. The seven volume (eight including 'The Outlying Fells') of Alfred Wainwright's 'A Pictorial Guide to the Lakeland Fells' is probably the most well known and comprehensive description of all the various approach walks to the summits. To appreciate the wealth of information and the attention to detail in these hand-written books, it is necessary to spend some time walking the fells in their company. Their preparation – by a man who did not drive – was truly a labour of love. The contributors to this book acknowledge their debt to all three of these authors.

In recent years there has been an explosion in walking guides to the Lake District, including Bill Birkett's 'Complete Lakeland Fells' identifying 541 fell tops. Many of these guides are more selective in nature, covering either walks in a particular area or choosing the author's favourites. Others cater for specific groups or interests such as walks for motorists or naturalists.

Is there room for another guide? We believe there is. *The Lakeland Fells* provides a guide to all the mountains in the National Park in one volume. For each mountain or hill it describes quality routes to the summit. The descriptions are complemented by sketch maps and colour photographs which help to locate the walk and indicate the type of terrain covered. All the contributors have sought to describe what they consider to be the most interesting routes – which may not necessarily be the shortest and are rarely the standard 'tourist' route. The walk descriptions may include references to the geology, flora and fauna of the fells and to their associated historical, archeological, literary and cultural association to help the user become more familiar with this rich and diverse landscape. Some of the fells have been grouped together to provide longer circuits. Others are described singly for the benefit of those requiring shorter walks. The descriptions and photographs have been prepared at different times throughout the year enabling the contrast between winter snowscapes, spring freshness, summer hazes and autumn colours to be fully appreciated. Finally, the book has been produced by members of The Fell and Rock Climbing Club, the leading mountaineering club in the Lake District whose members have a wide and comprehensive knowledge of the area. This walking guide also complements the Club's publication since 1922 of the definitive rock climbing guides to the Lake District.

How to use this guide

At one time, walkers used to compile their own lists of fells over 2,000 or 2,500 feet, then made a point of visiting them all. Some regarded only hills over 2,000 feet as 'mountains' but there is no hard and fast definition of the word mountain. 'Fell' is a local word of Scandinavian origin which is synonymous with 'hill'. For practical purposes fell, hill and mountain are interchangeable but the word 'top' is reserved for those lesser summits which are distinctly subsidiary to a nearby higher fell.

Wainwright's guides include 214 fells over 1000 feet in height and many thousands of walkers now regard his list as definitive. Our purpose in compiling this guidebook is to design a comprehensive and varied selection of walks which enable walkers to reach all the major fells by routes which are enjoyable, aesthetically pleasing and well within the capacity of the average walker. We have avoided strict rules for inclusion of this or that summit based on minimum lateral separation or minimum height difference. In choosing the routes, there has never been a tendency to include as many tops as possible in the round: this means that some fine classic walks, such as the Fairfield Horseshoe, have not been explicitly included although such routes are always pointed out in the text.

With the advent of metric maps, 1000 feet converts to 304.8 metres and for greater convenience we have chosen to make a cut-off point at 300 metres. The decision as to which fells to include is not an easy one owing to the proximity of many summits along ridges. Our list seeks to identify all those fells over 300 metres, with public access and lying within the National Park. In a few respects this differs from Wainwright's list. For example, we have added Iron Crag, Carling Knott, Knock Murton, Ponsonby Fell and Swainson Knott in the Western Fells. In the Southern Fells both Broad Crag and Ill Crag have been added as separate fells in their own right. A decision was taken to include Bakestall (on Skiddaw) and Mungrisdale Common (behind Blencathra) as fells with a separate status, in spite of the fact that they are ignored by many other guidebook writers. This is not only because they are in AW's list and many readers would object to their absence but also because it was found that satisfying routes to them could be devised.

Unfortunately, difficulties with public access, particularly in the Far Eastern Fells, have led to the omission of some hills including those around Crookdale. There is also no public right of way onto The Nab. The final result of these decisions is a total of 243 summits and 139

Far Eastern Fells   Those lying east of the Ullswater – Kirkstone Pass – Ambleside – Windermere line

Eastern Fells   Those lying between the St John's in the Vale – Thirlmere – Dunmail – Ambleside line and the Far Eastern Fells

Central Fells   Those lying within the perimeter of the Kewick – St John's in the Vale – Thirlmere – Dunmail – Ambleside – Langdale – Langstrath – River Derwent – Keswick line

Southern Fells   Those lying south and west of the Wasdale – Sty Head – Langstrath – Langdale – Windermere line

Northern Fells   Those lying north of the Cockermouth – Keswick – Penrith line

North-Western Fells   Those lying within the horseshoe formed by the River Cocker – Crummock Water – Buttermere – Honister Pass – River Derwent – Derwentwater – Bassenthwaite

Western Fells   Those lying within the horseshoe formed by River Cocker – Crummock Water – Buttermere –Honister Pass – Sty Head – Wasdale

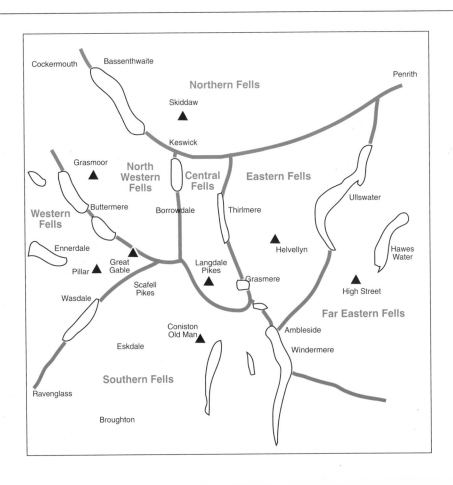

Ill Bell and Froswick

route descriptions.

The boundary of the National Park extends beyond the boundary defined by Wainwright's guides. To the east and to the south there are significant groups of lower hills which still reach over 300 metres. Many of these are described in Wainwright's *Outlying Fells* and we have identified 17 separate fells for inclusion in our list.

Castle Crag in Borrowdale presents a dilemma. This was the lowest hill in Wainwright's list at 985 feet (just 300 metres) but more recent maps have demoted it to only 290 metres. We feel its 'mountain-in-miniature' character and impressive location justify its inclusion as the lowest of our summits – a suitably idiosyncratic decision which befits any attempt to categorise these wonderful hills of Lakeland!

To make cross-referencing with other guides easier we have divided the hills into seven geographic areas which correspond with those used by Wainwright's guides as extended to the perimeter of the National Park (see table and map opposite).

The heights used throughout this guide have been taken from the OS 1:25,000 metric maps. These are given in metres with approximate conversions to feet; as one metre is 3.2808 feet, the approximation may be one or two feet either way. Those walkers who are more familiar with Wainwright's imperial heights will find differences of up to 30 feet in heights as a result of more recent aerial surveys.

Times for ascending a summit or completing a walk have been worked out on a variation of Naismith's Rule allowing one hour for each 4 kilometres on the map and one minute for each 10 metres of ascent. This should be comfortable for average walkers. No allowance has been made for rest stops or the extra time required by bad weather, route finding or difficult terrain.

Abbreviations and conventions

E, SW, ENE	the 16 cardinal points of the compass
OS	Ordnance Survey
GR	grid reference
NT	National Trust
FC	Forestry Commission
NWW	North West Water
AW	Alfred Wainwright
km	kilometre of distance
metre	metres of horizontal distance, not to be confused with –
m	metres of vertical height
ft	feet of heights (used only in mountain title)
hr and min	hours and minutes to reach a place (written as '2hr 45min')

Each entry describes a circular walk which, in the opinion of its author, offers the most interesting traverse of the fell. Where two or more mountains are located closely together, the description may link these summits in one walk. We have deliberately described walks of differing length but all are within the competence of people who have some walking experience. More experienced walkers will feel able to link two or three of the walks together for a more extended route. None of the walks involves any rock climbing. Sections involving steeper ascents or descents, or some scrambling are clearly indicated.

Each entry begins with the height and grid reference of the mountain. All the fells are to be found on one of the four OS Leisure Sheets at a scale of 1:25,000 or the OS Touring Map at a scale of 1:63,360. Entries describe the starting point, means of access to the hillside and sufficient information for you to be able to follow the route. Where appropriate, reference is made to historical, geological, literary and cultural connections in the hope that these will increase your enjoyment of the walk. The route descriptions in the guide should not be regarded

as a substitute for a good map. An appreciation of the surrounding landscape and good route finding (particularly in bad weather) depend on carrying an up-to-date map and knowing how to use it.

At principal summits on the walk, an indication is given of the distance travelled from the start, the height gained from the start (*not* the height of the fell), and the time likely to be taken by a competent walker without rest stops. At the end of each entry, the total distance and time taken are given. Alternative approaches are suggested at the end of each entry, as are ideas for extending the walk to other fells.

Finally, whilst all reasonable care has been taken in preparing and describing the routes in this book, using definitive footpaths and bridleways and other commonly used paths across open land, it should be remembered that most land in the Lake District is privately owned. The description of a route in this book is not meant to signify a right of way. In all cases, the latest edition of the 1:25,000 Ordnance Survey map should be consulted to verify the existence of recognised rights of way. Whilst much land owned by the National Trust in the Lake District (and shown on the OS maps) is freely open to the public, this is not always the case. If in doubt about access, please ask the landowner first.

Walkers are asked to behave responsibly at all times and to follow the Mountain Code. Those with dogs should take particular care throughout the year and especially during the lambing period from February to May. Even well behaved dogs cause distress to sheep when running on the hills and as sheep farming is such an important part of the local economy, dog owners must keep their animals under close control at all times, on the higher fells as well as the lower ones.

The editors believe the information in this book is accurate at the time of writing. We would be pleased to learn of errors, changes and omissions for inclusion in later editions. Please send any comments to the editors at The Archway, 17 St John Street, Keswick, Cumbria CA12 5AE.

The geomorphology and geology of the Lake District

The shaping of the Lake District's hills and valleys, and the origin of the rocks which compose its mountains, represent separate and dramatically different periods of time. The hills, lakes and valleys are mainly the result of glacial events of which the most significant from the point of view of the scenery, took place during the relatively recent glacial (Devensian) event between 25,000 and 10,000 years ago. The bedrocks record a much longer and more exotic series of events in earth history, extending back more than four hundred million years.

During the last half million years, glaciation has affected the Lakes area in the form of repeatedly advancing and retreating ice sheets, culminating in the present inter-glacial stage during which human civilization has developed. At its most extensive, ice covered the Lakes in a way similar to the present-day Greenland ice-cap. The ice from Scotland, which filled the Irish Sea Basin, covered virtually the whole of the Lake District area, occasionally exposing scattered peaks as nunataks or rocky mounds projecting from the ice. Ice from the Lakes area was diverted over Stainmore and Tyne gaps and transported erratic boulders, notably of Shap granite, eastwards over the Pennines. Melting

of the ice was followed by a buoyancy response of the earth's crust which elevated the northern England uplands. Melting ice also raised sea levels to flood the valleys of the Solway and West Cumbria coast. Most of the characteristic glacial erosion features, including corries and lakes in U-shaped, over-deepened valleys, originated during the last glacial stage. The ice sheets deposited huge quantities of rock debris as moraines, several of which dam lakes, and a blanket of boulder clay which obscures bedrock over much of the lowland areas. Swarms of aligned drumlin hillocks along the Eden Valley testify to the direction of the ice flow.

During and after the ice melt some 10,000 years ago, water run-off became a main agent of erosion and rivers cut deep V-shaped valleys into moraines, unconsolidated boulder clay and softer bedrock, notably the Skiddaw Slates. River debris was washed into lakes to create deltas like the one separating Derwentwater and Bassenthwaite, on which Keswick stands. The end of glaciation was also marked by widespread landsliding, now stabilized, examples of which are to be seen in many places.

The walker on the Lake District fells views a landscape shaped mainly by the events which

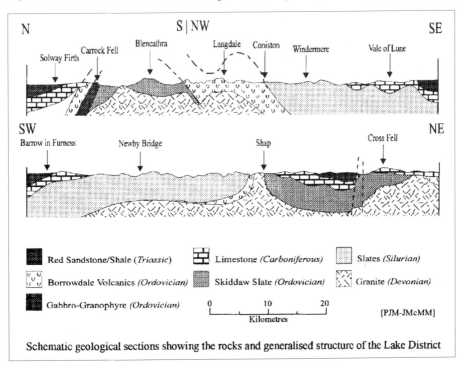

Schematic geological sections showing the rocks and generalised structure of the Lake District

took place as the ice shrank to valley glaciers and then to isolated corries before finally melting away, leaving the becks and rivers which became the main agents shaping the modern landscape.

The bedrock of the area contains the record of one tenth of earth history. The Borrowdale Volcanics, which are a mixture of consolidated ashes and lavas erupted from marine volcanoes, form the spine of the Lake District high ground and were the source of much of its mineral wealth from copper ores to slates and graphite. Intrusive igneous rocks are less common but the Carrock Fell gabbro-granophyre complex and the granitic rock outcrops of Shap, Skiddaw, Eskdale and Ennerdale protrude from the roof of a much larger subterranean, granitic body emplaced during the Caledonian mountain building period three to four hundred million years ago.

Flanking the central Borrowdale volcanic belt, which contains the Scafells, Helvellyn and Langdale Pikes, are the Ordovician slate mountains of the northern Lakes (including Skiddaw and Blencathra) and the gentler Silurian slate hills of south Lakeland. The Ordovician slates were deposited as black fossiliferous muds on the floors of deep sea basins and canyons. Evidence of massive submarine landsliding is common and, with the Borrowdale Volcanics, these rocks are a record of dynamic seismic and volcanic conditions associated with plate collision, similar to those of the Japan area today. Although they represent somewhat shallower conditions, the Silurian strata are also of marine origin.

Flanking the slate, volcanic and granitic core of the Lake District Dome are Carboniferous Limestone and Coal Measures strata which record a period of several hundred million years during which the area was covered by shallower, clear tropical seas resembling the Bahama banks. This was followed by deltas on which the coal forests grew. In turn, the Coal Measures were overlain by windblown dune sands and flash flood deposits of the Permian and Triassic deserts. Permo-Triassic dinosaurs must have looked east, from what is now the Lake District, across the red dunes of Appleby, to the faulted Cross Fell escarpment. They must also have felt the earthquake tremors which marked the beginning of the Atlantic rift as North America began to separate from Europe.

It was only during the tropical climatic conditions, perhaps 10 to 20 million years ago, that the Lake District assumed its distinctive domal form and the first uplands began to emerge from the surrounding areas of Carboniferous Limestones, Coal Measures and the Permo-Triassic red desert sandstones. These Tertiary times were followed, in geological terms almost as an afterthought, by the Quarternary glacial events which have done so much to shape the morphology we know today.

It would be wrong to think of the Lakes as a static system. Quite the contrary! Earthquakes occur as faults continue to move. Magnitude three and four events have affected Carlisle, the central Lake District and the northern Irish Sea area in recent years. Significant rock falls continue such as that of Kern Knotts on Great Gable, and landslip areas including Dove's Nest Crag in Borrowdale have become de-stablised in recent years. Sea level change continues apace, and natural erosion is moving huge quantities of rock debris seaward as any Lake District river bed can testify.

In short, the Lakeland walker is viewing but one moment in the continuum of change as ice sheets come and go, the land sags beneath their mass, and sea levels rise and fall. On the global scale, crustal plates move, the Lake District's earthquakes are but one symptom of the continuing separation of Europe and North America at an average annual rate approximately equivalent to that at which finger nails grow. The climate continues to change inexorably, by natural processes and the Earth's poles (magnetic and rotational) migrate among the wandering continents as rocks deform and new mountains form. The Lake District has, in its time, been a deep ocean floor, a belt of volcanic islands, a shallow coral fringed sea, a muddy forested delta, a red dune covered desert and a tropical savannah. It has migrated towards the geographical pole and into the tropics, while the earth's magnetic field has reversed its polarity several times, leaving a complex record in these rocks on which we walk.

Walking in the hills and valleys, there are endless geological and landscape features to be seen, all of which give the geologist the evidence necessary for interpretation of the Earth's history and, more importantly, the processes which shape our planet.

Daffodils by Ullswater

The natural history of the Lake District

This section describes some of the main aspects which govern the flora and fauna found within the Lake District. It does not attempt a complete listing of all individual species.

The composition of the soil is governed largely by the nature of the underlying rock and by the leaching of nutrients. In many areas, lime is absent. Apart from the rim of carboniferous limestone, the greater part of the Lake District is covered by acid soils which provide insufficient nourishment for many plants. Exceptions occur where the valley bottoms contain exposed or relatively shallow areas of volcanic rock and locally lime-rich soils develop. In such areas, and on high rock ledges and steep gill sides, rich mountain flora can be found.

To live high in a mountain area, plants must adapt. Summer conditions can be bad but winter can be arctic. Man and grazing animals have both had their impact. So too has the introduction of large areas of alien conifer plantations. High winds expose plants to excessive drying-out. In a mountain area, the soil is generally shallow and does not hold water easily. To adapt, the rose root has developed fleshy leaves and the campion has an extensive root system. Bilberry and least willow are low in stature to resist wind. Most of the fellsides are covered by grasses of various types with species of moss in wetter areas and coarser grasses on the slopes. Extensive grazing by sheep has reduced the heather which has been replaced by bracken on many lower slopes.

Until comparatively recently, the fellsides below 500m were covered with woodland – oak on the drier slopes and birch and alder on the wetter ones. Examples of these ancient woodlands can still be found in the higher reaches of the more remote valleys (such as Keskadale). Such woodlands gradually disappeared as they were cut for farming and sheep grazing. The dry stone walls were built to contain sheep whose grazing has subsequently eliminated many species of grass and plant.

The natural rock gardens of the high fells are a great delight. In addition to alpine plants, several species from the lower slopes have also found their way there. The globe flower supplies splashes of gold along ledges; cranesbill, red campion, moss campion, angelica and hogweed add to the display. Small spring flowers are to be found in plenty: wood anemone, wood sorrel, violets and the early purple orchid. The time of flowering varies from year to year but June and July are often best for the rock gardens. The purple saxifrage festoons the crags in April. Rarer plants such as the shrubby potentilla, alpine catchfly and mountain avens can be found in less accessible spots.

Lakeland fauna too must come to terms with the preponderance of water. Water-based life is found in three main habitats – lakes, tarns and streams. Nearly all the rivers and streams in the district flow fairly rapidly; consequently their beds tend to be stony. Any animal which can establish itself in these streams has a constant supply of food being carried past it. By contrast, many of the mountain tarns are shallow and sluggish resulting in an absence of food. Most of the lakes and lower tarns contain fish (pike, perch and trout), water bugs and beatles, frogs and toads. Char also occurs in one or two of the larger lakes, particularly Windermere.

There are around 10,000 species of insect in the Lake District. Earthworms are absent in any quantity, their place and function being filled by the larvae of insects. There are few ants. The absence of lime prevents the growth of snails, but slugs are common. Various grass moths occur and over 22 species of butterfly and moth have been recorded.

A few golden eagle have now returned to breed in the mountains. Another notable species is the peregrine falcon which can nest on inaccessible ledges. The buzzard nests in the valley woodlands. Crows, jackdaws and ravens are also common. On a fine summer day, skylarks can be heard at over 750m on the High Street ridge. Drystone walls are a haven for wrens and redstarts. Ring ouzel, although not common, breed in gills and deserted quarries. One winter visitor to the mountain tops is the snow bunting: small parties appear each winter to feed on the seeds of the heathrush which bears its fruits on

stalks projecting through the snow. Both red and black grouse are resident but not in large numbers due to the lack of heather.

On the lower tarns and lakes, ducks and geese are common. The most conspicuous winter visitor is the whooper swan. The common sandpiper is a regular breeder along with the curlew and, to a lesser extent, the heron. The dipper is seen along shallow tree-lined river valleys amongst broken water and moss-covered stones.

After the myxematosis epidemic of the 1950's, the rabbit is common once more. The brown hare is present but in lower numbers than previously due to hunting. The field vole is plentiful wherever there is coarse grass; it is a most important item in the food chain and without it, the buzzard would be rare. The red squirrel has declined steadily since the 1970's.

The fox's reputation for cunning is part of the legend of the Lake District. Its survival is assured due to its impregable lair amongst rock falls at the foot of the crags. It is sometimes seen by day on passage from one valley to another and will ascend to the highest areas in pursuit of prey. Badgers are found in low lying areas. Otters are confined to the larger rivers running to the west coast. Pine martens are still present but this shy animal is rarely seen.

The Lake District is one of the best areas for the study of our native deer because of the variety of habitat and the animals' determination to survive in an area which is relatively densely populated. Red deer require the cover of woods and consequently are to be seen in the limestone areas to the south west, Grisedale Forest, Martindale and on the fells to the east of the Helvellyn range. Roe deer are most frequent on the Solway mosses, in the woods around Armathwaite in the Eden Valley and around Keswick. Herds of fallow deer have been kept in public parks such as Holker Hall and Dalemain and some stragglers have established themselves in dense limestone woods near Arnside and on Whitbarrow Scar.

Castlerigg Stone Circle

A history of man in the Lake District

There is frequent evidence on the surface of the hills and dales of the Lake District of man's activity in previous times: relics of pre-history, of Roman occupation, of viking settlement, of medieval and later mining, of 17th and 18th century agriculture, and of the 19th century tourist influx.

The first evidence of human activity in the district comes from the coastal lowlands and limestone fringes in the form of mesolithic flint scatters dating to around 5-7000 BC. These hunter-gatherer folk also began the first small-scale disturbance of the forest cover. The first farmers established neolithic settlements in the coastal lowlands in about 4000 BC. Stone axe-factory sites dating from around 2-3000 BC are to be found on the slopes of Pike o'Stickle and on Scafell Pike. Feeling the sharpness of the chippings in the refuse heaps at these sites is a very good way of crossing the centuries back to those times. These axes were exported as far as Bournemouth and Shetland. Also surviving from the same period is the magnificent stone circle at Castlerigg, outside Keswick, built for a still unknown purpose, though certainly not by 'Druids'. Later Bronze Age cremation sites are

to be found on Bannisdale Moor (near Coniston) and hut circles and field circles of the same period on Stockdale Moor (between Ennerdale and Wasdale). These would have been peopled by Celtic-speaking Britons, the Cymri of Cumberland, the original natives of the area. These early inhabitants were responsible for accelerating the deforestation of the area, since there is evidence of a much higher tree-line. The only Iron Age remains of any significance are the remnants of a splendidly sited hill-fort on Carrock Fell. There is good environmental evidence that the climate deteriorated during the late Iron Age (500 BC - 0 BC) precipitating the abandonment of many upland settlements.

The Romans came in about 80 AD and left evidence of a strategic network of roads and forts. The most spectacular fort site is that of Hardknott, guarding a road which connected Ambleside to the port of Ravenglass. The most interesting of the roads, though only the line of its route can be seen, is that running across the top of High Street. Evidence of other Roman settlements can be found outside Cockermouth, at Papcastle, and outside Penrith at Brougham. The Romans withdrew by the end of the fourth century AD. There are few physical relics of the Celtic period but there are Celtic elements in a number of place-names: for example, Glencoyne preserves the word *glyn* (= valley), Penruddock the word *pen* (= summit). Anglian settlers arrived around the fringes of the Lake District from 600 AD and from 900 AD Scandinavian pirates first raided, then settled, intruding right into the innermost valleys of the Lake District, re-naming almost everything with Norse names. This colonisation went on until the end of the 13th century. The wide open fellsides are the result of deforestation begun in pre-historic times and carried on by these Norse settlers.

Following the Norman Conquest, great monasteries were founded, of which Furness Abbey is outstanding in its importance. It owned extensive sheep pastures in Borrowdale and Eskdale and in the Furness fells in the south, while St Bees owned much of Ennerdale. Many more forest areas were cleared in medieval times to create their sheep farms. These were the years of Scottish raiding, to meet the threat of which pele towers or fortified homesteads were built round the fringes of the Lake District: for example, at Dacre, Kentmere and Muncaster. Tradition has it that the local Herdwick sheep are ancestors of sheep washed ashore from the wreck of a ship in the Spanish armada, though their ancestry may go back much further to neolithic times. During the 16th century the mineral resources of the area began to be exploited. German miners were brought to Keswick to search for gold and silver, copper, lead and iron, in the Newlands Valley and on the slopes of Cat Bells; other mines were opened round Caldbeck and Coniston. This mining industry must have been responsible for further deforestation. These were the years of the charcoal burner, an activity which has died out only very recently. From a slightly later period (1660-1760) come the distinctive pack-horse bridges of the Lake District on the old pony routes through the central mountains: such bridges survive at Stockley Beck, Wasdale Head, Throstle Garth and Watendlath. Also distinctive and from much the same period of time are the old Lakeland farmhouses, built by the statesmen, or independent yeoman-farmers. The most interesting and best preserved example is the home of the Browne family at Townend, Troutbeck, now owned by the National Trust. The walls on the fellsides, which are almost as characteristic a part of the Lake District scene, belong to the end of the 18th century and are mostly due to the enclosure movement of that time. They are historical monuments built with considerable skill and enormous effort. They are under great threat and should be treated with care; it is rarely necessary to climb a wall.

The Lake District was then opened up and re-discovered in the middle of the 18th century. The first to see the area with modern eyes was arguably the Rev Dr John Brown (1715-66), who had been brought up in Wigton and who published a *Description of the Lake at Keswick* in 1766. Brown was followed by Thomas Gray, who toured Ullswater, Borrowdale and Grasmere in 1769, and then by Thomas West, whose *Guide to the Lakes* in 1778 marks the real beginning of the tourist influx. All this was due to a change in mental attitude associated with Romanticism, which could regard mountains with admiration rather than with loathing, and, more mundanely, with the development of turnpike roads, which made travel to the Lake District both easier and safer.

The history since then up to our own times has been of a conflict of interests, of a spread of hotels and wealthy villas in the early 19th century, of incursions by roads, railways and reservoirs, and of the attempts by the National Trust, the Lake District National Park and other conservation bodies to preserve the landscape against these various threats and yet to allow a way of life for its local inhabitants.

Lake District weather and the walker

We all grumble when it rains as we are hoping for a fine day on the hills with panoramic views and warm sunshine; but that rain is essential to keep the lakes fresh, the becks gurgling and the waterfalls cascading into rocky pools!

Seathwaite is often mistakenly described as the wettest place in England, with around 131 inches of rain each year. Not so: it is far wetter up on the fell tops where as much as 180 inches have been recorded. The rainfall is high because the prevailing moisture-laden westerlies are forced to rise over the mountains and as they do so, the lower temperatures cause the water vapour to condense out as raindrops, or hailstones or snow if it is really cold. With good waterproof gear in the rucksack, today's walkers need not be deterred by the prospects of rain, but if preferred, they can often find attractive low-level walks where it is drier: at Rosthwaite the average annual rainfall is 100 inches, yet at Keswick just six miles down the valley, the figure is only 57 inches.

Walking in poor weather can sometimes bring special rewards, as when a curtain of clouds parts to reveal the hidden view, or when a magnificent rainbow appears. A striking phenomenon is the 'brocken spectre', which occurs when the sun casts a shadow of the walker on a low bank of cloud with an apparent halo around the head. Wave, and the spectre waves back!

In general, the climate is mild, due to the proximity of the sea and the influence of the Gulf Stream. Severe winters are unusual, to the disappointment of those who like to ski or engage in winter mountaineering, both of which can be alpine in character and requires special equipment. Walking can normally be enjoyed on the Lake District fells all the year round. In summer, May and June are usually the driest months, with the traditional holiday month of August often being wet. With the typical variability of mountain weather everywhere, there can be June floods and August droughts too.

There are some facts about weather that walkers should be aware of. First, temperatures normally decrease with altitude by about 1°C for every 100 metres. This means there may be a 10° difference between sea-level and the highest tops. Secondly, wind speed increases with altitude so that a moderate wind in the valley can be strong to gale force on the high fells. Thirdly, wind-chill is an important factor to recognise: an air temperature of 5°C with a wind speed of 30km/hour will produce an equivalent temperature of -3°C on the skin.

Low cloud and hill fog can cause problems and no-one should be out on the fells without a map, a compass and the ability to use them. A rare condition in winter is a white-out when snow on the ground and thick white cloud combine to remove all visibility: it is impossible to determine the horizon or the slope of the ground. Keep throwing an object ahead of you into the snow to provide a focus for your eyes.

Summer thunderstorms with lightning can be worrying on an exposed ridge. Watch for towering cumulus clouds building and producing anvil-shaped tops. If you are caught out, and your skin begins to tingle, get away from the ridge quickly and adopt a crouching or kneeling position to reduce height. Never shelter beneath a tree.

As a service to walkers, the National Park Authority provide a twice-daily updated weather service based on information from the Meteorological Office. This is available 24 hours a day by phoning 017687-75757. Weather bulletins are posted daily throughout the year in information centres and many outdoor shops and at some popular car parks. In doubtful weather, and particularly in winter, it makes sense to check the forecast and change your plans if necessary. The hills will always be there for another day!

24 hour Lake District Weatherline
017687-75757

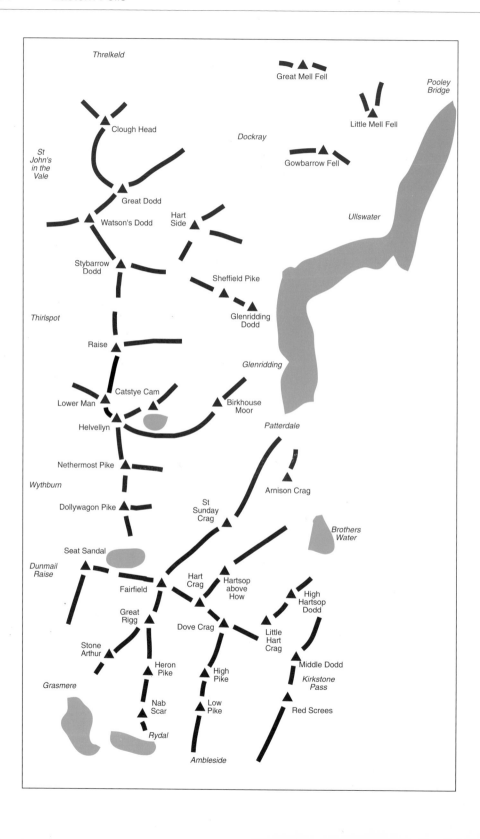

Threlkeld

Great Mell Fell

Pooley Bridge

Clough Head

Dockray

Little Mell Fell

St John's in the Vale

Gowbarrow Fell

Great Dodd

Hart Side

Ullswater

Watson's Dodd

Stybarrow Dodd

Sheffield Pike

Glenridding Dodd

Thirlspot

Raise

Glenridding

Catstye Cam

Lower Man

Birkhouse Moor

Helvellyn

Patterdale

Nethermost Pike

Wythburn

Arnison Crag

Dollywagon Pike

St Sunday Crag

Brothers Water

Seat Sandal

Dunmail Raise

Hart Crag

Hartsop above How

High Hartsop Dodd

Fairfield

Great Rigg

Dove Crag

Little Hart Crag

Stone Arthur

Middle Dodd

Heron Pike

Kirkstone Pass

Grasmere

Nab Scar

High Pike

Low Pike

Red Screes

Rydal

Ambleside

Section 1

The Eastern Fells

The Eastern Fells was the first of AW's pictorial guides to be published in 1955 and it set the standard for the rest of the series. At the end of the book he tells readers how great his pleasure was in writing and drawing about the mountains he loved; a pleasure that is echoed today by the many appreciative walkers who still peruse his books both on the hill and in the armchair.

The area of the Eastern Fells is a clearly defined one, bounded in the west by Thirlmere and the road over Dunmail Raise and in the east by Kirkstone Pass and Brothers Water, the two boundaries meeting in the south at Ambleside. The northern limit is the Threlkeld to Troutbeck section of the Keswick-Penrith gap. Between these boundaries lies a massive area of high ground forming a long north-south ridge, the highest point of which is Helvellyn at 950m.

Forty years on, many observations made by AW remain true: Helvellyn is still the most popular summit; the Dodds north of Sticks Pass are relatively unfrequented and the whole territory continues to give enjoyable walking to ever-growing numbers of people.

Clough Head from Threlkeld

Clough Head 726m, 2381ft, GR 334225

Clough Head, the most northerly hill of the Helvellyn Range, commands the broad valley of the Greta and the Glenderamackin rivers. Its western flanks are steep and craggy, and much quarried.

A start can be made from Threlkeld. There is a NT car park in Blease Road and other possibilities in the village. From the church (GR 322254) take a footpath south across the A66 and on to a minor road leading over the river and disused railway to a solitary house, Newsham (GR 331247). Go through a gate on to the fell and follow a path of sorts south to above the quarry and on to the site of a prehistoric settlement. Continue south uphill on a pathless but open grassy fellside, to the top of Threlkeld Knotts at 514m. From here, a slight descent leads to the base of the steep craggy flank of Clough Head. A footpath makes an upward traverse through this steepness. From the top turn east up the broad grassy ridge to the summit (4km, 630m, 2hrs).

To descend, follow the fine open ridge NE to White Pike and then go down steeply past a curious heap of rock to the Old Coach Road. Stay on this back to the vicinity of the prehistoric settlement and then join the outgoing route at Newsham. Resist the temptation to head straight down to Newsham from the Coach road, the going there being wet and tussocky (9km, 3hrs 20min).

A nearer though less attractive starting point is the car park near the former railway station (GR 321246). Follow the railway track to join the minor road to Newsham.

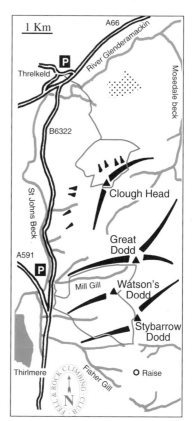

The Dodds from Helvellyn

Stybarrow Dodd 843m, 2765ft, GR 343189
Watson's Dodd 789m, 2588ft, GR 336196
Great Dodd 857m, 2811ft, GR 342206

Dodd is the old name for a rounded grassy hill, of which these three are the highest of all fifteen or so in the Lake District. The walk along the high-level ridges connecting them is easy and particularly rewarding, both on account of the extensive views and because they are unfrequented. In springtime they are the haunts of dotterel and golden plovers. These tops are more usually reached from the east where the approaches are more gradual, but the route from the west gives glimpses of rocky ravines as well as close-up views of the splendid and impressive Castle Rock of Triermain.

Park in the NWW car park at Legburthwaite on the west side of the St John's in the Vale road. Walk south along the road to the telephone box at Stanah and turn left, crossing a high wall by a wooden stile. Cross the leat (capturing water for Thirlmere from Ladknott and Mill Gills) and a footbridge. A path rises up steeply by the side of Stanah Gill, with views of its tumbling waterfalls. On reaching a sheepfold, the steep part is over and the path continues easily to Sticks Pass. Turn left, almost due north, to reach a minor top and then head NE to reach the upright blue slate slab marking the highest point of Stybarrow Dodd (5km, 676m, 2hr 25min).

After appreciating the extensive views, join the path which lead NW to Watson's Dodd, slightly offset from the line of the ridge. To reach Great Dodd, the line is now NE, rising about 54m after an almost imperceptible descent. In mist, take care to avoid the path which forks left here to contour round Millgill Head. The large shelter cairn on the top is 100 metres further south than the highest point but is a better spot for views (8.5km, 772m, 3hr 25min).

To descend, head SW then west to Little Dodd, avoiding the main path which curves around to Calfhow Pike and Clough Head. Little Dodd is no more than a rounded protuberence, but from it you should be able to spot a cairn, ESE, which is the next point to aim for. There is no descent path but the ground is mainly short grass and easy underfoot. As the distant hills disappear from view, Castle Rock looms larger, with the overhanging north face on the right. When the ground steepens, a path develops and leads to the only possible crossing place of Mill Gill, between the upper and lower ravines. Go left over the neck of ground connecting Castle Rock with the fell, through a narrow open gateway and down to reach the leat at a point where it emerges from a tunnel. Turn right and follow the path along the upper edge of a small copse of larches. After crossing a slate stile, go down at the side of the wall to reach the road exactly opposite a path into the car park (12.5km, 4hr 25min).

Great Mell Fell from Troutbeck

Great Mell Fell 537m, 1760ft, GR 397254

The larger of a pair of isolated conical tops in North East Lakeland is a pleasant place to escape from the crowds on more renowned hills. It offers an easy ascent with great views south towards the centre of the District and north toward Blencathra. The peak can conveniently be climbed along with its smaller neighbour in an easy afternoon's outing.

Park on the northern side of the minor road that runs from Penruddock to Matterdale End at the point where a rough track runs up and around the lower slopes of the hill (GR 407247). There is room here for about three carefully parked cars. Follow the track to a gate on the right with a sign proclaiming you are on the right hill. Pass through this and turn left to tackle the steep oak and ash covered slope (no real path) to where the trees open out and the angle eases. Continue in the same line through a stand of pine trees and on again through sparse larches. Cross an area of tussock grass and arrive at the small summit cairn on a minor grassy knoll. The map indicates that this is a tumulus but more to the point, where did the collection of sandstone boulders that make up the cairn come from?

To descend, retrace the final part of the ascent and then bear away to the right (southwards) down steep bracken-covered slopes to join a good path at the edge of the fields. This descends to meet the track used at the start of the walk at a stile. The car is a few minutes further away through the wood (3km, 270m, 1hr 15min).

Little Mell Fell

Little Mell Fell 505m, 1657ft, GR 423240

The smaller of a pair of isolated conical hills in NE Lakeland offers as uncomplicated an ascent as you will get anywhere in the District. The peak can conveniently be climbed along with its bigger neighbour in a short day. Wainwright considered the hill hardly worthy of the title 'fell' but this seems just a little unfair. Either way it's on the list so you will have to go and do it anyway!

Park at the high point of the road from Matterdale End to Watermillock where there is room for half a dozen cars on the southern side of the road (GR 424236) opposite a buried water tank.

Cross the road, pass over a stile and a short distance further, another. From here there are two choices, attack the steep grassy slope dead ahead via a shallow gully feature, or follow a long zig-zag that initially heads out to the right around the sky line before cutting back to joint the direct route where it's angle begins to fall back. The summit is marked by a stone-built triangulation point and views that are rather restricted because of the flat nature of the hill top. Take a walk around the rim to appreciate the full panorama. The descent should not require a description (1.5km, 120m, 40mins).

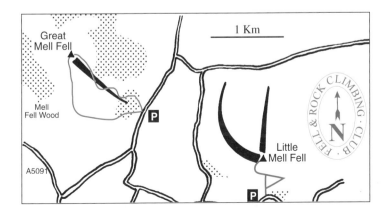

Hart Side 756m, 2481ft, GR 359198

View from Hart Side to Great Mell and Little Mell Fells

The highest point on this walk is known as Green Side or White Stones (795m) and is really a subsidiary summit of Stybarrow Dodd. All these tops are grassy and unexiting in themselves, the highlight of this walk being the long traverse path used in the approach from Dockray; this gives extensive views of Ullswater and curves impressively round the upper reaches of Glencoynedale. Several other tops are included in the round. One of them, Birkett Fell (722m), named in honour of Lord Birkett, bears a plaque in the summit cairn. The whole area is delightfully quiet and unfrequented.

Start the walk in Dockray where there is a small layby opposite the signposted footpath at GR 393215. Follow the wide track as far as the stepping stones but instead of crossing these take the indistinct path on the left in a SE direction, keeping on the east side of Common Fell. The path becomes more distinct when it meets the wall which it then follows. Leave the wall to branch right at a cairn for the path contouring around Glencoynedale. As the path turns the corner above Nick Head turn right to go up by the grassy ridge, passing a large disused quarry as the ridge flattens out. A grassy trod continues to the top of Green Side, marked as White Stones on the map (6.5km, 505m, 2hr 30min).

Follow the high ground NE across a shallow depression to reach Hart Side, which has a strange ditch excavated across the top. Then either make straight for Birkett Fell, or if preferred turn right and follow the line of the high ground to the lesser top of

Hart Side (741m, no cairn). Then turn left (NE) to Birkett Fell. To descend follow the wall which runs SE until it crosses the spur of Brown Hills. Go through the wall and walk along the Brown Hills ridge, continuing over Swineside Knott (533m) and Watermillock Common (542m). There is no path and some marshy ground to contend with. From the last top, named Common Fell, drop down to the east to join the path used on the ascent and follow this back to the start. Or bear right to include the additional tops of Round How (387m) and Bracken How (340m) (13.5km, 4hr 25min).

The approach route described can also be used for a walk over the Dodds, continuing from Green Side to Stybarrow and over Watson's, descending from Great Dodd by Randerside and down to the old coach road, following this back to Dockray (16.5km, 675m, 5hr 15min).

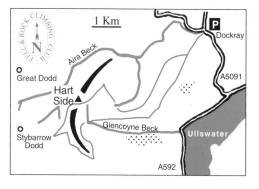

Gowbarrow Fell from near Sandwick

Gowbarrow Fell 481m, 1579ft, GR 407218

Although of modest height Gowbarrow Fell is a delightful place abounding in rocky knolls and green winding paths which give superb views of Ullswater. Owned by the National Trust since 1906, the area is famed for Aira Force, a series of waterfalls that cascade down a deep ravine carved through the volcanic rocks by Aira Beck. Do not be put off by the crowds; the falls are well worth seeing and the hordes are soon left behind.

Start the walk from the NT carpark at GR 400200. Go up either of the main paths to the falls, continuing up the east side after the second bridge. Or if you are feeling adventurous stay on the west side and cross 'The Strid', where one bold step across the narrow ravine is easily made when the rocks are dry. At the gate in the boundary wall turn steeply uphill and follow narrow winding paths towards the north and NE, joining a good path which comes up from Dockray and closely follows the wall. At this stage Ullswater is hidden and the views are over Dockray to Great Dodd. The summit lies about 150 metres from the wall (3km, 320m, 1hr 20min).

Descend ENE from the top towards a corner in the boundary wall where there is a stile. Cross this and go NE over some tedious hummocky grass to the top of Great Meldrum (437m). Continue NE to a stile in the corner and follow the path up to the forest gate, bypassing Little Meldrum which is enclosed in a forested area. An unnamed top at 424m (GR 425234) is easily reached. From this top descend south easily

on grass, picking a way through the bracken to join a good path coming up from Watermillock church. Turn right along this contouring path, where the bracken can be very high in late summer, to re-enter the Gowbarrow estate by the remains of an old hunting lodge.

The excellent continuing path gives fine views, particularly after rounding a corner above Yew Crag where there is a cairn on a viewpoint by a memorial seat. An alternative is to branch right at this point and go over Green Hill before completing the circuit (10.5km, 3hr 25min).

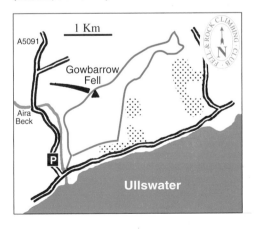

Sheffield Pike from Dockray road

Glenridding Dodd 442m, 1450ft, GR 381176
Sheffield Pike 675m, 2214ft, GR 369182

Sheffield Pike and its outlier Glenridding Dodd form a distinct barrier between the valleys of Glencoyne and Glenridding. There are steep crags on all sides except the west; the eastern end of the indefinite but steep ridge of the Dodd ending in the precipitous Stybarrow Crag on the edge of Ullswater. The traverse of both tops gives an excellent walk which deserves to be better known.

Park in a wide layby immediately north of Stybarrow Crag on the west side of the road at GR 387179 where the path begins and follow it up into the woods. When it almost disappears bear right and keep at the upper side of a broken wall. When another wall is met turn left and go up steeply at first with the wall on the right hand side. When the ground levels out the line of an old path is picked up leading to a place where the wall can be crossed. This is slightly awkward as there is a fence on top. The old path now rises steeply through bracken and leads to a shoulder from where the east ridge can be followed to the large and hummocky top. A fine tall cairn shows the best view of Glenridding and the upper reaches of the lake.

A path leads easily down to the col at the foot of the SE ridge of Sheffield Pike. The good path up this ridge is easy to follow and gives an enjoyable route, with the distinctive pyramid of Catstycam constantly catching the eye. After gaining the top of Heron Pike the gradient becomes more gradual and there are several small tarns in some boggy ground. On the summit cairn is a distinctive boundary stone with initials H, M, ER and the date 1830. (H is for the Howard estate of Greystoke and M for the Marshall estate of Patterdale).

To descend, go due west to reach Nick Head and turn right to follow the excellent path down the Glencoyne valley. Near the row of ten cottages known as Seldom Seen the path becomes a cart-track. To avoid some road walking, take the path on the right when the track bends sharp left. This path rises over a spur in the woodland before joining the road a short distance from the layby (7km, 580m, 2hr 45min).

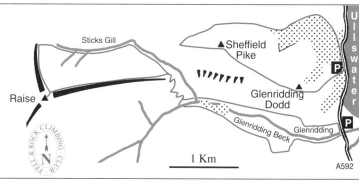

Raise from the east in winter

Raise 883m, 2896ft, GR 343174

Raise lies on the main watershed of the Helvellyn massif between Stybarrow Dodd and Whiteside Bank and is often included in a long circular walk which includes all the main tops. The area is popular with skiers, the only tow in the Lake District being on the northern slopes. The route in this book has been chosen for its comprehensive view of the Greenside leadmining area. This is an activity which has left scars on the landscape but is of great historical interest. The ascent route is by an old chimney flue built in the 1830's, constructed to carry gases from the smelter to a chimney one mile away. Incidentally, AW made one of his rare mistakes in describing this as a 'disused aqueduct', although a number of aqueducts or leats will be observed in the area.

From Glenridding take the Mires Beck route past the campsite as far as the ladder stile. Turn right and follow the grassy path outside the wall to the footbridge over Glenridding Beck above Greenside. Turn left, then right to join the waymarked path up towards Sticks Pass. This path zigzags up through scattered juniper bushes below the steep rocks of Stang End. After a sharp bend left and then right leave this track to follow the collapsed remains of the old flue. This gives easy walking right up to the remains of the chimney itself. Disused since the second World War, the vegetation here has still not recovered from toxic leakage from the flue. Continue uphill in the same direction (slightly south of west) to reach the top of Raise (6km, 735m, 2hr 45min).

The descent north to Sticks Pass and then east by Sticks Gill is a well-trodden route down to a desolate area of tips and spoil heaps which may still yield samples of galena and other minerals to the diligent searcher. After crossing a footbridge the track continues down past the flue and follows the route of ascent down to Greenside. The old mine buildings now all have a new lease of life as outdoor pursuits centres and a youth hostel. Follow the narrow lane down to Glenridding (13.5km, 4hr 35min).

An alternative ending to this walk is to include Sheffield Pike by leaving the Sticks Pass route where it makes a sharp right turn by the spoil heaps and take the path rising gently to Nick Head. Descend by Heron Pike and the SE ridge, ending with a rather steep descent at the side of Blaes Crag (14km, 860m, 5hr).

Red Screes

Red Screes 776m, 2545ft, GR 396088
Middle Dodd 654m, 2145ft, GR 397096

This southern gatepost of Patterdale can seem quite intimidating when the sheer mass of its flank is first viewed from the Kirkstone Pass, indeed a direct assault of the SE flank is a tough undertaking. However a rewarding day is to be had by taking the less frequented but still well defined path via Caiston Beck; the walking is moderate and never exceeds a 1 in 3 gradient.

Starting from a small parking bay 400 metres south of Caudalebeck Farm on the A592, cross the road and walk 50 metres S to find a stile and finger board marking the beginning of the path. The well spaced marker posts take you across the water meadows, over a wooden bridge, then through a stile to the fellside proper. The steadily rising path keeps parallel with the beck, passing a disused level and pleasant little cascades to reach the head of Scandale Pass where you turn SE and follow the dry stone wall side to its conclusion.

At this point do not be tempted to follow the major track directly for the summit but hold your course until you hit the ridge then follow it SW for a minute or two to gain the cairn at Raven Crag. As the vista unfurls to reveal the panorama of the Southern Lakes and Morecambe Bay you will agree it was worth the extra effort. Walking NE you will enjoy the bold profile of Ill Bell and Froswick to your right whilst a meander westwards will give you the opportunity to study the whole of the Fairfield Horseshoe before continuing to the little tarn and trig point for a well earned rest.

In all but inclement weather, the descent NE along the ridge of Middle Dodd is too tempting to miss, the path being well established although a little steep in places. As you progress more and more spectacular fells come into sight as the view towards Ullswater is unveiled. As you reach the cross wall at 410m you may be inclined to keep to the ridge or even worse traverse off rightwards towards the Kirkstone Pass. This is not to be advised, as this section of the fell is a muddle of minor crags and stumble holes just waiting to ensnare the tired and the unwary. Instead follow the faint track NW to rejoin your ascent path in the foot of Caiston Glen, thence safely back to the road side (7km, 2hr 45 min).

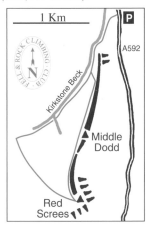

Catstye Cam 890m, 2919ft, GR 348158

Sometimes called Catchedicam, this is one of the most perfectly shaped peaks in Lakeland, but is often overlooked by walkers in preference for its loftier neighbour, Helvellyn. When seen from the east it presents a fine pyramidical shape. Linked to Helvellyn by the ridge of Swirral Edge, it gives a fine view of the Red Tarn corrie. Often combined with an ascent of Helvellyn, the north west ridge of Catstye Cam provides a worthwhile outing on its own.

The starting point is in Glenridding (GR 385169). This road is followed through the village and up the valley to Greenside Mine. The mine is vast with the old entrance into the Lucy Tongue level being just above the present buildings. The extent of the levels range from 240m above this level to 400m below, the lowest point being below sea level. The lead mine closed in 1962.

The valley dog-legs left and the path weaves up past the workings. Continuing on the right of the valley, the scars of mankind are now left behind and this fine valley beckons with the shapely Catstye Cam standing guard. Next to Catstye Cam are the remains of Kepplecove Tarn. The dam was formed to provide water power for the Greenside mines. In 1927, the dam burst, causing much damage down the valley. The dam was replaced and was used to supply water which was led by the watercut along the flanks of Catstye Cam, down the valley to a power station just above Glenridding. Electricity thus generated was carried by cables to the mine.

The NW ridge of Catstye Cam above is not as formidable as it looks. Cross the beck near the dam and make for the base of the ridge. The summit is unseen until the last

The NE ridge of Catstye Cam

moment when the full panorama comes into view (6km, 740m, 2hr 45min).

The descent is by the grassy east shoulder. This gives a good view into the gully on the NE face which can provide a fine, easy climb under snow conditions and has been skied on at least one occasion. At the foot of the shoulder the main path leading from Red Tarn and Helvellyn is joined and followed back down the valley across the flanks of Catstye Cam. Continue on the true right of the valley. Just before reaching Glenridding the path drops down to cross Rattlebeck Bridge and joins the valley road near the Travellers Rest inn (12km, 4hr 15min).

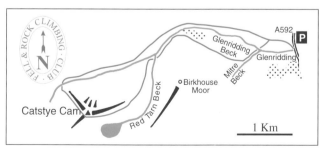

Helvellyn from Striding Edge in winter

Birkhouse Moor 718m, 2355ft, GR 364160
Helvellyn 950m, 3118ft, GR 342151
Lower Man 925m, 3034ft, GR 337155
White Side 863m, 2831ft, GR 338167

The height and the accessibility from both sides has long contributed to the enormous popularity of Helvellyn. It was visited by Thomas Budworth, one of the earliest guidebook writers, in 1792. Dorothy Wordsworth mentions that Coleridge arrived at eleven o'clock one night in August, having walked over Helvellyn. More people climb this mountain than any other in the Lake District so do not expect to find peace and quiet, although strategies such as dawn starts in mid-week may pay off. The Helvellyn range

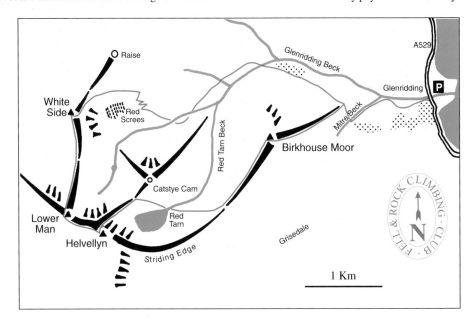

is a massive one, forming a long ridge between Thirlmere and Ullswater. There are numerous ways to the top from east and west, those from the east offering the most dramatic scenery, the cirque containing Red Tarn being the finest in the Lake District. Thousands reach the summit from all directions in summer; in winter Striding Edge covered with ice and snow makes a fine mountaineering excursion for those suitably experienced and equipped.

The ascent by the NE ridge of Birkhouse Moor is unfrequented until it joins the standard route by Mires Beck and there are outstanding views throughout. The scramble up Swirral Edge on firm clean rock is delightful and the descent is by a well-graded path.

Start from the car park in Glenridding. Leave the main road by the track to the campsite on the south side of Glenridding Beck. Turn left at a T, signposted to Helvellyn by Mires Beck, then go straight on at the second junction. After a ladder-stile turn right towards Greenside and after 120 metres go left up a steep grassy slope to reach a good path. Turn right and almost immediately find a place to start going up the ridge. There is no path, but it is easy to choose a way up grassy ramps between rocky outcrops. A cairn is reached on the apparent top of Birkhouse Moor, the ridge

Striding Edge in summer

flattening out before joining the Mires Beck path and rising on to the true top (3.5km, 558m, 1hr 50min).

Continue walking along the ridge. When the Hole-in-the-Wall (now a stile) is reached there is a choice of ways by either Striding Edge or Swirral Edge. For the latter, which is recommended as less crowded and less eroded, turn right and follow the path across the outlet of Red Tarn and up to the col between Swirral and Catstycam. At the top turn left to reach the trig point and summit shelter (6.5km, 789m, 3hr).

Follow the edge of the high ground (NW) over Lower Man (925m) and then north to White Side. Continue towards Raise (NE) and five minutes later take the right fork which descends to join the main

track down from Keppel Cove. At Greenside, cross the footbridge over the beck and take either the lower path near the wall or a higher parallel track. Join the outward route to return to the starting point (15.5km, 5hr 20min).

A circular walk over Helvellyn from the west begins at the FC Swirls car park 1km south of Thirlspot at GR 316169. The route up the side of Helvellyn Gill is exceedingly steep until the top of Browncove Crag. Thereafter the walking is easy over Lower Man and Helvellyn. Continue south past the shelter for about 700 metres where a cairn marks the descent path to Wythburn (pronounced Wyb'n). Return to Swirls by the forest track (11km, 770m, 4hr 10min).

Dollywagon Pike from Fairfield

Nethermost Pike 891m, 2923ft, GR 344142
Dollywagon Pike 858m, 2814ft, GR 346131

These summits are near one of the busiest paths in Lakeland but are rarely visited and solitude can be enjoyed here as many walkers tramp past with their eyes fixed on nearby Helvellyn. The summits may be incorporated with an ascent of Helvellyn but the route described here avoids the crowds on that loftier neighbour and approaches the peaks from the east up the attractive Grisedale valley.

The starting point is in Glenridding (GR 385169). Follow the track up the south side of the beck past the village hall. Where the track divides, take the left branch which ascends to a number of houses at Wetside. Arrows direct you up the fell path to Lanty's Tarn. This delightful tarn is just below the summit of Keldas (311m) which is well worth a short detour to enjoy not only the fine view of Ullswater but also up Grisedale to the objective of this walk. The path now drops slightly into Grisedale and the splendour of the valley is seen, with Nethermost Pike and Dollywaggon Pike at the head. This track was created by miners at Eagle Crag Mine many years ago. The ridge dividing Nethermost Cove and Ruthwaite Cove is guarded by Eagle Crag below which the spoil heaps bear witness to more than a century of mining activity. The clean south crag now gives a number of good rock climbs. Our way avoids a frontal assault of the ridge by taking

the faint miners' path leading up into Nethermost Cove. The inner sanctuary of the Cove, despite is closeness to Striding Edge, can provide a haven of peace. The route crosses the beck and makes a way up the slope onto the ridge on the left, above Eagle Crag. The ridge at this point is quite wide and leads on to the finale of the walk. The ridge now narrows and steepens to finish with an arete, like a miniature Striding Edge. Above this, the terrain suddenly changes to the flat summit area of Nethermost Pike (8km, 740m, 3hr 15min).

Helvellyn lies to the right but today's route bears left. Following the main crest, pass over High Crag and then drop down before the final climb up Dollywagon Pike.

From here it is all downhill. The 'motorway' descent to Grisedale Tarn weaves down a well worn path but our route follows the less frequented ridge called The Tongue which descends NE dividing Ruthwaite Cove and Cock Cove. This route should be avoided in bad weather. Spout Crag cuts across the base of the ridge at which point you should drop into Ruthwaite Cove. The old packhorse track, which works its way back down Grisedale, has for years linked Grasmere with Patterdale. This is joined at Ruthwaite Lodge. Originally built as a smithy and

Dollywagon Pike from Grisedale

bothy for the miners, this building is now a climbing hut and has recently been rebuilt after a fire.

Cross the beck and follow the track which develops into a road down the S side of the valley.

Continue to join the main road at Grisedale Bridge and follow this and the path along the base of Keldas back to Glenridding (19km, 6hr).

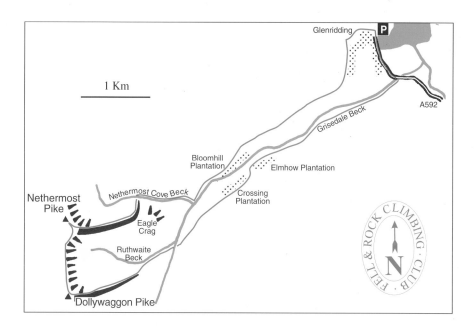

St Sunday Crag from NE ridge of Dollywagon

St Sunday Crag 841m, 2756ft, GR 369134
Birks 622m, 2040ft, GR 380144

St Sunday Crag dominates the head of Ullswater. Its summit lies on the long ridge which strikes NE from Fairfield and its craggy northern face forms the south side of Grisedale. From its lofty height, fine views are available over Ullswater.

This walk takes you up the full length of Grisedale and returns over St Sunday Crag and its outlier Birks. The starting point is in Patterdale (GR 398158) where parking is available opposite the Patterdale Hotel. Follow the track from the centre of the village westwards around the fellside to Grisedale. This track eventually reaches the Grisedale valley road which is followed. Nethermost Pike is at the head of the valley with Helvellyn on the right. The road gives easy walking along the valley floor as far as Elmhow.

Towering above, the slope of St Sunday Crag rises 600m to the summit and dominates its side of the valley from here onwards. A track now continues into the upper reaches of the valley. On the right stands Eagle Crag with signs of man's endeavours around its base. The track pleasantly ascends the left side of the valley before crossing the beck to gain Ruthwaite Lodge. This was originally used as a smithy and bothy for miners but is now a climbing hut. Continue up the valley to Grisedale Tarn nestling between the slopes of Dollywagon Pike and Fairfield. Our route avoids a direct ascent of these slopes by aiming for the col of Deepdale Hause between Fairfield and St Sunday Crag. Cross the outflow of the tarn and gain a track which ascends to this col; here the upper reaches of the valley of Deepdale can be seen – a relatively unfrequented place deserving attention on another day. The ascent of the ridge to St Sunday Crag's summit is straightforward (10km, 725m, 4hr).

Continue along the ridge dropping quickly to a col. The path bears left here but continue upwards along the ridge to the summit of Birks. The fell drops away and the view over Ullswater is worth contemplating. Follow a path downwards through craggy Thornhow End to rejoin the approach path from Patterdale (15km, 5hr 30min).

Arnison Crag

Arnison Crag 433m, 1420ft, GR 394150

Unnoticed by many visitors to Patterdale and ignored by most walkers aiming for higher summits, Arnison Crag gives an attractive short walk with fine views, well-suited to either a summer evening or a winter day.

From the car park opposite the Patterdale hotel, turn left and take the first track right after passing the post office. Turn left at a public footpath sign and keep on this path as far as the wall bounding Glemara Park. Turn left and go uphill outside the wall. Either keep on this path or after passing Oxford Crag go up on to the ridge and re-join the path later. When the bracken is high it is best to stay by the wall. As the top is approached, look out for the path which doubles back left and then goes steeply up to the little rocky summit. A post on the left marks a lower summit which gives good views over the valley to the western flank of Place Fell (1.5km, 283m, 50min).

Descend south and then west and pick up a grassy trod which leads over some undulating ground to Trough Head. A rather unique iron ladder stile gives access over the high stone wall into Glemara Park. A pleasant path gradually descends this valley with lovely views of the head of Ullswater. Great Mell Fell is prominent in the north with Sheffield Pike and Glenridding Dodd in the middle distance. Cross Hagg Beck and keep descending until a wide path is met. Turn right and follow this back to the starting point (5km, 1hr 40min).

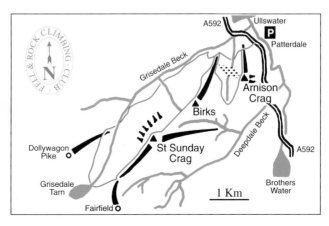

Seat Sandal and Fairfield from Helm Crag

Seat Sandal 736m, 2415ft, GR 344115

The charms of Seat Sandal are hidden to viewers from Grasmere who only see the smooth and grassy western flanks: to the east is a steep craggy face, well seen from the flanks of Fairfield across Grisedale Tarn. Being an isolated hill it is an excellent viewpoint and a quick there-and-back ascent is easily made from Dunmail Raise. A more rewarding route is to use one of the paths on either side of Great Tongue up to Grisedale Hause and to descend by the south ridge.

Park near Mill Bridge on the A591 just north of Grasmere. Go up the made path on the north side of Tongue Gill for 600 metres then cross both bridges to continue up the east side, this being the shorter and easier of the two paths. On reaching the hause, a fine view opens up over Grisedale Tarn. Leave the main path and climb steeply left to the rocky outcrop which marks the summit (5km, 636m, 2hr 20min).

To descend, head SW and follow the tongue of land curving south and descending back towards Mill Bridge. Before you lies Grasmere village with its patchwork of green fields; to the east, the ranges of hills slowly diminish as height is lost. There is hardly any path on this ridge line. A continuous descent to the start is not possible. At a cross-wall, a sign diverts you eastwards along the edge of the NT property to reach Little Tongue Gill. Descend the obvious footpath and return to the start (9km, 3hr 25min).

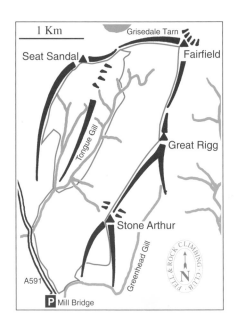

Cofa Pike and Fairfield from the NE

Stone Arthur 500m, 1640ft, GR 348092
Great Rigg 766m, 2513ft, GR 356104
Fairfield 873m, 2864ft, GR 359118

Fairfield is set amidst the rugged scenery of the Borrowdale Volcanic rocks in the central fells, its craggy northern face contrasting with the rounded approach from Grasmere which offers classic views of the southern lakes. Whilst this is a strenuous route, paths are clear and difficulties are only likely to be encountered in poor conditions, when descending over steep, icy ground can be treacherous and a compass is needed to check the way off the summit plateau.

Take the minor road alongside the Swan Hotel on the A591 just outside Grasmere. After 200 metres, turn right at the signpost to Greenhead Gill and Alcock Tarn. After pasing through a gate follow the path on the left which climbs very steeply beside the wall before turning across the fellside to gain the shoulder leading north to the outcrop at Stone Arthur, where there are splendid views W across Easedale to the Langdale Pikes and SW to the Coniston fells.

Continue along the shoulder to a cairn on the main ridge just below Great Rigg for a superb southerly panorama over Lake Windermere and Coniston Water, with Morecambe Bay in the distance. An easy stroll of some 1.5km brings you onto the wide basalt summit plateau of Fairfield (4km, 820m, 2hr 30min). To the NW lie the spectacular crags of Nethermost Pike and Helvellyn, the softer profile of High Street forming the skyline to the east. The sharp descent W to Grisedale Hause is steep and loose in places, requiring extra care. From the rim of the combe the route turns south down Tongue Gill along a well laid track past Tonguegill Force and back to the A591. A short walk along the road to the left returns you to the starting point (10km, 4hr).

The ascent from Deepdale Bridge in Patterdale (GR 399144) via the Hartsop above How ridge and Hart Crag is also recommended, returning NE over St Sunday Crag (12.5km, 4hr 40min).

Hartsop above How

Dove Crag 792m, 2598ft, GR 374105
Hart Crag 822m, 2696ft, GR 368113
Hartsop above How 580m, 1902ft, GR 384120

Hart Crag and Dove Crag both lie on the eastern arm of the Fairfield Horseshoe, a classic long round from Rydal or Ambleside. Our route approaches the tops by lovely Dovedale and returns by the long ridge which descends from Hart Crag over Hartsop above How and down to the valley. We leave the popular but stony and loose path to Dove Crag to go up a narrow grassy shelf giving superb and intimate views of the steep east face.

Park at Cow Bridge between Patterdale and Brotherswater, GR 403133. Walk along the path by the lake and after passing Hartsop Hall turn right along the permissive fell path leading up into Dovedale outside the fell wall. This is a gradual ascent with fine views especially after leaving the woods. Keep on the main path until two streams have been crossed, then leave it as it turns steeply uphill and follow the stream up the narrow grassy valley heading south. There is some irksome tussock grass and the gradient is quite steep, but the views of the face of Dove Crag are ample reward. When a small tarn is passed the going becomes easier and suddenly you top out on the broad ridge with a panorama of Lakeland fells spread out before you. Turn right to reach the top of Dove Crag in about 300 metres (5.5km, 634m, 2hr 45min).

Continue NW along the ridge, dropping down to a broad col and then up the rocky slope to Hart Crag. From the northern edge of the long top are fine views of Scrubby Crag and the Step. A cairn shows the way down to the short and steep east ridge which is rough

and rocky but with an easier alternative on the right. Walking along the broad ridge to Hartsop above How and over Huggill Brow and Gale Crag is a delight, looking across Deepdale to St Sunday and over the main valley to Place Fell, Angletarn Pikes and other Far Eastern Fells. A stile over the wall on the right leads to a steep short cut back to the car park, but for easier walking keep to the main path which, after crossing a wall and a fence, divides into two. Take the right branch which joins the road about 800 metres north of Cow Bridge. A permissive path avoiding the road leads back to the car park (12.5km, 5hr 25min).

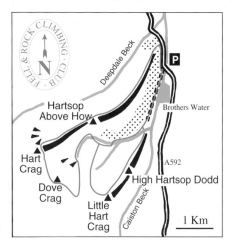

Little Hart Crag 637m, 2089ft, GR 387100
High Hartsop Dodd 519m, 1702ft, GR 393107

High Hartsop Dodd is barely a separate summit, yet when seen head on from the valley floor it gives the striking impression of a towering pyramid, steep on all sides. Little Hart Crag, the higher of the two, has a rocky double summit and some steep flanks but is rarely seen to such advantage as its lower satellite. The approach to Little Hart Crag by Stangs ridge gives outstanding views of Dove Crag.

Park at Cow Bridge near Brotherswater (GR 403133) and walk along the track at the side of the lake to Hartsop Hall. Keep on the main path into Dovedale, crossing the footbridge over Dovedale Beck at the end of a level grassy section. The path now rises at a moderate gradient through patches of bracken, following the banks of the beck if you choose the path variants on the right. After crossing a ladder stile over a wall, leave the path to go left through a gap in an old fence and gain the Stangs ridge. There is no path, but after a short section of bracken the going is straightforward, if steepish in places.

The ridge rises in steps to an unnamed but distinct top of about 460m, then after crossing a flattish depression continues as a series of grass-covered knolls, probably morainic. Skirt the first of these if preferred, but make sure to include the last one for a sudden arrival above the precipitous Stand Crags. Descend to the corner of a fence near the top of Hoggett Gill and go uphill a little way to find the narrow trod which contours across several tributaries

of this. Go up the continuation of the ridge to reach the flat area of Bakestones Moss. A well trodden path follows the old fence to the left and and after passing the branch down to Scandale Pass continues to the first and highest top of Little Hart Crag (6.5km, 507m, 2hr 30min).

Go NE and over the lower top, then down a rake to join the main path which bypasses this top. The gentle stroll down the grassy ridge to High Hartsop Dodd is a delight. Although the descent at the end is steep there is a clearly defined path and where it has become eroded and loose it can be avoided on grass. The views are outstanding, with Angletarn Pikes on the skyline and Brotherswater below. Go to the right of the barn at the foot of the ridge and join the signposted path back to Hartsop Hall (9.5km, 3hr 20min).

Descent from High Hartsop Dodd

Nab Scar 440m, 1443ft, GR 355072
Heron Pike 612m, 2007ft, GR 356083

These two tops lie on a prominent north-south ridge which leads ultimately to Fairfield. It is possible to complete the 'Fairfield Horseshoe' (the watershed of Rydal Beck) by ascending this ridge and descending the next ridge to the east over Dove Crag and High Pike. Dividing the walk into smaller sections enables the less serious walker to explore some of the delights of these fine ridges.

The circuit starts from the lane alongside Rydal Church where there is limited parking. Further parking is available in the two NT car parks alongside Rydal Water. Walk up the lane past Rydal Mount, the last home of Wordsworth from 1813 until 1850, to the open fell. Here a well defined path climbs easily up the slopes of Nab Scar which seemed so steeply wooded when viewed from the roadside. A wall is crossed shortly before a series of nobbles on the ridge any one of which could be regarded as the top. From here, easy walking up the ridge leads to the summit of Heron Pike (2.5km, 550m, 1hr 30 min). There are fine views south and west over Windermere and the Langdale and Coniston Fells.

It is possible to continue along the ridge to Great Rigg and Fairfield. A direct descent NNW leads towards Greenhead Gill and a path descending to the Swan Hotel on the A591 near Grasmere. Descents to the east down steep ground towards Rydal Beck should be avoided. To return to Rydal, retrace your steps back along the ridge for 400 metres and go right (W) at a muddy pool and follow a small stream down to Alcock Tarn. This pleasant, former

reservoir lies in a fold in the hillside. Take the path leading SW from the end of the tarn which descends a wooded spur giving fine views over Grasmere and brings you to a minor road.

A detour right leads to Dove Cottage, the famous home of Dorothy and William Wordsworth. For Rydal, turn left up the minor road. At its highest point, another short detour to the right leads to White Moss Common with exceptional views over both Rydal Water and Grasmere. The minor road continues and becomes a pleasant, wooded track traversing the lower slopes of Nab Scar above the main road and leading to Rydal Mount once again (7km, 3hr).

Pool on Heron Pike, with Great Rigg and Fairfield behind

Low Pike and High Pike from the slopes of Red Screes

Low Pike 508m, 1666ft, GR 374078
High Pike (Scandale) 656m, 2152ft, GR 374088

These two tops lie on the ridge which forms the eastern approach to the Fairfield Horseshoe – a route which continues over Dove Crag and Fairfield before returning to Ambleside over Great Rigg and Heron Pike. An easier and shorter walk to these two fells described here is possible by returning alongside Scandale Beck. The route offers a good opportunity to study the ingenuity of Lakeland walls.

From the central car park in Ambleside, walk up Smithy Brow (the road to Kirkstone Pass) and go first left along Nook Lane to Low Sweden Bridge. A delightful track then ascends through fields to reach the open hillside. The path keeps to the east of the ridge and it is necessary to climb a rocky outcrop without difficulty to reach the summit of Low Pike. The path follows the substantial wall along the ridge northwards to High Pike (4.5km, 600m, 2hr 10min). A direct descent to Scandale Beck from the ridge should be avoided as the ground is steep and rocky. Instead, continue northwards along the ridge to within a few hundred metres of Dove Crag. Take a narrow path eastwards at a small cairn and traverse across to the prominent High Bakestones cairn. A descent is then possible across a rock-strewn slope to tiny Scandale Tarn and Scandale Pass where a good path leads down into Scandale Bottom. The walk back

through the valley reveals more magnificent examples of the craft of the stone wall builders. The track eventually reaches the old packhorse bridge at High Sweden and then enters woodland to return to the Kirkstone Pass road and Ambleside (13km, 5hr 10min).

Section 2

The Far Eastern Fells

The boundaries of AW's *Far Eastern Fells* are Kirkstone Pass and Ullswater in the west and Swindale, Mosedale and Longsleddale in the east. In this book, the area has been extended eastwards to the National Park boundary thereby including nine summits which are in *The Outlying Fells*. Unfortunately, the landowners do not wish to encourage access to The Nab in Martindale and there are no public rights of way around Crookdale and Bannisdale.

AW did the walks for his book in the years 1955 to 1957 and says that he rarely met anyone in his explorations from dawn till dusk. Today there are certainly more walkers about, but it is still possible for seekers of solitude to have some success in this area especially out of season. Even on bank holidays, the more remote hills are quiet and peaceful, but the High Street ridge and the area around the head of Ullswater are best avoided at such times.

Heughscar Hill

Heughscar Hill 375m, 1230ft, GR 488231

Overlooking the northern end of Ullswater is this apparently rather insignificant fell. Its ascent however, gives a wonderful view along the length of the lake and over the Eden Valley. On the west side, a limestone scar gives an indication of the core rock quite different from the Borrowdale Volcanic Series in the central Lakes area.

The ascent of Heughscar Hill starts at Roehead (GR 478236), the roadhead just above Pooley Bridge. Through the gate a track leads up onto the fellside. Beyond Moor Divock is an expanse of open ground with the track leading eastwards to a road above Helton. To the south a long wide ridge ascends towards High Street.

This area is steeped in history. High Street itself is thought to have been the course of the Roman road from Galava (near Ambleside) to Brocavum (just south of Penrith). This track would have used the high ground to avoid the wooded valleys and passed by Heughscar Hill. Imagine a Roman foot-soldier resting beside that limestone scar and looking at the view, possibly feeling closer to his home in Spain with the same familiar core rock. On Moor Divock itself, signs of intensive habitation during the Bronze Age are evident by the

number of burial cairns and tumuli. What was the ring of stones known as the Cockpit (GR 483223) use for? Was this a meeting place or a place of workship? The users would have been people more attuned to nature than today's 'technological' man; what knowledge do these stones hold?

This place is a 'must' during any ascent of Heughscar Hill and requires a slight detour. The track is followed up the fellside to a junction with the main 'Roman Road'. Follow the track to the Cockpit and savour its atmosphere. The ascent is now obvious.

Follow the path eastwards to rejoin the track across Moor Divock and make a direct climb to the summit. The panorama from the cairn is spectacular but the view westwards over Ullswater is improved by keeping to the edge, which is followed northwards to the limestone scar which gives the fell its name. Descend north to gain the track just below and follow this back to Roehead (5km, 150m, 1hr 30min).

Heughscar Hill can also be reached from Askham taking the track SW from the fell gate at GR 507235. After going through a second gate, incline up grass to the corner of a plantation and continue to the top of the hill.

Knipescar Common

Knipescar Common 342m, 1131ft, GR 527191

The name of the Lowther family crops up throughout the Lake District. Lowther Castle, near Askham, on the east of the Lakes is now derelict but shows the wealth accumulated from mining activities in the west of the county. Several farms in the area are owned by the family. The River Lowther flows out of Wetsleddale, just south of Shap, and after joining Haweswater Beck continues northwards passing the delightful village of Askham and through a wooded vale before joining the River Eamont at Brougham, just south of Penrith.

Just to the east of the River Lowther, near Bampton Grange, Knipescar Common commands a

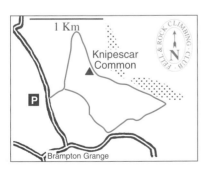

fine position giving a view up towards the dam holding back the waters of the now flooded Mardale. Its distinctive limestone scar bears witness to the difference in the underlying rock structure from the Borrowdale volcanic rock on the other side of the valley.

Althoughthe Scar can be ascended directly by the grassy slopes of Knipescar Common, a pleasant circular walk is recommended. Park alongside the unfenced road between Bampton Grange and Knipe and cut across the lower slopes to join a public footpath by a wall corner at GR 523189. Follow this SE to the point where it almost joins the road, then turn NE along the vague line of an ancient lane, bearing right to a squeeze stile concealed behind a hawthorn copse, then continue to the ruined Low Scarside, a fine house built in 1674. Above and behind the old house go up through a gated field to reach open ground. Finding a way through the intricate maze created by sheep through the gorse bushes is an interesting exercise. On reaching the grass track next to the boundary wall, turn left to enjoy almost 2km along the Scar, with panoramic views to east and west and some fine examples of dissected limestone pavement. Descend from the northern end by sheep trods following the wall (5km, 1332m, 1hr 30min).

Bonscale Fell

Bonscale Pike 524m, 1719ft, GR 450200
Arthur's Pike 532m, 1745ft, GR 461207

Both Arthur's Pike and Bonscale Pike are only minor elevations on the western edge of the long, gentle slopes that form the norther extremity of the High Street ridge. Towards Ullswater however, they present steep craggy faces separated by the rocky ravine of Swarthbeck Gill. The traverse of both the tops from Howtown makes a delightful easy walk with outstanding views.

Driving down the narrow lane to Howtown is best avoided in high season and an attractive alternative is to travel by steamer from either Pooley Bridge or Glenridding. There is parking opposite the public launch site at the Outdoor Centre.

Go through the access gate next to the entrance to the Centre and cross the field diagonally towards a house. Turn right along the path outside the wall towards Mellguards. A grassy path begins here and leads up in a few zig-zags and then diagonally to the head of a dry stream. At the top, turn left (N) along a path which becomes a grassy groove near the top of Bonscale Pike (2km, 370m, 1hr 10min). The best views are from the tall cairn at the edge of the steep ground.

From Bonscale Tower on the northern edge, head SE towards a prominent sheepfold in Swarthbeck Gill. A good path then leads obliquely NE up the grass slope towards Arthur's Pike which is slightly offset from the main path. Return to the main path and follow it NE for 2km to reach a major cross path. Turn left and follow this gently downhill to return to the starting point (10km, 3hr 15min).

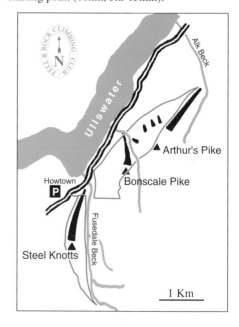

Steel Knotts

Steel Knotts 432m, 1417ft, GR 440181

The highest point of this walk is Gowk Hill (470m) which is a spur on the western side of Wether Hill; Steel Knotts is a fine narrow ridge leading up to it from Howtown. This ridge separates Martindale from the quiet hidden valley of Fusedale and the walk along the crest is an exhilarating one with fine views.

Parking at Howtown is not easy but early in the day it is usually possible to use the small layby at the bottom of the road leading to Sandwick at GR 439194. Cross the valley outside the intake wall to join the path from the church. Turn left and when the path begins to descend start going up the ridge by a small marker post. The initial ascent is rather steep but perfectly easy. Higher up the gradient becomes gentle and gives pleasant walking. The main summit sports a fine rock outcrop (2km, 284m, 1hr).

Continue along the narrow ridge over the intermediate top of Brownthwaite Crags and on to Gowk Hill. This is a grassy top with no cairn (3.5km, 398m, 1hr 40min). From the top cross over some marshy ground and go through a broken wall to join the main path and turn left downhill. The path forks right and rises slightly by a ruined house and then descends into Fusedale by the attractive little ravine of Groove Gill, which it crosses by a slate bridge. When the enclosed fields are reached the gill is crossed twice and the concrete road followed for a short distance. When this road bends sharp right, leave it and follow the wall left to return to the start (7.5km, 2hr 40min).

The same route over Steel Knotts and Gowk Hill is also recommended as an approach to Wether Hill and Loadpot Hill to give a more strenuous walk. From Gowk Hill it is hard going up steep ground to the main ridge. The easiest way is not to make a beeline for Wether Hill but to bear right up a slanting shelf to the groove which arrives at Keasgill Head. After this it is pleasant walking along the ridge over Wether Hill and Loadpot Hill, bearing left for Arthur's Pike. Return to Howtown by the gradually descending path from the junction at GR 473220 (16.5km, 659m, 5hr 15min).

Hallin Fell

Hallin Fell 388m, 1271ft, GR 433198

Though relatively small, this superbly positioned mountain has fine views over Ullswater and into secluded Martindale. With the road passing over the adjacent Martindale Hause giving ease of access, it is a popular and well-climbed mountain. Our route starts from this col (GR 435192), initially walking around the base and ascending the fell from the lakeside.

Take a path which slopes down the side of Hallin Fell towards Ullswater. Gain a popular path traversing around the base of the mountain. The lake steamer can often be seen at the pier in Howtown Bay. The path gives access to the lake shore. Hallinhag Wood on the NW side of the fell is enclosed by a wall barring access to sheep: its natural lushness shows what the Lakes were like before the introduction of sheep. Just before a gate at the west end of the wood, a path strikes up leftwards. Where the path levels out, take a direct line up the fellside to the summit (3km, 240m, 1hr 20min).

The distinctive cairn dominates the summit but the view in all directions is superb. A descent can be made in a number of ways all going southwards back to the col (4km).

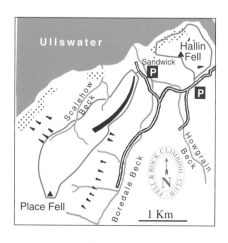

Place Fell from Hartsop above How

Place Fell 657m, 2154ft, GR 406170

Easily approached by many paths and in a superb position to the southeast of Ullswater, Place Fell is a much-loved mountain with panoramic views. There are gentle grassy slopes on the extensive upper reaches but it is rough and craggy on both sides, with little tarns near the top and lovely waterfalls in Scalehow Beck. One of the most beautiful of Lakeland's low level paths runs along the foot of its western slopes, from Sandwick to Patterdale.

Park at Sandwick on the verge of the unfenced road, approached along the east side of the lake from Pooley Bridge. Go up the steep grassy north end of Sleet Fell (378m) and on up to the top of High Dodd (501m). Descend to the col ahead on which is a sheep fold. Continue uphill in the same direction (SW) on the main path. Bear right along the obvious scooped track to the eastern shoulder and after passing a tarn

the rocky summit is reached (4km, 487m, 1hr 50min).

Descend to The Knight, following a narrow trod (black dots on the map) roughly NW at first and then north. Deer are frequently observed in this area. Continue past The Knight still in a northerly direction until the ground begins to rise towards Bleaberry Knott. At this point start going down to the NE to a sheepfold (GR 410183). Cross Scalehow Beck above the falls and go straight across the main track to follow a delightful path above High Knott with lovely views of the lake. This path leads straight to the unfenced road where the walk began (8km, 2hr 50min).

A more traditional route is to climb Place Fell from Patterdale by Boardale Hause, descending by the main path to the foot of Scalehow Force and returning by the lakeside path (12km, 509m, 5hrs).

Angletarn South Pike from the north

Brock Crags 561m, 1840ft, GR 417136
Angletarn Pikes 567m, 1860ft, GR 413148

The double rocky tops of Angletarn Pikes are seen to advantage from many of the fells in the Patterdale area. In turn, they are perfectly situated for panoramic views of nearly all the hills in the north-eastern Lake District. Angle Tarn, which lies at the foot of the south Pike, is particularly attractive with its small islets, indented shoreline and little crags on the western side.

Park at the end of the road in the hamlet of Hartsop. Take the sign-posted bridleway towards Hayeswater but fork left towards the filter house at the cattle grid. As this is reached, double back left along the pipeline track, no longer an eyesore as described by AW 40 years ago, but a pleasant green path. At the stream confluence you can see the remains of the supports for a water-course and the wheel-pit for a 30ft waterwheel, used as a power source for draining the Low Hartsop mine.

After about 600 metres, turn right up the obvious grooved path climbing the hillside diagonally. At about the 500m contour pass a cairn and take a faint grassy path on the left as the main path levels out. Go through a gate in an old fence and continue through a gateway in the second wall. Turn immediately left here to reach Brock Crags on a vague path which initially follows an old wall and leads through the cluster of small tarns to the tall cairn (3.5km, 256m, 1hr 20min).

Return to the path by the gap in the wall and follow it N to join the main 'highway' passing Angle Tarn. At the foot of the rocky south Pike, take to a grassy trod leading up to the top from the east side. Retrace your steps a little way and cross the col to the higher north top, also approaching this from the east (5.5km, 353m, 2hr).

Descend easily NE to pick up a pleasant little-used path leading to Boardale Hause and follow another pipeline track back south towards Hartsop. When you have crossed the footbridge below the waterfalls of Angletarn Beck, either go left and over the stile to a footpath, or through the gate and follow the stony lane (10km, 3hr 10min).

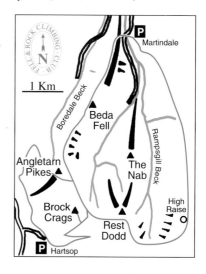

Beda Fell from Hallin Fell

Beda Fell 509m, 1669ft, GR 428170
Rest Dodd 696m, 2283ft, GR 432137
(**The Nab** 576m, 1889ft, GR 434152)

This high level walk along grassy ridges in the quiet and unspoilt area of Martindale gives easy and enjoyable walking with superb views. The area, with its two valleys separated by The Nab, gives sanctuary to a herd of red deer and you may be rewarded by a sight of some of these magnificent animals. Take great care not to disturb them by keeping to the described route and note that this does not include The Nab. However, permission to climb The Nab may be given if requested in advance by contacting Dalemain Estate Office.

The approach to the start is along the east side of Ullswater from Pooley Bridge. Park near Martindale Old Church at GR 434184. Walk over the bridge to Winter Crags farm and go uphill behind the slate signpost to Sandwick to find the path sloping up behind a wall. This leads to the ridge, joining another path from Garth Heads farm in Boardale. Walking up this ridge is fairly steep at first but quite delightful. The second and higher top of Beda Fell is passed followed by several more ups and downs along the ridge before crossing the good path from Patterdale to Martindale. (Those wanting a shorter walk can descend from here to Dalehead Farm.)

The main walk continues along the ridge, approaching Angletarn Pikes but keeping on the east side above the crags enclosing Bannerdale. Angle Tarn comes into view and then the path descends to join the main track near the tarn's edge. (Detours to take in Angletarn Pikes and Brock Crags may be made from here.) Follow the main path through a gate and along the east side of a wall, leaving it after a few minutes for a minor path making towards Rest Dodd. This vague path continues up an indefinite east ridge but gives out before reaching the top (7.5km, 570m, 3hr).

Continue the walk by following the wall SE across a marshy saddle and on up towards The Knott. Turn eastwards to Rampsgill Head and then follow the ridge northwards to the top of High Raise (10km, 809m, 3hr 50min). The way now lies north along the main High Street ridge and over Red Crag, a slight rise on the ridge at 711m. Keep to the crest of the ridge for another 1km. Near Keasgill Head, take the descending path NW, bypassing Gowk Hill before rising slightly over Brownthwaite Crag and sloping down the hillside back to Martindale (16km, 5hr 20min).

Hallin Fell and Loadpot Hill from Ullswater

Wether Hill 670m, 2198ft, GR 456167
Loadpot Hill 671m, 2201ft, GR 457181

Although these two tops may be traversed when following the whole of the High Street ridge they provide a worthwhile walk in themselves. The attractions lie in the combination of easy walking on grass while enjoying the superb panorama across the Eden valley to the Pennines in the east and closer views of the Helvellyn range in the west. Good visibility is a necessity for full enjoyment.

The approach to the start is by a narrow lane from Bampton with few passing places, or from Helton through some unfenced ground but with five gates. There is some parking on the grass verge near a barn at GR 497183.

Cross Cawdale Beck by a clapper bridge SW of Moorahill Farm and follow the grassy path up the ridge of the Hause. Keep to the original old path partly in a grassy groove, passing a large cairn before traversing the minor top of Low Kop (572m). Keep in the same direction, crossing High Kop where there is an old boundary stone and joining the main ridge path north of Keasgill Head. Either keep to the main path or find the narrow trod which crosses the flat southern top of Wether Hill and rejoins the main path by the summit cairn (6km, 360m, 2hr 10min).

Continue northwards along the main path, passing the old ruined chimney of Lowther House to the summit of Loadpot where there is a trig point. From the nearby cairn incorporating a boundary stone strike eastwards along the broad ridge, soon picking up a descending trod. Choose any line, aiming roughly towards Knipe Scar. In about ten minutes

cross another trod diagonally and after passing a ruin (bield) make towards the edge of the broad ridge overlooking Cawdale. Drop down into the valley by the wall enclosing a narrow strip of woodland to avoid Carhullan farm and return to the starting point (11.5km, 4hr 35min).

A circular walk can also be made from Howtown ascending by Steel Knotts and descending by Arthur's Pike. See entries under these headings for further details.

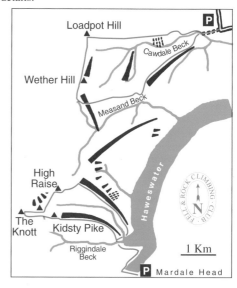

High Raise ridge from Naddle Forest

High Raise (Martindale) 802m, 2631ft, GR 448135
Rampsgill Head 792m, 2598ft, GR 443128
The Knott 739m, 2423ft, GR 437127
Kidsty Pike 780m, 2560ft, GR 447126

High Raise and Rampsgill Head lie on the long High Street ridge; the other two tops are offset, Kidsty on the east and The Knott on the west. This route approaching the tops by the long south-east ridge is attractive for the views of Whelter Crags and has the added bonus of being little used. By including The Knott in the round fine views to the west are obtained. Two interesting diversions may be made. One is to the observation point in Riggindale when the Golden Eagles are nesting in early summer; the other to the British hill fort perched on Castle Crag.

Park at the head of Haweswater and follow the path round to Riggindale. Just after crossing the stone packhorse bridge over Randale Beck turn left at the corner of a plantation. Follow an old path, at first partly lost in bracken which leads up by some old fence posts and through a gateway in a wall. Leave the path half-right to make for the first dip in the skyline. When this col is reached, the British fort is five minutes away on the other side. Continue up the ridge over the minor bump of Lady's Seat, veering left to a ruined building. Either go up the steep but continuous grass slope ahead and then bear right or make your way up among the rocky outcrops near the edge of Whelter Crags. When the angle eases make for the subsidiary top of Low Raise (754m). A substantial cairn and a low shelter are a surprise considering the grassy nature of the terrain. There are magnificent views of Cross Fell and the Eden Valley to the east. A vague path leads on to High Raise which is almost on the main ridge path (7km, 580m, 2hr 30 min).

Follow the wide path SSW on to Rampsgill Head. (Note that from the col between the two a contouring path veers left towards Kidsty, a recommended short cut in bad weather.) To reach The Knott, go west from Rampsgill along the edge of the cliffs to strike the main path up from Patterdale and then it is a short pull up taking two minutes or so. Return to the path and follow it by the wall along the Straits of Riggindale to reach the branch path going north-east around the head of Riggindale to Kidsty Pike. The descent eastwards along the broad grassy ridge is straightforward. At Kidsty Howes the well trodden path is muddy after rain and can be avoided by grassy slopes further east. Re-join the lakeside path near the bridge to return to the starting point. (13km, 4hr 30min).

Rough Crag and High Street from across Haweswater

High Street 828m, 2716ft, GR 441111
Mardale Ill Bell 761m, 2496ft, GR 447101

The top of High Street is the culminating point of a long north-south ridge along which ran the course of the Roman road from Ambleside to Penrith; a fine walk today for the superfit. The plateau near the trig point was used in more recent times as a shepherds' Meet each July for the exchange of strayed sheep and to enjoy cakes and ale and a bit of horse-racing. Although this ceased in 1820 it is still known as 'Racecourse Hill'.

There are many routes to the top but the one chosen for this book is one of the finest walks in the Lake District: the long ridge of Rough Crag separating Riggindale from Mardale and the deep circular tarn of Blea Water. Although steep in places, there is a clear path and the views are superb.

Park at the head of Haweswater, an early start being advisable on Sundays. Go through the fell gate and turn right at the end of the wall on a signposted footpath. Cross the footbridge and turn right and after reaching the wooded area double back left just before the lakeside path goes through the wall. There are several false tops before the 628m top of Rough Crag is reached, with views improving all the time. From this vantage point the suggested alternative route of descent from Mardale Ill Bell can be inspected. In early summer if you are lucky the walk along the ridge can bring the rewarding sight of the golden eagles who nest in Riggindale.

From Rough Crag there is a slight descent to Caspel Gate, where there is no gate but a small tarn which dries up in drought. The ascent continues quite steeply up the rocky ridge of Long Stile where hands are needed but there is no difficulty. Near the top the path is a little loose but can be avoided on grass. A cairn marks the edge of the plateau and is a key reference point if descending this way. Continue roughly SW to reach the wall and follow this left to the trig point (4.5km, 604m, 2hr 10min).

Follow the wall south along the path as far as a prominent cairn and then turn left on a well-defined path giving easy walking all the way to Mardale Ill Bell. If preferred you can follow the escarpment edge for exciting views, but this involves rougher walking and a greater height loss. The summit cairn is slightly to the left of the path. To descend by the standard route return to the path and follow it SE then east to the Nan Bield pass on which is a huge windbreak cairn. From the pass a delightful but stony path leads down to the attractive little tarn of Small Water.

The alternative way down from Mardale Ill Bell by the Northeast Spur is interesting and quite adventurous, but is not recommended in mist or for inexperienced walkers. Although described by AW 30 years ago (as an ascent route) there are few signs of use and the author has never met nor seen anyone there. Care is needed as there are many crags and

High Street from Rampsgill Head

although it is easy to avoid them backtracking is sometimes involved. Grass slopes lower down lead to the path by Small Water. Cross the stepping stones near the outlet and follow the well-used path back to the car park (9km, 620m, 3hr 10min).

This walk is easily linked with Harter Fell to make an excellent long walk by continuing uphill from the Nan Bield Pass, walking over Harter Fell and descending to the head of Haweswater by the Gatesgarth Pass. See the entry under Harter Fell for further details.

A pleasant way to climb High Street from the west is to start at Low Hartsop (GR 409131) and follow the path up Hayeswater Gill and over The Knott, continuing along the ridge over High Street to Thornthwaite Crag and descending either by Pasture Beck or the long arm of Grey Crag.

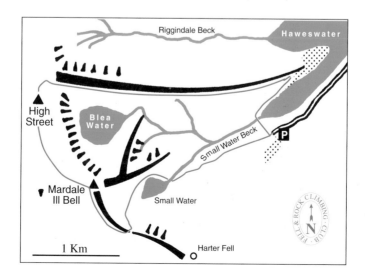

Gray Crag

Gray Crag 699m, 2293ft, GR 427117
Thornthwaite Crag 784m, 2572ft, GR 432100
Stony Cove Pike (Caudale Moor) 763m, 2502ft, GR 418100
Hartsop Dodd 618m, 2027ft, GR 411118

This is a delightful high level walk with commanding views of the High Street massif to the east and the Fairfield and Helvellyn ranges to the west. When the hordes are on their way up to High Street via The Knott, this alternative walk offers seclusion. The section between Thornthwaite Crag and Stony Cove Pike is unfortunately a return to the fast track.

Start at the car park at Hartsop (GR 410131). Take the good track through the gate to Hayeswater, keeping on the right of the gill, when the track divides. After about 1km you come to a gate leading to the open fell. Go through this and climb steeply SE towards a vague gully feature; a broken down wall acts as a guide. Go up the grassy 'gully' ignoring sheep tracks running across the slope. Eventually you come across a faint track heading south, leading to a fine rugged ridge and the summit of Gray Crag (2.3 km, 520m, 1hr 30min). Continue south on the crest of the ridge with magnificent views - particularly of Lake Windermere through Threshwaite Mouth. A little climb leads on to Thornthwaite Beacon (4.3km, 650m, 2hr 10min). From the Beacon head NW before going steeply down the eroded path to Threshthwaite Mouth. A steep climb up a delightful rocky section leads to Stony Cove Pike. From the summit rocks follow the wall west for 200 metres, when the wall turns to your left, head straight on to Caudale Moor. You soon leave the hordes behind and can sit

overlooking Caudale Valley from above the steep slopes of Caudale Head – a beautiful secluded spot. Following the edge of Caudale Head move in an easterly direction across tussock grass to meet up with a wall. Follow this north to Hartsop Dodd with a magnificent view of Ullswater (8.7km, 850m, 3hr 35min). From the summit head steeply down the crest of a spur. Zig-zag downward until you come to a wall, head NE down the steep grassy slope and return to Hartsop (10.5km, 4hr).

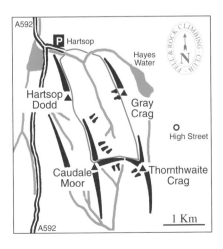

Harter Fell from Ill Bell

Harter Fell (Mardale) 778m, 2552ft, GR 460093

The craggy face of Harter Fell dominates the skyline above Mardale Head at the southern extremity of Haweswater. This outing is ideal for a short day or summer evening, with an extensive summit panorama from Scafell Pike in the west to Cross Fell, the highest point of the Pennines, in the east. The walk uses two ancient pack horse routes, with a rugged but easy ascent through magnificent scenery to Nan Bield Pass and a gentle stroll back from Gatesgarth Pass.

The flooding of Mardale in 1935 to form the reservoir engulfed the community of Mardale Green which lay at the head of the valley, but in drought conditions the bridge in the village emerges from the waters. Eagles nest in Riggindale and for some years the RSPB has set up a public viewing facility in the area, where deer are also seen regularly.

From the Mardale head car park take the Kentmere bridleway which climbs steadily to the outlet of Small Water. The path passes three old stone shelters by the tarn to navigate the steep, boulder strewn northern side of the glacial combe in a wide arc, reaching a wind break on the summit of Nan Bield Pass. Here the walker is rewarded with a view of Kentmere reservoir surmounted by Ill Bell, Froswick and Yoke.

The route then ascends the shoulder to the SE, emerging on the round, open summit of Harter Fell at an unusual cairn, having a skeleton of mangled iron railings (2km, 530m, 1hr 30min). Turn NE and descend gently over easy ground for 500 metres to a second cairn by a boundary stone which offers the best views over Mardale. In poor visibility, keep the fence on your right. The track continues SE over Little Harter Fell to descend to Gatesgarth Pass, returning to Mardale Head by the byway beside Gatesgarth Beck (5.5km, 2hr 20min).

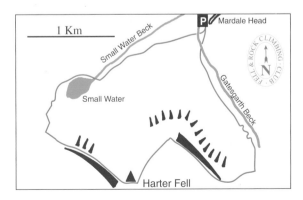

The view from Hare Shaw to High Street

Hare Shaw 503m, 1650ft, GR 497131

Hare Shaw is a small fell overlooking the beautiful valley of Swindale and the desecrated valley of Mardale. The Haweswater Reservoir is now the dominant feature of the latter and attracts hordes of visitors, particularly when low. They hope to see the remains of the hamlet, Mardale Green, that existed before water for Manchester resulted in the building of the reservoir.

The walk starts at Mardale Head car park. This is a stunning spot as you have been transported into the heart of the Eastern Fells. Around you are High Street, Mardale Ill Bell, Harter Fell, Artlecrag Pike and two important passes. From the car park take the lake side path below the road. After just over 1 km you will cross a small beck by a stone bridge. Follow the path up to the road and continue along the 'Old Corpse Road' as it zig zags its way up the hill. This hilly track was used to transport corpses from Mardale Green for burial at Shap. This practice ceased in 1729 with the building of Mardale Church and cemetery. As the track levels out it crosses Rowantreethwaite Beck (posts mark the route). Leave the path here and head due north to the cairn on Rowantreethwaite Crag. Head NE past Ritchie Crag to a broad ridge feature. This is across boggy ground and leads with more bog hopping past Woof Crag to the bulk of Hare Shaw and the summit cairn (4.6km, 300m, 1hr 40min). From the cairn, head NW into a broad marshy area and follow the stream until it meets a wall. Keeping to the south side of the steam follow it to some waterfalls. Follow a vague track SW to Guerness Gill. A small hillock marks the entrance to the gill. Cross the gill via an excellent bridge (pipeline nearby). A slight climb, 20m, leads to a track heading diagonally down the hill to the road. Be careful on leaving the gill not to go too high, only a slight climb is necessary and the track is marked with concrete posts. Once on the road you can go through a gate and make your way to the reservoir path and thence Mardale Head (10km, 3hr 15mins).

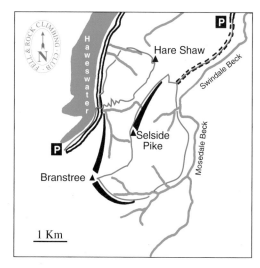

Selside Pike from Rough Crag

Branstree 713m, 2339ft, GR 478100
Selside Pike 655m, 2148ft, GR 490112

These two fells near the head of Haweswater are little visited and give enjoyable walking away from the crowds. There is no unsightly erosion but much water-logged ground and good boots will be appreciated. The flat grassy top of Branstree has little of interest in itself, the cairn on nearby Artlecrag making a better objective. It can be climbed from the Haweswater road by the north ridge with a descent to Gatesgarth Pass, but this circular route from the quiet and peaceful valley of Swindale has much more to recommend it. Selside Pike is seen at its best. An east facing corrie heads the valley, with steep crags encircling a dry tarn bed known as Dodd Bottom.

Swindale is approached from Shap and Bampton by a narrow road. Park at GR 522142 where there is a sign warning 'No car park beyond this point'. There is some unofficial parking at Truss Gap, but the narrow lane is much used by farm traffic and is best traversed on foot.

Walk up the valley road to Swindale Head farm, enjoying fine views across to Gouther Crag. Continue up the bridle path through the moraines, with views of the waterfalls, where the path begins to rise more steeply. As the angle levels out the path becomes

vague in the boggy ground. Aim to the right of a rocky knoll and pick up the path again on the upper side of a broken wall. The path becomes vague again as the bridge across Mosedale Beck comes into sight but the cart-track from Mosedale Cottage (now a bothy) is soon found.

Continue past the bothy and around a corner, then leave the path and head up easy grass slopes to reach the wall and follow it NW to the top of Branstree (3hr 15min). If in cloud, turn right when the fence is met and follow it with confidence all the way to Selside Pike. In clear weather, make for the cairn on Artle Crag, then re-cross the fence and aim for Selside Pike via the flattish unnamed top at 673m, passing a prominent survey post built by Manchester Corporation.

From the top of Selside Pike on which is a large hollow cairn go roughly NE down the broad grassy ridge along a path which becomes intermittent. Lower down it is better defined and joins the Old Corpse Road midway between two marker cairns. Turn right and follow this down to join the road near Swindale Head farm, a high ladder stile leading to a short cut at the end (16km, 530m, 5hr).

High Wether Howe from Mosedale

High Wether Howe   531m, 1742ft, GR 516109

This walk looks into the lonely uper reaches of Mosedale and poses some interesting navigation problems on the return to Swindale.

Drive up Swindale until you reach a cattle grid where a slate let into the wall advises 'No car park beyond here'. Park on the grass on the right. Walk up the road to Swindale Head and continue on the bridleway signed to Mosedale. Follow the rough track over a plank bridge and through moraines until the slope rises ahead. The path is easy to lose here and you may be forced left towards the stream. To avoid this, keep straight on uphill from the marker post, swinging left of a rocky outcrop and then back right to pick up the bridleway which follows the line of an old wall. Pass through the fence at an iron gate and descend to the stream confluence in Mosedale Beck which is crossed by a bridge. A narrow path follows Little Mosedale Beck for a short way and then swings left to zig-zag up the fell. When the path disappears at a fence, go NE along the ridge to Scam Matthew and then NNW for 400 metres to High Wether Howe (7km, 300m, 2hr 30min).

The return crosses the desolate, gently-sloping ground to the north-east. It is crossed by buggy tracks and the footpaths are not evident. Walk ENE to Seat Robert along a ridge with rocky outcrops. Continue descending in the same direction towards White Crag. Turn left and follow an indistinct, boggy path WNW for over 2km to the corner of a wall around Gouther Crag. A small cairn to the right marks the start of a steep decent into Swindale, initially grassy and then rocky, leading to a fine bridge and the road at Truss Gap (14km, 5hrs).

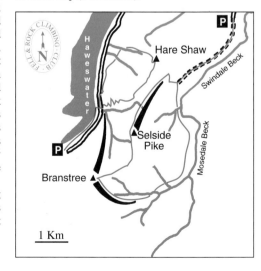

The cairn on Whiteside Pike

Whiteside Pike 397m, 1302ft, GR 521016

Whiteside Pike is the southernmost peak of what has been called the Bannisdale Horseshoe; the other tops from Cappelbarrow round to White Howe being rounded and grassy and uninteresting to walk upon apart from distant views on a good day. The Bannisdale valley is, however, charming, usually deserted and home to many birds and flowers. Private land makes a walk around the Horseshoe impractical at present but the ascent of Whiteside Pike, a pleasant rocky summit, makes a good short excursion.

Turn off the A6 north of Kendal at a substation (GR 530997) and park at a bridge just after the road to Mosergh Farm branches off to the left. Walk up the Mosergh road for 400 metres then turn right, before the farm, onto a bridleway. This leaves the walled lane after another 600 metres but to climb Whiteside Pike, follow the lane straight on to a gate which gives access to the open fell. A way can now be made north across bracken and heather to the summit.

Routes into Bannisdale begin from Bannisdale Beck Bridge, 2km further north up the A6. There are no public rights of way in or around the valley and permission for access should be sought locally.

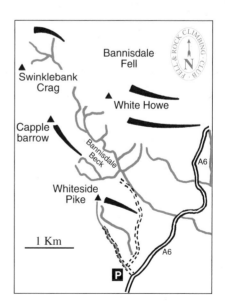

On Kentmere Pike in winter

Kentmere Pike 730m, 2394ft, GR 466078
Shipman Knotts 587m, 1926 472063

There are many ways to reach these summits. They form part of the Kentmere round and can also be ascended from High Street and Mardale to the north. This walk describes a less common route starting from Sadgill in Longsleddale (GR 483057). Park where the bridge crosses the River Sprint. Follow the old quarry road on the east bank of the river past Buckbarrow Crag to a wooden stile at a sheepfold (GR 478085). Cross the wall and follow the path through the disused Wrengill Quarry workings taking care, particularly on the steep ramp to some ruined quarry buildings where a large engine block may be inspected.

The path narrows and passes beside a narrow ravine. By two stone pillars swing left onto the south bank, avoiding the deep pot and waterfall. Follow the lumpy ridge between the stream ravine and a deep hole on the left. The ridge runs onto the fellside and walking SW, the line of a wall is followed to join the main wall along the Kentmere Pike ridge to the top (5km, 545m, 2hr 10min). This route affords good views of the quarry workings but would be dangerous in poor visibility. In such conditions, continue past the stile, along the track before turning left through a gate to follow the quarry perimeter wall and fence; follow this SW to the ridge.

Continue SE along the ridge wall to reach the 626m cairn. The wall becomes a fence which is followed southwards over Shipman Knotts and down a steep rocky section to the junction with the Kentmere–Longsleddale brideway. From this point, the circuit and ascent of Green Quarter Fell can be followed if a longer walk is required. Otherwise, turn left and follow the bridleway back to Sadgill (10km, 3hr 30min).

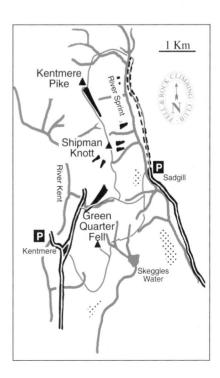

The head of Kentmere from Green Quarter Fell

Green Quarter Fell 426m, 1397ft, GR 469041

Although this fell is a featureless moor, it has the virtue of being unfrequented and of giving superb views of the Kentmere valley. It can be circumnavigated by paths well-marked on the map and the ascent uses part of the circular tour before making a bid for the top.

From the parking area at Kentmere church, walk back along the road to Lowfield Lane and follow this to Green Quarter. Turn right along the bridleway signposted to Longsleddale. After 400 metres, veer left at a low stump (footpath marker). The path rises round the hillside through several fields and gates until it eventually leads north-east. Where a fence cuts off the corner of a field, a gate allows access to the open fell on the left. Ascend NNW to reach the highest point (3.5km, 260m, 1hr 20min). The only way off which does not cross fences or walls is to retrace one's steps to the gate in the fence. Turn right to return directly to the start. Alternatively, continue left and follow the bridleway NE following the posts. This track joins the Kentmere–Longsleddale track at GR 482051. Turn left to return to Kentmere. The main track reaches the road 1.5km north of Kentmere village. Alternatively, a path descends SE more directly to Green Quarter from the highest point (10.5km, 3hr 20min).

The other way of appoaching Green Quarter Fell is from Sadgill in Longsleddale.

Looking across Longsleddale to Tarn Crag

Grey Crag 638m, 2093ft, GR 497072
Tarn Crag (Longsleddale) 664m, 2178ft, GR 488078

Longsleddale is a favourite stamping ground for the lovers of solitude and this round of Tarn Crag taking in Grey Crag and Great Howe provides a pleasant introduction to the area. After a short, stiff initial pull the walking becomes a leisurely stroll in easy terrain more reminiscent of the Pennine moors than of the Lake District

From Sadgill (GR 484056) go through the field gate on the right and walk NE uphill to a hurdle incorporating a stile in the wall. Continue uphill, through bracken, following the left-hand fork of a tiny gill which leads to the upper slopes of Great Howe. Continue north on gentler ground across moorland until you reach a fence crossing the upper reaches of Galeforth Gill. The fence may be crossed by a makeshift stile in the NE corner. Proceed NE without a path to the summit cairn of Grey Crag from where there are fine views of Borrowdale, Bannisdale and the Pennines.

From the cairn, go NW over moorland and the peaty outfall from Greycrag Tarn to the cairn on Tarn Crag from where there are views of Longsleddale and Windermere (3km, 515m, 1hr 35min). In the dale bottom there is plentiful evidence of the valley's former mining and quarrying history.

To descend, go NW down a grassy slope following a gill with a fence above on its north bank. Disused Wrengill Quarry lies across the valley. Another quarry site marks the foot of the slope; turn left to take the downhill track south back to Sadgill (7km, 2hr 45 min).

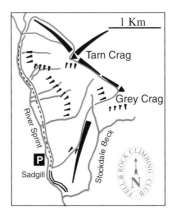

Ulgraves on Brunt Fell from the A6

Brunt Knott 427m, 1400ft, GR 484006

This is the highest point in an area of upland immediately east of Staveley in the lower Kentmere valley. There are other tops to Potter Fell and Ulgraves further east but they have no obvious means of access or rights of way.

From the north end of Staveley village, cross Barley Bridge and turn left up Hall Lane for 1.5km to a signed path on the right leading through a field towards Ghyll Bank. Just before the farm, follow the track right for 300 metres to a track junction and go left to Brunt Knott Farm. Follow the yellow footpath markers through the two gates at the farm. A wide stony track zig-zags uphill towards an iron gate and stile in the top right-hand corner of a rough pasture. After the gate, swing left and go straight up the fell in a NW direction. This is hard pounding until you reach the shallower, hummocky, summit slope leading to the stone-built trig point (3.5km, 327m, 1hr 25min). The surrounding walls and absence of public footpaths limit any continuation walk and you will need to return by the same route.

The hill can also be climbed from the other end of the approach path in Longsleddale, starting from the lane leading to Tenter Howe and Bridge End farms.

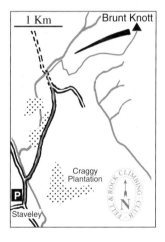

Yoke, Ill Bell and Froswick from Mardale Ill Bell

Froswick 720m, 2362ft, GR 435085
Ill Bell 757m, 2483ft, GR 437077
Yoke 706m, 2316ft, GR 438067

This is a walk of contrast: a walk along the famed Roman Road and pathway for invading Scots (beaten back on the Troutbeck slopes) along High Street and the lofty Ill Bell ridge. This cuts a north/south swathe joining the high fells in the north to the green foothills of the south.

The walk starts next to Trout Beck near Church Bridge GR 412027. There is parking for several cars next to the minor road on the north bank of the beck.

From here walk due south on the main road for 200 metres and then head steeply uphill on the Garburn Road track. At GR 416027 take the (possible) line of High Street in a northerly direction and initially downhill. (It is possible to avoid this ascent and descent by taking the shortcut from Troutbeck through Limefitt Park onto this track.) Follow this up Troutbeck and then Hagg Gill. As you continue up the valley you will see the steep bracken covered slopes of Park Fell, the route heads up this – watch out for mountain bikers. After a rather steep climb you come onto the more open approach slopes heading towards Thornthwaite Crag (8.2km, 580m, 3hrs). An option is to continue to this summit. Our route turns due south along the ridge to the delightful rocky summit of Froswick. Continue in a southerly direction to the high point of the route, Ill Bell (10.5km, 800m, 4hrs). This is a particularly scenic position, with wonderful views of Windermere to the SW and Kentmere with the Nan Bield Pass at its head, to the east. From here follow the path on the crest of the ridge southwards to Yoke and back via some rather boggy sections to the Garburn Road. This is followed to the main road and Church Bridge (17.5km, 5hr 50mins).

Troutbeck Tongue from the Garburn Pass track

Troutbeck Tongue 364m, 1194ft, GR 422064

As you head over Kirkstone Pass on the A592 from Troutbeck you will undoubtedly notice the great Ill Bell ridge but pause for one moment and look more closely into the valley. A small fell, an off-shoot of the larger Thornthwaite Crag, the Tongue, stands proudly overlooking the valley. From its summit you get a splendid view of Lake Windermere and the fells of the southern lakes, many covered in a coat of trees – Claife Heights and Grizedale Forest.

The walk starts from Town Head, GR 414037, and follows the private Ing Lane (footpath only) towards Troutbeck Park Farm. This is a short walk but it does involve a fairly steep ascent. Follow the lane until you reach Hagg Bridge; from here take the footpath up Hall Hill to a gate in the wall and go through onto a good track. Go along this in a northerly direction until you go through a gate in a fence with a barn to your east. Now the hard work starts. Go through the gate and, following the line of the fence, head steeply uphill. When the fence turns due south keep zig-zagging uphill. After a while the slope eases and you will see the summit cairn of The Tongue (3.7km, 240m, 1hr 20min). Rest and admire the view. This ascent is awkward in summer/early autumn due to the profusion of bracken on the slopes. It is best done in spring before the bracken takes hold. The descent is the reverse of the above or follow a vague track north. After about 300 metres turn east and zig-zag down a vague gully feature in the face. Follow the track back to Town Head (7.5km, 2hr 15min).

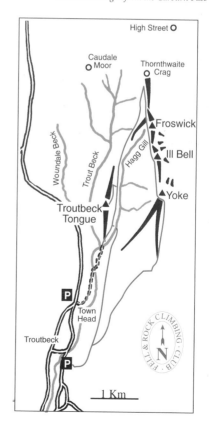

Wansfell above Windermere

Wansfell 487m, 1597ft, GR 404053

Overlooking a large expanse of open country south of Kirkstone Pass, this low fell has one of the finest views in Lakeland. In fact the best viewpoint is from Wansfell Pike at 484m and more than 1km SW of the highest point of the fell. The walk starts directly from Ambleside town centre and after a steep ascent descends to Troutbeck before returning along the slopes of the hill. The route is an excellent round, on good tracks all the way.

Start from the market hall in the centre of Ambleside and ascend the steep road behind Barclay's Bank. After 400 metres take the footpath on the left alongside the ghyll, a Victorian walk, staying on the right hand side. At the top, double back for 50 metres and join the road by a revolving gate. Ascend for a further 400 metres into farmland and over an iron ladder stile onto the fellside. Climb steeply on a good track and restored path directly to the excellent rocky summit of Wansfell Pike (2.5km, 434m, 1hr 20min).

To include the highest point of Wansfell (Baystones on the map), go over the stile and walk NE alongside the wall for 1300 metres. From the summit turn south and follow the wall to reach Nanny Lane at GR 403040. Otherwise, to continue the circuit from Wansfell Pike descend east to Nanny Lane. Turn right down this green lane to reach Troutbeck village by a farm. Turn right and walk along the road to the Post Office by the village green. Turn immediately right along Robin Lane which rises gently round the hillside with several seats and excellent views of Windermere.

After 1500 metres fork left down towards High Skelghyll farm. Turn right along a road through the farm, then along a trackway through woodland and past Jenkins Crag (NT), descending to Ambleside by the Mountain Rescue headquarters. Turn right to return to the town centre (12km, 3hr 45min).

The round can also be done from Troutbeck, but parking there is more difficult and this is not recommended.

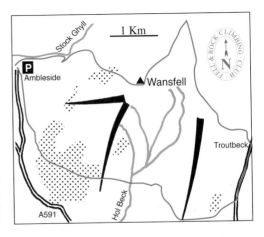

Approaching Sour Howes and Sallows

Sour Howes 483m, 1584ft, GR 428032
Sallows 516m, 1691ft, GR 437040

Despite its name, this is a pleasant walk for a short day or when the weather is too bad for the high hills; it gives extensive panoramic views to the west and north.

Start at the end of Browfoot Lane, above the River Kent, at GR 448004 where there is limited parking for one or two cars. Head NW along the stone track for 1km to a three-fingered signpost by a gate. Follow the Kentmere sign through the right-hand gate. Pass through several gates with the wall on your left; pass a small sparse copse on the right; with the wall now on your right, stay with the track at the next gate. After 30 metres fork left and keep to the left of the prominent trees to reach a wall junction at GR 441026.

Keep the wall on your left, now head west uphill through bracken to another wall corner with a gate. Pass through the gate and immediately strike NW up the hillside to the top of Capple Howe. Head west for 200 metres and cross a stile marked by a tall post. Now head NW uphill over minor false tops to the summit of Sour Howes marked by a small cairn (4.5km, 260m, 1hr 30min).

Follow the distinct path to the north, with fine views into the head of Troutbeck, eventually meeting a stone wall which is kept on your right until a fence and stile is reached. Cross this and head east to the summit of Sallows with its miniscule cairn (6km,

320m, 2hrs). Descend ESE with the path to stone grouse butts in an area of wet ground and reeds. From here, head south, skirting the edge of Long Crag to reach a metal gate in the fence at GR 443031. Go through the gate into pasture land and head downhill to the sheepfold and gate in the opposite corner. Pass through this gate and cross Park Beck to follow the bridleway to the rowan trees on the skyline passed earlier in the day, then retrace your steps down the bridleway to the start (11km, 3hr 25min).

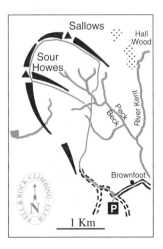

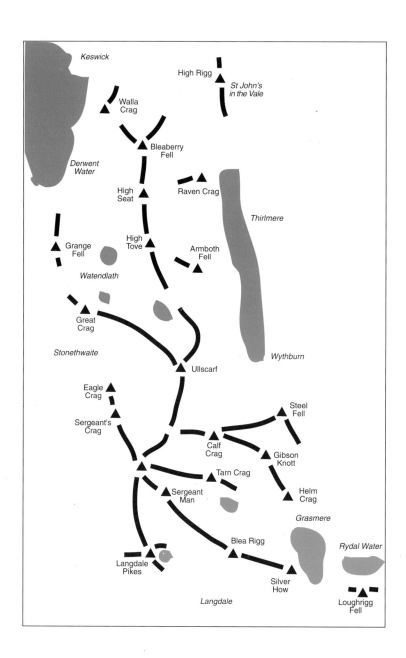

Keswick

High Rigg

St John's
in the Vale

Walla
Crag

Bleaberry
Fell

Derwent
Water

High
Seat

Raven Crag

Thirlmere

Grange
Fell

High
Tove

Armboth
Fell

Watendlath

Great
Crag

Stonethwaite

Wythburn

Ullscarf

Eagle
Crag

Steel
Fell

Sergeant's
Crag

Calf
Crag

Gibson
Knott

Tarn Crag

Helm
Crag

Sergeant
Man

Grasmere

Rydal Water

Blea Rigg

Langdale
Pikes

Silver
How

Loughrigg
Fell

Langdale

Section 3

The Central Fells

The natural boundaries of the Central Fells in the east are St John's Vale, Thirlmere and Dunmail Raise. In the west they are Derwentwater, Borrowdale, Langstrath and Stake Pass, twisting east through Great Langdale to Ambleside. The best known mountains in this area are the Langdale Pikes but there are many more attractive fells of modest height. High Raise is the highest summit and north of this there is a change in the terrain, related to a change in the underlying rocks from Borrowdale Volcanics to Skiddaw Slates. The ground becomes more grassy and level so that after rain it is often boggy.

In the notes at the end of Book 3, AW deplores the changes that constantly take place and makes guidebooks out-of-date, suggesting that the books will 'progressively be withdrawn from publication after a currency of a few years'. As we all know, this did not happen. In fact some of his unique diagrams are still invaluable, an example of this being Eagle Crag 4 which shows the route of ascent in a way which cannot be done on a conventional map.

Walla Crag from Derwentwater

Walla Crag 379m, 1243ft, GR 277213

This prominent hill overlooking Keswick makes an easy short walk from the town and the panoramic view from its belvedere is a fine reward.

Start from the town centre by walking up the Market Square past the Moot Hall and leaving by the road on the left. This becomes St John Street leading past the cinema and church. After 650 metres, at the foot of Manor Brow, turn right into Springs Road and follow this to its end. A signed footpath leads through Springs Farm, forking right at the first bridge, up past the adjacent television mast, through a gate to cross the stream again at a second bridge. On reaching the narrow lane beyond, turn right towards Rakefoot and at the end of the lane re-cross the stream to reach the open hillside leading to the fine, rocky top of Walla Crag (3km, 290m, 1hr 15min).

There is an exceptional view over Derwentwater and Bassenthwaite, taking in the Newlands fells, Skiddaw and Blencathra. From the stile just beyond the top of Walla Crag, take the path to the right which follows the wall down into the impressive chasm of Cat Gill. This path drops steeply and care is required in the wet. At the bottom, turn right to reach the NT car park in Great Wood. Cross the car park and the Borrowdale Road beyond to reach the lake shore. Turn right and follow the delightful shore path around Calfclose Bay. A detour away from the shore is required at Stable Hills but the path continues past Friar's Crag and the boat landing to reach the road leading back into Keswick (8km, 2hr 30min).

From the stile beyond the top of Walla Crag, another path straight ahead leads to Bleaberry Fell and High Seat. After 500 metres this path forks; the one to the right traverses the hillside towards Ashness Bridge and the Watendlath road with a longer return back along the lake shore. A pleasant alternative would be to return by launch from the landing stage at the bottom of the Ashness road.

High Seat above Watendlath

High Seat 608m, 1994ft, GR 287180
Bleaberry Fell 590m, 1935ft, GR 286196

The ridge to the east of Borrowdale is less frequented than its scenic much photographed alternative to the west. The reason may be that this eastern ridge is broader and boggier, but it offers an interesting upland area harbouring grouse and red deer as well as sheep and walkers.

A good starting point is the ample car park in Borrowdale's Great Wood (GR 272213). Cross the stile and follow the path south, across Cat Gill and below impending Falcon Crag to Ashness Bridge with its famous view over Derwentwater, Keswick and Skiddaw. From the bridge go up the right (south) side of the beck. The path leaves the beck to climb a steep bank, then rejoins its southern branch above a waterfall. Another half-hour of walking brings you to High Seat, a little rocky outcrop in a spreading moorland (4km, 530m, 1hr 50min).

Go north for 1.5km following the ridge-line, avoiding the bogs as best you can, to the pleasant summit of Bleaberry Fell. A path descends north west towards Walla Crag which is an excellent viewpoint overlooking Keswick, Derwentwater and Bassenthwaite. At the wall just before the summit of Walla Crag, turn left and descend steeply alongside Cat Gill to return to Great Wood car park (9km, 3hr 15min).

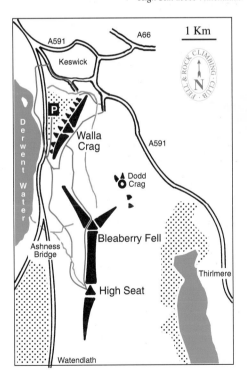

High Rigg 354m, 1161ft, GR 309220)

High Rigg from the path to Castle Rock

This low ridge forms the true west bank of St John's Beck which drains from Thirlmere and is sometimes referred to locally as Naddle Fell. The traverse of the grassy tops is an easy, pleasant walk with fine views northwards towards Blencathra and southwards towards Thirlmere and Helvellyn.

The NWW car park in the trees at Legburthwaite makes a convenient starting point. From the far end of the car park, turn left on the old road the reach the A591. Go right for 100 metres and cross the stile on the right beyond the river. A good path branches left to climb to the ridge. The ridge itself consists of several low tops which can be traversed to the main summit; the path keeps to the west of the highest points to make a more even approach to the summit (3km, 235m, 1hr 15min). From here a short descent northwards leads to St John's Church and Youth Centre. The stile opposite leads towards Low Rigg and Tewet Tarn with fine views towards Blencathra. From the church turn down the road for 50 metres and take the track on the right which follows the foot of the slope through St John's in the Vale to pass Low Bridge End Farm and return to the start (8km, 2hr 30min).

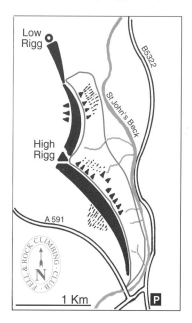

Raven Crag 461m, 1520ft, GR 303187

Raven Crag, Thirlmere

This outcrop crag overlooking the Thirlmere dam is a somewhat detached outlier of High Seat. It is better known by some for its rock climbs on the steep buttress rising above the forestry. Thirlmere reservoir was formed by enlarging the former Leathes-Water and opened in 1894 to supply water to Manchester. The area around Raven Crag itself features in WG Collingwood's saga of Norse times called *Thorstein of the Mere*.

The forestry plantations make access to the fell difficult. Park at the road junction on the west side of the dam (GR 307189) and walk north along the road for 100 metres. Turn left onto a path through a signposted gate into the forestry and ascend steeply. The path crosses two forestry roads and emerges onto the ridge above at a clearing. At the sign take a narrow track south which leads up the back of Raven Crag to emerge on the summit (1km, 270m, 45min). From just in front of the cairn there are good views down Thirlmere and over the Helvellyn fells. Return to the clearing by the same path; all other routes are steep and dangerous.

From the clearing two detours are possible. A path leads west to a small defensive hill fort amongst trees overlooking Shoulthwaite Gill. An ascent can also be made north through trees to the minor top of The Benn. A faint track may be picked up leading to this treeless top. From both detours return to the clearing and descend to the road by the ascent route. Total distance and time for the walk with both detours is 3km and 1hr 30min.

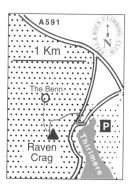

High Tove and Armboth Fell from Ullscarf with Blencathra behind

High Tove 515m, 1689ft, GR 289165
Armboth Fell 479m, 1571ft, GR 297160

The shores around Thirlmere have been much changed since such writers as Symonds and Wainwright attacked the insensitive burying of the valley sides by impenetrable plantations to protect Manchester's water supply. North West Water has done much to increase public access to the land and to soften the forestry with more sensitive planting. This short walk explores the hillsides above the quieter western shore road – although it is best reserved for a lengthy dry spell as the ridge above remains as boggy as ever.

From Armboth car park, close to the site of former Armboth village, submerged for a century beneath the reservoir, a signed track climbs alongside Fisher Gill towards Watendlath. Above the tree-line, gentle slopes lead directly to the cairn on High Tove (2km, 330m, 1hr). From here, a descent south-east over wet ground followed by a short rise leads to Armboth Fell, any one of whose mounds could be the highest point. Continuing south-east, descend towards Launchy Gill. This stream can be followed into the forestry where a narrow path leads down the right (south) bank of the stream beside impressive waterfalls and a picturesque bridge to reach the road. Between the road and the lake shore, a pleasant path returns to Armboth through glades carpeted with bluebells in springtime and offering attractive views across the lake (6km, 2hr 10min).

These two tops can also be reached by a shorter ascent eastwards from Watendlath. The walk along the ridge can be continued beside the fence either northwards over High Seat or southwards towards Blea Tarn and Ullscarf.

Grange Fell

Grange Fell 410m, 1345ft, GR 265162

Writing in 1769, Thomas Gray was appalled by the wilderness of Borrowdale and would go no further than Grange. Yet today, the sylvan glades, rocky outcrops and stunning views of Grange Fell are perceived as the very essence of Borrowdale's intimate beauty. This is a relatively low hill to delight the exploring walker.

From the Bowderstone car park south of Grange (GR 253168) take any of the paths leading NW and then W through the birch trees past an old quarry and towards Troutdale. Before the second wall, turn right to climb uphill to the left of the impressive Great End Crag. The steep, well-made path eventually turns back on itself to reach the open top of King's How, a memorial to Edward VII. Here, the whole of Borrowdale is laid out at your feet. A myriad of sheep tracks criss-cross the hummocky fell beyond. Paths lead down SW to cross a fence, then a wall before ascending to Brund Fell, the highest point (2.5km, 370m, 1hr 20min). Retrace the last 300 metres of ascent and continue down the path

towards Rosthwaite. On reaching the trees and a wall, turn right to follow the path down through woods to the road. A gate on the right allows 500 metres of road walking to be avoided. Where the route looks improbable, seek a hidden passage up and to the right; this leads to the track to the Bowderstone. This is a huge glacial erratic boulder perched on its apex and under which, you can shake hands! The path continues along the "dreadful road", so feared by Gray, past Quayfoot Quarry to the start (5.5km, 2hr 15min).

Grange Fell can also be climbed easily from Watendlath. Cross the packhorse bridge following the track to Rosthwaite and veer right to follow a track near the wall leading to the summit.

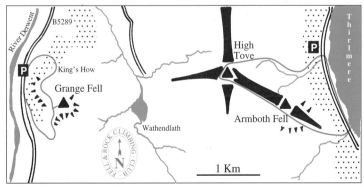

Great Crag from Green Combe

Great Crag 456m, 1496ft, GR269147

Although easily climbed in a couple of hours, Great Crag and the surrounding area invite leisurely exploration. Usually done in a circuit from Rosthwaite via Stonethwaite and Dock Tarn, this fell can also be combined with Grange Fell. This alternative route starts from the picturesque hamlet of Watendlath; the narrow access road is often choked, so an approach on foot or by bike is recommended.

Leave the village by the pack horse bridge and skirt the tarn's NW shore to join a little lonnin. Follow this, turning gently uphill just after a gate and stream. The track ahead avoids the wetland bog myrtle and soon reaches a gate through the intake wall. Ascend

the pitched path until a broken wall on the right points the way to the summit cairn (2km, 140m, 45min).

Turn SSE and pick an intricate route along the broken ridge past Dock Tarn, crossing the main path and Willygrass Gill to a tiny col near High Crag. A wall corner allows access to this little knoll with its splendid view up Langstrath. Head east across wet and open moor to the scoured rocks of Lord's How (from where a minor track leads to Ullscarf). Contour beneath Coldbarrow Fell and cross the outflow immediately below Blea Tarn. Turn left and head back to Watendlath down the rough bridleway with a steep descent at the end (8km, 3hrs).

Ullscarf 726m, 2381ft, GR 292122

Situated on the watershed between Borrowdale and Thirlmere, Ullscarf is a moorland plateau rather than a prominent peak but, despite including some of the boggiest land in the region, it offers fine walks from both valleys and its summit cairn commands a superb panoramic view. From Borrowdale ascents can be made on good paths via either Watendlath or Stonethwaite but the circuit from Thirlmere offers an interesting route over varied terrain.

From the FC car park at Dob Gill Bridge (GR 316139), take the waymarked track beside Dob Gill to Harrop Tarn, an attractive spot set amongst trees

and crags and noted in season for its display of water lilies. From the tarn, follow the 700 year old bridle path signed to Watendlath, which climbs up through conifers until it emerges on the open hillside at a gate. From here, the path is far less frequented than the waymarks lower down would suggest.

Ascend on a clear track through bracken, then over moorland where slabs have been placed over the boggier sections and reach the skyline at a gate in a boundary fence overlooking the descent to Watendlath. Follow this fence south past Standing Crag and then SW over high moorland to reach the

On Ullscarf looking towards Skiddaw

summit plateau (4km, 540m, 1hr 55min).

From the summit, an enjoyable trackless descent can be made down the western flanks of the fell but this is not advised in poor visibility. Given clear conditions, head W over tussocky grass to a cairn visible on Black Knott. Continue on this line past three small pools and keeping close to the skyline, descend the now craggy hillside bearing NW to reach the cairn on Nab Crags; this is a fine viewpoint overlooking Wythburn. A path now leads to the Beacon at the end of the Nab Crag ridge below which a good track leads back to the road either via Harrop Tarn or over Birk Crag (9km, 3hr 15min). In poor weather, follow the fenceposts south from the summit to the col at Greenup Edge and walk down Wyth Burn to the road.

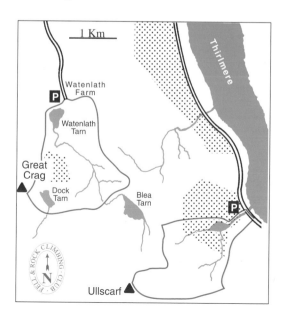

Eagle Crag from the Stonethwaite valley

Eagle Crag 520m, 1706ft, GR 276121
Sergeant's Crag 571m, 1873ft, GR 274114

Sergeant's Crag is partly hidden from view on the approach from Stonethwaite and it is Eagle Crag which catches the eye with its sheer north-facing crags on one side and steep Heron Crag on the other. It is hard to believe there is a walking route up this magnificent prow. From Eagle Crag there is a view of the deep gully which splits the west face of Sergeant's, and which was climbed in 1893 by OG Jones.

There is parking by the traditional red telephone box in Stonethwaite if you arrive early enough. Cross the bridge and turn right along the path signposted to Greenup Edge, with Eagle Crag in view all the way. At the confluence of the two streams turn right over the footbridge and then immediately left over a stile in the wire fence. Go through a gate in a stone wall and after passing a second wall, strike steeply up the hillside. A path develops and leads to a wooden stile in the top corner of the enclosure where the wall abuts against a crag. A good path leads up below this crag then doubles back left into an open gully which gives a short easy scramble. A diversion may be made at the top for a view of Eagle Crag. From the top of the gully, an intriguing path along a series of rocky ledges is followed to the right. Finally the summit cairn is reached by doubling back and forth along a number of grassy ledges.

Follow the trod to a rock step by a wall and continue along the easy ridge to the top of Sergeant's Crag (3km, 1hr 20min). Go towards High Raise and after about ten minutes walking, take a minor path on the right. This shepherd's track heads towards Brown Crag and contours above a side-stream before making a diagonal descent towards the foot of Stake Pass. Easy walking along the valley path, passing the beautiful rocky pool of Blackmoss Pot leads to a footbridge and so back to Stonethwaite (11km, 490m, 3hr 40min).

The start of this route can be used for an ascent of High Raise, returning by Greenup Edge and Lining Crag. This gives a more strenuous walk with an ascent of 680m.

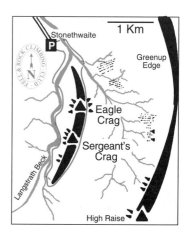

Pike o'Blisco and Coniston fells from near Sergeant Man

Sergeant Man 730m, 2394ft, GR 286089
High Raise (Langdale) 762m, 2499ft, GR 281095

High Raise is an elongated plateau considered by many to be the centre of the Lake District. It commands a fine panoramic view from Blencathra westwards round to Helvellyn, reaching as far north as Criffel and south to Ingleborough. In contrast, its neighbour Sergeant Man is a compact, rocky knoll and a circuit of both tops from Grasmere offers a fine mountain walk mostly on good paths.

From the car park in Easedale Road (GR 334081) turn right along the road to a footbridge and follow signs to Easedale Tarn. A large boulder and iron bench mark the site of the refreshment hut which once stood here to serve visitors to the tarn. Climb steadily up the track with the stream to your right. At a cairn (GR 292085) turn right. (It is worth continuing ahead for some metres to enjoy the views over Stickle Tarn far below.) Return to the path which now rises amongst rocky outcrops to reach the summit of Sergeant Man.

The trig point marking the summit of High Raise, though not visible from Sergeant Man, lies some 800 metres away across open moorland. Head NW, keeping left of an iron post standing out from a pile of stones ahead, to reach a track leading to the trig point (6km,

690m, 2hr 45min). From here, descend NNE alongside the remains of a boundary fence to join the Borrowdale to Grasmere path in the dip at Greenup Edge. Follow this path right towards Grasmere, crossing a boggy depression to reach a hause at the head of Far Easedale. A good track leads back down this valley to Grasmere (13km, 5hr 30min).

From the head of Far Easedale, this circuit can be continued over Calf Crag, Gibson Knott and Helm Crag. An alternative ascent from Grasmere can be made up the ridge between Easedale and Far Easedale, over Tarn Crag.

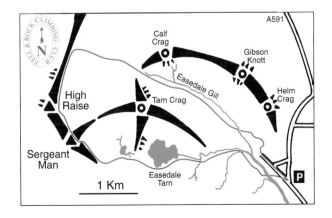

The Langdale Pikes

The Langdale Pikes
Loft Crag 680m, 2230ft, GR 277071
Pike o'Stickle 709m, 2326ft, GR 274073
Pavey Ark 700m, 2296ft, GR 285079
Harrison Stickle 736m, 2414ft, GR 282074
and **Thunacar Knott** 723m, 2372ft, GR 279080

Perhaps the most popular group of fells in the entire Lake District, and deservedly so, the Langdale Pikes are the archetypal image of Lakeland landscape. They display startling contrasts of style. Some sweep serenely down to the valley floor, others stand as majestic guardians of a popular tarn whilst Thunacar Knott retains a watchfull aloofness from the less visited hinterland.

The walk described here has a second focus - the exploration of Dungeon Ghyll. The savage and confined features of this twisting watercourse cannot be appreciated from the valley, but this route follows much of the watershed of the ghyll and gives the walker the opportunity to gaze at the diversity of this often unheeded attraction.

The walk starts from the car park near the New Dungeon Ghyll Hotel which is also easily reached by public service bus. Take the track leading to Stickle Gill but, 50 metres behind the cottages and hotel, take the left fork (westwards). After a further 150 metres of gentle rise across the fellside to a stile and another fork where you should take the right branch (NW) and continue uphill to a second stile and yet another branch. Here you go left (westwards) again to cross the Dungeon Ghyll and start climbing a good, rugged track with the ghyll on your right. This fine streamed

is narrow and steep-sided for almost all of its fall and there are lots of waterfalls and craggy waterslides which make it an entertaining scramble after drought conditions.

After a short section of rocky staircase you reach a level area which is useful for getting your breath back and enjoying the developing views of Windermere, Lingmoor Fell, Blea Tarn and beyond to Wetherlam. The slope relents and, as the surface changes to coarse grass, the track swings leftwards (NW) towards Gimmer Crag whose upper part can be seen in profile. However the path soon swings right (N) and starts climbing quite steeply between Loft Crag (the true summit of Gimmer) and Thorn Crag (not identified on the map)

The angle eases quite suddenly as you reach the gentle, marshy coombe which is the collecting area for Dungeon Ghyll - and it couldn't be more different! Turn left here and follow the track as it zig-zags generally westwards to the summit of Loft Crag. You can rest now with the length of Mickleden 500 metres below and the knowledge that most of the uphill work is over.

A short, enjoyable walk along the ridge (NW) leads to the long scree chute - sadly worn and no longer recommended as a descent route - with its

Harrison Stickle

prehistoric stone axe factory. Pike o' Stickle, unmistakable in front of you, is most easily climbed by a ramp across its NE flank followed by a short scramble. The top commands tremendous views of the Coniston fells and, across the valley, a whole sweep of high fell from Pike of Blisco, past Crinkle Crags and Bowfell along to Great End. It is a great place to sit and absorb the magnificent Lakeland atmosphere (3.5km, 660m, 2hr).

Thunacar Knott is easily reached by walking N then NE, staying on the higher ground which is likely to be drier. The summit is relatively undistinguished, less visited and all the better as a vantage point for watching activity round the other tops.

The short walk east to Pavey Ark is given more interest by the small tarns and outcrops along the way but, from this side of Pavey, you wouldn't guess at the steep drop on its SE side - very definitely rock-climbers' country. Below, Stickle Tarn lies placidly in its mountain setting and is entirely in keeping with its surroundings, even though its level was raised by the dam to provide water reserves for the former gunpowder works at Elterwater.

The route from the bare, craggy summit of Pavey Ark to Harrison Stickle goes firstly south-west then south. There are lots of barren rock slabs, cairns and many paths winding about. Harrison's is the highest of the Pikes and a very fitting

end to the high level walking. It is a magnificent viewpoint for the lower part of Langdale, right out to Windermere and beyond.

When your appetite for grand scenery is sated, walk NW briefly before taking the worn track SW into the upper part of Dungeon Ghyll. Here you will find a path leading SE which soon brings you close to the loose-looking rock pillars which guard the entrance to the turbulent part of the ghyll's descent. As this good track winds down the fellside, there are more opportunities to look into the depths of the ghyll. This path returns to the valley bottom where the walk started (10km, 780 metres, 3hr 30min).

The Langdale Pikes can also be ascended by obvious paths up Stickle Gill to Stickle Tarn.

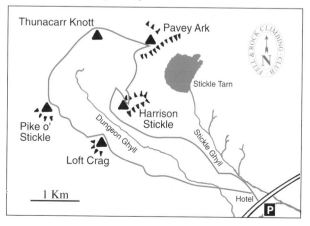

Steel Fell

Steel Fell 553m, 1814ft, GR 319111

This attractive fell forms the prominent steep ridge behind Helm Crag when viewed from the A591 travelling north over Dunmail Raise. The large cairn on the summit of this road pass is reputed to mark the burial site of Dunmail, the last King of Cumberland around 945 AD.

From the Travellers Rest inn on the A591 (limited parking on the verge), take the minor road to Low Mill Bridge and Ghyll Foot. Follow the private, unmade road up Green Burn over two cattle grids to a gate. A path on the right ascends steeply through fields to the open fellside. The path continues past a rocky knoll up the steep grassy ridge to the summit cairn and boundary fence (3km, 460m, 1hr 30min).

On a clear day there are magnificent views northwards over Thirlmere and southwards towards Windermere.

Either return the same way or continue westwards along the ridge fence past a small tarn. Continue on a less distinct path trending south-west then south for 1km on rising ground to a cairn at GR 297102 from which a good path descends into Far Easedale Gill to join the Easedale road. When on the level, look for a junction marked by boulders and turn left onto a track past the youth hostel and turn left again on the minor road to return to Low Mill Bridge (11km, 3hr 40min).

Steel Fell can also be ascended by Steel End in Wythburn, or, more directly, from the summit of Dunmail Raise. The return route can be extended to include Calf Crag, Gibson Knott and Helm Crag.

Tarn Crag (Easedale) 550m, 1804ft, GR 303093

Tarn Crag is probably one of the least ascended summits in the area yet it is a delightful hill commanding fine views to the south and east. Its dominant feature is the rugged skyline overlooking Easedale Tarn: the fellside plunges steeply down to the waters of the tarn which in certain conditions can be dark and foreboding. The ascents are mostly clearly defined on steep but relatively easy ground.

From Grasmere, take the Easedale road over Goody Bridge and into Far Easedale. Continue past the guide post to Helm Crag and up the valley. Cross

Far Easedale Gill at the footbridge and after a further 100 metres turn left up a path going west and climb steeply up the south-east ridge past a prominent rock tor, over Greathead Crag to the summit (4km, 470m, 1hr 50min). To return, walk SW along Slapstone Edge to descend the good track past Easedale Tarn and Sourmilk Gill to Grasmere (9km, 3hr 10min).

Tarn Crag can also be climbed from the outflow of Easedale Tarn if approached by Sourmilk Gill. The ridge walk can also be extended to include High Raise and Sergeant Man.

Helm Crag summit rocks

Helm Crag 405m, 1328ft, GR 327093
Gibson Knott 420m, 1377ft, GR 319099
Calf Crag 537m, 1761ft, GR 301104

These three summits are all tops on the curving ridge behind Grasmere between Far Easedale Gill and Green Burn. They are best traversed as a ridge walk starting and finishing in Grasmere. For travellers on the A591, Helm Crag is most famous for its distinctive summit rocks, known variously as the Lady and the Piano, or the Lion and the Lamb depending on the profile. The ascent of Helm Crag alone makes an interesting short walk. The fuller traverse provides an interesting ridge walk, full of rocky outcrops, crossing undulating ground with good views.

From the centre of Grasmere, take the Easedale road over Goody Bridge to Easedale House. Turn right up a short track to a gate. Go through the gate left to a finger post and follow the obvious track climbing steeply up the fellside. This path has been repaired in places to combat serious erosion on the steeper sections. Continue upwards to the summit ridge adorned at either end of an impressive rocky chasm by towering blocks of stone (2.5km, 340m, 1hr15min). Take particular care if scrambling on the summit rocks in wet weather.

To traverse the ridge, walk north-west along the undulating ridge over Gibson Knott. A less distinct path leads in a further 2km to the outcrop of Calf Crag. Continue west to a boundary fence and turn left to reach the main path which descends Far Easedale

Gill and joins the approach route shortly before Grasmere village (11km, 4hr).

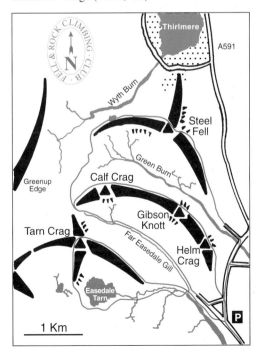

Blea Rigg from the east

Blea Rigg 541m, 1774, GR 301078
Silver How 394m, 1292ft, GR 325066

This walk, popular in all seasons, is on good dry paths throughout and combines a walk up Easedale with a good ridge walk and fine views of the central fells; there are no steep ascents. Blea Rigg is an unexceptional fell but the area is varied and justifiably a good family walk.

From Grasmere take the Easedale Road alongside the art studio out of the village. The public road ends at a gate after 500 metres. Immediately before the gate, cross the stream on the left over a footbridge and walk through meadows signposted Easedale Tarn (NT). Keep on a good track alongside the stream and a wall past several fields and through two gates. After 1km the path swings left and starts to ascend the fellside alongside Sourmilk Gill leaving Easedale but with excellent views of the north side of the valley. Climb steadily for 700 metres until Easedale Tarn appears with the crags of Blea Rigg behind. Part way along the side of the tarn take a cairned path S diagonally up the hillside which leads to the main track along the ridge between Easedale and Langdale. On reaching this track go right. After 500 metres go right E for another 200 metres up and round the rocks to the summit of Blea Rigg for an excellent viewpoint of the Langdale Pikes and higher fells (4km, 460m, 1hr 45min).

Retrace your steps and follow the broad ridge generally SE on a meandering path for 2 km passing several minor tarns and hillocks along the way and avoiding the descent paths to either Easedale or Langdale. Ascend to the grassy summit of Silver Howe with its spectacular views of Grasmere and Rydal. Then descend steeply N over the summit crag, fork right off the main path and go east round the crag and down a short ravine for 200 metres to a good track by a wall. At this T-junction turn left (N) alongside the wall and descend the hillside to a gate, then on a track to the road by the boathouse on Grasmere lake. Turn left for the village (8km, 3hr).

These summits can also be ascended by several paths from the Langdale valley.

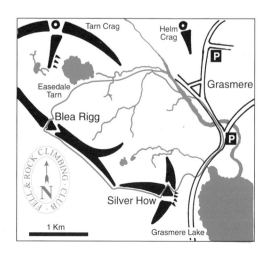

Autumn colours on Loughrigg Fell

Loughrigg Fell 335m, 1099ft, GR 347051

Loughrigg is a centrally placed belvedere for almost the whole of the southern Lake District. It is deservedly one of the most popular fells. Loughrigg was a favourite walk of Dorothy and William Wordsworth when living at Grasmere and references to the fine views can be found in their diaries and writings.

From the NT car parks on the A591 between Rydal Water and Grasmere cross the river Rothay by the wooden footbridge. Continue up through the trees to the wicket gate and so on to the path known as Loughrigg Terrace. Turn right in the direction of Grasmere and keep on the terrace path for about 1km. Just before entering a wood, take a steep path to the left heading for the summit. This path has been well pitched and is usable in all weather conditions. The ascent brings you first to the Grasmere cairn and then more gently to the summit trig point (3km, 245m, 1hr 15min). It is possible to descend quickly to the west to the Red Bank road but it makes a better walk to complete a circuit of the high ground. Head SE from the summit down a trough and then along the western escarpment to Ivy Crag (GR 353043), a good viewpoint for the Coniston and Langdale fells. Beware the multiplicity of paths and knolls which confuse the sense of direction. From Ivy Crag, retrace your steps for 200 metres to a depression where a path leads

down gradually to the east, heading as it were, for Wansfell Pike which can be seen beyond Ambleside. On reaching a flatter area, cross a small stream and turn left to pick up a path now going north, as if for Nab Scar. This leads down gently to the trees and back to Loughrigg Terrace. Quite near the path junction is a huge (unsafe) cave. Turn west, where a choice of paths lead back to the wicket gate, and through the woods to the river bridge and car park (8km, 2hr 30min).

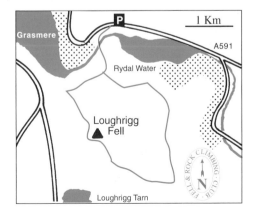

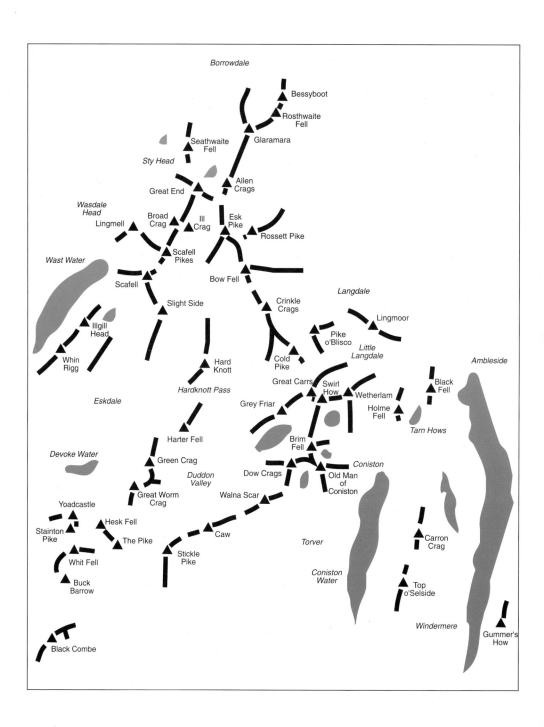

Borrowdale

Bessyboot

Rosthwaite
Fell

Glaramara

Seathwaite
Fell

Sty Head

Allen
Crags

Great End

Wasdale
Head

Broad
Crag

Ill
Crag

Esk
Pike

Lingmell

Rossett Pike

Scafell
Pikes

Wast Water

Scafell

Bow Fell

Langdale

Slight Side

Crinkle
Crags

Lingmoor

Illgill
Head

Pike
o'Blisco

Little
Langdale

Ambleside

Whin
Rigg

Cold
Pike

Hard
Knott

Great Carrs

Swirl
How

Wetherlam

Black
Fell

Hardknott Pass

Grey Friar

Holme
Fell

Eskdale

Tarn Hows

Harter Fell

Brim
Fell

Devoke Water

Green Crag

Duddon
Valley

Dow Crags

Coniston

Old Man
of
Coniston

Great Worm
Crag

Walna Scar

Yoadcastle

Hesk Fell

Caw

Torver

Carron
Crag

Stainton
Pike

The Pike

Stickle
Pike

Coniston
Water

Top
o'Selside

Whit Fell

Buck
Barrow

Windermere

Gummer's
How

Black Combe

Section 4

The Southern Fells

This group of high fells is bounded by Wasdale in the west and by Langstrath, Great Langdale and Yewdale in the east. The main massifs are Scafell, Bow Fell and the Coniston fells. In this book, 12 additional tops have been included, mainly in the Ulpha and Dunnerdale fells and extending to Black Combe, but there are also two tops east of Coniston, and Gummers How which is east of Windermere.

The higher fells are all rugged volcanic rocks giving dramatic scenery with steep crags (much favoured by rock climbers), rocky tops and exhilarating ridges. In contrast, the lower fells in the south west are rounded and grassy but have a special appeal to those who like solitude in the hills.

Bessyboot from Castle Crag

Bessyboot 540m, 1771ft, GR 258125
Rosthwaite Fell 630m, 2067ft, GR 254114

These fells provide an airy, interesting walk along the undulating ridge which separates the Borrowdale valley from its branches to Stonethwaite and Langstrath.

Starting from the road junction to Stonethwaite (parking along the side road), walk past Borrowdale church and through the farm beyond to reach a stony lane leading south-westwards. After 200 metres, a signpost points the way uphill on a permissive path to Bessyboot. The valley floor is soon left behind as the path meanders steeply but pleasantly upwards, giving increasingly expansive views of the middle part of the valley. As you reach the ridge top, you can skirt or climb numerous little hummocks before reaching the summit of Bessyboot. For a relatively low fell, this is a remarkable viewpoint with the hills of Buttermere, Newlands, Langdale and Coniston in sight, as well as the Eastern Fells, Blencathra and, of course, Skiddaw.

Continue past the oddly named Tarn at Leaves generally southwards and be aware that the track down into Combe Gill is indiscernible on the ground. The next 1km rises slightly, but not continuously and among the general bumpiness there are three distinguishable tops. The most dramatic, though not the highest, is Rosthwaite Cam which you will need some ingenuity to master. The highest point of Rosthwaite Fell lies just beyond (3km, 540m, 1hr 45min).

As the line of the ridge curves SW and then W, you arrive at Combe Door. In misty weather it is difficult to be certain of your position and your best plan may be to continue westwards and take the track from Glaramara down past Thornythwaite Fell. However, in clear conditions, or with accurate navigation, you can descend just left (west) of a dramatic chasm which runs almost due northwards into Combe Gill. There is an intermittent track with a few cairns. On reaching the corrie floor, descend the E bank of the gill by a path which skirts the lower slopes of Bessyboot and so rejoin the approach route returning to Stonethwaite church (9km, 3hr 30min).

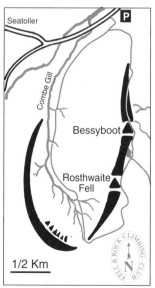

Seathwaite Fell 632m, 2073ft, GR 227097

Seathwaite Fell and Sprinkling Tarn from below Great End

This unassuming fell is set in an amphitheatre of Lakeland's highest tops. Unlike many of its bigger neighbours, its summit is not a barren expanse but an interesting, undulating area which is fun to explore.

From Seathwaite, walk up the valley to Stockley Bridge and turn right, towards Styhead. Once clear of the intake wall, you will see the vegetated buttress of Aaron Crags to the south and an obvious gully just to its right. Zig-zag up towards the gully, where a faint track will occasionally be found. The going is steep in places but not difficult. As you gain height and escape the narrow confines, you find yourself level with the top of Aaron Crags. Do go across and take a break there; it is the best view for the upper Borrowdale valley. The confluence of Styhead and Grains Gills lies far below. Away to the north, Derwentwater is set idyllically between the western ridge dominated by Dale Head and the eastern, Glaramara, ridge. Blencathra and Skiddaw provide a serene backdrop.

Tearing yourself away from this outlook to complete the ascent, you find that it is your turn to be dwarfed and overlooked. Allen Crags, Great Gable and particularly Great End (with its sought after winter gully climbs) stare down. You can enjoy the gentle meandering to the top with the added pleasure, in summer, of finding asphodel, saxifrage and bedstraw along the way (3km, 510m, 1hr 40min).

An interesting return is to continue southwards past the eastern side of the lovely Sprinkling Tarn and pick up the top of the path down Grains Gill. This has more appeal than the easy highway from Styhead (7.5km, 2 hr 50min).

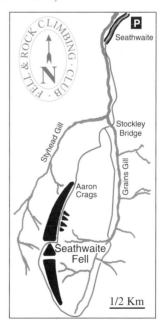

Glaramara from High White Stones with Gable behind

Glaramara 783m, 2568ft, GR 246105
Allen Crags 785m, 2575ft, GR 237085

A walk full of contrasts, this excellent but relatively long outing leads towards the heart of the Lake District fells. A steep approach is rewarded by superb mountain scenery with a choice of finishes.

From the NT car park at Seatoller, follow the road back to Borrowdale and turn right immediately after crossing the River Derwent at Strands Bridge along the track signed to Seathwaite. After a short distance, by the end of the stone wall, cross a stile on the left and follow the winding path up into the valley.

Pass through a gate from where Comb Door, the distinctive notch in the skyline, can be clearly seen. Continue until the path starts to head up towards the ridge. Do not follow this but look for a minor path, indistinct at first, that keeps to the bottom of the valley. Follow this path towards the obvious gully below Comb Door. Climb steeply alongside the gill to the head of Comb Door, the view suddenly opening out as you reach an area of level ground. From this flat area turn west and follow the path steeply up to another flat area. Glaramara is directly to the SW but your feet will stay drier by keeping to the right of the wet ground. The summit can be attained either by a short scramble on the north side or by contouring round to the west side for an easy line to the top (4k, 670m, 2hrs10min). Follow the path, generally SSW over numerous rises and depressions and past several small tarns to Allen Crags (6.5k, 2hr 45min).

A straightforward path descends steeply to the stone shelter below Esk Hause and from here there is a choice of routes. If time or energy is limited, turn NW down the valley of Grains Gill to Seathwaite and along the road to Seatoller (7km from Allen Crags). A less frequented but much longer route is to descend the Langstrath valley. From the stone shelter descend SE to Angle Tarn. Follow the tarn's outlet stream, changing banks as necessary. From the bridge at Tray Dub follow the good path on the W bank to Stonethwaite and the valley road to Seatoller (18km, 6hrs).

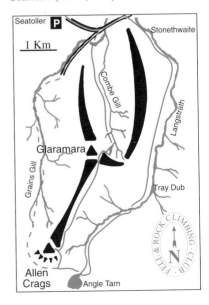

Lingmell in spring sunshine

Lingmell 800m, 2624ft, GR 209082

Lingmell is a westerly outlier of the Scafell massif. Its uniformly steep flanks overlook the irregular patchwork of green fields at Wasdale Head and its slightly detached position makes it an ideal viewpoint for a panorama of all the Wasdale fells.

From the green at Wasdale Head take the Sty Head track past the church and through Burnthwaite Farm. Cross the footbridge beneath Gable and after 200 metres, when the main path begins to rise, branch right to walk alongside Lingmell Beck which is crossed after a further 1km. A path forks right away from the beck to climb alongside Piers Gill on its left-hand side. This impressive watercourse has cut deeply into the northern slopes of Lingmell. At half height, the ravine splits with one branch rising evermore steeply to the summit crags and another branch taking a dog-leg turn to the left. Do not be tempted to try the bed of the gill as there are few escape points. The path follows the edge of this gash, round the dog-leg until it eventually joins the Corridor Route from Sty Head to Scafell Pike. Cross Piers Gill easily at this point and ascend westwards to Lingmell Col from which an easy walk up the ridge leads to the summit (5km, 730km, 2hr 30min).

On a clear day the views across to the Gable screes, into Mosedale, and down Wasdale are exceptional. The descent down the south-west ridge from the summit is at a uniformly steep angle and is a test for any knees! At the wall, turn right to take a diagonal path across the flanks of the fell to a bridge over Lingmell Beck. The path continues across fields to the road and so back to Wasdale Head (8km, 3hr 20min).

Lingmell may also be included in a circular route over Scafell Pike, ascending or descending Brown Tongue alongside Lingmell Gill.

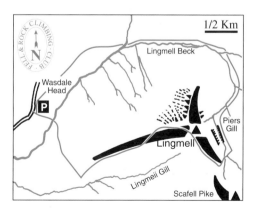

The Scafells and Yewbarrow from Red Pike

Great End 910m, 2985ft, GR 227084
Ill Crag 935m, 3068ft, GR 223073
Broad Crag 930m, 3051ft, GR 219076
Scafell Pike 978m, 3208ft, GR 216072

This walk enables the competent hill-walker to roam in the domain of the rock climber. The four summits, one of which is the highest ground in England, each have spectacular views of the extensive crags on either side of the summit ridge. The walk should not be under-estimated as the ground is rough and boulder-strewn in places and in poor weather, accurate use of a map and compass is essential as it is all too easy to stray onto dangerous ground.

Park at Wasdale Head. From the green, follow the stony walled track NE towards the mass of Great Gable ahead and passing a small church. At Burnthwaite Farm, signs guide you through the farmyard towards the open fells. Continue east following the obvious path across pasture-land, through several gates to reach the narrow, wooden bridge spanning Gable Beck. After another 300 metres, the path splits: the left-hand stone track traverses the scree-covered hillside of Gable to reach Sty Head; the right-hand grass path is an old packhorse route which follows the stream and is a preferable way to arrive at Sty Head.

This grass path follows Lingmell Beck for 1km to its junction with Piers Gill. Cross the beck on stones and continue up a small spur to follow the path as it gains height towards Sty Head. There are magnificent views of the Wasdale Valley and, in particular, from the higher reaches of the path a keen

eye should be able to pick out the silhouette of Napes Needle among the southern crags of Great Gable. From Sty Head, the view suddenly unfolds to produce a panorama of the northern Lakeland fells with Sty Head Tarn nestling at your feet.

The route to Great End goes east, following the stony track to Langdale via Esk Hause. After 400 metres the path crosses a small stream by a large boulder. Leave the path and go right heading across grass slopes in a southerly direction to follow an intermittent path up the steep ridge known as 'The Band'. There is no fixed route but height is gained easily by picking your way through various outcrops and boulders to reach the halfway point signified by a slight dip at the head of Skew Gill. Continue steeply upwards through more outcrops, pausing to admire the views of the Langdale Pikes to your left. Eventually the slope eases as you arrive at the NW cairn. The true summit cairn of Great End is 200 metres SE mounted on top of a boulder of huge proportions (5.5km, 830m, 3hrs).

From the summit, head south down rocky ground which soon leads to a col. Now head SW up easy ground at first, but soon becoming rougher due to large boulders. At the end of the boulders, the summit of Scafell Pike comes into view as the ground again eases. It is worth making a detour at this point to the south to reach the summit of Ill Crag whose extensive

Scafell Pike and Esk Buttress from Upper Eskdale

views down the Esk valley provide an insight into another hidden area of Lakeland. Head NW from this summit to rejoin the well-worn path and continue across it to take in the summit of Broad Crag. This is reached by a scamble over boulders and scree but the effort is well-rewarded by the spectacular view northwards to the Great Gable massif. Return to the main path again, continue SW down rough ground to the final col before the summit slope. A short distance of steep, uphill ground leads finally to the summit of England (8km, 1020m, 3hrs 45min).

Leave the summit by heading NW again over boulders to reach the col under Lingmell's summit. Here turn right to follow a well-worn path across the top of the spectacular chasm of Piers Gill. After crossing the head of the gill, stay with this path on

fairly level ground passing some small tarns on your left to continue along the 'Corridor Route', crossing the head of Greta Gill, then the bottom of Skew Gill to return to Sty Head. The easiest route of descent is SW via the outward zig-zag packhorse route to the valley bottom. Once back in the valley and through Burnthwaite Farm, spare a few moments to visit the beautiful church set amongst yews, with its memorials to former mountaineers.

Great End and Scafell Pike can be climbed from Borrowdale via Sty Head and from Langdale via Esk Hause. A long approach is possible from Brotherilkeld in Eskdale. The shortest and steepest route to the summit is from the Wasdale NT camp site, via Lingmell Gill, Hollow Stones and the rocky col of Mickledore.

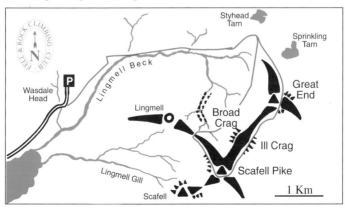

Scafell from the slopes of Lingmell

Scafell 964m, 3162ft, GR 207065
Slight Side 762m, 2499ft, GR 210050

Scafell has formidable crags on its northern and eastern flanks, with only one or two walking routes through them. To the south and west there are stony and unrelenting slopes, but the approaches from Eskdale are particularly interesting and scenically rewarding.

A good starting point is by Wha House (GR 201009) where there are some small parking places. Take the cart track leading NE to Taw House and on through fields to Scale Bridge. Cross the bridge and go up the beck side on a path that leaves the main valley then swings NE through two or three boggy hollows, past Silvery Bield into Upper Eskdale, a fine empty strath with the crags of the Scafells towering over it.

Continue through some sheepfolds and past Sampson's Stones to Cam Spout (GR 219058) which takes about 2 hours. Now go up beside the waterfall, NW, towards Mickledore, the col between Scafell and Scafell Pike. Before reaching the col, and before arriving under the beetling crag of Scafell East Buttress, turn west up a rocky path to Foxes Tarn, the Lake District's smallest named tarn, and on up to the summit plateau. This path is now a made-up staircase.

Before heading for the summit cairn it is well worth touring the tops of the north-facing crags to look down Deep Ghyll into Hollow Stones and across to Lingmell, Great Gable, Pillar and the northern fells of the Lake District. From the summit cairn you can look south to Black Combe, the Duddon estuary, and sometimes Blackpool Tower and Ingleborough, while to the west lies Sellafield and in clear weather the Isle of Man (9km, 880m, 3hr 45min).

Descend south along the crest of the ridge, a scenic route, to Slight Side and Horn Crag, then down past Quagrigg Moss and Catcove Beck, through various hollows and outcrops to the road by Wha House (16km, 5hr 30min).

Another way to reach Cam Spout is from Brotherilkeld (GR 213014), following the river Esk into Upper Eskdale. This involves getting across the Esk at some point, which is easy enough except in times of spate.

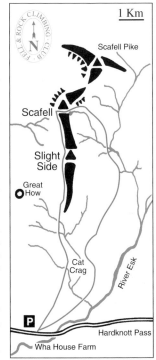

Ill Gill Head above the Wastwater Screes

Whin Rigg 535m, 1755ft, GR 152034
Illgill Head 609m, 1998ft, GR 169049

This exhilerating but easy traverse above the craggy ramparts of the Wasdale Screes and the return via Burnmoor Tarn and Miterdale provides contrasting views of 'stern and sterile' Wasdale with valleys where man has left his mark since pre-historic times.

Leave the Santon Bridge – Eskdale Green road at GR 119013 and take a path north signed 'Plumgarth' which rises steeply through FC woodland to the open summit of Irton Pike. Follow the path NE, at first through woods, until it joins a major path across the fellside. Continue rising between Miterdale Forest and the crumbling granite pillars of Greathall Gill towards the two cairns of Whin Rigg (4km, 430m, 1hr 45min).

Continue easily along the ridge for 2km, past small pools on the col, to Illgill Head's twin tops. Savagely split ravines to the NW give glimpses of Wast Water below and the pyramid of Yewbarrow above. To the NE, Kirkfell, Gable, Lingmell and Scafell fill the horizon.

Small, pink garnets may be found ESE of the Illgill Head cairns but descend ENE and after 1km turn south towards Burnmoor Tarn. Here, to pasture his flocks, Neolithic man began the clearance of the oakwoods which has resulted in these acid and impoverished soils. Turning SSW above the rock-cupped head of Miterdale, the path rises gently along Tongue Moor to the intake wall. Look across the slot of Miterdale to Low Longrigg beyond – the site of Bronze Age stone-circles and burial cairns. Go through the wall-gate and descend fields across other (ruinous) walls to the distant stile where flanking woodlands converge. Cross the stile and proceed down the valley, past Bakerstead Barn and on to Low Place. Follow the track sign-posted Eskdale Green for 750 metres but, where it forks left towards the stream, keep straight ahead on the green bridleway into Miterdale Forest. In 500 metres bear slightly right and pursue the gravelly track which crosses the bridleway and winds for 1.5km in the forest across a clearing and Keyhow Coppice. Turn briefly left, then right (N) onto the road which leads back to the start (16.5km, 6hrs).

A shorter circuit is possible from the N end of Wast Water by traversing the rough path along the foot of the Screes and climbing the path alongside Greathall Gill; follow the summit ridge as described back to Burnmoor and descend to Wasdale Head (13km, 4hrs 15min).

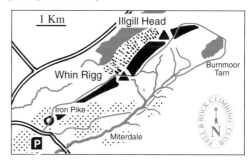

Esk Pike in winter

Bow Fell 902m, 2959ft, GR 245064
Esk Pike 885m, 2903, GR 237075
Rossett Pike 650m, 2132ft, GR 249076

Bow Fell is a major peak in the heart of the District and considered by AW to be one of the half dozen finest hills in the Lakeland, surely recommendation enough. A steep approach leads to an exciting traverse through impressive territory and on to a spectacularly positioned summit.

Starting from the NT car park at the Old Dungeon Ghyll follow the road to Stool End from where the track leads to the open fell. This rises up the broad ridge of the Band, steeply at first and then more gently as a height of 550m is reached. It is possible to bear left at the end of the gentler section to reach Three Tarns and then turn north for the summit, but the most satisfying approach is to continue up the crest of The Band until the narrow path of the Climber's Traverse veers away horizontally to the right. This is followed as it undulates below the steep wall of the cliff known at Flat Crags, whilst ahead lies the rocky tower that is home to Bow Fell Buttress, one of the Lake District's most popular low grade rock climbs. Once beyond Flat Crags (sparkling spring on the right) it is possible to turn left and scramble up the blocky gully located on the right side of the impressive sheet of rock known as the Great Slab. Above this point the summit is reached by a short rocky scramble (5km, 780m, 2hr 40min).

From the summit follow the path that descends diagonally to the north to reach the iron stained area of Ore Gap and from where a direct ascent leads to the top of Esk Pike dead ahead. From here there are two possibilities, either return to Ore Gap and drop down to the north or continue in the same direction as on the ascent to arrive at Esk Hause. Both ways reunite above Angle Tarn which is skirted round and from here a short ascent leads to Rossett Pass with the summit of Rossett Pike just a few minutes away to the left. A return to the pass leads to the top of Rossett Ghyll down which the descent lies, either following the vague line of the old pony track in its big zig-zag or more directly down the well-beaten track. A pleasant stroll along the flat bed of Mickleden takes you back to the car park (13.5km, 5hr).

The central position of Bow Fell means that it can also be approached from Cockley Beck and Brotherilkeld to the south (via Lingcove Beck), from Wasdale to the west (via Sty Head), and from Stonethwaite to the north (via Langstrath).

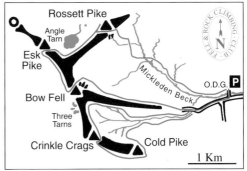

Crinkle Crags from Pike o'Blisco

Crinkle Crags 859m, 2818ft, GR 249049
Cold Pike 701m, 2299ft, GR 263036

This magnificent outing takes in some of the most interesting high level fell walking in Langdale as well as offering a close vantage point for one of the Lake District's most dramatic gorges. Start at the Old Dungeon Ghyll Hotel, easily reached by public bus but with limited pay and display parking.

From the road just beyond the hotel, take the track signposted 'Oxendale and the Band' to Stool End Farm. On leaving the farm take the left fork, signed 'Band'. After about 150 metres at a second fork, ignore the obvious track leading rightwards to the Band and continue into Oxendale. The path through the sheepfold is waymarked on its left, then continues past a footbridge. At the end of the intake wall, climb the fellside briefly to an easy track which leads to the confluence of four gills and another footbridge. Once across this, the path starts to climb quite steeply WNW, offering views of the impressive waterfall in Buscoe Sike on your right. Continue across the Sike to discover the justly named Hell Gill, a quite sensational chasm with a fine, though steep path just beyond. Higher up, there are opportunities (for the sure-footed) to edge across for a glimpse of the sinuous streambed far below. Beyond the chasm, the track changes in character to an easy walk (boggy in places) which steepens to join the track up the Band just below Three Tarns.

The track over Shelter and Crinkle Crags wends its way generally southwards, missing most of the tops. How much more fun to zig-zag over the myriad rocky knolls and feel the real nature of this elevated playground with its contrasting views of Langdale and Lingcove Beck.

The descent from Long Top (the highest Crinkle) to the last one should be taken in a direct line only by competent scramblers as there is a 3-metre wall to climb down. Most walkers will prefer to start on a 250° bearing and follow an eroded track leftwards to the foot of the difficulties.

From the last Crinkle, a broad, gentle track leads down towards Red Tarn. A short way down, above a steeper section, walking on a 140° bearing will lead you on a faint path across moorland to Cold Pike with its array of small, rocky tops. The easiest descent route is NW to rejoin the broad track which is then followed eastwards. From the Red Tarn area, a major descent path goes northwards, past Brown Howe, then NE into Oxendale where it joins the outgoing route at the first footbridge (11.5km, 823m, 4hr 20min).

Pike o'Blisco above a sea of cloud

Pike o'Blisco 705m, 2312ft, GR 271042

A fine rocky peak whose summit cairn can be seen from the valley car park. The ascent involves some very easy rock scrambling if the easiest line is avoided. The round trip from Langdale is a half-day outing but an ascent of the peak can also be used as a starter for a tour westwards on to Crinkle Crags, Bow Fell and beyond. For a less energetic outing it is possible to head eastwards to include an ascent of Lingmoor Fell.

Starting from the NT car park at the Old Dungeon Ghyll follow the road along the valley to Stool End, where the path leads out onto the fell. Continue alongside the boulder-filled stream in Oxendale to a memorial footbridge (two plaques) which gives access to the lower slopes of the hill. A steep climb leads up an excellently refurbished track to the prominent shoulder of Brown Howe. From here the path rises more gently, above the upper section of Browney Gill and below the rocky outcrop of Black Wars, to arrive at the col close to Red Tarn. Here Pike o'Blisco lies to the left, Cold Pike to the right and the Coniston Fells are seen for the first time, through the col. From this point the summit is again visible if you know where to look. A well-marked track (though not obvious as such from below) zig-zags through the many rocky outcrops that dot this slope to arrive at the twin rock summits. The one to the north is marginally higher (4km, 600m, 2hrs).

The descent drops down to the east steeply at first and a couple of awkward rocky grooves require care. The path then flattens out and leads without incident to the top of Redacre Gill, down which the final section of the descent lies. This is steep but easy; follow the (still steep) road back to the car park (7.5km, 600m, 2hr 50mins).

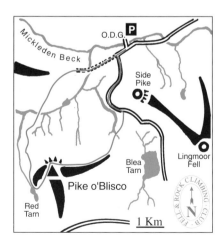

Lingmoor Fell 469m, 1538ft, GR 303046

Lingmoor Fell from Upper Langdale

This long, rounded hill separates Great Langdale from Little Langdale and provides panoramic views of the higher peaks of Langdale and Coniston. The variety of woods, heather moorland and quarries contributes to a varied and interesting walk without any difficulties.

From the NT car park in Elterwater village cross the bridge and turn right (NW) on a quarry road above Langdale Beck. In 400 metres fork right alongside the beck and after another 200 metres, before the footbridge, fork left up into the quarry workings. Follow signs carefully right and right again past the slate cutting sheds and then left of the spoil heaps. On reaching a road cross it, then go uphill in a SW direction ignoring the waymark and continuing on the wide track through mature oak woods to a small quarry with good views of Great Langdale. Proceed up a well-graded track to a prominent yew tree and make a sharp turn left, going uphill to a stile in a wall. Turn right over the stile along the open hillside, initially alongside the wall and then W over undulating rising ground. In 800 metres join a ridge with a fence which leads to the summit cairn (4km, 409m, 1hr 40min). The best views of the Langdale Pikes are seen a little further along the ridge.

To complete the circuit, follow the ridge alongside the fence and wall NW, rough in places, to reach the foot of Side Pike. At this point turn sharp left and descend steeply towards the road, bearing right to reach the cattle-grid along a footpath. Follow the good path down to the NT campsite. Take the path which leaves the site to the east on the lower slopes of the fell at first and then along Great Langdale Beck for 3km to Chapel Stile. Just before the village cross the river on a packhorse bridge, walk right along the road to Wainwright's Inn and cross the beck on a footbridge. Turn left alongside the beck to return to the start of the walk (12km, 4hr 40min).

This is a favourite family walk for all weathers with plenty interest. A shorter walk and possibly even more rewarding is to return along the ridge to enjoy the views in the opposite direction. Another good walk can be made from the NT car park at Blea Tarn.

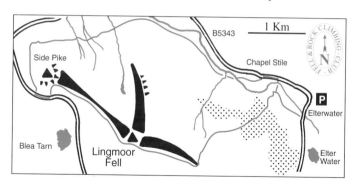

Wetherlam from Great Carrs

Wetherlam 762m, 2499ft, GR 288011

Wetherlam is well separated from the rest of the Coniston Fells and is an attractive mountain with several interesting lines of ascent. It is also particularly rich in disused mines and quarries. Some of the copper mines are at least 400 years old and well worth exploring on the surface. A guide book can be purchased locally. Many of these workings are very deep, the support timbers are rotted and they can be extremely dangerous to enter.

This walk is short in distance, but quite challenging. There is a large car park at Low Tilberthwaite. Leave this by the steps at the rear and walk up the track through disused slate quarries. Take the right fork down to the Gill and cross the footbridge. A sign cautions: 'Footpath steep and dangerous beyond this point'. Properly shod walkers may ignore this and make a worthwhile detour upstream to view Tilberthwaite Gorge from a purpose-built vantage point.

From the 'Steep and dangerous' notice, climb out of the gorge and over a stile to join the old miners' track. Turn left and follow this along the rim of the gorge. Where the ravine ends, fork left over a footbridge. Upstream are the reddish spoil heaps of Tilberthwaite Mine. Ahead, a ridge called Steel Edge is the route of ascent. A deep cleft cuts into the rock

where a vein of ore was once excavated: climb up beside this onto Steel Edge. The path on the crest is grassy at first, but the upper section is steep. The rock is ideal for scrambling and easier underfoot than the loose, stony path. About half an hour from the mines, Steel Edge joins the south ridge of Wetherlam at a small tarn. Follow the well-trodden footpath for 1km to the summit cairn (3km, 612m, 1hr 45min). From the top there are good views north to Little Langdale and Blea Tarn, and south-east over the whole South Lakes region to the Pennines.

Descend by the steep path down Wetherlam Edge. In mist it is important to find the track (30 degrees E of N) as there are crags to the N and E. After about 1km, the ground flattens at Birk Fell Hawse. The popular path forks right and down, but it is easier on the feet and knees not to be tempted by the pull of gravity but to keep ahead over Birk Fell, descending comfortably on grass through some old larch trees to Hellen's Mine. The mine track forms a beautifully constructed route back to the valley, past Tilberthwaite Mine. In descent, keep above the gorge to Low Tilberthwaite Farm. Note the spinning gallery outside the first floor of the farmhouse (7km, 2hr 45 min).

Wetherlam may also be climbed from Coniston via Levers Water.

Swirl How 802m, 2631ft, GR 273005
Great Carrs 780m, 2558ft, GR 270009

Swirl How is much visited on a popular circuit from Coniston Old Man to Wetherlam. It's northerly outlier, Great Carrs, is less frequented. This moderate

walking route starts and ends in the quiet little valley of Greenburn, which offers the advantages of solitude and interesting copper mines.

Swirl How and Great Carrs from Wetherlam

There are few parking places in Little Langdale; one area for a few cars is just west of the Blea Tarn-Wrynose Pass junction. Cross the valley by the lane from Fell Foot Bridge to Bridge End and continue upwards to join the old mine track up Greenburn. Follow this track up to the disused workings. Greenburn copper mines were in operation until the 1940s, so the ruins of the pumping and processing plant are unusually extensive and worth inspecting.

Continue up the valley. The footpath soon disappears, but keep high enough up the SE slope to avoid the bog in the valley bottom. Greenburn Tarn will be seen below. Formerly the reservoir for the mine, the tarn has been much reduced in size since the dam burst. Once in the upper combe, with the crags of Great Carrs ahead, turn south up the slope to ascend about another 150m to Swirl Hawse, between Swirl How and Wetherlam, which is marked by a large cairn. This is the junction of popular routes up Wetherlam, down to Levers Water and up Prison Band onto Swirl How. Take the latter for a steep ascent over rocks and stones to the summit (6km, 693m, 2hr 40min).

From Swirl How to Great Carrs follow the top of Broad Slack for about 10min. A cross and some metal remains commemorate the place where a Halifax Bomber crashed on October 22nd 1944 on a night exercise. Other fragments of the aircraft are scattered down Broad Slack. The summit of Great Carrs is a much pleasanter place to sit than Swirl How, with natural sheltered grassy seats looking down into Greenburn.

The descent is a rare delight: just over 3 km of gentle, easy downhill walking on grass over Little Carrs, down Wet Side Edge and over Rough Crags. After descending the steeper lower end of Rough Crags, bear right towards Greenburn, or left towards the road over Wrynose. Note, however, that there are no public rights of way through the fields behind Fell Foot Farm. In hot weather, the pools in Greenburn Beck just below the mines are superb for bathing (11km, 4hr).

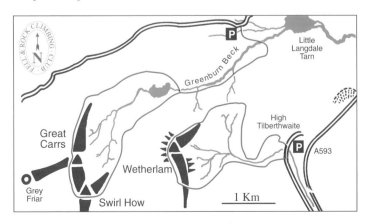

The Old Man of Coniston and Brim Fell from Wetherlam

Brim Fell 796m, 2611 ft, GR 271986
The Old Man of Coniston 803m, 2634 ft, GR 272978

The vast bulk of Coniston Old Man dominates Coniston village. Its flanks are scarred by huge slate quarries, two currently being worked. The combination of scenic grandeur with Victorian prosperity brought several eminent characters to Coniston. John Ruskin, the artist, writer and social reformer, lived at Brantwood, with its superlative views of the Old Man. His neighbour the historian Collingwood had four grandchildren who were taught to sail on Coniston Water by Arthur Ransome, inspiring the writing of *Swallows and Amazons*. While the Old Man is an object of pilgrimage for most fit visitors to Coniston, Brim Fell is often overlooked as a mere hump on the ridge and OS maps leave the summit unmarked. This walk is a challenging route up Brim Fell, which continues over Coniston Old Man but avoids the over-popular tourist routes.

The circuit starts and ends in Coniston village. From the bridge over Church Beck, walk up to the Sun Hotel and turn sharp right beyond it. Follow the path marked 'YHA' up beside the beck to Miners' Bridge in the Coppermines Valley. Keep to the path up the fell without crossing the beck; after about 1km this joins a disued quarry road. 30 metres up the road, turn right along an old quarry track cut horizontally under a crag. A working quarry is a vast hole below to the right. Pass through a disused slate quarry and up some rock steps to an upper valley, aptly named Boulder Valley, strewn with large boulders including the enormous Pudding Stone. Stop here to look for the next stage in the route. At the rear of Boulder Valley, the beck tumbles about 150m down from Low Water. The ascent route passes above the crags to the right of this waterfall up a green diagonal from lower right to top left (the top of the falls). It may look a little alarming from the Pudding Stone but, although steep, it is a perfectly safe route and no scrambling is involved. Cross the footbridge and walk NW across the valley to the foot of the crag and ascend on steep grass and then stony spoil from an old copper mine. The mine passage, complete with iron rail tracks and the rusted remains of a trolley, is about half way to Low Water. Continue steeply up to Low Water, in about 50min ascent from the Pudding Stone.

At Low Water, turn 20 degrees W of N and walk up a grass slope to the col between Raven Tor and Brim Fell summit. Walk west gently uphill over grass and rocks to the rounded top of cropped turf and stones, surmounted by a conical stone cairn. Fifteen minutes to the south along the ridge is the summit of Coniston Old Man (5km, 755m, 2hr 30min). This is capped by a massive man-made stone platform, with a substantial cairn on top. A triangulation point looks down on Low Water.

In mist, the heavily used footpath to Low Water (and thence down the old quarry road) is easy to find. However, it is very steep and loose underfoot. A

On the ridge between Coniston Old Man and Brim Fell

pleasanter descent in clear weather is almost due south down the nose of the mountain. Routes are easily picked out down grass between the rocks. It is inadvisable to stray too far west, where there is a steep drop, while to the east, the huge eyesore of Bursting Stone quarry, is best avoided. At the Walna Scar bridleway at the foot of the mountain, turn east for 1.5km to the fell gate (A shorter alternative to this walk would begin and end at the car park here). To avoid walking down the tarmac, take the footpath south from the fell gate, above the wall. At the fourth (wooden) gate, an ancient bridleway runs across a field and down a lane, past some cottages. The disused railway line, which formerly linked Coniston to the coast at Foxfield, provides an easy walk back into the village (11km; 753m; 4hr).

Coniston Old Man and Brim Fell may both be included in fine circular ridge walks over Dow Crag or Swirl How.

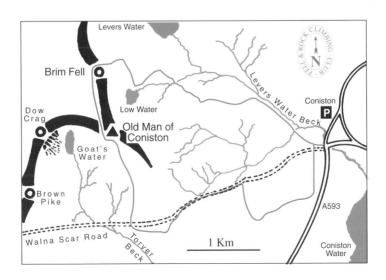

The 'Matterhorn Rock' on Grey Friar

Grey Friar 770m, 2526ft, GR 260004

Although Grey Friar is linked to the main block of the Coniston Fells by a broad grassy ridge, it is the most remote and least visited of the group. This circular walk from the Duddon Valley is varied, interesting, yet unfrequented. In consequence, paths are sometimes faint or non-existent, but the route is of moderate difficulty and not hard to find.

There is a parking place on the road through the Duddon Valley above the Stepping Stones (Fickle Steps) (GR 231975). From the rear of this, take a path downhill towards Tarn Beck and bear left on a waymarked path into a wood. Here the path runs behind a cottage, to emerge from the trees near a footbridge over Tarn Beck. Cross the bridge and the stile beyond it and follow a clear track uphill through the bracken. Continue through a wall and past a sheepfold to join the main NWW access road about 500 metres before Seathwaite Tarn. Cross the dam and footbridges and continue along the NW rim of the tarn to a disused mine. Keeping above the boggy valley bottom, traverse around Brock How. The route follows the course of Tarn Head Beck and there is no path, but the going is quite straightforward. Two more disused mines, with ruined buildings, are passed. Higher up, a little optional easy scrambling in the watercourse is possible. At the top of the steepest ascent, a delightful little double waterfall tumbles over the lip of Calf Cove.

Still following the stream, cross the Cove to the grassy plateau of Fairfield between Great Carrs and Grey Friar. From Fairfield, a well-trodden track leads SW uphill to the summit (7km, 603m, 2hr 45min). A

cairn on a rocky outcrop marks the highest point.

In mist, the direction of descent should be chosen carefully as there are crags east and north of the summit. Take a line SW down grassy slopes for about 1.5km, then turn due south and make for Seathwaite Tarn dam. Bear right before the dam to keep above the bog by the beck and look for a footpath which is indistinct in places, but leads down into the valley. Near the bottom it veers north away from Tarn Beck to avoid the falls. Turn downstream in the bottom to the footbridge which was crossed at the start of the day and retrace the path to the car park.

An alternative route up Grey Friar from the Duddon Valley is a steep ascent from Cockley Beck. The summit can also be included in a ridge walk from Swirl How to Coniston Old Man. (12km, 4hrs).

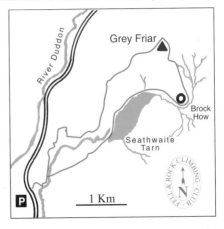

Sunset, Dow Crag

Dow Crag 778m, 2552ft, GR 262978
Walna Scar 621m, 2037ft, GR 258963

Dow Crag rising above Goat's Water is one of the most spectacular sights in the Lake District. This circular walk combines this deservedly popular approach to Dow Crag summit with a descent over the less-frequented ridge of Walna Scar.

Park in Torver about 200 metres north of St. Luke's Church. Take the lane signposted to Coniston Old Man and Walna Scar and follow this waymarked bridleway past the climbing hut at Tranearth. Fork right at Banishead slate quarry (disused), crossing Torver Beck by a footbridge to ascend the path between waste heaps. This track skirts a huge quarry pit containing a dark lake in its depths which is fed by a spectacular waterfall. Continue up to meet the Walna Scar Road at a large, untidy cairn. Keep straight on up the grass and follow the path up the Cove for about 1km, while the view of Dow Crags ahead becomes increasingly impressive. After a short, steep rocky section the path suddenly emerges at Goat's Water.

Keep to the E side of Goat's Water and ascend steeply to Goat's Hawse. Turn

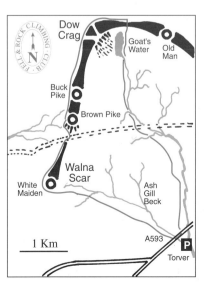

W and follow the path up the ridge to the summit, where it will take a short, easy scramble to achieve the rocky cockpit at the top (6km, 670m, 2hr 35min). Goat's Water appears almost vertically below.

Follow the ridge S over Buck Pike and above Blind Tarn to Brown Pike. A short, steep descent leads to the crest of the Walna Scar Road, between the Coniston and Duddon valleys. Keep SW on the grassy ridge to Walna Scar. The highest point is unmarked, but the subsidiary rocky top of White Maiden has a small cairn looking down into Broughton Moor Slate Quarry just below.

From this cairn finding a route down to the E presents no difficulties, although there is no path. At Gill Beck turn downstream to Ash Gill Beck quarry and continue down the footpath. After crossing a boggy area, take the waymarked path left over a stile, not the more obvious gate straight ahead. This path becomes a pleasant grass track and then a lane. At the first house, follow the marked path around it, and below its grounds turn sharp left to regain the road (12km, 4hr 10min).

Harter Fell from above Boot

Harter Fell (Eskdale) 653m, 2142ft, GR 219997

This shapely peak dominates the Eskdale scene and is one of the few summits in the Lake District that cannot be reached without taking your hands out of your pockets.

Start from the foot of Hardknott Pass in Eskdale where there are limited parking possibilties. (GR 212012). Walk up the road for about 200 metres to the top of a small copse (possible parking here too) and then turn south across the beck, following a path which traverses the hill in a SW direction for about 1km before climbing south to a boggy upland drained by Spothow Gill. Just before reaching the edge of Dunnerdale Forest turn NE and up to the rocky summit (3.5km, 559m, 1hr 50min). Harter Fell commands fine views into Upper Eskdale and of the Scafells, Bowfell and the Coniston Fells.

From the summit go NE to the top of Harknott Pass. Cross the road and follow the path which curves around the northern side of Hardknott Castle, the Roman fort Mediobogum, before descending to join the road leading down into Eskdale (8km, 3hr).

An entertaining variant on the ascent is to strike up to the summit from halfway along the traversing path, thus scrambling on easy rocky outcrops most of the way up. Harter Fell can also be climbed from Birks Bridge or from Wallowbarrow in Dunnerdale, or, of course, from the top of Hardknott Pass.

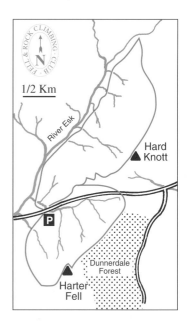

Eskdale from Hard Knott Fell

Hard Knott 549m, 1801ft, GR 232024

Hard Knott looks like the coiled shell of a large snail when viewed from Brotherilkeld. This circular walk involves a direct ascent to the fell's false summit, (Border End), a tour northwards to and beyond the summit, and a return down Eskdale. Difficulties can be subtly avoided. It provides a rich link with Roman antiquity.

Park near Brotherilkeld public telephone box (GR 212012). Walk east, up the walled road, to where it begins to zig-zag up open-hillside to Hardknott Pass. Locate a path on your left and take it to 'Mediobogdum', the Roman fort; walk through its gates and across the parade ground:

"Aloft, the imperial bird of Rome invokes
Departed ages, shedding where he flew
Loose fragments of wild wailing, that bestrew
The clouds, and thrill the chambers of the rocks"
(Wordsworth, Sonnet XVII, River Duddon)

Ascend to the first of three rock bands ahead which can be turned easily on the left. In between bands walk directly upwards. Approaching the third band you have two choices. First, you can turn it to your left, or, if a dry spell has prevailed, keep right to where the band becomes 12 metres of gently angled rock, above a narrow, briefly horizontal, grassy slope. Make a simple scramble upwards; did Roman legionnaires go this way for look-out duties?

Proceed to the first of Border End's three cairns. Eskdale Needle is NNE below you. Walk on from the first cairn to its neighbour. South is the Duddon "Soothed by the unseen river's gentle roar".

Hard Knott's summit lies NE of Border End. Avoiding projecting sharp ribs of rock, a twenty minutes walk leads across a plateau to its cairn. A ridge of high fells surrounds you northwards. You can opt to shorten the walk by going south to the road at Hardknott pass and descending to Eskdale. To continue, walk north, keeping to the highest ground to avoid bog. Head for the junction of Mosedale and Lingcove beck (OS GR 234043). Then return SW down a track to Lingcove bridge (GR 227036). The Brotherilkeld track heads south.   On nearing Brotherilkeld farm observe NT direction signs and skirt fields by way of a path that runs parallel to the River Esk (9Km, 480m, 3hr 10min).

Green Crag from Birkerthwaite

Green Crag 489m, 1604ft, GR 200983

This rocky hill, an outlier of Harter Fell, is a prominent feature of the Eskdale landscape. The approach is varied and quite rough in places.

Start from the carpark by the Ratty railway terminus at Boot (GR 173007). From the crossroads in Boot go south to the river and east along the riverbank to a footbridge (formerly a continuation of the railway to a mine). Follow a path NE to Low Birker farm. The path forks to the right just before the house, rising in a series of bends to pass an old stone peat house. The track continues along a terrace with fine views over the valley, then swings SE round a corner where the view of Birker Moor opens up. When the path divides keep to the lefthand branch which rises a little and keeps to reasonably dry ground beween Tarn Crag and Low Birker Tarn. Go east round the base of Tarn Crag to join a poor path heading slightly east of south, until after about 1.5km it is possible to strike east for the top of Green Crag (5.4km, 430m, 2hr 5min).

From Green Crag follow the main ridge north over the rocky summits of The Pike, Crook Crag and Great Winscale. Make for the 328m top of Kepple Crag (GR 197998) before descending right (east) to pick up a path which leads down to Penny Hill farm. Go west along the lane to Doctor Bridge, cross it and take the delightful riverside path back to Boot (11km, 3hr 30min).

These summits may also be reached from Wallowbarrow in Dunnerdale, via Grassguards.

Great Worm Crag 427m, 1400ft, GR 194969

This sprawling hill is not much visited but gives fine views over open country into Eskdale and Dunnerdale.

Start from the Birker Moor road, at or near Winds Gate (GR 185957) where there are several possible lay-bys. Head NE over bare fell-side to the summit (1.5km, 170m, 40min).

Continue north and north-west over Little Worm Crag and Long Hill, then descend west along Highford Beck to join the path from Birkerthwaite to Brown Rigg. Follow this path south back to the road (5.5km, 1hr 40min).

Top of Great Worm Crag, looking west

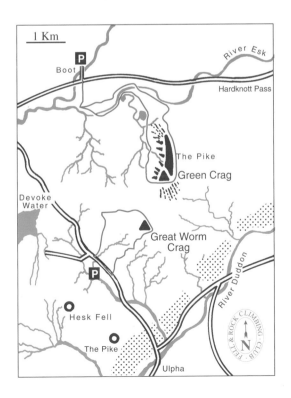

Rowantree Force on Stainton Pike

Stainton Pike 497m, 1632ft, GR 153943
Yoadcastle 494m, 1610ft, GR 157952

Stainton Pike is the highest point on the ridge running south from Devoke Water. From anywhere on the ridge there are extensive views of the coastal plain and the Esk estuary and this alone makes the ascent worthwhile. Seldom visited, there are few well defined paths and the gradients are gentle.

A good round walk taking in all the principal summits on the ridge starts where the bridleway to Devoke Water leaves the Broughton to Eskdale Green fell road (GR 171977). There is ample roadside parking here. Take the Devoke Water track, passing the boat house and continuing along the south side of the tarn. As the track nears the tiny island of Watness Coy, a faint path can be taken which leads away from the tarn and starts to gain height. Keep to the dry ground and aim for the western skyline, a prominent boulder providing a reference point. Once on the

ridge go up to the summit of White Pike (442m) which is marked by a fine dry stone cairn. Leave the cairn and head SE towards the triangular peak of Yoadcastle but, as it gets nearer, traverse round the base to its south end; Stainton Pike can then be reached by walking along the broad ridge to the south and crossing the fence by a gate at Holehouse Tarn. The top is marked by a large cairn (5.5km, 268m, 1hr 50min). Retrace your steps across the fence and head northwards to reach the summit of Yoadcastle and then on to Woodend Height from where the way back to the car can be seen. Head over Rowantree How and make a beeline for the boat house and the track back (10km, 3hr).

An alternative, longer ascent can be made from the western side by starting along the lane at GR 117938 and following the bridle way which leads past Whitfell and continues on to Ulpha. If using this route detour from the path and visit Rowantree Force with its delightful double waterfall which is the highlight of the walk. The summit is reached by following the fence from the top of the falls to Holehouse Tarn, then through the gate to the summit. Continue over Yoadcastle and White Pike, descend to Devoke Water and follow the bridleway past the pre-historic settlement of Barnscar to Dyke Farm (13.5km, 4hr).

Hesk Fell from The Pike

Hesk Fell 477m, 1564ft, GR 176947
The Pike 370m, 1214ft, GR 186934

Hesk Fell is the large rounded, grassy hill that lies to the south-west of the moor road from Ulpha to Eskdale Green. It is rarely visited because it holds very little of interest to the walker and, therefore, there are hardly any paths to the summit. A redeeming feature lies in a number of ancient enclosures which can be found on the south side of the summit plateau. The Pike, in contrast, is a fine little peak with steep crags south, west and east and excellent views of the Duddon valley.

The start for this trudge is at GR 179963 where the tarmac road to Woodend leaves the moor road. There is parking on the grass verge for two cars, which should be ample. Walk along the road towards Woodend to a gate, then go up the open fell with a wall on your right. When the wall bears away to the NW go straight up the hill due south. The summit is on a flat plateau and its location is a matter of personal guess work. There is a good view of the Scafell group and the Eskdale Fells (2km, 247m, 55min).

Continue over the summit heading SE until a wall is met with a stile at GR 182943. A return to the start can be made from here by following a series of sheep tracks along the wall, contouring round the hillside to join the Woodend road at the gate.

For the main walk, cross the stile and follow the wall down to a col, then up to the top of The Pike. Return to the col and follow a bridleway to the NE joining the road at Crosbythwaite and follow it back to the car (7.5km, 2hr 15min).

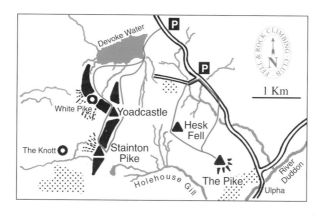

Whit Fell from The Pike

Whitfell 573m, 1879ft, GR 159930
Buck Barrow 549m, 1801ft, GR 152910

These two fells lying in the far south of the Lake District offer the walker little in the way of interesting features; there are no great crags or sharp ridges but what you do get is good easy walking country with hardly any rocks to hinder progress. These are hills for people who like their own company and can rely on themselves for navigation, as you will seldom see anyone else on your travels nor will you find good paths to follow or cairns to show you the way. Gradients are easy and the views superb.

The most satisfying walk to be had starts on the east side of the fell road from Ravenglass to Broughton where it is crossed by a bridleway at GR 130907. There is only parking for two cars here but there is ample space 200 metres up the road towards Buckbarrow Bridge. Head up the bridleway which is a delightful, well engineered green track winding up the fell over the Whit Crags with Buckbarrow Beck on your right. After reaching the 530m contour the track fades but continue NE onto a broad grassy plateau. A small cairn on Burn Moor is passed after which there is a slight descent to a wide col. The summit cairn of Whitfell can be clearly seen from here so make a beeline up the grassy slopes to the top which is marked by a large, well made cairn with an OS column on the NE side (4km, 356m, 1hr 40min).

The view is expansive from the Duddon Estuary, the Coniston group, Bow Fell, the Scafells, Pillar and then on to the coastal plain of West Cumberland. In fine weather the route to Buck Barrow can easily be seen returning to the wide col and then contouring SW then S around the headwaters of Logan Beck until the rocky summit is reached. In bad weather it is better to retrace your steps to the top of Burn Moor from where Buck Barrow is due south. Kinmont Buck Barrow is next visited by going east crossing a wall and on to a rocky top. Return to the starting point by descending SW to a broken wall which can be followed back to the fell road (9km, 450m, 3hr).

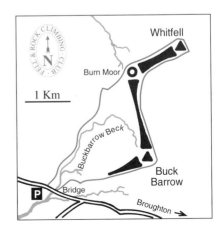

Stickle Pike from Caw

Caw 529m, 1735ft, GR 230945
Stickle Pike 375m, 1230ft, GR 212927

Although Caw and Stickle Pike are quite low, both have fine little conical summits and their outlying position ensures excellent views. This moderate circular route explores the unspoilt area above Broughton Mills, which is relatively little visited.

Start at Stephenson Ground (GR 235931). There are several parking places on the road between Hawk Bridge over Appletreeworth Beck and Water Yeat Bridge on the River Lickle. At Stephenson Ground Farm, take the bridleway signposted to Walna Scar. Follow this track above the Lickle for 2km, where it passes through a gap in the highest wall onto the open fell. Turn left up the side of the wall. Continue along the wall until it turns sharp left; then keep straight on beside a small stream. The conical summit of Caw is directly ahead. The easiest approach to the steep-sided summit is round to the north side, where there is a path. A conspicuous white triangulation point marks the highest of two tops (3km, 310m, 1hr 20min). The top of Caw is a fine vantage point, especially for the Duddon Valley. SW about 2km away is the cone of Stickle Pike.

Descend carefully on the SW side of Caw, which is steep grass and rocks. Where the ground flattens a bridleway SE down Long Mire provides a short cut back to Stephenson Ground. For Stickle Pike, take Park Head Road, a track used by four-wheeled vehicles. Turn right when this forks (GR 216929) to reach the summit of the road from Broughton Mills to the Duddon Valley. Stickle Pike is well-frequented by people who park at the top of this pass. Cross the road and ascend the broad, grassy path to gain another 60m to Stickle Tarn, a pretty little mountain tarn. From here it is a steep ascent for another 50m to the top, which is marked by a fine cairn. There are good views back towards Caw.

To descend, take a path through the bracken just below the tarn outflow to a small, deserted quarry and follow the quarry track back to the road. Turn right down the road through Hoses farm and 400 metres later take the bridleway left across a field to Stainton Ground (ruined). The path continues beyond the farm buildings up a dry gully and from the col at the top, contours easily round the fell to Jackson Ground. Regain the road here and complete the circuit to Stephenson Ground (10km, 3hr 20min).

Caw may also be ascended from Seathwaite in the Duddon Valley, or as a continuation of a ridge walk from Walna Scar.

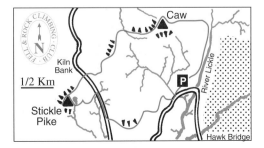

Crinkle Crags from Pike o'Blisco

Black Combe from Walney Island

Black Combe 600m, 1968ft, GR 135855

Black Combe and its tops form the southernmost whaleback of the Western Fells; with shattered slatey cliffs to the SE and glacially-sheared slopes to the west, the fell offers moderate gradients but some rough walking along its broad ridges. Visit Black Combe in clear weather to appreciate the vast views it commands (from Criffel to Snowdon and from the Irish coast to Cross Fell) and to seek out Swinside stone circle below its NE toe.

Park near Whicham Church (GR 135826) and follow the lane WNW towards the white Kirkbank Farm; turn north beyond the farm up a grassy highway rising steadily onto the heathery ridge. After 3km, turn right off this track up a minor path to reach the summit cairn and shelter. A tiny tarn lies just to the south (3.5km, 560m, 1hr 50min).

A faint path descends gently NE with the craggy amphitheatre of the combe over the lip to the right; from a col, the path rises to meet another path ascending from Whicham Mill at GR 149874. Descend gently SSE to the cairn on the grassy outlier of White Combe. Return to the path junction and turn WSW following round the (sometimes boggy) broad ridge top for 800 metres. At GR 144868 join a clear path descending generally westwards in a broad loop around Little Fell. Look across to Barfield Tarn where pollen evidence suggests that by 3000 BC neolithic man had felled the forests and was cultivating cereals. Continue on the path contouring low round the western flanks of the massif, crossing tumbling becks below mini-waterfalls and with fine sea views. Take the A595 briefly beyond Whitbeck, then follow a contouring path back past Kirkbank Farm to Whicham (10km, 620m, 5hr 15min).

Don't miss Swinside Stone Circle (GR 172882). From the path junction on the ridge you can descend steeply ENE along Swinside Fell but this leaves unpleasant road walking back to the start. Alternatively, drive along the A595, turning left onto the Corney Fell road and parking near Cragg Hall; walk up the farm track to the circle. The 57 stone circle was probably a site for religious assembly raised by early Bronze Age inhabitants.

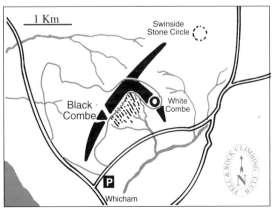

Black Crag from Tarn Hows

Black Fell 323m, 1059ft, GR 340016
Holme Fell 317m, 1040ft, GR 315006

These two fells can be ascended easily in a circular walk. Despite their relative insignificance, they both command extensive views in all directions from their summits. The route comprises easy walking on well defined footpaths and farm tracks.

From the NT car park at GR 323999 cross the footbridge over the stream and follow this to picturesque Tarn Hows. Turn left at the outflow and follow the west shore to the north end of the tarn to a signpost for Arnside; follow this track to the stile. Turn right onto the walled farm track and follow this, turning left at the NT Ironkeld signpost. Cross the stile and follow the rising track through the forest to a gate. Turn right 20 metres after the gate onto a narrow cairned path rising up the fellside to the summit of Black Fell. Retrace your outward route and take the gravelled path on the east side of Tarn Hows to the outflow and descend to the car park (7km, 225m, 2hr 15min).

To ascend Holme Fell, walk south from the car park along the A591 for 200 metres and turn right at Yew Tree Farm. Follow the signed path through three gates onto the lower fellside. Fork left at the cairn adjacent to several large boulders and follow the steeply rising path to a large cairn on the col. Turn left and climb the track to the cairns on the twin summit; the further summit above a short crag is the highest. Both are magnificent viewpoints. Retrace you route back to the car park (4km, 220m, 1hr 20min).

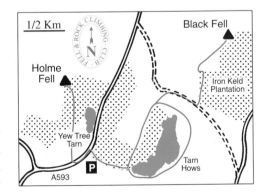

The rocky top of Carron Crag

Carron Crag 314m, 1030ft, GR 325943

Almost hidden in the depths of Grizedale Forest, Carron Crag raises a surprisingly rocky summit well clear of the trees and with a splendid all-round view. The Coniston Fells, Helvellyn and Fairfield lie to the north, while down below is the sheltered Grizedale valley. This walk is mainly within the forest boundaries but there are many open views. An added bonus is that the route passes some of the specially commisioned forest sculptures.

A convenient starting point is an unmarked car park 300 metres south of Satterthwaite at GR 337919. Walk NW along Moor Lane ignoring branches to the left until a forest road is met. Follow the marker posts with green tops (part of the Silurian Way forest trail), passing a shelter and picnic tables and then re-joining the road. Keep on the road as it swings round a corner, passing a carved water-wheel on the left. Pass a 'running table' sculpture and keep on the road to some steps by a marker post and turn left uphill into a delightful area of deciduous woodland. The route becomes a wide track through open ground, reaching a path junction near a splendid Ancient Forester. Go through the gate ahead and follow the good path to the top (4km, 236m, 1hr 25min).

Follow the continuation of the path NE then north down to a forest gate. Turn left on the wide forest road and follow this gently downhill. Ignore a branch left and later another on the right. Almost immediately after this turn sharp left on a major forest track. Follow this SW for 1.5 km and then keep straight on along a narrow path when the track bends left, enjoying fine views across the lake to the Coniston hills. The path leaves the forest at a stile by Park Crags and a waymarked path continues over open ground, descending a little to Low Parkamoor. Go past the house and keep straight on uphill to join a path coming up from High Nibthwaite. Turn sharp left and follow this rising track past the ruined High Parkamoor and on across a boggy area. Turn right at a junction and make for the forest gate at GR 314924. After crossing a forest road there is a cleared area where a rough path crosses several side-streams draining into Farra Grain Gill. Cross another road and continue descending on a path which leads down to Moor Lane and so back to the start (13km, 3hr 40min).

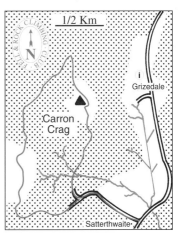

Top o'Selside from across Coniston Water

Top o'Selside 335m, 1099ft, GR 309919

Top o'Selside is the highest point of the stretch of rough moorland that lies between the east side of Coniston Water and the Rusland valley. It is surrounded on three sides by trees: to the east and north are the conifers of Grizedale and to the west lie beautiful deciduous woodlands. These trees form a barrier to free access to the hill and the easiest approach is from the south at High Nibthwaite. Once access is gained, it is best to keep to the paths as the whole fellside is covered with thick bracken, heather and rough tussock grass which make for slow progress. Do not be put off by this, as the ascent of Top o'Selside on a clear day is well worth the effort for the dramatic views.

Start in the hamlet of High Nibthwaite. Parking here is a sensitive issue so if you cannot park next to the telephone box it is better to use the wider sections of the lakeside road to the north of the village, or the NT car park about 1.5km up the road. Go up the short lane on the east side of the village behind the telephone box and through the gate at the end. Turn left on a rising track with the woods on your left. There are delightful views of the whole length of Coniston Water. Follow the track onto the open fellside for 2km. When a point is reached at GR 303917 overlooking Peel Island a broad grassy path can be seen on the right. Take this then immediately head off left up the hillside on a green path which climbs directly to the summit cairn (4km, 320m, 1hr 40 min).

There are extensive views over all points of the compass from Ingleborough in the south with the Howgills, Fairfield and Helvellyn and, of course, the Coniston Fells. Descend east on a path skirting round the north side of a tarn then turning south over Arnsborrow Hill (322m) to join the well defined track which contours the west side of the fell at GR 306903. Follow this track south until a wall is reached by a gate. Stay on the north side of the wall and descend steeply to the west across Caws Beck and down through bracken back to the lane at High Nibthwaite (9k, 350m, 2hr 50min).

Access can also be gained to the fell from the Grizedale Forest Visitors Centre using forest tracks although this way does not offer views and is spoilt by the work of man in the forest and a large area of moor which has been churned into thick mud and ruts by four-wheel drive vehicles.

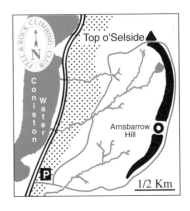

Gummer's How

Gummer's How 321m, 1054ft, GR 390885

The superb views from Gummer's How more than compensate for its lack of height on this popular tourist walk. An easy, pleasant path leads to the summit from where one can look along Windermere and past the southern fells to Skiddaw in the north, the Pennines in the east and, in the south, the channels and estuaries of Morecombe Bay.

There is a car park on the minor road from Newby Bridge to Bowland Bridge and a gate leads onto the fellside 100 metres further up the road. A good track, with a man-made surface in much of the lower part, ascends through willows and birches. The gradually steepening path leads, via a short rocky section where a number of minor variations are possible, to the summit. It is only as you approach the trig point that the extent of the view becomes obvious. The best view of Windermere is obtained from 50 metres west of the highest point.

It is possible to make a short circular route by descending NE towards a group of larch trees, passing a steep little valley on the right. The path turns east then south-east and winds down, through a grove of old, windswept larches, and joins the line of ascent at the corner of a wire fence. A curved line of slates set on end direct you downhill and back to the road (2km, 96m, 45min).

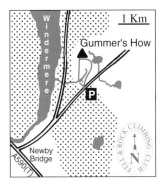

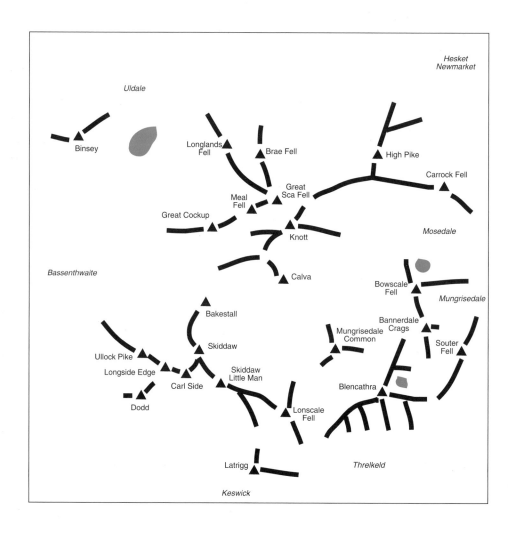

Hesket
Newmarket

Uldale

Binsey

Longlands
Fell

Brae Fell

High Pike

Carrock Fell

Great
Sca Fell

Meal
Fell

Great Cockup

Knott

Mosedale

Bassenthwaite

Calva

Bowscale
Fell

Mungrisedale

Bakestall

Mungrisedale
Common

Bannerdale
Crags

Skiddaw

Souter
Fell

Ullock Pike

Skiddaw
Little Man

Longside Edge

Blencathra

Carl Side

Dodd

Lonscale
Fell

Latrigg

Threlkeld

Keswick

Section 5

The Northern Fells

This area north of Keswick is a mountainous mass entirely separate from other Lake District hills and completely surrounded by roads. Although Skiddaw and Blencathra dominate the area and are more popular than ever, the Caldbeck and Uldale Fells are still remote and almost as quiet as when AW produced his book in 1962. The only fell on which he saw other people then was Carrock Fell. As for the rest, 'nobody, not a soul, not once.'

To many walkers an added interest in this area at the 'Back o' Skidda' are the remains of the mineral mines especially in the Roughton Gill area. Some of the tracks and paths used today were put there by the miners who AW suggests may have also been responsible for some of the exotic names on the map – names like Trusmadoor, Brandy Gill and Candleseaves Bog and many more.

Looking down to Scales Tarn from Sharp Edge

Binsey 447m, 1466ft, GR 225355

Binsey with hang glider

This minor outlier of the north-western fells offers a short excursion in a relatively little known but very attractive part of the Lake District.

From the A591, turn east at Bewaldeth on the narrow road to Uldale and park at Fellend Farm. From here, a path leads NW across a field to reach the open fellside above. Ascend over trackless ground covered in grass and blueberries to reach the top (1.5km, 218m, 45min). The profusion of cairns and tumuli on the summit comes as something of a surprise after the approach. Return by the same route or continue over the top to follow a faint track ESE to the road junction at GR 236351 and then turn right along the pleasant rural road to the farm (3.5km, 1hr 15min).

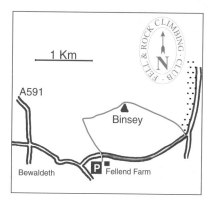

Skiddaw from above Thirlmere

Lonscale Fell 715m, 2344ft, GR 285272
Skiddaw Little Man 865m, 2837ft, GR 267278
Skiddaw 931m, 3054ft, GR 260291
Bakestall 673m, 2208ft, GR 266307

Skiddaw is the highest peak in the northern Lakes and the fourth highest in the whole District. The ascent is quite straightforward and some may consider it mundane, though the wonderful panorama to the south from high on Skiddaw more than makes up for this. The route described offers a complete circuit of the mountain and has the twin advantages of starting at 300m and of getting the hard work for the day over with early on.

Start from the parking area at the top of the Gale Road behind Latrigg (GR 281255). The path leads initially through fields and a fenced 'corridor' then out onto the open fell just below the stone cross of the Hawell Monument, a local family of shepherds. From here the route steepens and a steady ascent is needed, following a good track and a wire fence to a gate at the site of the ruined refreshment stop of the Skiddaw Hut. Above this more steep work is required, now following a wall until it trends to the right into the narrow valley of Whit Beck. Ignore the main path heading straight up the hill and follow a narrower affair into the valley on the right, by the wall. Continue by the stream finally climbing out of the valley to

arrive on the broad col between Lonscale Fell and Skiddaw Little Man. The summit of the former lies just over the crest to the east a few minutes away and is easily reached by following the wire fence (2.5km, 410m, 1hr 20min).

Return to the col and then follow the path and fence up over the rounded shoulder of Jenkin Hill and on to the steep cone that is the summit of Little Man, crossing the main 'highway' that skirts round this at a gate. Cross the high point taking in the view to the south, considered by Wainwright as possibly the finest in the whole Lake District, and continue down to the NW to join the main path to the summit ridge of Skiddaw. Pass over the South Top and follow the near horizontal ridge to the main summit (6.25km, 735m, 2hr 40min).

Continue along the ridge, over the North Top and descend open slopes to a wide col with old sheep folds from where a short ascent leads to the top of Bakestall. From here follow the fence steeply down to Dash Beck (do not trend to the left as there are cliffs below), and then turn right to follow the well-made track, an old supply road, all the way to lonely

Skiddaw from Helvellyn

Skiddaw House. This was originally a row of old shepherd's cottages and is now a seasonal Youth Hostel set amongst its stand of windblown trees. The route continues as a wet path round into the deeply incised valley cut by Glenderaterra Beck, contouring the slopes of Lonscale Fell to round the ridge. Finally a good track leads gently down into the valley of Whit Beck and up a short incline back to the car parking area (15.5km, 5hr 20min).

Alternative routes to the summit of Skiddaw are from Bassenthwaite via Ullock Pike or from Millbeck via Carl Side.

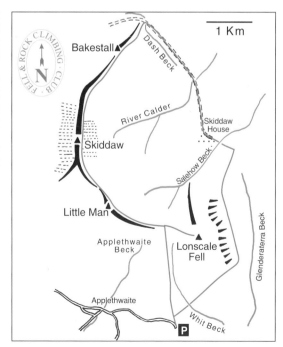

Ullock Pike from Watch Stones

Ullock Pike 690m, 2263ft, GR 244287
Longside Edge 734m, 2408ft, GR 249284
Carl Side 746m, 2420ft, GR 255281
Dodd 502m, 1646ft, GR 244273

These four tops offer an interesting circuit, starting and ending amongst mature trees and including a fine miniature ridge traverse between the three highest points. On a clear day there are excellent views over Bassenthwaite and Derwentwater to the central fells, to the Galloway hills and to the Isle of Man. This is also an approach route to Skiddaw.

Start from Dodd Wood car park on the A591 at Mirehouse. Go north along a footpath which runs parallel to the road for 2km. At the Ravenstone Hotel turn right uphill on a steeply climbing footpath through the trees and onto the ridge above. The path then ascends pleasantly SSE on the crest of the steep-sided ridge to Ullock Pike giving fine views over Southerndale to Skiddaw and over Bassenthwaite to the fells beyond. Continue easily along the ridge to Longside Edge. From the dip 200 metres beyond this summit veer right from the path to ascend the grassy slopes to Carl Side (5.5km, 680m, 2hr 30min). The path going NE from here leads to the summit of Skiddaw involving another 215m of ascent in 1.5km.

Descend south on the steep path towards Millbeck. After 1km, fork right at a prominent white quartz outcrop to descend to the col with Dodd and cross the fence back into the forest. The roadway to the right leads down Skill Beck to the car park. From the col cross the road to follow another upward rising roadway and signposted path west to the summit of Dodd. Return by the same route and follow the green waymarked path in either direction to return to the car park (10km, 3hr 50min).

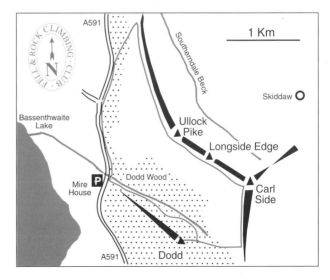

Latrigg from Wescoe

Latrigg 368m, 1207ft , GR 279247

The three stunted trees on Latrigg's grassy crown are a familiar landmark when approaching Keswick from the east. Although a low outlier of mighty Skiddaw, it is such a popular hill and commands such a wide panorama that it deserves its own entry. There are many approaches, of which the quickest is from the car park at the end of the Underscar road (15 min) but the recommended ascent uses a wide path made popular by Peter Crosthwaite, one of Keswick's first tourist guides.

Start at the Leisure Pool in Station Road, Keswick. From the rear of the pool turn left and walk along Brundholme Road for 400 metres past one road junction. Turn right into Spoony Green Lane and cross the A66 by a bridge. The path climbs up the side of the hill ahead. After crossing the first stream, a choice of grassy paths lead up steeply through bracken on the right to reach the summit directly. For a more leisurely approach stay on the main track until 350 metres beyond the second stream crossing, a path doubles back to the right traversing the slope to reach the summit (3km, 278m, 1hr 15min). The record for the annual fell race from Keswick to this point and down again is less than 18 minutes!

The view is breathtaking. From Blencathra and the Pennines to the north-east, past St John's in the Vale, Helvellyn, Bow Fell, the Scafells, the Newlands fells, round to Bassenthwaite and Skiddaw in the north-west. And at your feet, the hillside drops away steeply to reveal all of Keswick with Derwentwater and wooded Borrowdale beyond.

There is a path which descends south steeply towards Keswick. An excellent alternative is to walk along the summit path to the wall. Go through the gate and take the path leading ENE down the gentle ridge to reach the narrow road end near Brundholme House. Either, go right along the road to the starting point or better still, cross the road and descend the gravel track past Brundholme House to the River Greta. A gate on the right leads onto the old Penrith-Keswick-Cockermouth railway line which is followed to the right alongside the river back to the start (9km, 2hr 45min).

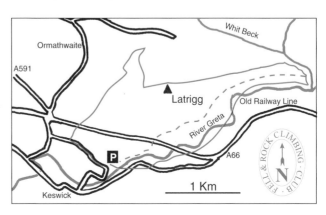

Blencathra from Swirral Edge

Blencathra (Saddleback) 868m, 2847ft , GR 323277

Blencathra lies above the village of Threlkeld and derives its alternative name of Saddleback from its profile when approaching along the A66 from Penrith. The magnificent, deeply cut ridges on the southern side contrast sharply with the hidden, rounded slopes to the north. This route encompasses good paths, a fine scrambling arete and wonderful views.

Park on the minor road below Mousthwaite Comb or, if full, in a lay-by near Scales Inn. Ascend into Mousthwaite Comb alongside Comb Beck across wooden tread boards to keep feet dry and prevent erosion. The path ahead rakes up from left to right to a col between Souther and Scales Fells. At the col cross the ridge and follow the path west as it contours along the side of Scales Fell and up towards Scales Tarn. This moody little tarn is reached after 2km: sunshine seems to make it happy but shadow brings out its dour look.

A further short climb to the north brings you to Sharp Edge. This excellent scramble can be followed on the crest itself. (Avoid the lower path which can be dangerous, loose and slippery: this has led to accidents.) The ridge is exposed in places and should not be attempted in bad weather. The final, steeper headwall leads up corrugated rocks and particular care is needed here in the wet.

From the top of Sharp Edge the path leads left around the top of the corrie, past a distinctive memorial cross laid out on the ground in white quartz stones, to reach the main summit shown on the map as Hallsfell Top (4km, 650m, 2hr 5min). The views over Scales Tarn towards Cross Fell, High Street and Helvellyn are particularly fine, whilst from the summit there are excellent views south and west over St John's in the Vale and Borrowdale. The summit ridge continues gently south west around the deeply cut corries above Threlkeld to Knowe Crags. Excellent alternative ascents are possible up any of these fine ridges from Threlkeld.

Returning to the main summit, there are a choice of descents. The shortest routes lie east down the easy ridge of Scales Fell or southwards down the more attractive ridges of Hall's Fell or Doddick Fell.

For a longer circuit revealing different aspects of this complex mountain, return northwards towards the top of Sharp Edge, crossing Atkinson Pike above Foule Crag. The path avoids this obstacle on its north-west side by descending Blue Screes before continuing round to the north and offering a different profile view of rocky Sharp Edge. From the col, two paths descend the Glenderamackin valley: the path on the right rejoins the approach route below Scales Tarn whilst that on the left follows the stream to a bridge at White Horse Bent from where a short ascent may be made back to the col and Mousthwaite Comb (11km, 4hr 15min).

Mungrisdale Common and Blencathra

Mungrisdale Common 633m, 2077ft, GR 312292

Mungrisdale Common is a spongy moorland outlier of Blencathra. It is not a separate summit, except by Wainwright tradition, but it gives an interesting walk in unfrequented country.

Start from the car park just beyond the Blencathra Centre, above Threlkeld (GR 302257); this gives a helpful starting height of 300m. Walk along the level path-cum-road towards Skiddaw House for 2km. Two streams descend from the right about here. Leave the road where the second of these, Sinen Gill, crosses the road; the road itself turns away to the left at this point. There are no paths from here on. It is, however, a simple matter in clear weather to head upwards NE on the northern side in Sinen Gill; the south side is much rougher ground. After about 150 metres the hump of the summit appears as a goal. On the way up you pass to your left a curious split rock called The Cloven Stone; it affords shelter to sheep and acts as a parish boundary. The slope flattens out and the summit cairn should be visible across the moor (4.5km, 333m, 1hr 40min).

The best, if fairly energetic, way to make a circular walk is to head SE across the moor to Foule Crag and then walk across the top of Blencathra and back down Blease Fell to the car park (10km, 4hr). If you can arrange transport, it is also possible to walk across to Bannerdale Crags and down to Mungrisdale or down the

Glenderamackin and over Mousthwaite Col to Scales. The River Caldew to the north is too deep to cross, except in its uppermost reaches.

This is not a walk to do during wet weather as much of the going is marshy, or in mist as the lie of the land is indistinct. However, it gives very good views to the Borrowdale fells and across to Lonscale Fell and Skiddaw.

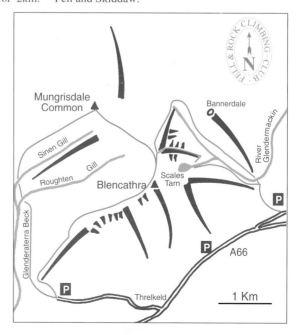

Great Calva from the track above the Blencathra Centre

Great Calva 690m, 2263ft, GR291312

The pyramidal shape of Great Calva can be viewed from a long sweeping bend on the A66 between Skiddaw and Blencathra. Its summit cone gives an appearance similar to Mt Fuji but in reality Great Calva is a very docile replica. Almost enveloped in heather, its apparent remoteness can often ensure the mountain to oneself. Perhaps its main claim to fame is being included in the Bob Graham Round – the mammoth circuit of 42 Lakeland peaks in a day.

The route starts at the beginning of the track leading past Dash Falls to Skiddaw House. From the car park near Peter House farm (GR 249323) a roadway leads south-east towards the Dash valley. The track ascends beside this dramatic waterfall. To the north-west, Binsey stands alone; to the west the slopes of Skiddaw sweep upwards and to the east lie the heathered slopes of Little Calva, our way of return. Walk on to Skiddaw House nestling next to the only trees in Skiddaw 'Forest'. Great Calva rises gradually to the north. Follow the track NE until a bridge is crossed. The thick heathered slopes above are troublesome and only eased by the occasional grassy patch. Eventually, the struggle diminishes and the summit area gained. An initial false summit is one side of the cone, followed by the main summit a short distance further (6km, 480m, 2hr 20min). The view in all directions is spectacular. The view north over the Solway to Scotland is new and rewarding.

The descent follows the new fence north-west then across somewhat boggy ground to Little Calva. The lack of path makes the going difficult and it is best to follow the fence which drops steeply to rejoin the approach path just above Dash Falls and thus back to the start (10km, 3hr 20 min).

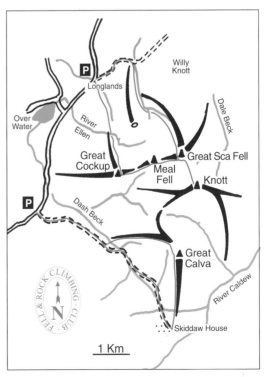

Comb Height on Knott above the River Caldew

Great Sca Fell 651m, 2135ft, GR 291339
Knott 710m, 2329ft, GR 296330
Meal Fell 550m, 1770ft, GR 283337
Great Cockup 526m, 1725ft, GR 273333

These fells surround the headwaters of the infant River Ellen. They comprise smoothly rounded, grassy hills with occasional deeply eroded ravines on their flanks and give gentle walking in unspoilt country.

Longlands Bridge (GR 267359) is a quiet and pleasant start point. After crossing the stile, walk NE up the old fell road for about 1km. An old bridleway will be seen on the right as you turn east. Follow this path up the valley of Charleton Gill to the stream's head. A broad grassy track is then seen coming down in gentle meanders from a point to the north of Little Sca Fell. Follow this until the last 30m of ascent, when it is necessary to head south for the summit (cairn). Ten minutes walking on the beginnings of a genuine fell-walkers' path brings you to Great Sca Fell (small cairn, 5km, 450m, 2hr).

It is easy to go wrong here in mist. A due south bearing brings you to a faint track leading to Knott; in clear conditions a well-defined shoulder can be seen coming down from the summit. Follow the faint track over wet ground until you reach the firm, grassy higher slopes. The path fades when you need it most but upward progress SSE brings you on to the wide,

close-cropped summit plateau and the cairn (6.5km, 510m, 2hr 30min). 'Knott' is an old-English word for a rocky summit – surely a misnomer here. There are good views across the Solway and south to the central fells.

Retrace your steps until almost back at the summit of Great Sca Fell. Then drop steeply westwards down a regular but knee-jarring slope to a marshy col below Meal Fell. A short ascent brings you to a large shelter-cum-cairn on the top (8km).

It is possible to descend to Longlands from here down the NW flanks but Great Cockup is very close. To reach it, aim SW for the south point of Trusmadoor. From the col at the head of the defile, climb up the obvious slaty edge, leading to the grassy flat top of Great Cockup (9km, 630m). There is a spectacular view of Dead Crags on Skiddaw.

Descend the slopes northwards (or retrace your route to Trusmadoor) to reach the headwaters of the River Ellen. Cross the stream to a pleasant level path which leads past a sheep-fold and hut back to Longlands Bridge (13km, 4hr 15min).

On Brae Fell

Longlands Fell　483m, 1584ft, GR 276354
Brae Fell　586m, 1922ft, GR 289352

These two fells, minor by size and lacking in major features, nevertheless provide pleasant open walking, unspoilt by path erosion on the hill or traffic below. They can be combined in one walk or ascended separately as alternative approaches to Great Sca Fell.

If taken together, the best starting point is Longlands Bridge (GR 267359). Cross the stile by the gate and walk north east on the old bridleway until nearly at the derelict farmstead of Sworley. It is possible to start ascending the north ridge of Longlands Fell from any point along here. You soon find yourself on a broad track leading by an easy gradient to the summit (2km, 260m, 55min). There are good views to the Solway and Criffel.

Continue along the ridge, over Lowthwaite Fell. Traverse the moss to the head of Charleton Gill and pick up an old bridleway leading to the col below Little Sca Fell. This latter is a quick extra summit if you wish. At the broad col a pleasant elevated path with good views to the north and west leads direct to the large cairn on the summit of Brae Fell (4.5km, 2hr 30min).

To descend the pathless ground to the ford at Charleton Wash, head NW towards the distant marker of Criffel. The grass is tussocky but the gradient is gentle. The attractive ravine of Charleton Gill can be crossed at a narrow point or avoided on easier slopes to the north. From the ford, descend the path beside the intake wall back to Longlands Bridge (7.5km, 3hr 30min).

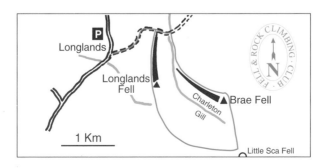

Carrock Fell from near High Row

Carrock Fell 660m, 2165ft, GR 342336
High Pike 658m, 2157ft, GR 319350

These two fells, which encircle Carrock Beck with their ridges and which both bear the marks of much mining activity in the past, are the north-eastern outliers of the northern fells. They give easy walking with gentle gradients.

Park either on the grass at the ford across Carrock Beck on the side road to Calebrack walking down to Stone Ends Farm for the start, or park on the grass opposite Stone Ends itself. The path up the fell begins at the quarry-like remains of Carrock End mine (not to be confused with Carrock Mine in Mosedale) and goes up a grassy rake, veering left for the first 100 metres. The rake comes to an unpleasant patch of scree, goes up by it , and crosses it at its top to reach a point below a grandly placed rowan tree on a crag. It is a mistake to continue to the left here, as the ground above is tussocky heather; instead, climb straight up the grassy gully and come out on a level with the top of Carrock's lower crags. A peregrine nests on these crags in season; geologists will find gabbro here. A well-defined path leads upwards past a sheepfold to the east peak (good views over the Eden valley to Cross Fell) and then across the stony plateau to the main cairn (2.5km, 450m, 1hr 25min). An elliptical ring of stones surrounds the summit; these are the remains of the walls of the largest known iron age hill fort in Cumbria.

Drop down the western side of the summit and walk WNW, following a broad ridge. There is now a clear path, skirting north of Miton Hill, but the going underfoot can be marshy. After about 3km, the path

joins an old path coming from Great Lingy Hill (shelter hut) to the south: in mist this area needs care as there are few landmarks and the terrain is confusingly humpy. Turn north-east, following the bridleway for a short distance till it meets a faint path coming down from High Pike. Walk up the broad ridge to the summit (large cairn, seat and shelter on the north side) (6km, 550m, 2hr 25min).

From the summit descend due east (no path). After 400 metres, regain an old bridleway. Go north along this for 400 metres until the old working of Driggeth Mine appears below. Descend through these to the bridleway which leads down to Carrock Beck and its ford (9km, 3hr 20min).

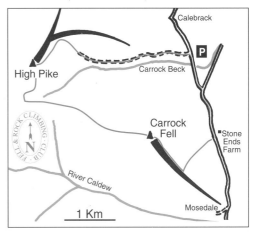

Bannerdale Crags

Bowscale Fell 702m, 2303ft, GR 333306
Bannerdale Crags 683m, 2241ft, GR 335291

These two hills make a most attractive circuit around some high craggy valleys and the route can be done in either direction. The north to south traverse is recommended as it gives views towards Sharp Edge on Blencathra and the walk can be extended to other tops. Leave your car at either unspoiled Mungrisdale village or at Bowscale 1.5km further north: this short section of road has to be used at either the beginning or the end of the walk.

From Bowscale take the signposted track west which rises gently across the lower slopes of Bowscale Fell above the river Caldew. Height is gained gradually until hidden Bowscale Tarn is reached nestling beneath its steep perimeter rim. Cross the outflow stream and climb the steeper narrow path on the right which zig-zags up to the ridge. The slopes above are rounded and grassy; make your way south on a faint path around the rim of Tarn Crags and up to the summit of Bowscale Fell (4km, 500m, 1hr 50min).

There are no obvious paths leaving the cairned summit. Descend south for 250 metres to reach a path along the high rim above the steep walls of the empty valley of Bannerdale. This path leads on towards the top of Bannerdale Crag in under 2km but avoids the highest part of the connecting ridge which is wet and boggy. A high cairn stands on top of the crags above Bannerdale but the true summit is 50 metres to the west.

The best return route follows the spur ridge towards the River Glenderamackin on the east. This river actually drains the fell on three sides. The descent requires particular care in mist and should not be used in icy conditions. Do not go due east from the high cairn as this leads over the crags. Instead continue SE around the top of the crags for another 150 metres, past a rocky gully and find the path leading down the spur. This is steep at the start but all the rocky steps can be passed easily on the right side. The path continues past old mine workings, along the spur and drops down onto the broad track alongside the River Glenderamackin; follow this down to reach Mungrisdale village (9km, 3hr 15min).

There are several alternative approaches from Mungrisdale. It is possible to ascend Bowscale Fell either by the east ridge or The Tongue, both of which lead directly to the summit. From the Glenderamackin path there is a track leading up Bannerdale which reaches the ridge 250 metres south of the summit. From Bannerdale Crags it is also possible to descend SW along the main ridge and cross the River Glenderamackin at a footbridge near the intriguingly named White Horse Bent. After a short climb to the ridge above, a return to Mungrisdale can be made over Souther Fell.

Souther Fell from Mungrisdale

Souther Fell 522m, 1712ft, GR 355291

Souther Fell is a long ridge of medium height, lacking in character itself but acting as a good viewing point. The fell has a curious legend attached to it: apparently a ghostly army was seen marching across it in the summer of 1745.

Please note that there is no public access through the intake fields at the north-eastern end, by the Mill Inn, and also that it is not possible to ford the River Glenderamackin along its northern flank; these factors create problems in making a circular route from Mungrisdale which is nevertheless the obvious start point.

Park either in the public car park opposite the village hall or in the lane by the telephone box. Take the path through the gate at the head of the lane and follow it along the north bank of the Glenderamackin, heading at first as if for Bannerdale Crags. Cross the stream coming down from Bannerdale (difficult if in spate) and then carry on up the broad but occasionally wet track towards the col between Blencathra and Souther Fell. This section of the valley is particularly attractive with fine views and a delightful waterfall. Just before the top, drop down to the stream and cross it by a broad wooden bridge; the path then slants back up to the col above Mousthwaite Combe.

From the col follow a grassy trod up a gentle incline and over the flat top, keeping on till you reach a small cairn towards the NE end (4.5km, 290m, 1hr 40min): a large cairn to the left near the SE end appears to mark nothing in particular. There are excellent views back to Sharp Edge on Blencathra. Remembering that there is no way off the fell by

continuing down the ridge, it is necessary from the summit to head down NE (bearing 60 degrees) towards a large collection of farm buildings at Beckside. After 100m of descent, pick up an old track descending diagonally through the bracken, coming out on the back road from Scales just above Beckside, near the first gate. A short walk along the road brings you into Mungrisdale (6km, 2hr 30min).

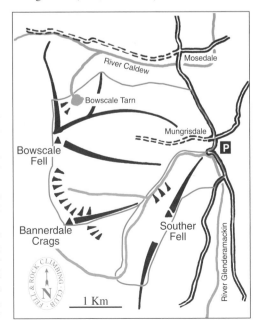

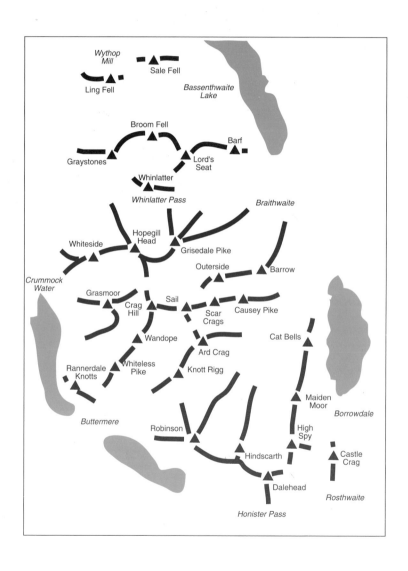

Section 6

The North Western Fells

The clearly defined boundaries of this compact area are the river valleys of the Derwent and Cocker. The whole territory is fine walking country with many splendid ridges and some little-known corners. To AW these were the most delectable of all the fells.

Most of the underlying rocks in this area are Skiddaw Slate which is not much exposed but is responsible for the smoothness of surface and the absence of tarns. Only towards Borrowdale are volcanic rocks evident; nowhere more so than at Castle Crag, the only top below 300m to be included in this guide because of its special mountain characteristics.

Sale Fell from the south

Sale Fell 359m, 1177ft, GR 194297

Sale Fell is a fine viewpoint on the northern edge of the North Western Fells, looking across the West Cumbrian plain to the Scottish hills and over to Skiddaw in the east. There are two lesser tops, Lothwaite (345m) and Rivings (335m) and all are covered with soft green turf sprinkled with brightly coloured wild flowers in summer. The walking is delightfully easy and the gradients gentle.

The walk begins from the Kelswick road east of Wythop Mill, where there is parking for a few cars (GR 185293). Walk along the lane to Kelswick, forking right at the farm through a gate/stile. A grass track leads down to the site of an old church pulled down in 1865 but where an annual service is still held every August. Continue in the same direction along a shady lane below the oaks of Chapel Wood. Take a left fork and continue rising gently uphill. After passing a gated path on the right look for a narrow path on the left leading to the grassy col between Rivings and Lothwaite. A short diversion right leads easily to Lothwaite.

Now return to the col and continue to follow the pleasant grassy path along the high ground curving round Sale Fell. Make a slight diversion left to take in the top of Rivings with its large cairn. Cross two stone walls and some old cultivation strips to reach the top of Sale Fell (4km, 240m, 1hr 25min). From the double top follow the broad grassy ridge as it descends in a westerly direction towards a wall. Turn left at the wall and the green track leads gently down towards Kelswick and so back to the starting point. If preferred a steep short cut can be made by following the wall straight down instead (5.5km, 2hr).

Ling Fell

Ling Fell 373m, 1223ft, GR 180286

Lonely little Ling Fell does not, in all fairness, offer any serious challenge to the walker but it has got a certain charm in spite of its size. You can be up and down in an hour if you like, but taken at an easy pace with a good long leisurely picnic at the top it can offer a very pleasant afternoon away from the rat race and give a genuine feeling of being part of 'The Great Outdoors'.

From Wythop Mill take the south loop in the road to Eskin until you come to a double farm gate at GR 183291 where there is room to park a couple of cars on the grass verge. Pass through the right hand gate to find a well established track or Corpse Road leading you westwards. After about 1km the track begins to curl around the steadily steepening fellside eventually leading you westwards until it levels out at the remains of a group of grouse butts. Strike SE at this point to follow one of the faint paths to the summit. This is the spot for a bit of practice in orientation and if the day is clear a competition to name as many of the Lakeland Fells as can be seen.

Continue on over the top and descend steeply east to a track above a stream. Follow this left to the start (3km, 1hr).

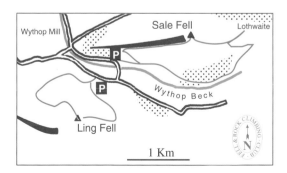

Barf

Barf 468m, 1536ft, GR 214268

Barf is a rugged little fell of classic proportions. This tough scramble by way of its south eastern defences will leave you either loving or hating its very existence. The walk is ideal for a stiff early morning constitutional in its own right or, as is more usual, a testing opening round as a preliminary to a traverse of the North Western Fells.

From the path opposite the Swan Hotel take the path branching right from the minor road. Once past the smaller white painted pinnacle known as the Clerk the wear and tear is reduced as the steepness of the ground takes its toll. The majestic Bishop in his fine white raiments now dominates the view but few humans ever undertake the scramble up scree to meet him in person. As the path crosses Beckstones Gill you may think you have found the easy way in by the back door but not so; you will have to work your way up a steep and seemingly relentless course, at times using your hands to scramble up two or three rocky sections. As you emerge from the wooded gill you will be glad to find a more affable path with a gentler gradient trending rightwards across open slopes which leads you easily to the summit cairn (1km, 370m, 1hr). From here you will see a whole medley of differing views from the wide open spaces of the Solway Firth and Lorton Vale in the north and west to the high rugged profiles of Grasmoor, Helvellyn, Blencathra and Skiddaw in the south and east.

Unless you are contemplating an excursion to further fells the only safe descent is by reversal of your previous course (2 km, 1hr 30 min).

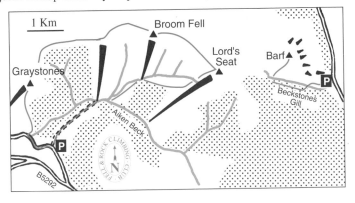

Lord's Seat from Broom Fell

Graystones/Kirk Fell 456m, 1496ft, GR 178264
Broom Fell 511m, 1676ft, GR 196270
Lord's Seat 552m, 1811ft, GR 204266

Although it could be said that these three tops lack the character of typical Lakeland Fells they do provide a pleasant half day's outing with less of the hustle and bustle to be found on the loftier fells. The clockwise traverse is preferred giving a steep way up and gentle descent, but of course the route is easily reversed. Graystones is also known as Kirk Fell on some maps.

There is a sizeable car park at the turn-off for Darling How at GR 181255 on Whinlatter Pass which makes a useful starting point. Walk 200 metres along the forestry road and take the track to Scawgill Bridge quarry; follow the path up the side of the forestry wall easing the angle of ascent by longer and longer zig-zags as the density of the bracken allows. Pausing to get your breath back on the little outcrop of Graystones you begin to appreciate the tranquillity of your surroundings as your gaze wanders over the Vale of Lorton past Fellbarrow and onwards to the sea beyond Distington. After losing a little height to skirt Darling How Plantation head ENE to climb steadily to the cairn of Broom Fell. A more or less level south easterly kilometre takes you easily on to Lord's Seat (4.5km, 460m, 2hr). The summit itself is quite unremarkable but you can quite often have the place to yourself and it is a fine vantage point to take in all the sights of North Western Lakeland.

Return via the path which takes you generally west and then SW between Aiken and Darling How plantations. Alternatively if you can make suitable transport arrangements continue east to take in Barf by the easy way and hence obtain even better views of Bassenthwaite Lake and beyond (8km, 2hr 50min).

Whinlatter

Whinlatter 525m, 1722ft, GR 197249

This less frequented hill, with its steep side overlooking Whinlatter Pass, is not particularly impressive to look at but offers good views towards Grisedale Pike and makes an interesting short walk. Start from Whinlatter Visitor Centre which offers displays and forest walks suitable for all the family.

From the Visitor Centre, walk 300 metres up the road to the top of the pass. At the edge of the forestry turn right up a forest road for 500 metres to a crossroads and clearing. Take the roadway on the left which leads to the open hillside. Cross the stile and take the faint path which follows the fence up to the ridge and then strikes east for the summit (2km, 220m, 50min). Wainwright suggests the east top is the highest point but the latest maps show the west top to be eight metres higher. The path continues to the east top but thick forestry and fencing inhibit alternative descents. From just beyond the main top it is possible to follow the wall down north over heather towards Aiken Beck where an opening in the fence leads onto the forest road. This isolated valley gives good walking through trees and open slopes. Turn right on the road which winds its way up to a col near Tarbarrel Moss before descending to the Visitor Centre. When the crossroads is reached again, a choice of routes leads back to the start; the path straight ahead is the shortest (6km, 2hr 10min).

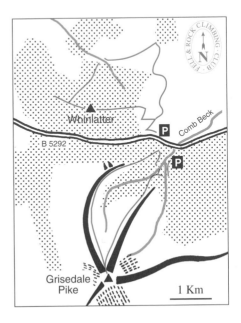

On Grisedale Pike with Skiddaw in the distance

Grisedale Pike 791m, 2595ft, GR 198225

The shapely triangular peak of Grisedale Pike is a dominating feature of the Keswick fells. It sends out three ridges. The east ridge is certainly the most popular route but it is very eroded and it is often difficult to park near Braithwaite. The north east ridge provides the quickest and easiest route to the summit, with the advantage of a large car park at Revelin Moss just below the top of Whinlatter Pass. It is important on this walk to keep to forestry paths and not to stray into the forest or cross fences. An up-to-date map is available from Whinlatter Visitor Centre.

Take the way-marked path (white arrows) on the south side of the car park, following the markers along the forest roads above the beck, until a stile leads on to the path up the NE ridge. This path is grassy in its lower stages, becoming stonier higher up. It follows the crest of the ridge by the remains of a wall, maintaining a steep angle of steady ascent. The consolation is that it starts high and is short in distance (2km, 490m, 1hr 20min).

The most convenient alternative way down from the summit is to descend the north ridge over Hobcarton End. In mist, take a true N bearing to make sure you get on the right ridge, as there is no obvious path at first; in good conditions, a line of cairns is obvious below. Descend over shaley ground at first, eventually picking up a path through bilberry and heather. Cross a fence by a stile and head for the summit of Hobcarton End with fine views to the Galloway coast. The path down leaves the ridge just before the summit of Hobcarton End, heading down east through bilberries to the right of the prow of the ridge. Drop down to the upper limit of the forest, keeping above it till a gap in the forestry appears. The old path has been preserved in the new plantation but it is narrow; it is particularly important to keep to the path here. The path descends to the forest road: turn right and follow the forest roads to the approach path and back to the car park (5.5km, 2hr 30min).

Hopegill Head from Whiteside

Whiteside 707m, 2319ft, GR 170219
Hopegill Head 770m, 2526ft, GR 186222

These tops lie between Crummock Water and Whinlatter Pass in an area of Skiddaw Slate. Typically the rock is broken and fragmented, not good for climbing but providing some dramatic scenery. Hopegill Head (also known as Hobcarton Crag) has an impressive line of cliffs where rare alpine plants grow. This circular walk includes an airy traverse of the ridge between the two tops, rightly described by AW as exhilarating. The ascent is quite strenuous up rough and rocky ground.

Park at Lanthwaite Green on the Buttermere road. A grassy path leads to a crossing of Liza Beck which emerges from Gascale Gill. When the path turns a corner to enter the Gill, turn left and go up the steep and rocky path to Whin Ben. The angle eases a little here but care is still required on account of loose rock. From Whiteside, follow the rim of the crags to Hopegill Head (3km, 650m, 1hr 50min).

From Hopegill Head continue in a northerly direction towards Ladyside Pike from where there is a long gradual descent, easy underfoot, along the ridge to the north west. Towards the foot of the ridge, keep on the left side of an old wall. The angle steepens and it is a relief to reach a good grassy path descending gently to the left, just above the road. Veer left to cross Hope Beck and pick up the path outside the intake wall to Lanthwaite Green (12km, 4hr 15min).

For a shorter walk which includes the delectable ridge between the two tops, turn SE from Hopegill Head. Gradually bear away from the edge of the crags to follow the easy path over Sand Hill and down to Coledale Hause. The path which descends Gascale Gill is unmistakable and gives a pleasant walk (8.5km).

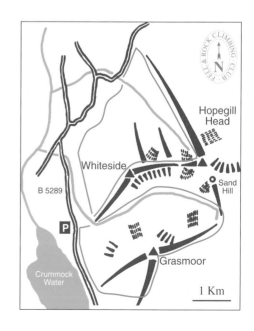

Grasmoor from Red Pike

Grasmoor 852m, 2795ft, GR 175203

The massive bulk of Grasmoor dominates Crummock Water. Its steep sides appear to repel all approaches, although there are scrambling routes leading directly to the summit from both Lanthwaite Green and Rannerdale Bridge. This route picks an easier way from the car park by Lanthwaite Green Farm (GR 158207) on the B5289 Lorton - Buttermere road.

Head ENE across Lanthwaite Green towards the gap of Gasgale Gill between Grasmoor and Whin Ben. Cross the Liza beck by a small footbridge and turn right to follow the stream on its N bank all the way to the head of the gill at Coledale Hause. The gill narrows initially with steep crags on the left side; two easy scrambles are necessary on the path. The valley widens below the sweeping northern slopes of Grasmoor and the shattered rocks of Gasgale Crags falling from the Whiteside ridge. A ruined sheepfold is passed before the path rises more steeply to reach Coledale Hause – the Picadilly Circus of the North-Western Fells.

The main path continues south towards Wandope. Follow this path for 200 metres before crossing the stream and heading up the broad slopes of Grasmoor in a south-westerly direction to follow the ridge around the edge of Dove Crags. There are splendid views of Whiteside as you approach the broad, grassy summit plateau with its large cairn (5km, 702m, 2hr 30min).

Follow the broad path around the head of Cinderdale Beck towards Crag Hill and Wandope for 250 metres until a faint path strikes right to descend the very fine Lad Hows ridge with more fine views over Crummock Water. Towards the bottom, keep close to the beck which leads down to the road. Turn right along the road for 1.5km to return to the start (9km, 3hr 30min).

This walk can easily be extended from Lanthwaite Green by taking in Whiteside and Hopegill Head, and from Coledale Hause by including Crag Hill, Wandope and Whiteless Pike.

Whiteless Pike

Wandope 772m, 25332ft, GR 188197
Whiteless Pike 660m, 2165ft, GR 180190

This route offers a spectacular circuit with dramatic views into a hidden cove and incorporates a little-known classic mountain ascent.

Park just outside Buttermere at GR 173172. Cross the road to the footpath sign and follow the path to the left of the white cottages heading NE up Mill Beck. This good footpath follows the valley floor gaining height at an easy gradient. After 1.5km keep to the left fork in the path, climbing slightly uphill, to cross a feeder stream in a further 600 metres. Stay with the footpath for a further 1km to cross Third Gill, pausing occasionally en route to admire the view of the Buttermere fells behind. The path continues providing views of Sail and Causey Pike ahead with Skiddaw in the distance. About 200 metres before Addacomb Beck make your own way steeply uphill in a NW direction through bracken aiming for the rock outcrop on the ridge rising from your right. At this outcrop the dramatic view into Addacomb Hole

is revealed in front of you and traces of a footpath appear to help you wind your way through further rock outcrops and Alpine flowers to arrive suddenly at the summit cairn of Wandope (6km, 670m, 2hr 45min).

Linger a while on the summit to absorb the panoramic views of the major Lakeland summits before heading W across tufted grass and descending gradually to a cairn at GR 184196 which marks the start of Whiteless Edge. The path now heads SW to the summit of Whiteless Pike along a narrow, airy ridge where care is needed in strong cross winds.

Leave the summit in a southerly direction by a well-defined path descending initially through a rocky area with more fine views towards Great Gable and the Scafells. The path soon reaches grass slopes and leads easily back to join your outward path near the white cottages (10km, 4hr).

Rannerdale Knotts 355m, 1164ft, GR 167182

Rannerdale Knotts from Low Ling Crag

If the Norman army had used a guidebook like this when it tried to quell the Norse settlers of West Cumberland, it would not have been falsely diverted into the waiting ambush in Rannerdale. In April, Rannerdale's blue hue lends credence to the legend that the local profusion of bluebells springs from a soil well fertilised by Norman blood. (The Battle of Rannerdale is told by Nicholas Size in *The Secret Valley*.) Beauty comes in small packages they say, and this fell within its modest height delightfully presents a self-contained hill, unlike some of its more lofty competitors.

Start in Rannerdale (GR 163183), where there is parking for several cars. A direct ascent is possible, but the charms of Low Bank are best discovered more gently: 'Go slowly, my friend, so that you may see how much there is in me, and not I how little there is in you.' So, proceed NE along a level track, through a gate into Fletcher's Field, and then gently rising as you pass below Dale How to the junction of Squat Beck and Rannerdale Beck in High Rannerdale. Pass through a gate on the right. Climb gradually up to the col, resisting the temptation to short cut sharply right onto Low Bank. From the col between Low Bank and Whiteless Pike enjoy the view of Buttermere before turning your back on it to follow the rising, undulating ridge of Low Bank. The summit is at the far end, not

at the intermediate cairn (3.5km, 250m, 1hr 15 min). From the craggy top, to which the name Rannerdale Knotts is correctly applied, a panorama of three lakes is revealed. Descend from a prominent notch in the rock down a groove heading NW, before swinging left (poor path) towards Crummock Water. After some steep ground gain the old road, and any of several tracks leading back to the modern road (4.5km, 1hr 45 min).

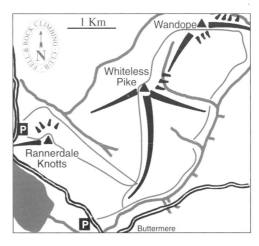

Causey Pike and Crag Hill from Barrow

Scar Crags 672m, 2204ft, GR 208207
Causey Pike 637m, 2089ft, GR 218209

The knobbly top of Causey Pike is a recognisable landmark from many fells in the northern Lakes and its distinctive shape and steep front nose is most impressive when seen from Keswick. Scar Crags forms part of the continuation leading to Crag Hill and eventually to the possible circuit of Coledale. This moderate walk makes an interesting round offering fine views over Newlands and Derwentwater.

Start from Stoneycroft Farm just above Stair on the road leading to Newlands Hause from Braithwaite. Parking for several cars is available on the verge and above Uzzicar Farm. From the bridge, follow the old mining track alongside Stonycroft Gill on its north bank. This continues to the head of the little valley from which an ascent of Outerside can also be made. The path continues SW to ascend through an old cobalt mine to the well defined col between Sail and Scar Crags. Turn left and climb another 65m to reach the summit of Scar Crags (4km, 532m, 2hr). This ridge is well defined with steep sides which form heather covered rocky aretes on the south side well seen from Ard Crags.

The ridge continues easily to Causey Pike in just over 1km, crossing several bumps on the way. Causey Pike is the unmistakable final bump. The descent from this fine vantage point is down the steep and obvious nose of the mountain. The start is rocky but presents no great difficulty. The flatter ground at Sleet Hause is reached with some relief. Here, there is a choice of routes. A path descends left to take a

more direct route to the bridge and starting point on the road but it is preferable to continue along the ridge on a path to Rowling End and then descend this second nose above Ellas Crag to the same point (7km, 3hr).

A traverse of these hills in the other direction can be continued over Sail and Crag Hill or over Outerside and Barrow. The former involves a return via Coledale to Braithwaite from which it is necessary to walk along the road to the starting point.

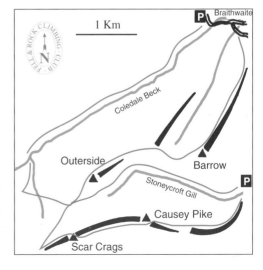

Causey Pike ridge above Outerside and Barrow

Barrow 455m, 1494ft, GR 227218
Outerside 568m, 1863ft, GR 211215

These two fells form a lower inner ridge within the circuit of higher fells surrounding Coledale. This walk provides good examples of the mining history which has been associated with Keswick for over 400 years. The Company of Mines Royal was established with support from Elizabeth I and her senior minister. Miners were brought from Germany to live in Keswick and work the copper and lead mines in Borrowdale and Newlands.

From the centre of Braithwaite village (where sensitive parking is required), take the narrow Newlands road for 100 metres and turn right up the drive to Braithwaite Lodge. Skirt the buildings via a gateway on the right to a signposted and stiled crossing of paths. Continue up through another gateway to the open fell where a short ascent leads to a sign indicating the ridge track. Follow this through bracken and then heather to reach the top of Barrow (2km, 350m, 1hr 10min). At a nick on the ridge, evidence of former mines and their discarded spoil can be found on the slopes on either side. From the top, descend west a short way to Barrow Door and ascend the other side of the col by a thin path to Stile End. Here the path turns to the left and descends again to Low Moss.

Care is required in mist since the paths are faint and several sheep tracks traverse towards Stonycroft Gill. Keep going WSW and the ground soon starts to rise again. A path leads more steeply up the ridge to Outerside (4km, 590m, 2hr).

Descend the other side of the top to a level area at the head of Stonycroft Gill. From here an ascent can be made SW past more mine workings to reach the main ridge leading over Scar Crags and Causey Pike but this involves a return walk along the road to Braithwaite. Alternatively turn right off the path and traverse rough grass slopes west for 350 metres to join a path descending alongside Birkthwaite Beck. This zig-zags down towards Force Crag Mine and crosses Coledale Beck just below the mine. A level gravel roadway then leads out of Coledale. A path leaves the roadway on the right just before its end to bring you back to the edge of Braithwaite (9km, 3hr 15min).

The route can be shortened by using any of the paths from Barrow Door, Stile End and Low Moss which descend past High Coledale. Barrow and Outerside can also be climbed from Stair in Newlands by the track up Stonycroft Gill.

Crag Hill

Crag Hill (Eel Crag) 839m, 2752ft, GR 193204
Sail 773m, 2536ft, GR 198203

Crag Hill forms the hub of the North Western Fells. It is rarely climbed on its own but combined with one of several possible circuits. From Braithwaite, it can be linked with Grisedale Pike and Hopegill Head or with Causey Pike and Scar Crags. From Crummock Water and Buttermere, it can be combined with Grasmoor, Wandope and Whiteless Pike. This route takes you into the heart of these fells leaving you with plenty of options for extending the walk if you wish.

Starting from Braithwaite, where there is a car park at the foot of Whinlatter Pass, take the land-rover track along the N side of Coledale Beck for 4km to Force Crag Mine. Cross the beck by a bridge and follow the track more steeply up to Coledale Hause.

A direct scramble is possible due S through Eel Crags to the summit of Crag Hill. For a gentler ascent, follow the main path SSW alongside the stream for 500 metres and then branch left up grassier slopes to the top (6km, 735m, 2hr 45min). Descend the narrow E ridge to a col followed by a short rise to Sail. Another descent along the ridge leads to a second col. It is possible to continue easily along this ridge to Scar Crags and Causey Pike. From the second col descend left through old mine workings and follow the path into upper Stonycroft Gill beneath Outside. After 2km, fork left beneath Stile End to reach the Barrow Door col and follow this path NE down the ridge past High Coledale to return to Braithwaite (12km, 4hr 35min).

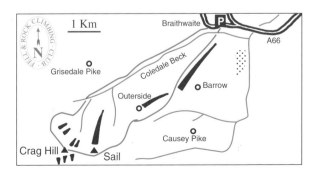

Ard Crags from Rigg Beck

Ard Crags 581m, 1906ft, GR 207198
Knott Rigg 556m, 1824ft, GR 197189

The traverse of this fine little ridge in Newlands offers a less frequented alternative walk when all the surrounding fells are swarming with summer crowds. The ridge between the two distinct summits has steep flanks throughout its length. Two remaining woods of Lakeland sessile oaks can be found above Rigg Beck and in Keskadale. The steep slopes forming the valleys on either side have protected the heather from over-grazing and in late summer all the surrounding slopes are extensively covered with a deep purple spread.

Start at Rigg Beck where a small quarry offers parking for several cars. Take the good path up Rigg Beck for 700 metres to the final field boundary on the left. Cross the stream and climb due south to gain the ridge. From here a grassy path through bracken ascends the ridge west over Aikin Knott to reach the almost flat ridge of Ard Crags (2.5km, 415m, 1hr 20min). There are fine views of the steep broken flanks beneath Scar Crags and Causey Pike to the north and down to Keskadale and Newlands to the east.

A descent down either flank from the summit is not advised. Continue SW along the ridge for 1.5km, dropping slightly to a col and rising again to Knott Rigg. From this summit, turn back sharply to go east past two small fenced-in bog holes and descend a most enjoyable narrow path through thick heather along the ridge forming the SE boundary of Ill Gill. From Keskadale Farm, return to the starting point by following the narrow road which can be busy in summer (8km, 2hr 50min).

The summit of Knott Rigg can also be reached by an easy ascent from Newlands Hause (1.5km, 223m, 50min). The continuation to Ard Crags will need to be reversed to avoid a lengthy return along the road.

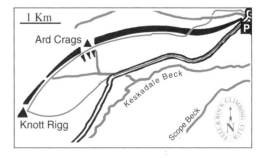

Cat Bells from Hindscarth

Cat Bells 451m, 1479ft, GR 244199

More people have probably been introduced to fell walking on Cat Bells than on any other Lakeland hill – including the present writer! It is a justifiably popular summit occupying an enviable position between island-studded Derwentwater and the green fields of Newlands. From its fine ridge there is an impressive view of higher surrounding fells in every direction. This is a hill for young and old alike which continues to delight in all conditions.

For a leisurely walk of great enjoyment, choose a warm sunny day and take a picnic. Start from Keswick landing stages by taking the launch across Derwentwater to Hawse End. This gives a magnificent approach in which you can anticipate the ridge in all its glory. On leaving the boat walk up the path to the road at the foot of the ridge close to a steep double bend and cattle grid. For those with less time, start at the small car park on the short road leading to Gutherscale Farm. Follow the path up onto the crest. Earlier severe erosion has been reversed by the construction of this path so please do not take short-cuts across the corners. Once on the ridge there are fine views to left and right. As with so many hills the first 'top' is a false one, revealing an almost level part of the ridge leading to the final steeper climb to the summit (2km from road; 310m, 1hr). This is one of the very few fells without a summit cairn – perhaps the volume of visitors taking away souvenir rocks has

depleted it! Rest awhile to take in the view.

To complete a circular walk, continue south along the ridge which descends to a col. From here you can ascend Maiden Moor 2km to the south or descend paths on either side of the ridge. On the east side the initial descent is steep. Shortly before reaching the road at Manesty, an older grass road is crossed. This terrace provides a pleasant way of traversing the hillside and returning to the starting point (6km, 2hr). If returning to Keswick by boat, walk north from Manesty along the tarmaced road for 1km, past Brackenburn (the former home of author Hugh Walpole), until open land allows you to reach the lakeshore and the landing stage at Brandelhow Bay. It is also delightful to walk along the lakeshore path to the starting point at Hawse End through oak woods and fields which were the first purchases of the National Trust in 1902.

A descent from the col by a path on the west side is also recommended. Descend 500 metres through former Elizabethan mine workings and look out for a path going right near the stream. This crosses the lower slopes of Cat Bells past Skelgill Farm to the starting point at the foot of the ridge (5km, 1hr 45min). This slope and path is the home of Mrs Tiggy-Winkle in the Beatrix Potter story of that name.

High Spy from Dalehead

Maiden Moor 576m, 1889ft, GR 237182
High Spy 653m, 2142ft, GR 234162

This is a walk of contrasts, from the wooded valley of the River Derwent to the rugged grandeur of the higher fells.

From the NT car park at Rosthwaite continue along the road to Yew Tree Farm and follow footpath signs to Grange. Cross the river by the bridge and follow the broad riverbank path through woods beneath Castle Crag. On reaching the metalled road turn left to Hollows Farm and pass through the farmyard following the path north. At a stone wall (red gate with a 'Private' sign) turn left and skirt the wood, crossing a small stream. The path continues by a fence and stone wall on the edge of the wood to Manesty. Here, a path climbs diagonally right to reach the saddle between Cat Bells and Maiden Moor. At the saddle, turn left to ascend the main ridge. After 1km, branch rightwards, following the edge of the plateau to the summit of Maiden Moor: an insignificant cairn set in featureless grassland but with superb views to the west. (5.5km, 493m, 2hr 20min).

From the summit an obvious path leads south to the impressive cairn on the summit of High Spy. Continue on, southwards, descending the ridge until the path turns slightly to the west. From this point it is possible to descend the fellside directly to the fence above Rigghead Quarry thereby avoiding the very wet ground between Dalehead Tarn and the quarry. Descend through the old quarry workings and follow Tongue Gill down into the main valley. Cross the

intake wall at a gate and descend through fields to recross the river at the stone bridge and so back to Rosthwaite (12km, 4hrs).

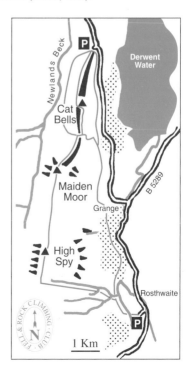

On Robinson, looking down to the Newlands Valley

Dalehead 753m, 2470ft, GR 223153
Hindscarth 727m, 2385ft, GR 216165
Robinson 737m, 2417f, GR 202169

This is an excellent circuit of no great difficulty and with a variety of contrasting viewpoints. The path leading into the combe below Dalehead was constructed over 400 years ago when the mines of the Newlands Valley made it one of the most important industrial centres in Britain.

Limited parking is available at Littletown (GR 232195) by Newlands Beck. Cross Chapel Bridge and turn left through a gate and along the lane, forking left at the church, to Low Snab Farm. Pass through the farmyard and follow the track down to the beck. Cross the bridge and follow the old mine road south into the valley. A short way past the prominent spur of Castle Nook, fork right (cairn) and cross the beck at the junction with Near Tongue Gill. Follow an indefinite shelf SSW across the hillside, crossing the ravine of Far Tongue Gill, and continue on the now obvious grass path which zig-zags up to the Dalehead mines. From the mine the path cuts east above crags to reach the ridge leading to the summit of Dalehead (5km, 610m, 2hr 15min).

Continue WNW, along the obvious path until it starts to climb the shoulder of Hindscarth. From here, follow a narrow path north onto the ridge and summit of Hindscarth.

Retrace your steps south until it is possible to cut the corner again, SSW, back to the ridge of Littledale Edge. Continue along the ridge, following the fenceline NW until the path turns north at a small cairn, where a magnificent view of Crummock Water,

Loweswater and the Solway coast suddenly unfolds. A short distance north from this point is the summit of Robinson (9km, 860m, 3hr 45min).

To descend, follow the line of cairns NE along the broad ridge above Robinson Crags. Three short rock steps above Blea Crags add to the interest and lead onto the grassy ridge of High Snab Bank. Just before the end of the ridge turn right and go down a steep slope towards a small group of trees and the track to Low High Snab Farm. Follow the road back to the starting point passing Newlands Church which is well worth a visit (14km, 5hrs).

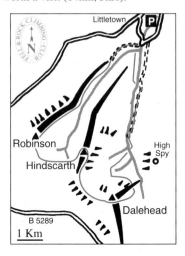

Castle Crag from the south

Castle Crag 290m, 951ft, GR 249159

The 'Jaws of Borrowdale' have lost a few feet in height since Wainwright listed Castle Crag as the 214th and last of his Lakeland Fells. The OS maps of the time showed this miniature hill to be the imperial equivalent of exactly 300m. Despite more recent surveys lowering the height, Castle Crag is so characteristic of the intimacy and beauty which define the attraction of the Lake District to walkers that we feel it is worthy of a special place in this guide. It is a true Lakeland Fell combining all the elements of its taller neighbours in one perfect, miniature mountain. In AW's own words, "the loveliest square mile in Lakeland".

Rosthwaite, in the heart of Borrowdale, makes an ideal starting point for this exploration. There is a car park down the side road opposite the shop. Walk further down this road, past the village hall and turn right at the farm to reach the river. Cross this by the bridge 200 metres to the right. Follow the river bank right via a stile until in 200 metres the path veers left over a small slab bridge. 100 metres further, another stile gives access to a path which climbs the hillside through trees to the ridge. From a further stile, the path makes a final climb through piled quarry waste to the summit just beyond the disused quarry (2km, 200m, 1hr). The top is an ancient fort which commands superb views of Derwentwater and Skiddaw. A stone plaque commemorates the men of Borrowdale killed in the First World War.

To descend, retrace your steps through the quarry waste to the stile over the wall. Here, go right and descend the path over more waste slate to reach the old road at the bottom. Follow this down right towards Grange until you reach the river again. Here the old road continues ahead to Grange but to return to Rosthwaite turn right and follow the path alongside the river. This delightful path amidst Borrowdale's magnificent oak trees leads back to the starting point (5.5km, 2hr). A detour away from the river avoids an awkward river-side outcrop. Just beyond a wall, at the highest point on the path, there is a junction of tracks. The one to the left leads to Rosthwaite but a short diversion to the right leads to the two caves inhabited during the summers between the two World Wars by Millican Dalton the self-styled 'Professor of Adventure' who offered a guiding service to visitors.

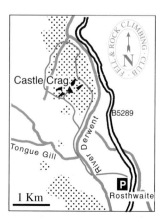

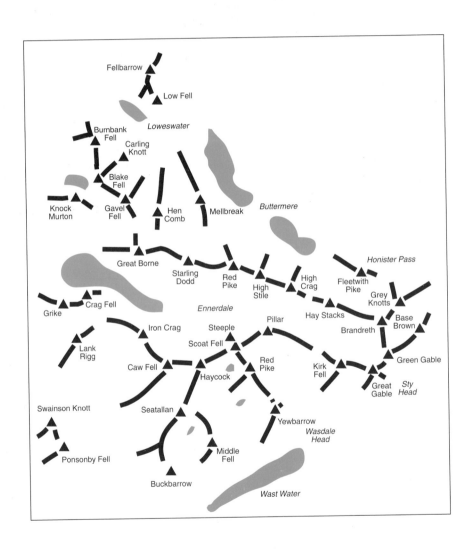

Section 7

The Western Fells

This area includes all the hills in a rough triangle bounded by the Crummock/Buttermere and Wasdale valleys and by Styhead pass. It includes some of the famous summits around Wasdale Head – the birthplace of English rock climbing – as well as the more lonely valley of Ennerdale. In the west we have extended the area to the National Park boundary and added several new tops including Knock Murton, Iron Crag and Swainson Knott.

In 1965, on finishing his Book 7, AW announced his future plans for a series of Lakeland *Sketchbooks*, for *Fellwanderer* and for 'A pictorial guide to the Pennine Way', but firmly rejects any idea of 'The Outlying Fells'. He came round to the idea in the end, this book appearing in 1974 describing 56 walks. These have not only delighted those who can no longer reach the higher tops but provide many ideas for enjoyable short walks on many occasions.

Sphinx Rock, Great Gable

View from Low Fell to Crummock Water

Low Fell 423m, 1387ft, GR 137226
Fellbarrow 416m, 1364ft, GR 132242

The wedge of low grassy hills separating Lorton Vale from the Loweswater trench offers an afternoon's easy stroll embracing scenes of perfect sylvan loveliness from the Low Fell area, and sweeping seaboard prospects from the Fellbarrow dome.

Half-way along the road skirting Loweswater is a sign 'Mosser - unfit for cars' (GR 125219). Walk up the Mosser road, leaving it at a stile behind a signpost to Foulsdyke. Turn immediately left over a beck then strike straight up, right of a fence, to join Darling Fell's NW ridge at an iron corner post. Loweswater's sublime beauty demands dalliance here. A faint track beckons up right to a stile and the cairned crest of Darling Fell. Now accompany the fence on the left down to Crabtree Beck's marshy basin. Hereabouts, a dam burst in 1828 destroying lakeside property and drowning two people. The main dwelling happily survived and is notable as the birthplace of John Burnyeat, an early Quaker. Follow the fence up to Low Fell ridge. Don't cross the stile, but turn right for 200 metres to enjoy the artistic symmetry of the vista from the cairned knoll at spot height 412m. Return to the stile and a broad track north to Low Fell's summit cairn and an intimate outlook over Lorton Vale.

Continue northwards on the fine undulating path. Watching Crag on the right is worth a short diversion from the main route which ascends to a stile and fence adjoining a ruined enclosure. Cross the stile, then desert the Thackthwaite-bound bridleway by using a thin trod off left, countouring Sourfoot Fell, then descending to an isolated stone wall.

Continue northwards alongside the wall over Smithy Fell. Fellbarrow's OS column is reached after two more stiles (5km, 490m, 2hrs). In any weather the superbly detailed coastal panorama is as compelling as the nearby Hatteringill Head's cairn is tempting for an optional visit.

From Fellbarrow's top, amble WSW (no path) down broad slopes of tussocky grass to a cart-track which crosses Mosser Beck. An iron gate permits access to the Mosser/Loweswater road (GR 122238). Veer left and eventually climb the stile at the second signpost on the right. The attractive path becomes a metalled lane avoiding Miresyke farm by cutting suddenly down right to Loweswater's most westerly car park (9km, 3hrs).

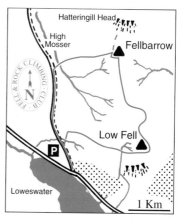

Knock Murton from Kelton Fell

Knock Murton 447m, 1466ft, GR 095191

This delightful fell is splendidly situated on the edge of the high ground. It offers views of the high fells of Ennerdale and Buttermere, whilst maintaining a broad outlook over the coastal plain and an insight into industrial history.

Start from the small car park in the hamlet of Felldyke, walk through to the Dockray Nook Lane and follow this for 20 metres until you can turn right onto the track to Cogra Moss. This soon enters trees, but there are views of the Moss and surrounding fells, sadly disfigured by conifers. Near the eastern end of the Moss, the track narrows; take the path which rises through a forest break, due south. This leads to forestry roads; either may be taken south-westwards as they join lower down by the forest edge, at the site of the former administrative buildings of the Knockmurton Mine. Work started here in 1852 to extract hematite (iron ore) at up to 5000 tons per year, though economic reserves were exhausted by 1911. Below the surface, the fell is criss-crossed by veins, cross-cuts and adits at several levels. Turn NE at the gate and climb the open fell until you can take a good miners' track leftwards and explore some of the abandoned workings. From here the track of the Rowrah and Kelton Fell Railway is clearly visible. The railway was built in 1874 as a response to the high cost of carting and its disastrous effect on the local lanes. The rails were eventually lifted in 1934.

Meander up the fellside generally north-eastwards until the fine summit cairn and shelter are reached. You will realise then why this lovely little hill should be climbed on a good day and not as a bad weather alternative. If you descend on a bearing of about 310 degrees, you come to a signposted footpath leading almost north through the forestry, back to the Cogra Moss track. The last few metres are quite steep and provide an unexpected sting in the tail (6km, 320m, 2hr).

A much easier route is from the road near Cross Rigg, but this would be over almost before you began and misses out on Cogra Moss and its atmosphere.

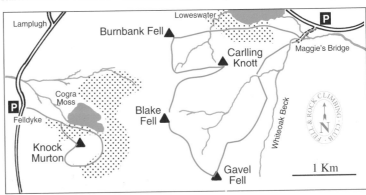

On Burnbank Fell

Burnbank Fell 475m, 1558ft, GR 110209
Carling Knott 544m, 1784ft, GR 117203
Blake Fell 573m, 1879ft, GR 110197
Gavel Fell 526m, 1725ft, GR 117185

This group of Loweswater Fells are grassy, heathery hills with few paths, which make for rough going. The good views to the Solway coast and the Buttermere valley and the fact they are little frequented make them a worthwhile destination.

Start from the NT car park at Maggies Bridge (GR 135211), taking the track to Watergate farm and Holme Wood. In the wood turn left on a narrow path rising diagonally to a kissing-gate at the top. Turn right on the wide track and follow it across Holme Beck, then take a narrow trod heading SW above the beck. Step over an old fence and, after crossing a side stream, swing north onto the broad shoulder of Burnbank Fell. Follow this SW to the small cairn at the fence corner which marks the summit. Fine views of the Solway Firth, southern Scotland and the Isle of Man can be enjoyed on a clear day.

Turn south and follow the fence up the ridge towards Blake Fell. After about 1km and at the 500m contour, turn NE towards Carling Knott across an escarpment of low crags for about 750 metres, to the highest point which is crowned with a small but well-built shelter cairn. Good views of the valley can be obtained by going another 500 metres to the lower summit marked as Carling Knott on the map. Return along the ridge SW towards Blake Fell and follow the fence which passes 20 metres east of the summit cairn, from where there are views of the 'pudding basin' shaped Knock Murton (6km, 517m, 2hr 20min).

From here descend the south-east ridge, following the fence, for around 500 metres and at a fence junction go down to the boggy saddle of Fothergill Head. Follow the fence again up to the summit of Gavel Fell, the last and probably the quietest of the day's four summits.

There are two ways of effecting a return. In fine weather the best is to follow the NE ridge all the way down over heathery ground, mostly pathless, to join a wide track where it crosses the ridge at the 270m contour. Alternatively, and preferable in poor weather, follow the fence running NE from the summit to the same track above Whiteoak Beck. In either case follow it down to High Nook Farm and back to Maggies Bridge (11km, 3hrs 45min).

Mellbreak, Buttermere and Loweswater

Mellbreak 512m, 1679ft, GR 149186

The most self-sufficient and stately of that select handful of Lakeland tops having no bonds with other summits is undoubtedly Mellbreak. Steep on all sides, it is crag-rimmed facing Crummock Water and particularly rocky round the Loweswater end. The traverse, with a lakeshore return, provides a richly-varied walk of outstanding beauty.

Branch right below Loweswater Church and Kirkstile Inn to free parking just over Church Bridge at GR 141208. Walk south from the farm along a stony lane to a gate and bridleway fork. Ascend the 100 metre ride ahead between conifers to grassy slopes. Keep ESE up an improving path through bracken to a cairn below a bright-hued scree run. Some 200 metres above is a prominent scree gap dividing two large outcrops. Start up the left-inclining scree path and, avoiding excursions left, make for this rock gateway, enjoyably negotiated by staircase scrambling on its left side. Alternatively, climb the easier, cosier rift further right before veering up left to an exquisite viewpoint, the first promontory. A steep scree path soon leads to the grassy second promontory which gives even more breathtaking views, especially by moving 5 metres SE. Continue up the winding ridge-track through heather to the plateau and north summit cairn at 509m (2km, 389m, 1hr). Continue on the green way down to a saddle,

then up again to reach Mellbreak's highest point, a bare shield of rock with a few stones at 512m. Fifty metres south is a bigger cairn with sublime views of Buttermere.

Remaining right of a line of old fence posts, descend on a faint path deviating increasingly right to bypass steep ground. Cross the western flank of Scale Knott, then a fence, to curve right down to the main Floutern Tarn track alongside Black Beck. Push on down keeping left of this to Crummock's unfrequented western shore path. Here, near a footbridge, turn left to pass the dramatic High Ling Crag and its alluring peninsula. Further on, the trail descends to lake-edge shingle some 200 metres past the off-shore triangular Iron Stone. Leave the path and slant up the fellside for 100 metres to join another, parallel, track which develops into a well defined green passage rising NW to a wall running lakewards. Follow the wall, bending NW and fringing the delightful Green Wood to a gate above High Park GR 144203. Ignore the gate to climb left, among trees, up a bridleway which swerves right, hugging the wall enclosing Flass Wood, then a fence, back to the 100 metre ride. Descend this to the chosen parking place (10km, 3hr 15min).

Confirmed non-scramblers may spurn the north ridge entertainment to join the circuit at Mellbreak's saddle, attained directly from Mosedale near GR 143186.

Hen Comb from above Whiteoak Beck

Hen Comb 509m, 1669ft, GR132181

A gentle, individual hill, nicely separated from its neighbours and set among pleasant and relatively unfrequented fells.

Start from the Kirkstile Inn (GR 141209) and follow the bridleway southwards past Kirkgate Farm, eventually forking right beyond a gateway towards Mosedale. Just before the end of the conifers to the left of the track, the stone wall on the right curves away to reveal an ancient gate. Go through this fine relic with the respect it deserves and the care it needs and take a path down to Mosedale Beck which is crossed by paddling or boulder-hopping. Climb the hillside beyond the beck, close to the trees until the slope eases and you encounter a wire fence. You need to cross this fence at some stage but you may leave it a while. Once over it, head westwards to the ridge and start to enjoy views into the secluded Whiteoak Beck. There are footpaths on the fellside but it always seems more fun to stick to the line of the ridge all the way to the summit.

Linger a while and enjoy the situation; views of Loweswater and into the wide Buttermere valley; the broad sweep of Great Borne along to Red Pike; the isolated steepness of Mellbreak and, to the north, the rambling pleasantness of the Fellbarrow group. The descent is down the easy, trackless southern slope to pick up the path round the head of Mosedale Beck. The easiest way back is to follow the path down Mosedale but a worthwhile alternative is to take the more southerly track below Gale Fell and walk eastwards to Crummock Water. An enjoyable lakeside path will take you to Low or High Park and the Lane to Kirkstile (Return down Mosedale: 8.5km, 390m, 2hr 45min; return by Crummock Water: 10.5km, 410m, 3hr 15 min).

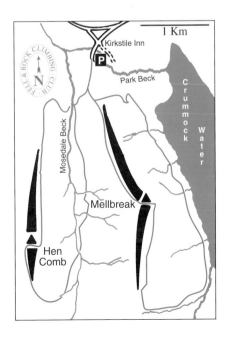

Bleaberry Tarn and the track to Red Pike from High Stile

Red Pike (Buttermere) 755m, 2477ft, GR 161154
High Stile 807m, 2647ft, GR 170148
High Crag 744m, 2440ft, GR 180140

An excellent outing along the Buttermere Fells, the steeper sections present no difficulties while easy ridge walking links the principal summits. The walk, starting and finishing in Buttermere village, provides superb views down to the valley and across Ennerdale to Pillar.

A signposted bridleway, to Buttermere Lake and Scale Bridge, starts on the S side of the Fish Hotel. Follow the track to the bridge, cross the river and turn right along a pleasant path that rises above the shore of Crummock Water. At the first large cairn turn directly up the slope to reach a good path continuing NW. This higher line is dryer than the lower alternative.

Gradually the path swings west where, at a gap in the wall, substantial man-made steps lead up alongside the beck. (From the wall make a short detour to view Scale Force, the highest waterfall in the Lake District.) Climbing the steps, notice the distinctly coloured rocks and soil, indicating the presence of Syenite.

From the top of the steps keep to the path alongside the beck onto the open slopes below Starling

Dodd. A little way beyond the last rowantree a worn path rises to the SE crossing heather moorland and arriving abruptly at Lingcomb Edge. Follow the edge SSE, gradually ascending to the summit of Red Pike (5.5km, 650m, 2hr 20min). A short descent to the south followed by a climb on the edge of the escarpment above Chapel Crags brings you to the highest point of the walk, High Stile.

Continue along the edge, following a broken line of metal posts. The path crosses the top of Eagle Crag from where one can look back to the jumble of buttresses that make up Grey Crag. Soon, the summit of High Crag is reached (8k, 640m, 3hr 20min).

Continue down Gamlin End on a reconstructed path which rises briefly over Seat before the steep descent to Scarth Gap. Turning back N, descend on a good path below the rock walls of High Crag to a small plantation. Take the left fork and follow the west shore of Buttermere through Burtness Wood. At the north end of the lake go through a small gate on the right, cross two wooden bridges and follow the track back to the village (14k, 4hr 50min).

Great Borne 616m, 2020ft, GR 124164
Starling Dodd 633m, 2076ft, GR 142158

Both Starling Dodd and Great Borne are on the long line of fells forming the northern boundary of Ennerdale. Both summits are unfrequented and may be enjoyed in solitude. The approach from Buttermere

by the lonely wilderness of Mosedale gives impressive views of the north face of Great Borne above Floutern Tarn. This walk is fairly strenuous, with paths rocky in places and boggy in others.

Great Borne from Ennerdale

The new NT car park in Buttermere is free to members and there is another pay carpark next to the Fish Hotel.

From Buttermere village follow the signposted path to Scale Bridge and on to the foot of Scale Force. This is cairned and easy to follow, turning uphill in one or two places to avoid boggy ground. From the bridge over Scale Beck at the foot of the waterfall go straight on up Mosedale. There are many boggy patches in this valley but the path diverges from that shown on the map to avoid the worst, then turns sharp right to cross Mosedale Beck. After this the path begins to rise more steeply until the flat ground between Floutern Tarn and Floutern Cop is reached. Cross the col (boggy) to the foot of Steel Brow and go up steeply by the fence. When the angle eases, either continue to follow the fence or keep to the edge of the steep ground and then move back right to reach the top of Great Borne (8km, 506m, 2hr 50min).

Return to the fence and follow it down to the SE. The path then heads straight towards Starling Dodd crossing the two tributaries of Clews Gill. A fresh-water spring bubbles up by the path at the point where the final rise to Starling Dodd begins. From the top go down to the col and then up again towards Little Dodd. Leave the path after passing a cairn to follow a narrow trod to the left which joins the prominent path descending into Scale Beck.

The path is easy to follow and keeps close to the beck as it tumbles over rocks into little pools, tempting resting places on a hot day. Lower down there are fine views into the gorge and of the waterfall from above. From the bridge at the foot of the falls follow the main path back to Buttermere (18km, 5hr 40min).

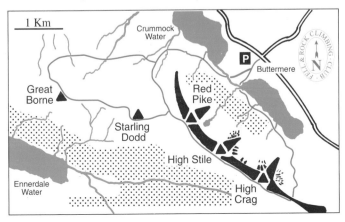

Hay Stacks 597m, 1958ft, GR 193131

Hay Stacks from Buttermere

For many fellwalkers, Hay Stacks will always be remembered as the chosen final resting place of Wainwright, the most well-known of all Lakeland guidebook writers. In his own words: "Haystacks stands unabashed ... in the midst of a circle of much loftier hills, like a shaggy terrier in the company of foxhounds ... but not one of this distinguished group of mountains ... can show a greater variety and a more fascinating arrangement of interesting features." The traverse of the main summits, on its own or as part of a longer walk along the Buttermere/Ennerdale watershed, is a marvellous expedition.

Starting from Gatesgarth Farm at the head of Buttermere, cross the fields to a footbridge near the head of the lake. Avoiding the path around the lake, take the good path up past the young plantation and rocky slopes beyond to reach Scarth Gap. From here, go left up the end ridge, over rocks and scree to reach the highest top (3km, 500m, 1hr 40min). The path continues ESE past several minor rocky tops, the delights of Innominate Tarn and the outflow of Blackbeck Tarn before traversing round in the direction of Fleetwith Pike and the quarry workings. This ridge is one to savour, full of twists and turns, nooks and crannies. On crossing the upper part of Warnscale Beck, you have several choices. You can continue on over Fleetwith Pike and down its prominent NW

ridge, or take one of the quarrymens' paths down either side of the stream. These lead to the flat green swathe of Warnscale Bottom from which an excellent track leads out to Gatesgarth (7.5km, 3hr 30min).

Hay Stacks can be reached by a long walk up Ennerdale towards Black Sail youth hostel, or from the top of Honister Pass via the old drum house path; this route, however, misses much of the interest. By reversing the route description, the walk can be extended over High Stile and Red Pike to give a satisfying long day out.

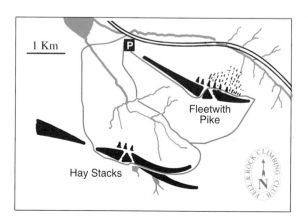

Fleetwith Pike from Buttermere

Fleetwith Pike 648m, 2125ft, GR 206142

The striking ridge that is Fleetwith Edge provides a direct line of ascent to the summit of Fleetwith Pike. The continuation path allows a fascinating glimpse of the extensive quarry workings above Honister Pass. A climb up the ridge is not as strenuous as it might appear from below.

Parking is available, for a fee, at Gatesgarth. Take the road towards Honister Pass for 130 metres at which point an indistinct path is followed in the direction of the prominent white cross on the hillside. A short scramble up to the cross allows you to read the inscription, a memorial to Fanny Mercer, accidentally killed in 1887. The rough and loose start can be avoided by continuing along the path into Warnscale and turning left up an obvious grassy gully to join the ridge higher up. A good path continues to Low Raven Crag where it disappears over short grass, becoming more obvious as height is gained. A worn path skirts the rocky knolls on the way to the top but it is more interesting to keep to the crest of the ridge over these rises. The summit is reached abruptly (1.5km, 541m, 1hr 20min).

Head east along the narrow path, keeping almost to the crest, with spectacular views down to Honister Pass. Cross the summit of Honister Crag, Black Star, and continue until the you reach the first quarry. Turn SW along a wide track of scree, through further workings and spoil heaps, passing on the left side of a quarry. Cross over another track and continue SSW over grass and heather, past a small cairn, to arrive above Dubs Quarry. The hut in the quarry has been converted into a camping barn and provides a useful shelter in bad weather.

Descend on the west side of the workings and join the narrow path heading west into the valley of Warnscale Beck. As the well-made path descends into Warnscale Bottom, views of Buttermere can be seen between small rocky spurs; the complete panorama eventually opens up as the path turns gradually north and returns to Gatesgarth (6 km, 2hr 30min).

Kirk Fell from Mosedale

Kirk Fell 802m, 2631ft, GR 195105

This is the lowest of the mighty circuit of Wasdale Head fells yet all the habitation and the thick stone-walled fields which give the valley head its distinctive character lie on the lower skirts of this large hill.

From the car park on Wasdale green, walk along the road to the inn. A wide track starts from the rear of the building and follows Mosedale Beck past an old packhorse bridge, through a gate, to reach the open fellside. For the fit, an unrelenting path ascends the nose ahead directly to the summit. An easier route continues left on the main track into wild Mosedale. After 1500 metres this path rises upwards to cross Gatherstone Beck (which can be awkward after heavy rain) and then follows the other side of the stream to reach Black Sail Pass. The same point can be reached by a long walk up Ennerdale past Black Sail youth hostel. From the pass, turn SE to make your own choice of scrambling route up the rocky rib of Kirkfell Crags without difficulty. Above, a line of fence posts across the rock-strewn slopes leads to the highest top (730m, 5km, 2hr 30min). Turn NE to follow the posts past Kirkfell Tarn and onto the second summit. The posts lead on east to the top of another rocky rib which is descended to Beck Head. Across the col lie the steep scree slopes of Gable. Several paths descend from Beck Head to Wasdale. A narrow track follows the stream whilst a more obvious one on the Gable slope descends the spur of Gavel Neese – a true test of your knees! – to reach the valley floor by the bridge on the Sty Head path. Return right through Burnthwaite Farm to the green (10km, 4hr).

This route can be done in either direction. From Beck Head, many walkers continue over Great Gable to Sty Head. From Black Sail, others continue over Pillar and Scoat Fell to complete the longer circuit of Mosedale.

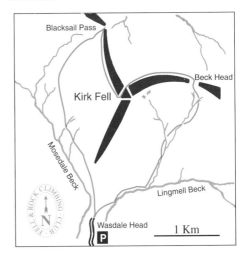

Base Brown 646m, 2120ft, GR 225114
Brandreth 715m, 2344ft, GR 215119
Grey Knotts 697m, 2287ft, GR 217126

Base Brown is an excellent viewpoint at the head of Borrowdale, many major summits being visible with the Scafells particularly prominent. The circuit including Brandreth and Grey Knotts gives a pleasant day with some basic route-finding and easy scrambling if taken in a clockwise direction from Seathwaite, where there is roadside parking. (Walking from the bus stop in Seatoller adds 4km, one hour return).

At the farm, go right under the archway (signed), cross the Ramblers Memorial bridge and climb the path on the south side of Sour Milk Gill with some easy scrambling near the top. 300 metres after passing through a gateway in the wall a short level stretch of path is reached. Looking upwards to the south a crag is seen, with the Hanging Stone (GR 227118) above a gully. Make your way up between the foot of the crag and a large detached mass of rock, below the Hanging Stone. Cairns show a path traversing left (east), passing two rowan trees. After the second tree turn back sharply right and follow grass rakes up to the NE ridge and from there easily to the summit (2.5km, 521m, 1hr 30min).

Leave the top in a SW direction until the path through Gillercomb is met. Continue beyond the col and junction with the path through Gillercomb to climb the shoulder of Green Gable. Turn north along the old boundary, dropping to the tarns at Gillercomb Head then rising again to the attractive rocky summit of Brandreth. Keep along the fence line to Grey Knotts where two tors dispute the highest point.

From the top of Grey Knotts go ENE to a fence and stile in a depression, then follow the fence NNE

For map, please turn over

down a steep gully to more open ground (GR 222128). Turn east across wet ground to the old spoil heaps at the head of Newhouse Gill. Descend the gully to a ladder stile crossing the wall and then follow an indistinct path winding between the old mine shafts of Newhouse Gill. These are the remains of the old plumbago mines which helped to start the pencil industry in Keswick. The path from Seathwaite to Seathwaite bridge runs beside the infant River Derwent; turn left for Seatoller or right for Seathwaite (11km, 4hr 10min).

There are two easier variations on this circuit. The first one is to keep on the main ascent path through Gillercomb as far as an NT signpost, then turn NE and follow the easy slope to the summit. The other is to descend from Grey Knotts to Honister and then follow the old mine road down to Seatoller, only a good option if that was your starting point.

The Hanging Stone on Base Brown

Great Gable and Green Gable from Allen Crags

Great Gable 899m, 2949ft, GR 211103
Green Gable 801m, 2627ft, GR 215107

Great Gable – or simply Gable to its many admirers – is a classic Lake District mountain. Despite being 51ft short of the illustrious group of 3,000ft summits, many would argue that its ascent offers one of the finest mountaineering days in England. As Wainwright has pointed out, there are few days in the year when the summit rocks remain untrodden. In consequence, you should expect all routes to be well used, particularly in fine weather and at weekends.

The shapely triangle of Great Gable with its long red screes draws the eye during the approach up Wasdale. During the long walk in up Ennerdale, the twin summits of Green Gable and Great Gable fill the head of the valley. Good ascents are possible from either valley head but the circuit here starts and finishes in Borrowdale.

From the road end at Seathwaite, walk through the farm and along the river to Stockley Bridge; cross the traditional packhorse bridge above deep pools in the river and take the pitched path climbing west up the hillside, through a gate in the intake wall and alongside Styhead Gill to Styhead Tarn (3km, 315m, 1hr 20min). This is part of an ancient route from the west coast across the mountains and was once used for smuggling. An alternative shorter but rougher way of reaching Styhead Tarn is to turn right in the farmyard, cross the river beneath Sourmilk Gill, then immediately left (south) along the riverside before climbing diagonally SW across rather wet fields to Taylorgill Force. The path scrambles up beside this waterfall to rejoin the Stockley Bridge path shortly before the tarn.

From here there is a choice of two ways to the summit of Great Gable. The most popular route continues past the tarn to another 500 metres to the mountain rescue box at the top of the pass and then climb NW to the summit. The repair work on this path by the NT won the B.U.F.T. upland path award in 1996. An alternative route, steeper but more rewarding in terms of rock scenery, is to ascend WNW from the tarn up Aaron Slack to Windy Gap and then climb left through broken rocks to the summit of Great Gable (5km, 765m, 2hr 35min).

For the best views, walk 100 metres away from the summit south to Westmorland Cairn for the view down Wasdale, or NE for the view down Ennerdale. On the summit rocks is a bronze memorial map showing the land over 1500ft including the summits of Pillar, Kirk Fell, Great Gable, Green Gable, Brandreth, Grey Knotts, Base Brown, Rosthwaite Fell, Glaramara, Allen Crags, Great End and Lingmell which the Fell and Rock Climbing Club purchased in 1923, in memory of those members who lost their lives in the First World War, and gave to the National Trust. Every year on Remembrance Sunday a simple two minute act of remembrance at this memorial is

Great Gable from Kirk Fell

attended by several hundred walkers.

When leaving the summit in any direction take particular care to select the right path as the proliferation of cairns can be very confusing, especially in mist. Descend NE, gently at first and then over steeper rocks to Windy Gap. Ascend the 50m to Green Gable and continue NE down gentle grassy slopes for 1km. (Avoid the main path which veers left here to traverse west of Brandreth to reach Honister). From the broad grassy col between Green Gable and Base Brown descend the path north into Gillercomb and then follow the pitched path steeply down alongside the foaming Sourmilk Gill back to Seathwaite Farm (9km, 3hr 40min).

There is a lengthy approach to Windy Gap from the NW up Ennerdale either from Gillerthwaite or from Buttermere over Scarth Gap. The ascent from Wasdale Head may be made by traversing the lower slopes to Sty Head to join the route described above, or more directly up Gavel Neese to Beck Head between Kirk Fell and Great Gable. The 5km approach from Honister Pass by way of the broad path to the drum house on Fleetwith and then traversing beneath Grey Knotts and Brandreth to Green Gable involves the least ascent but is also the least interesting.

To see the impressive crags of Kern Knotts and the Napes (including Napes Needle) take the Climber's Traverse path rising WNW from Sty Head. This route gives superb views of the crags but requires rock scrambling. To reach the summit, however, involves a steep and loose ascent of Little Hell Gate, or a continuation to Beck Head and then the well-trodden path from there to the top.

Pillar Rock from Westmorland's Cairn

Red Pike (Wasdale) 826m, 2709ft, GR 165106
Scoat Fell 841m, 2759ft, GR 160114
Steeple 819m, 2686ft, GR 157117
Pillar 892m, 2926ft, GR 171121

Dominating an illustrious and rugged quartet, Pillar, Lakeland's seventh highest peak, is an unmissable target for fit walkers. Its long sensational Ennerdale flank of cliffs and coves includes the renowned Pillar Rock, whilst the south, more shaven, face overlooking Mosedale bristles with craggy blisters. SW across Wind Gap looms Pillar's complex and (especially by the OS) under-researched neighbour, Scoat Fell, whose highest point is map-named, oddly, Little Scoat Fell. This gnarled, four-ridged mountain carries the final two summits: Steeple, a savage eminence on its NNW spur, and Red Pike, a cliff perch on the SSE arm. Most conveniently approached from Wasdale because of FC vehicular restrictions in Ennerdale, this magnificent, fairly strenuous round embraces some of Cumbria's wildest and grandest scenery.

Wastwater's head provides ample parking at a layby (GR 181075) or near the campsite. Walk Gosforth-wards on the road for 1.5km to fork right up a signposted grassy path joining a fence end and the main track up the apex of Yewbarrow's SW ridge. Labour up the Wastwater side of the ridge wall to a stile crossing near the first slabby outcrop. Start contouring, avoiding the right branch line up to Dropping Crag, and following the gentler way northwards, then NE up to Dore Head saddle (GR 175095). Now toil NW up a stony track through shelving outcrops to flatter, more turfy terrain. Above left juts a cairned knoll but Red Pike's cairn balances on the precipice lip 500 metres further on, right of the path (6.3km, 761m, 2hr 45min). The heady prospect includes fascinating aspects of all the Mosedale and Wasdale fells, and further out, the coastal plain.

Regain the trail, dipping gradually NW to a little cairned col. A short-cut to the Pillar group's backbone ridge curves clearly right (useful if the weather suggests pruning of ambitions), but for Scoat Fell's precise summit, ignore the map's dubious path hints and strike a bold line NNW, initially up a faint trod, then over a boulder field – marked only by four widely spaced cairns – to the mountain's cresting wall. Step over this at the nearest opening to discover the summit. Ennerdale's yawning trench impresses, as does the NW seaboard, but the choicest item is the rock cone of Steeple, seductive and seemingly readily available.

Walk 200 metres west along the wall's Ennerdale side to where the structure suddenly angles SW. A fair-sized cairn and small shelter point the way northwards to the Steeple arete. The track down is partly cairned, rough and exhilarating before 25m of simple clambering lead to Steeple's limited top. Ennerdale Water and the crags of Mirkiln and Mirk Coves look hypnotically attractive from this exposed eyrie.

Steeple

Return to Scoat Fell's wall and accompany it east, past its end and down steeply over a jumble of blocks to meet the curving path from Red Pike. Traverse the easy, virtually level, ridge to Black Crag's cairn, then weave down through more bulky boulders to Wind Gap. The loose rise opposite soon relents when cairns assist steerage to Pillar's rounded grassy plateau with its survey column, cairns and wind shelters (10km, 990m, 4hr 10min). The panorama is comprehensively majestic, with even the Isle of Man materialising in clear conditions. To see the blunt horn of Pillar Rock's short side rearing up from Ennerdale, walk beyond the shelter N of the survey column. Conquered in 1826, the apparently impregnable Rock remains a monument to man's earliest recorded venture on British crags.

Black Sail Pass, the next objective, is easily attained from Pillar's long ESE ridge and its string of old fence posts. The path is largely guided by the latter. The conspicuous cairn and subsidiary track seen off left just before Looking Stead signal the start of the spectacular High Level Route – a nimble wanderer's traverse of Pillar Rock/Pillar Fell via Robinson's Cairn and the rock wonderland of the Ennerdale face. After Looking Stead, the way trends gradually SE to Black Sail where a well-hammered thoroughfare plunges SW, following primarily Gatherstone Beck, then crossing it to enter Mosedale and the beaten lane SSE. Close to Wasdale Head Inn's yard, however, limit road-walking, if not thirst, by going over the old humped bridge and befriending Mosedale Beck's pretty west bank to Down-in-the-

Dale bridge (GR 184082). The starting point is 700 metres along the road (16km, 5hr 45min).

This classic round proves equally rewarding in reverse when the High Level Route offers an exciting alternative way up Pillar for the 'vertiginously unchallenged'. Remember, though, that Pillar is a major cloud compeller and that the Red Pike/Scoat Fell area can be particularly bewildering in thick mists. Pillar can also be ascended from Black Sail in upper Ennerdale.

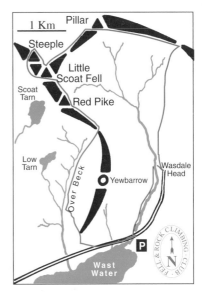

Pinnacles on Crag Fell

Crag Fell 523m, 1715ft, GR 097144
Grike 488m, 1601ft, GR 085141

Crag Fell is a prominent rocky hill which towers over the western end of Ennerdale. The Crag Fell Pinnacles stand out against the skyline and provide some minor rock climbs. Revelin Crag too is precipitous and one of the north-facing combes boasts some detached pinnacles reminiscent of the Quiraing in Skye. The tops of both fells are grassy and give easy walking with some fine views. Ben Gill drains the slopes between the two and forms a deep ravine seen to good advantage from the descent path. This route gives a moderately strenuous ascent.

Start from the FC free car park at GR 085154. Walk past the water pumping station and take the signposted path between two fences to reach the lakeside. Start walking along the lake looking out for the rising path (indistinct at first) to the col above Angler's Crag. Before continuing the ascent it is worth making the diversion to the top of Angler's for the views.

Leaving Angler's Crag follow a well-trodden path aiming towards the base of the Pinnacles, finding sheep trods leading left then right to reach the neck at the top. Go up the grass and bilberry slope above, steeply at first, to reach an almost flat shelf below a line of

crags. Scramble easily up to the top by a rocky corner on the left. Continue ahead until the direct path from Ben Gill is joined. Follow this to the summit cairn.

From Crag Fell go SW to reach a boundary fence and follow this across the 451m col and on to the top of Grike. Return towards the col, but gradually drop down left into the upper reaches of Ben Gill, aiming for the tongue of land between parallel branches of the gill. Step over the old fence and continue downhill to meet the main Crag Fell path. Turn left and follow this down to meet the forest track in the valley bottom, making use of an obvious short cut near the end. Turn right, then left before reaching Crag Farm to return to the starting point (8km, 2hr 45min).

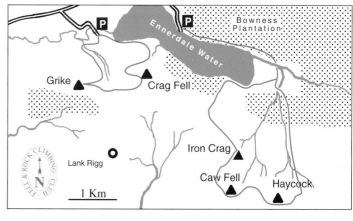

Haycock from Middle Fell

Iron Crag 640m, 2099ft, GR 123119
Caw Fell 690m, 2263ft, GR 132110
Haycock 797m, 2614ft, GR 145107

This circuit is in a quiet yet beautiful area of Cumbria and offers an energetic way to the high summits from a less popular corner of the Lake District, embracing dramatic views over the Scafell range and the Ennerdale valley.

From the Bowness FC car park proceed east along the FC road on the north side of Ennerdale Water for 3km until you reach a stone bridge on the right which crosses the river. Cross the bridge and follow the track to the forest edge taking the stile on the right and following the footpath westwards to the second wall (GR 123139). Strike up steeply SSW through pathless trees keeping close the wall/wire fence until you reach open ground. Head south keeping the wall to your left steadily gaining height and follow the wall to the skyline. When the wall turns sharply NW head due south ascending for 200 metres to meet another wall of classic proportions. Turn SE following this wall for approximately 1km, to the summit of Iron Crag (8km, 520m, 2hr 30min). An alternative direct route involving scrambling can be enjoyed by striking south from GR 122130 through the skyline boulders direct to the summit.

Retrace your steps NW following the wall for 200 metres to go through the gate and turn SE following the wall for 1km to its junction with a broken wall approaching downhill from the south. Head south following this broken wall to the skyline turning ENE to the summit cairn of Caw Fell. Continue to use the wall as a guide on your right hand side, head east, then SE along the ridge over the rocky summit of Little Gowder Crag to the summit of Haycock (12km, 720m, 3hr 35min). On a clear day there are impressive distant views of the Scafell range.

Descend steeply ENE for 400 metres to a col, again following a wall on your right. Now turn NNW down rough grass for 400 metres then descend NW into Great Cove to follow Deep Gill on the east side. The gill widens and becomes a series of picturesque cascades. At the forest edge cross the stile and follow the FC track to GR 131135. Cross the stream by a hidden bridge to gain the west side and descend though the forest following the blue waymarkers to the gate at GR 131138. Retrace your steps to the FC car park (20km, 6hr 15min).

Yewbarrow 628m, 2060ft, GR 173085

Looking down to Wast Water from Bell Rib, Yewbarrow

Yewbarrow's position as the last and lowest hill in the magnificent Mosedale horseshoe round belies its impressive position. With its steep flanks and prominent nose surmounted by a fine rocky crag Yewbarrow is frequently to be found in photographs looking into the head of Wasdale. This short route introduces the walker to the diversity of this mountain.

From the car park at Overbeck Bridge take the obvious path leading up the nose alongside a fence. Cross the fence at a stile and shortly afterwards the path ascends right through scree and rock to find a way through the crags. On regaining the ridge at the cleft of Great Door there are excellent views across to Scafell and down Wasdale. The summit ridge is surprisingly long and flat. From the summit (2km, 555m, 1hr 30min)), continue NNE along the ridge, past a second, lower summit. From here, a path descends very steeply, threading a way past Stirrup Crag to Dore Head. The way is well marked, although some scrambling will involve the use of hands. From the col, a choice of two paths lead back to the start. Both are initially grassy and indistinct. One follows the west bank of Over Beck, crossing it by a bridge in the lower reaches. The other traverses the flank of Yewbarrow to rejoin the upward route at the stile (6km, 2hr 30min).

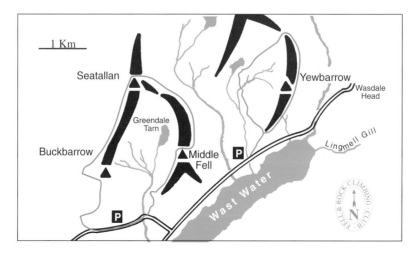

Buckbarrow

Middle Fell 582m, 1909ft, GR 151072
Seatallan 692m, 2270ft, GR 140084
Buckbarrow 420m, 1377ft, GR 136058

These three fells on the northern side of Wasdale provide an enjoyable walk in some of the less frequented areas of the Lake District, giving good views of the West Cumbrian coast and the higher fells which encircle the head of this wild valley. The three fells have different characters: Middle Fell is rough and rocky, Seatallan has a long grassy ridge, and the craggy southern face of Buckbarrow offers several rock climbs.

Starting from Greendale, 8km along the valley road from Gosforth, take the wide green path heading north towards Greendale Gill. When the path splits at around the 230m contour, take the right fork which climbs a grassy shoulder before crossing a bouldery patch. The path becomes fainter but is still followed in a NE direction over numerous false summits until 2km from Greendale, the rocky top of Middle Fell is reached. The view is dominated by the Scafells.

The route to Seatallan follows the path from the summit north, through the rocky outcrops to the very wet saddle above Greendale Tarn. A direct approach to the rounded top can be made due west from here, but it is easier underfoot and less strenuous, to head NW from the saddle towards Haycock until a prominent cairn is reached. Bear left onto the grassy shoulder and then head south for the summit (5km, 615m, 2hr 15min). The best views are of the West Cumbrian coast northwards from Black Combe.

The route, though all downhill from here, requires careful navigation especially in misty conditions, as this long grassy ridge is particularly featureless. The easiest way is to head SW to Cat Bields cairn, then SE to the prominent cairn on Glade How. A short distance to the south is the small rocky outcrop which marks the summit of Buckbarrow near the edge of the crag. Although the ridge from Seatallan has good views, Buckbarrow itself is a surprisingly unremarkable viewpoint. Head west from the summit down easy grass slopes to Gill Beck and follow a path down the east bank. A stroll of 1.5km left along the road leads back to Greendale (10km, 3hr 40min).

Lankrigg from Simon Kell Farm

Lank Rigg 541m, 1774ft, GR 092120

Lank Rigg is located in a remote and quiet corner of the Lake District, yet it offers some of the most stunning views of the higher Western Fells and also provides an unexpected insight into previous settlements. The walk is across wide expanses of open fell which requires careful navigation in poor weather.

Ample roadside parking can be found at the road junction at GR 055101. From here, proceed downhill on a good track and take the right branch at the fork to reach a wooden bridge over the river. After crossing the bridge, detour 100 metres upstream to see the ancient packhorse bridge known as Monks Bridge or Matty Benn's Bridge – a unique structure. Returning to the bridge, head SE and follow the track for 200 metres to a small hidden cairn on the left. Leave the track here and head east across open moorland, over Tongue How, passing various homestead ruins. As the ground begins to descend, strike NE heading for the skyline cairn of Boat How set amongst more ruins. From Boat How, head in a northerly direction, picking a way through small boulders to reach the skyline and summit (5km, 325m, 2hrs). Take your time to absorb the stunning views of the higher fells.

Leave the summit heading NE to the col and a cross path. Turn left (NW) and follow the path steeply downhill at first, staying on the hillside above Whoap Beck to reach the upper reaches of the River Calder (GR 087131). Turn W with the path and cross Comb Beck after 1km. Follow the stone track uphill to its junction with the minor road at GR 067130. Turn SW and follow the road for 3km to return to the starting point (12km, 3hrs 30min). In dry weather, an alternative route can be found by crossing the River Calder at its junction with Comb Beck and following the river south to Monks Bridge.

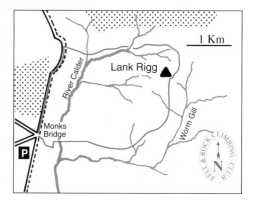

Ponsonby Fell from In Fell

Ponsonby Fell 310m, 1017ft, GR 082071
Swainson Knott 340m, 1115ft, GR 079083

Ponsonby Fell and Swainson Knott are summits on the south-eastern hillside of the Calder Valley. The Norman Calder Abbey lies in the valley below, with Calder Hall beyond: a contrast providing food for thought.

The walk starts at Stakes Bridge (GR 056067) which spans the river Calder, the 'mad beck'. Driving up the valley, park on your left just after crossing the bridge.

The name Ponsonby means 'Punzun's place'. In the 12th century Punzun was granted use of the local manor which later became well stocked with hares and partridges. Car parked, follow the sign Scargreen/River Calder. Take the public footpath up the northern bank of Scargreen Beck. After two stiles and a bridge join a track on the beck's southern bank. The path's final stage involves a detour to the northern bank, fording the beck twice. A metalled lane is joined (GR 064060), that leads up to Scargreen farm.

Just before Scargreen, ford the beck into a lane and proceed towards Laverock How. The bridleway to Ponsonby Fell branches off 150 metres above Laverock How via a wooden gate. Continue NNE to two wooden fieldgates and cross the stile. Walk NE to find a gate in a stone wall, using it to enter a field and journey parallel to the wall to a steel gate and open-hillside.

From the bridleway choose a grassy strip, between bulrushes, to Ponsonby Fell's summit and its small cairn. The view includes the combe of Haycock to the NE and Wasdale Screes to the east (4km, 245m, 1hr 30min).

From the summit descend almost due north to cross the old disused track linking Scalderskew to Calder Bridge. Go through the gate and over the stile, following the fence up the rough grassy slope, then heading NW to reach the enclosure on Stone Pike at 322m. From here, a slight descent north leads to a stile and on up pathless ground to the top of Swainson Knott, a small hummock on a grassy platform.

Descend westwards aiming for a gate which gives on to the north side of the wall bounding Needless Gill. On reaching the road, turn left and walk down the valley back to Stakes Bridge (9.5km 3hr 10min).

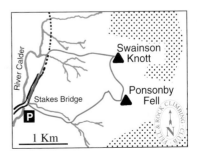

Ice on Stickle Tarn below Pavey Ark

Reference Section

La'al Ratty: train at Beckfoot station

Travel

The Lake District is easily accessible from anywhere in the UK with good road and rail connections enabling people to visit the National Park. Narrower roads and restricted public transport make travel within the Park less easy; these problems are often exacerbated during holiday periods and good weather weekends when traffic congestion can occur in and around any of the main towns and more popular valleys.

Air travel

The nearest airport with regular scheduled flights is Manchester. Carlisle has a small airfield for private aircraft; from time-to-time, smaller operators run services to/from London.
- *Manchester airport:* 0161-489-3000
- *Carlisle airport:* 01228-573641

Rail services

The West Coast InterCity line from London Euston to Glasgow Central covers the eastern side of the area. All trains stop at Oxenholme (near Kendal) and Carlisle. Some trains call at Penrith. From Oxenholme, a branch line serves Staveley and Windermere. Another line from Carlisle to Barrow connects many of the towns along the coastal plain and can be used to reach the western valleys. The Ravenglass and Eskdale Railway is a privately operated narrow guage railway line offering a scenic approach to Eskdale and is a popular tourist attraction.
- *British Rail train enquiries:* Carlisle 01228-44711
- *Ravenglass and Eskdale Railway:* 01229-717171

Roads

The National Park is served by a network of trunk roads around its perimeter. From the M6, use Junction 36 for the southern Lakes and Junction 40 for the northern Lakes. The A590 to Ulverston and Barrow gives access to the southern valleys and the A595 provides access to the western valleys. Whilst several of the valleys are linked by passes such as Honister, Newlands, Whinlatter, Kirkstone, Wrynose and

Steamer on Ullswater, below St. Sunday Crag

Hardknott, these routes all involve narrow roads, steep gradients and sharp bends. They are not suitable for caravans, trailers or coaches. In summer, they can be very busy with cars and minibuses; in winter conditions, snowfalls can quickly close them.

Information on road conditions is available on Ceefax.

Bus services

The main regional bus services are provided by *Stagecoach Cumberland*; service information is available at Tourist Information Centres and by telephoning 01946-63222.

Local valley services and tours, sometimes with stopping and picking up on request, are provided by several operators although the details change from year to year. Two services are provided by
* *Mountain Goat* (015394-45161) and
* *Lakes Supertours* (015394-42751 or 88133)

Lake cruises

Public launch services are operated on four of the larger lakes, calling at several jetties around the shore. For more information, contact:
* *Derwentwater:* Keswick Launch Company 017687-72263
* *Windermere:* Bowness Bay Boating Company 015394-43360 and Windermere Iron Steamboat Company 015395-31188
* *Coniston:* Coniston Launch 015394-36216 and Steam Yacht Gondala (NT) 015394-41288
* *Ullswater:* Ullswater Motor Yachts 017684-82229

Mountain bike hire

Several outdoor shops, garages and other businesses offer mountain bikes for hire in each of the main towns (and some villages). Enquire at the nearest Tourist Information Office for local details or look out for signs.

Accommodation

The Lake District offers a large supply of accommodation to suit every need and budget. This includes:

- Hotels (ranging in grade from many standard hotels to a few luxury ones) offering a range of facilities
- Guest houses providing homely accomodation from a night to a fortnight
- Bed and breakfast accommodation in private houses
- Farmhouse accommodation in the valleys
- Self-catering cottages, apartments and caravans
- Caravan sites – both static and mobile (though planning restrictions mean that the larger sites tend to be away from the central valleys)
- Camp sites
- Camping barns providing inexpensive, simple communal accommodation in converted barns
- Youth hostels, including private hostels as well as those operated by the YHA
- Climbing club huts (usually restricted to club members)

During school holidays and good weather weekends throughout the year, there is often a high demand for casual accommodation and advance booking may be advisable.

The Tourist Information Centres in each of the main towns produce and distribute accommodation guides with comprehensive information about most forms of accommodation (see opposite). They also operate an on-the-spot bed-booking service to find bed and breakfast and guest house accommodation for visitors.

Several companies organise self-catering bookings on behalf of private owners; many advertise in the national weekend newspapers or other travel guides. The larger cottage letting companies include Cumbrian Cottages (01228-599950), Grey Abbey (01946-693364), Holidays in Lakeland (015395-31549) and Lakeland Cottage Company (015395-30024).

Information about current caravan sites, camping sites and camping barns is obtainable from National Park Information Centres (see opposite); their location is often shown on recent OS maps.

Blake Beck camping barn

Information sources

Tourist Information Centres provide information on visitor facilities, public transport, local events and accommodation. Most Centres will make accommodation reservations for a small fee. Some smaller centres may have limited opening during winter months. Centres are located at:

M6 (northbound) Service Area, Forton (01524-792181)
M6 (southbound) Service Area, Killington Lake (015396-20138)
Church Street, **Ambleside** (015394-32582)
Duke Street, **Barrow-in-Furness** (01229-870156)
Glebe Road, **Bowness-on-Windermere** (015394-42895)
Carlisle Visitors Centre (01228-512444)
Town Hall, **Cockemouth** (01900-822634)
Ruskin Avenue, **Coniston** (015394-41533)
Main Street, **Egremont** (01946-820693)
Main Street, **Grange-over-Sands** (015395-34026)
Redbank Road, **Grasmere** (015394-35245)
Main car park, **Hawkshead** (015394-36525)
Town Hall, **Kendal** (015395-72645)
Market Square, **Keswick** (017687-72645)
Middlegate, **Penrith** (01768-876466)
The Square, **Pooley Bridge** (017684-86530)
Seatoller, **Borrowdale** (017687-77294)
Sellafield Visitor Centre, **Seascale** (019467-76510)
Main car park, **Glenridding** (017684-82414)
Main car park, **Waterhead**, Ambleside (015394-32729)
Market Place, **Whitehaven** (01946-695678)
Victoria Street, **Windermere** (015394-46499)
Washington Street, **Workington** (01900-602923)

The fells and valleys of Cumbria and Westmorland form the Lake District National Park. The Park authorities are responsible for planning matters, contribute to environmental and conservation measures, and provide visitor and educational facilities. A National Park Visitor Centre is sited at Brockhole on the A591 between Ambleside and Windermere (015394-46601).

Local National Park Information Centres provide information on public transport, accommodation bookings, access to the local countryside, and visitor facilities. Centres are located at:

Ruskin Avenue, **Coniston** (015394-41533)
Glebe Road, **Bowness** (015394-42895)
Red Bank Road, **Grasmere** (015394-35245)
Main car park, **Hawkshead** (015394-36525)
Lake Road, **Keswick** (017687-72803)
The Square, **Pooley Bridge** (017684-86530)
Seatoller, **Borrowdale** (017687-77294)
Main car park, **Glenridding** (017684-82414)
Waterhead, near Ambleside (015394-32729)

The National Trust run several Information Shops providing information about NT properties. Most shops have restricted winter opening hours. Shops can be found at:
Keswick: by the boat landings (017687-73780) and in Standish Street (017687-75173)
Ambleside: Bridge House
Grasmere: opposite church (015394-35621)
Cockermouth: Main Street (01900-824805)
Hawkshead: Main Street (05394-36355)

The NT Regional Office is at The Hollens, Grasmere (015394-35599)

For information on nature reserves, contact Cumbria Wildlife Trust, The Badger's Paw, Church Street, Ambleside LA22 0BU (015394-32476)

A 24 hour Lake District Weatherline service is provided on 017687-75757

commodity – leisure time. Climbing at that time was based around the higher hills and predominantly at Wasdale Head. The area was relatively accessible by railway and the hotel was strategically placed between Scafell, Great Gable and Pillar. For some years, it even boasted a resident Swiss mountain guide.

The early climbs mainly followed obvious gully lines, but as the sport developed, the pioneers were encouraged more and more onto the open faces of the crags. With limited opportunities for protection, some of these routes were considerable undertakings. In 1892, the now classic Eagle's Ridge Direct route was considered unjustifiable for a family man. By the eve of the First World War, a route was forced up the impressive Central Buttress of Scafell Crag by Herford and Samson. Central Buttress was ahead of its time, but tragically the pre-war generation was soon wiped out on the killing fields of northern Europe.

Rock climbing

The first people to climb the Lake District fells were the inhabitants themselves. There is little record of their exploits other than the place names they left and the occasional tantalising morsel – like the fact that the men of Borrowdale kept a stout rope for use in driving the eagles from their eyries. Rock climbing as a pastime began, arguably, on 27 June 1886 with the ascent of Napes Needle on Great Gable by Walter Parry Haskett-Smith. Climbing became not a means of getting to the summit but an end in itself.

At first, rock climbing was almost exclusively a middle class occupation. Many of the early pioneers were industrialists, scientists or students from the universities. They were relatively affluent and had that most precious

After the Great War, development was spearheaded by a few talented individuals. The next great impetus came when the benefits of modern society began to filter down to the masses and made the countryside accessible. Workmen like Bill Peascod and Jim Birkett, living on the fringe of the district, discovered the delights of the sport. However, it was not until the end of the Second World War that a great wave of development began. It was led by climbers from the great industrial cities; men like Brown, Whillans, Ross and Greenwood. They put up climbs of unprecedented severity that left the traditional climbing world gasping in their wake and significantly raised the standards of British climbing.

Mountain-biking on the Roman Road over Red Crag, High Street

Improvements in protection and a more sophisticated and disciplined approach to training brought further waves of advances and unimagined new technical standards. The pressures of numbers and the desire for new routes also saw the development of smaller crags and quarries. Now there are over 4,000 routes of all grades recorded throughout the Lake District in the Fell and Rock Climbing Club's definitive guides. Rock climbing today has progressed greatly from the sport carried on by the early pioneers, but the crags are still the same and the motivation is similar. The modern climber can still enjoy much the same experience as his or her predecessor. If you want to get started, contact a local climbing club or speak to climbers in your home area or sports centre with an indoor climbing wall. Climbing walls with public use can be found in Ambleside, Kendal, Barrow, Egremont, Cockermouth, Keswick, Carlisle and Penrith: ask in local climbing shops for information.

Mountain biking

Mountain biking is not an alternative, easy option to walking or scambling upon the Lakeland Fells; rather, it is a distinct way of exploring the countryside following bridleways and byeways where cyclists have a legitimate right of way. The ease and speed of cycling, particularly the downhill bits, makes the experience more akin to cross country skiing than walking. Contrary to the term 'mountain biking', which suggests the ascent of mountains, the essential element of mountain biking is being off-road. Challenging rides, and above all, enjoyment, can be found by exploring mixed terrain away from tarmac roads using ancient routes along green roads linking valleys and settlements. The ascent of a mountain may be incidental to this rather than the primary objective.

The attraction of the Lake District for bikers is that here can be found rides to suit all ages and abilities amongst stunning scenery from waymarked forestry gravel roads, to bridleways over high passes and even the higher summits. Although the bike will have to be carried over very steep and rocky sections, the summits of High Street, Helvellyn, High Stile, Skiddaw and

Black Combe can all be legitimately reached by mountain bikers. Such rides require a high level of fitness together with mountain navigational skills and appropriate clothing.

For those who prefer to remain in the saddle for most of the way, easier routes are generally found outside the central fells: for example, the marked trails in Grizedale Forest and the bridleways to the south and west of Torver and those around Tilberthwaite, Little Langdale, Langdale and over to Grasmere. Although some of these are very popular, as a general rule routes on the fringes are not so well known and fewer walkers will be encountered. In the Keswick area, routes of similar standard are to be found in Thornthwaite Forest, Whinlatter and along the former Keswick to Penrith railway line. This route may be linked to the Cumbria Way via Threlkeld and a bridleway on the east side of Glenderaterra Beck. For those seeking rides suitable for all ages, try the cycle track created by the West Cumbria Groundwork Trust along the old railway line between Ennerdale and Whitehaven.

An excellent area of high fell crossed by many rideable bridleways is to be found between Troutbeck, Kentmere and Longsleddale. A little further north is one of the best high mountain rides: the traverse of High Street from Troutbeck to Pooley Bridge – a distance of 15 glorious miles.

Although more usual in Scotland, bikes are an enjoyable way of reaching fells and crags at the heads of valleys, thereby avoiding long approaches on foot. Ennerdale, Langstrath, Kentmere, Longsleddale, Watendlath and Newlands are all examples of valleys where bikes may be used for this purpose. Although mountain biking is principally about being 'off-road', the many Lakeland lanes provide enjoyable riding preferable to the motor car – and less polluting.

It is important to start by seeking advice or by reading one of the many guidebooks available (see Reference Books). These describe routes, usually circular, graded according to their difficulty and providing information about distances and times. As many Lakeland valleys and passes are traversed by bridleways, it is possible to plan your own route with the help of an Ordnance Survey map. However beware,

some bridleways are extremely rough in places, making riding on two wheels impossible and in others – particularly those crossing high moorland and farmland – there is no evidence of their existence on the ground.

A new activity such as mountain biking, which has the potential to add to the existing problems of erosion, is bound to attract its critics. Only by responsible riding and respect for others will the risk of some bridleways being downgraded to footpaths be avoided. The Mountain Bike Code, prepared by the Countryside Commission and the Sports Council, should be followed at all times. The following advice applicable to mountain biking in the Lakes is based on this Code:

Rights of Way
• Bridleways – open to cyclists, but you must give way to walkers and horseriders.
• Byeways – usually unsurfaced tracks open to cyclists. As well as walkers and horseriders, you may meet vehicles which also have a right of access.
• Public footpaths – no right to cycle exists.

Other access
• Open land – on most upland, moorland and farmland cyclists normally have no right of access without express permission from the landowner.
• Pavements – cycling is not permitted on pavements.
• Designated cycle paths – look out for designated routes on forestry land, disused railway lines or other open spaces.

General information
Cyclists must adhere to the Highway Code. A detailed map is recommended for more adventurous trips. Follow the Country Code. Ensure that your bike is safe to ride and be prepared for emergencies. You are required to display working lights after dark. Reflective material on your clothes and bike can save your life. Ride under control downhill since this is when serious accidents often occur. If you intend to ride fast off-road, it is advisable to wear a helmet. Particular care should be taken on unstable or wet surfaces.

Ski-mountaineering on Gray Crag

Skiing and ski-mountaineering

The Lake District offers several possibilities for the skier who wants to extend his or her experience of the mountains. There are no commercial ski centres in the Lakes and the absence of predictable winter snow cover means that such centres are unlikely to be established. The Lake District Ski Club has a short permanent tow for use by members on the upper eastern slopes of Raise. Other local ski clubs own small portable tows which are set up each winter in different locations depending on the snow conditions. Contact the outdoor shops in an area for information about local ski clubs.

Snow conditions in the Lakes are variable. The first snowfall on the hills is usually recorded towards the end of November. It is often mid-January before snow lies on the hills and the period from mid-January to mid-March offers the best chance to find reasonable conditions. It is possible for snow to lie throughout the Lakeland fells, but those hills closer to the western coast tend to experience less prolonged snow cover, particularly on the lower slopes. The better snow conditions for skiing are often to be found on the more eastern hills.

Downhill skiers need to be fairly dedicated. It is a question of carrying skis and poles up to a summit, changing boots, and then enjoying one all-too-quick downhill run to the valley. Those with ski-mountaineering equipment can enjoy more of a tour by using skins to ascend onto one of the ridges and then touring along the ridge over several summits. Good days have been had on Skiddaw, Blencathra, the Helvellyn–Dodds ridge, the High Street ridge (from either Pooley Bridge or Troutbeck) and on some of the Kentmere hills. More dedicated skiers have been seen on the central fells but a good snow cover is required to cover the rocky terrain.

Cross-country skiing is possible in many areas depending on the conditions. All the ski-touring ridges are possible on nordic skis as well as several lower hills. If the snow is low-lying, it is also possible to use forestry roads through Grizedale and Whinlatter for cross-country skiing.

Skiing in the Lakes is an adventure. It's difficult to predict conditions until you get out on the hill. For those with an adventurous spirit, it can add a whole new dimension to their enjoyment of the fells in winter.

The sight of fell-runners lining up for a race is exciting: the anticipation not only of the battle for the lead but also for position right through the field; who is the fittest?; who is good uphill and who takes more risks in descent?; who has the better line and who knows the terrain, especially when the mist descends? The legends of fell running have left their mark – Bill Teasdale from Caldbeck, Joss Naylor from Wasdale and Billy Bland from Borrowdale – have dominated the podium in their time.

Feats of long-distance endurance have long attracted both walkers and runners. The four Three Thousanders (Skiddaw, Scafell, Scafell Pike and Helvellyn over 42 miles) has been a major

Fell running

The Lake District is renowned for such fell races as the Grasmere Sports, Fairfield Horseshoe and Ennerdale Horseshoe, but the pure joy of running on the fells is often not appreciated by walkers. A walker passed by a scantily-clad runner may comment on the apparent masochism involved but then appreciate the skills involved when the same runner disappears with apparent ease into the distance.

Fell running, like running in general, has become much more popular in the last few years. For many, the purpose of fell running is a training for a fell race; for others, it is just a means of covering the fells more quickly using lightweight gear and footwear, with no competitive intentions.

challenge for many. An average time for walkers is 16-18 hours but for the runners, 12 hours is the time to beat with a record time of under 8 hours. This route was first done in 1911 by Dr Arthur Wakefield. Height gained and not just peaks climbed were of interest. Eustace Thomas set off from the Moot Hall in Keswick and returned just under 24 hours later having ascended 27,000 feet; he wished to crack the 30,000 feet barrier, so continued with a circuit of the Grisedale Horseshoe and returned four hours later.

In 1932, Bob Graham, a hotelier from Keswick, climbed 42 peaks covering 72 miles and ascended 27,000 feet in a time of 23 hours 39 minutes. This 'Bob Graham Round' is the classic long-distance challenge for fell runners in the Lakes. It is attempted by many, usually on the weekends close to the full moon in June and July. Discussions ensue about the best way off Bow Fell, the use of a rope on Broad Stand, and getting lost on Great Dodd in the middle of the night as mist descends! Cars parked on Dunmail Raise in the evening, with supporters peering up to Steel Fell, bear witness to the hoped arrival of another group of runners.

The pleasure of a 'run' over the fells needs to be experienced. Compared to walking, the miles seem to fly by. A distant knoll or col soon arrives and the fells seem to unfold and become more alive. A good day's walk can be covered in just a few hours. Longer outings such as the Ennerdale Horseshoe or the Three Thousanders can be attempted with less weight.

Because the amount of equipment is kept to a minimum, there is a higher risk. Surprisingly, even in the big races, there are few accidents. However, if an accident does occur, the repercussions can be dire, even fatal. The fell runner must be aware of these dangers and take extra precautions with every step. Special equipment and footwear is available from outdoor and running shops.

A list of local fell races is normally posted in both Rock and Run (Ambleside) and Pete Bland Sports (Kendal).

Fell running is not for masochists. It requires a certain level of fitness, which, once obtained, makes it a pleasure to pass quickly over the fells whilst sustaining that fitness.

Conservation and the environment

The Lake District National Park, designated at such in 1951 and the largest of the ten in Britain, is visited by as many as 15 million people in any year. These enormous numbers, while a measure of the appeal of the unique area pose a constant threat to the very qualities that attract visitors in the first place. Indeed, the peace and tranquillity of half a century ago are rare, except out of season and on the more remote fell tops. The National Park authority (which owns over 8,000 hectares) and the National Trust (with over 16,000 hectares) protect the land in this very special area.

The NT holdings include 47 of the 87 areas classed as SSSI's and it also has 91 hill farms under their protection. These farms have contributed much to the landscape as it is today and the Trust helps with the costly maintenance of traditional buildings, walls and footpaths.

A major problem not yet resolved is the increasing numbers of cars which can block roads causing endless frustration and pollution. Local bus services in busy valleys are being encouraged.

The huge increase in fell-walking has caused severe erosion with many footpaths becoming dangerous because of loose stones, as well as forming unsightly scars on the landscape,

sometimes 30 metres wide. At first, some repairs to footpaths were done insensitively, giving rise to criticism that the cure was worse than the problem and that hillside tracks were being paved like urban paths. Now, years of experience using local stone, pitched and graded in the traditional manner have led to the production of a good practice guide. The British Upland Footpath Trust is a charity founded in 1993 to provide funds for the sensitive restoration of upland paths. They have instituted an award scheme to help promote good practice. The British Trust for Conservation Volunteers organises conservation working holidays where volunteers work under supervision to stone pitch eroded paths. The Friends of the Lake District is an active conservation body which campaigns on many issues are watches planning applications carefully.

You can involve yourself directly in conservation work by avoiding short cuts between zig-zags on graded paths; by using stiles and gates instead of climbing walls and fences; and by avoiding the most popular routes. You will find many little-used paths described in this book taking you into areas where visitors are few and the natural beauties of the area can be appreciated in solitude.

Long distance footpaths

The practice of going for long walks became popular some 200 years ago when Wordsworth, Coleridge and their friends made a regular habit of it. More recently, AW's Coast to Coast Walk became the first 'official' long walk passing through the area and now there are several more. Most of the later routes are 'unofficial' i.e. they consist of linked rights of way and other paths and have not been officially sanctioned.

Allerdale Ramble: This 55-mile walk from Seathwaite to Grune Point on the Solway Coast was devised by Harry Appleyard in 1976. It is a six-day walk with stages from 8 to 12 miles, leaving the Park after the third day near Cockermouth. A second edition of FR Harper's booklet is available from Tourist Offices. The route is mainly low level, but an optional variation includes Skiddaw.

Coast to Coast Walk: Alfred Wainwright's 190-mile walk from Ravenglass in the west to Robin Hood's Bay in the east was published in the early 1970's and has become increasingly popular over the years. The original route was not entirely on rights of way and some sections have now been re-routed. Michael Joseph (the copyright owners) have issued an amended edition. Paul Hannon has also produced his own version of the route in 1992 (Hillside Publications), taking on board all the changes that have taken place in the previous two decades. Owing to the popularity of the route, a wealth of accommodation is now available and there are even backpack shuttle services to ferry heavy packs on to the next night's destination.

The walk can be completed in 14 stages, but many people may find these overlong and prefer to plan their own shorter stages. Rosthwaite to Patterdale, for example, is 30kms and involves over 1200m of ascent, but could easily be split into two with a break at Grasmere.

The route enters the National Park at Nannycatch Gate en route for Ennerdale Bridge and continues through Rosthwaite, Grasmere, Glenridding, Patterdale, Burnbanks, Bampton and Rosgill to leave it again by the ruins of Shap Abbey. It is a fine walk through some of the best of the central Lake District.

Cumberland Way: Devised by Paul Hannon and first published in 1985, this 80-mile walk can be used in conjunction with Hannon's Westmorland Way and Furness Way to give a long, circular walk of three weeks duration. The Cumberland Way, from Ravenglass to Appleby, can conveniently be divided into six sections. The route lies mainly within the boundaries of the old county of Cumberland, which became part of Cumbria in 1974. Hannon is an admirer of AW and has unashamedly adopted his style. The route avoids mountain tops and can be followed with ease even in adverse weather conditions, but those who wish can easily diverge to take in various summits. The Way leaves the Park on Day 5, between Dalemain and Stainton.

Cumbria Way: A 70-mile walk from Ulverston to Carlisle and passing through the heart of the Lake District; this route is described by John Trevalyon on behalf of the Rambler's Association. It is divided into five stages with stops at Coniston, Dungeon Ghyll, Keswick and Caldbeck. Mainly a low-level walk, it is designed to show the great variety of landscapes with the county of Cumbria. Royalties from this publication go to the RA for work in securing access to the countryside.

Dales Way: This route from Ilkley to Bowness lies mainly in the Yorkshire Dales National Park. Only the final stage from east of Staveley to the finishing point is within the Lake District.

Furness Way: Another walk in the trilogy by Paul Hannon, this 75 miles covers the stretch between Arnside and Ravenglass in six stages and is almost entirely within the Park, which is entered on the first day just north of Brigsteer. The walking is generally easy, over varied terrain and includes some of the lesser-known areas of southern Lakeland.

Westmorland Way: A 98 mile walk from Appleby to Arnside described in seven stages. The third of Paul Hannon's walks (although the first to be written), this one is within the old county of Westmorland which disappeared in 1974 with the creation of Cumbria.

Yewbarrow from Nether Beck

Mountain safety

The following information is based on advice provided by the Lake District National Park.

Clothing

Conditions on the fells are often in sharp contrast to those in the valleys. Clothing should be comfortable: a warm insulating layer (not denim jeans) with a windproof outer jacket or waterproof suit for when it is wet. Avoid over-dresssing: sweat when cooling chills rapidly. Boots are usually the best footwear, especially in wet conditions, although lighter footwear may be adequate in fine weather providing you have a good sole to prevent slipping. Shoes with smooth soles or wellington boots can be dangerous, especially when descending. Carry spare warm clothing.

Equipment

The following items should be carried in a rucksack: map and compass (make sure you know how to use them); lunch and some extra energy-giving food; large polythene survival bag (bivvy bag); simple first aid kit; a whistle and torch; hat and gloves.

Plan

• Plan your route carefully.
• Allow one hour for every 4km and add one hour for every 500m of ascent, with extra time for rest and food stops.
• Set off in plenty of time to complete the walk.
• Obtain a weather forecast (017687-75757).
• Plan your walk with the ability of the weakest member of the party in mind.
• Leave details of your route with someone reliable before leaving.
• Report your safe return promptly.

On the walk

Be prepared to modify your route if necessary. Avoid steep scree slopes and take care when negotiating becks in spate. A party should walk at the pace of the slowest member and keep together at all times. Always be observant and maintain a group morale. Remember, most accidents happen in descent. Keep dogs under close control and, whenever sheep are likely to be near, on a firm lead.

Winter walking

Some extra precautions are needed when walking in the winter. Remember that daylight hours are shorter and walking conditions can be difficult. Your plan should not be too ambitious. Carry more extra clothing. Where conditions of snow and ice are likely to be encountered, each person should carry an ice axe and know how to use it. Boots are essential for winter conditions with soles that are rigid enough to prevent distortion on hard snow slopes. Under certain winter conditions, the wearing of crampons is essential for safe movement on the fells. Lightweight summer boots are not adequate. Avoid the risk of avalanches from gullies, cornices and steep slopes for 36 hours after a fresh snow fall and during periods of thaw.

In an emergency

• If you are delayed or descend into the wrong valley, inform your base or the Police as quickly as possible so that the Rescue Team is not called out unnecessarily.
• If you have to help a casualty, give first aid if necessary; make sure that breathing is unobstructed; dress wounds to prevent bleeding; keep the casualty warm, sheltered and safe from further injury. Also remember to protect yourself.
• Send for help. Dial 999 for the Police giving all the details including an accurate six figure grid reference of the location if possible. Remain at the telephone unless asked to do otherwise. The Police will alert the nearest Rescue Team.

Mountain rescue

Prevention is better than rescue. On the hill, turn back before the weather deteriorates or before you get lost. That way, there will always be another day.

Always carry waterproof outerwear, spare warm clothing, emergency food and nourishing drinks. On the fells, carry a bivvy bag in your party. Always carry a whistle, a torch with spare batteries, a compass and a map of the area. Practice navigation regularly using a map and compass. In winter, carry an ice axe and practice using it as a brake. Get instruction from more experienced walkers if you are in any doubt about using this equipment. Learn first aid.

In the event of an accident or other incident requiring emergency assistance, the following procedures should be followed.

Mountain rescue: You'll never know ...

- If a person is injured, make an assessment of the situation. Before touching or moving the patient, enquire and look to decide if the spine may be injured. Pain in the back or lack of sensation in the legs are suggestive. If the spine is thought to be injured, do not move the patient. Check whether the patient is conscious. If he or she does not respond to voice commands or pinching of the skin, you must assume the patient is unconscious. Place the patient in the recovery position (lying on the chest, one knee draw up, head to one side). Check that the airway is unobstructed. Carry out simple first aid.

- Make the injured person as comfortable as possible. Move away from any obvious dangers (e.g. falling stones, steep drop or rising water). If necessary, feed with hot drinks and nourishing food, but remember that, once evacuated, this may delay any operation that might be necessary. Put on extra clothes and get into a bivvy bag, sleeping bag or tent.

- If an injured person or lost group are out in the open, attempt to find shelter. Walls, boulders, stream banks and cairns can all reduce exposure to wind, rain and snow. Use tents or bivvy bags to provide protection.

- If your group is lost, benighted or trapped by bad weather, stop and find shelter. Take compass readings of significant features and use the map to determine your position.

- Ensure that all members of the party stay together. If you need to obtain help, send two reliable members of the party. Always ensure that at least one person remains with the injured person.

- A person going for help will need to know:
  - the number of people left on the hill;

Mardale Old Road and Harter Fell during a Haweswater drought

Helicopter approaching rescuers in Kentmere

- their location, preferably by using a grid reference and a description of the terrain;
- the nature of any injuries sustained.

• A person going for help should descend to the nearest and most accessible public or private telephone. Dial 999 and ask for the Police. Remain at that telephone and await further instructions.

• Mobile phones will often receive a signal when used on an open hillside or ridge in the Lakes. Assess the situation: is a rescue team really needed? If so, dial 999[SEND]

and ask for the police. When using a mobile phone, remember that the answering police station may not be a local one. You will need to provide more detail about the situation and your needs. Always give your mobile phone number to the police. Do not move away from your calling point as you are may lose the signal from the cell.

• When you get off the hill, tell anyone who is aware of your absence that you are now safe. This prevents them from worrying further and calling out the emergency services.

International distress signal

6 short blasts on the whistle repeated at one-minute intervals. In the dark, six torch flashes, repeated at one-minute intervals. Or any signal (e.g. flashes from a mirror) given six times in a minute and repeated at one-minute intervals.

Reference books

These are a selection of other comprehensive walking guides to the Lake District mountains. There are many other guides covering particular areas within the National Park. Also listed are some of the most significant past and present reference books to aspects of Lake District life and history.

Walking guides
Allen B, 1987, On High Lakeland Fells. Pic Publications
Allen B, 1995, Walking the Ridges of Lakeland. Michael Joseph
Birkett B, 1994, Complete Lakeland Fells. Collins Willow
Poucher W, 1960, The Lakeland Peaks. Constable
Wainwright A, 1955 onwards, A Pictorial Guide to the Lakeland Fells (7 volumes). Michael Joseph
Wainwright A, 1974, The Outlying Fells of Lakeland. Michael Joseph

Other guides
Ashcroft J, 1989, Mountain Bike Guide (Lake District, Howgills, Yorkshire Dales). Ernest Press
Bull A and Barnett F, Moutain Bikers Guide to the Lake District. Stanley Paul
Cram G, Eilbeck C and Roper I, 1975, Rock Climbing in the Lake District. Constable
Evans RB, 1982, Scrambles in the Lake District. Cicerone Press
Lindop G, 1993, A Literary Guide to the Lake District. Chatto and Windus
Fell and Rock Climbing Club, series of climbing guides

Lake District reference
Adams J and Ramshaw D, 1994, The English Lakes: the hills, the people, their history. P3 Publications
Collingwood WG, 1902, The Lake Counties. Frederick Warne and Co
Davies H, 1995, Wainwright – The Biography. Michael Joseph
Fell and Rock Climbing Club, 1986, 100 Years of Rock Climbing in the Lake District (Journal No. 70)
Gambles R, 1994, Lake District Place Names. Dalesman
Griffin AH, 1961, Inside the Real Lakeland. Guardian Press
Hankinson A, 1972, The First Tigers: The early history of rock climbing in the Lake District. Dent
Hankinson A, 1975, Camera on the Crags. Heinemann
Hankinson A, 1991, Coleridge Walks the Fells. Ellenbank Press
Oppenheimer LJ, 1908, The Heart of Lakeland. Sherratt & Hughes
Jones OG, 1900, Rock Climbing in the English Lake District. GP Abraham and Sons
Jones T and Millburn G, 1988, Cumbrian Rock. Pic Publications
Lefebure M, 1970, Cumberland Heritage. Gollancz
Pearsall WH, 1973, The Lake District: A landscape history. Collins (New Naturalist Series)
Rollinson W, 1967, A History of Man in the Lake District. Dent
Rollinson W, 1974, Life and Tradition in the Lake District. Dent
Rollinson W, 1978, A History of Cumberland and Westmorland. Phillimore
Shackleton EH, 1966, Lakeland Geology. Dalesman
Stainforth G, 1992, Lakeland: Landscape of imagination. Constable
Wordsworth W, 1835 (5th Edition), A Guide to the Lakes. (Several reprints available)

Maps
Ordance Survey Outdoor Leisure series (1:25,000) sheets 4, 5, 6 and 7
Ordnance Survey Tourist series (1:63,360) Lake District sheet
Harveys maps (1:40,000) Northern, North Western, Western and Eastern sheets

Scafell Pike and Scafell from Westmorland's Cairn

Wet days and off-days

The Lake District is well-known for its rain. Even during good weather spells, all but the keenest fell-walker may want a day off. Here are some suggestions as to alternative activities suitable for walkers and families. More information about all these facilities is to be found at local Information Centres (see page XXX). For ease of use, the suggestions are grouped around those valleys and towns most likely to form bases for visitors.

Ambleside, Windermere and Bowness
- Roman Fort, Ambleside
- Swimming Pool, Troutbeck Bridge
- Heron Corn Mill and Museum of Papermaking, Beetham, Milnthorpe
- Cartmel Priory and Gatehouse
- Levens Hall: Elizabethan house and garden
- Sizergh Castle, near Kendal: 14th century pele tower, historic house and gardens (NT)
- Townend, Troutbeck, Windermere: 'statesman' farmer's house built 1626 (NT)
- Hayes Garden World, Ambleside: award-winning garden centre
- Holker Hall and Gardens, Cark-in-Cartmell: excellent gardens, motor museum, regular events
- Stagshaw Gardens, Ambleside: woodland garden (NT)
- Abbot Hall Museum of Lakeland Life and Industry, Kendal
- Brewery Arts Centre, Kendal: modern arts complex
- Museum of History and Natural History, Kendal: includes Wainwright display
- National Park Visitor Centre, Brockhole, Windermere
- Windermere Steamboat Museum, Windermere
- Fell Foot Park, Newby Bridge: park and garden with boating facilities
- World of Beatrix Potter Attraction, Bowness
- Leisure Centre, Kendal
- Lakeside and Haverthwaite Railway, Newby Bridge

Grasmere
- Dove Cottage and Wordsworth Museum: former home of Dorothy and William Wordsworth
- Rydal Mount: William Wordsworth's last home
- Heaton Cooper Gallery, Grasmere: exhibition and sale of work by local artist

Hawkshead, Coniston and Duddon Valley
- Hawkshead Court House: 15th century building
- Hill Top, Sawrey: former home of author, Beatrix Potter
- Beatrix Potter Art Gallery, Hawkshead: exhibition of author's illustrations
- Grizedale Forest Visitor Centre, Grizedale: forest trails, sculptures and centre
- Hawkshead Grammar School: old school attended by William Wordsworth
- Brantwood: former home of John Ruskin
- Furness Abbey: ancient abbey
- Gleaston Water Mill, Ulverston
- Graythwaite Hall Gardens, Ulverston
- Dock Museum, Barron-in-Furness: history of steel shipbuilding locally
- Laurel and Hardy Museum, Ulverston: memorabilia of Laurel and Hardy
- Stott Park Bobbin Mill, Ulverston
- Park Leisure Centre, Barron-in-Furness

Eskdale
- Hardknott Roman Fort
- Eskdale Mill, Boot: water wheel corn mill
- Ravenglass and Eskdale narrow-guage railway: runs from Ravenglass to Boot

Wasdale and Ennerdale
- Ponsonby Farm Park, Ponsonby, Seascale: dairy farm with collection of rare breeds
- Egremont Castle (ruin)
- Ravenglass Roman Bath House
- Muncaster Castle, Ravenglass: historic castle and garden
- Sellafield Visitor Centre, Seascale: exhibition about the nuclear age
- St Bees heritage coast (RSPB managed)

Cockermouth
- Wythop Watermill, Embleton: wood-working museum and watermill
- Wordsworth House, Cockermouth: birthplace of famous author (NT)
- Workington Hall, Workington: historic house
- Cumberland Toy and Model Museum, Cockermouth

Temperature inversion over Bowfell, from Harrison Stickle

- Flying Buzzard and Vic '96 Steamships, Maryport: former steamship display
- Maryport Maritime Museum, Maryport
- Helena Thompson Museum, Workington: costumes, jewellery, social history
- Printing House, Cockermouth: history of printing
- Senhouse Roman Museum, Maryport
- Whitehaven Beacon: history of Whitehaven as a port
- Sports Centre, Cockermouth
- Sports and Leisure Centre, Workington

Keswick
- Trotters and Friends Animal Park, Bassenthwaite
- Keswick Spa swimming pool
- Mirehouse: historic house and gardens
- Lingholm Gardens, Keswick: formal and woodland garden
- Beatrix Potter's Lake District, Keswick: author's work in Lakeland conservation
- Cars of the Stars, Keswick: display of famous TV and film cars
- Cumberland Pencil Museum, Keswick: history of pencil-mking
- Keswick Museum and Art Gallery: intriguing Victorian museum

- Museum of Mining, Threlkeld: display of mining and quarrying
- Whinlatter Visitor Centre, Braithwaite: forest trails and forestry interpretation centre
- Castlerigg Stone Circle, Keswick: neolithic stone circle (NT)

Ullswater
- Lakeland Bird of Prey Centre, Lowther Castle
- Lowther Leisure Park, Penrith: multi-activity family leisure centre
- Brougham Castle, near Penrith (ruin)
- Penrith Castle (ruin)
- Dalemain House, near Penrith: historic house

Eastern Fells
- Keld Chapel, Shap (NT): small pre-Reformation chapel
- Shap Abbey (ruin)
- Kirkoswald Castle, near Penrith (ruin)
- Acorn Bank Gardens, Temple Sowerby, near Penrith: gardens, herbs and orchard (NT)
- Haweswater reserve (RSPB managed)

There are also a range of equestrian centres, water sports facilities, indoor climbing walls, swimming pools, golf courses and fishing waters in and around the Lakes.

Tick list of summits

This is a height order list of all the fells described in this book. There are a total of 243 summits of which 214 are described in Wainwright's seven volume *Pictorial Guide*. Fells listed by Wainwright in the *Outlying Fells* guide are denoted by * in the AW column. Hills without public access and where the landowner wishes to restict walkers have been omitted.

All heights shown are taken from the relevant OS 1:25,000 Leisure Sheet or Pathfinder Map. These have been converted to feet using a multiplier factor of 3.1408. The imperial heights may differ from those shown on earlier maps and in Wainwright's guides as a result of re-surveys by the Ordnance Survey and the less precise conversion from metric heights. Where exact heights are not recorded on the map, the height shown refers to the nearest contour.

	FRCC No.	AW No.	Fell	Metres	Feet	Grid ref	Section	Date
❏	1	1	Scafell Pike	978	3208	216072	S	_____
❏	2	2	Scafell	964	3162	207065	S	_____
❏	3	3	Helvellyn	950	3118	342151	E	_____
❏	4		Ill Crag	935	3068	223073	S	_____
❏	5	4	Skiddaw	931	3054	260291	N	_____
❏	6		Broad Crag	930	3051	219076	S	_____
❏	7		Lower Man (Helvellyn)	925	3034	337155	E	_____
❏	8	5	Great End	910	2985	227084	S	_____
❏	9	6	Bow Fell	902	2959	245064	S	_____
❏	10	7	Great Gable	899	2949	211103	W	_____
❏	11	8	Pillar	892	2926	171121	W	_____
❏	12	9	Nethermost Pike	891	2923	344142	E	_____
❏	13	10	Catstye Cam	890	2919	348158	E	_____
❏	14	11	Esk Pike	885	2903	237075	S	_____
❏	15	12	Raise	883	2896	343174	E	_____
❏	16	13	Fairfield	873	2864	359118	E	_____
❏	17	14	Blencathra (Saddleback)	868	2847	323277	N	_____
❏	18	15	Skiddaw Little Man	865	2837	267278	N	_____
❏	19	16	White Side	863	2831	338167	E	_____
❏	20	17	Crinkle Crags	859	2818	249049	S	_____
❏	21	18	Dollywagon Pike	858	2814	346131	E	_____
❏	22	19	Great Dodd	857	2811	342206	E	_____
❏	23	20	Grasmoor	852	2795	175203	NW	_____
❏	24	21	Stybarrow Dodd	843	2765	343189	E	_____
❏	25	22	Little Scoat Fell	841	2759	160114	W	_____
❏	26	23	St Sunday Crag	841	2756	369134	E	_____
❏	27	24	Crag Hill / Eel Crag	839	2752	193204	NW	_____
❏	28	25	High Street	828	2716	441111	FE	_____
❏	29	26	Red Pike (Wasdale)	826	2709	165106	W	_____
❏	30	27	Hart Crag	822	2696	368113	E	_____
❏	31	28	Steeple	819	2686	157117	W	_____
❏	32	29	High Stile	807	2647	170148	W	_____

	FRCC No.	AW No.	Fell	Metres	Feet	Grid ref	Section	Date
❏	33	30	The Old Man ofConiston	803	2634	272978	S	_____
❏	34	31	High Raise (Martindale)	802	2631	448135	FE	_____
❏	35	32	Kirk Fell	802	2631	195105	W	_____
❏	36	33	Swirl How	802	2631	273005	S	_____
❏	37	34	Green Gable	801	2627	215107	W	_____
❏	38	35	Lingmell	800	2624	209082	S	_____
❏	39	36	Haycock	797	2614	145107	W	_____
❏	40	37	Brim Fell	796	2611	271986	S	_____
❏	41	38	Dove Crag	792	2598	374105	E	_____
❏	42	39	Rampsgill Head	792	2598	443128	FE	_____
❏	43	40	Grisedale Pike	791	2595	198225	NW	_____
❏	44	41	Watson's Dodd	789	2588	336196	E	_____
❏	45	42	Allen Crags	785	2575	237085	S	_____
❏	46	43	Thornthwaite Crag	784	2572	432100	FE	_____
❏	47	44	Glaramara	783	2568	246105	S	_____
❏	48	45	Great Carrs	780	2558	270009	S	_____
❏	49	46	Kidsty Pike	780	2560	447126	FE	_____
❏	50	47	Dow Crags	778	2552	262978	S	_____
❏	51	48	Harter Fell (Mardale)	778	2552	460093	FE	_____
❏	52	49	Red Screes	776	2545	396088	E	_____
❏	53	50	Sail	773	2536	198203	NW	_____
❏	54	51	Wandope	772	2532	188197	NW	_____
❏	55	52	Grey Friar	770	2526	260004	S	_____
❏	56	53	Hopegill Head	770	2526	186222	NW	_____
❏	57	54	Great Rigg	766	2513	356104	E	_____
❏	58	55	Stony Cove Pike	763	2502	418100	FE	_____
❏	59	56	High Raise (Langdale)	762	2499	281095	C	_____
❏	60	57	Slight Side	762	2499	210050	S	_____
❏	61	58	Wetherlam	762	2499	288011	S	_____
❏	62	59	Mardale Ill Bell	761	2496	447101	FE	_____
❏	63	60	Ill Bell	757	2483	437077	FE	_____
❏	64	61	Hart Side	756	2481	359198	E	_____
❏	65	62	Red Pike (Buttermere)	755	2477	161154	W	_____
❏	66	63	Dale Head	753	2470	223153	NW	_____
❏	67	64	Carl Side	746	2447	255281	N	_____
❏	68	65	High Crag	744	2440	180140	W	_____
❏	69	66	The Knott	739	2423	437127	FE	_____
❏	70	67	Robinson	737	2417	202169	NW	_____
❏	71	68	Harrison Stickle	736	2414	282074	C	_____
❏	72	69	Seat Sandal	736	2415	344115	E	_____
❏	73	70	Longside Edge	734	2408	249284	N	_____
❏	74	71	Sergeant Man	730	2394	286089	C	_____
❏	75	72	Kentmere Pike	730	2394	466078	FE	_____

	FRCC No.	AW No.	Fell	Metres	Feet	Grid ref	Section	Date
❏	76	73	Hindscarth	727	2385	216165	NW	_____
❏	77	74	Clough Head	726	2381	334225	E	_____
❏	78	75	Ullscarf	726	2381	292122	C	_____
❏	79	76	Thunacar Knott	723	2372	279080	C	_____
❏	80	77	Froswick	720	2362	435085	FE	_____
❏	81	78	Birkhouse Moor	718	2355	364160	E	_____
❏	82	79	Brandreth	715	2344	215119	W	_____
❏	83	80	Lonscale Fell	715	2344	285272	N	_____
❏	84	81	Branstree	713	2339	478100	FE	_____
❏	85	82	Knott	710	2329	296330	N	_____
❏	86	83	Pike o'Stickle	709	2326	274073	C	_____
❏	87	84	Whiteside	707	2319	170219	NW	_____
❏	88	85	Yoke	706	2316	438067	FE	_____
❏	89	86	Pike o'Blisco	705	2312	271042	S	_____
❏	90	87	Bowscale Fell	702	2303	333306	N	_____
❏	91	88	Cold Pike	701	2299	263036	S	_____
❏	92	89	Pavey Ark	700	2296	285079	C	_____
❏	93	90	Gray Crag	699	2293	427117	FE	_____
❏	94	91	Grey Knotts	697	2287	217126	W	_____
❏	95	92	Rest Dodd	696	2283	432137	FE	_____
❏	96	93	Seatallan	692	2270	140084	W	_____
❏	97	94	Caw Fell	690	2263	132110	W	_____
❏	98	95	Ullock Pike	690	2263	244287	N	_____
❏	99	96	Great Calva	690	2263	291312	N	_____
❏	100	97	Bannerdale Crags	683	2241	335291	N	_____
❏	101	98	Loft Crag	680	2230	277071	C	_____
❏	102	99	Sheffield Pike	675	2214	369182	E	_____
❏	103	100	Bakestall	673	2208	266307	N	_____
❏	104	101	Scar Crags	672	2204	208207	NW	_____
❏	105	102	Loadpot Hill	671	2201	457181	FE	_____
❏	106	103	Wether Hill	670	2198	456167	FE	_____
❏	107	104	Tarn Crag (Longsleddale)	664	2178	488078	FE	_____
❏	108	105	Carrock Fell	660	2165	342336	N	_____
❏	109	106	Whiteless Pike	660	2165	180190	NW	_____
❏	110	107	High Pike (Caldbeck)	658	2157	319350	N	_____
❏	111	108	Place Fell	657	2154	406170	FE	_____
❏	112	109	High Pike (Scandale)	656	2152	374088	E	_____
❏	113	110	Selside Pike	655	2148	490112	FE	_____
❏	114	111	Middle Dodd	654	2145	397096	E	_____
❏	115	112	Harter Fell (Eskdale)	653	2142	219997	S	_____
❏	116	113	High Spy	653	2142	234162	NW	_____
❏	117	114	Great Sca Fell	651	2135	291339	N	_____
❏	118	115	Rossett Pike	650	2132	249076	S	_____
❏	119	116	Fleetwith Pike	648	2125	206142	W	_____

	FRCC No.	AW No.	Fell	Metres	Feet	Grid ref	Section	Date
❏	120	117	Base Brown	646	2120	225114	W	_____
❏	121		Iron Crag	640	2099	123119	W	_____
❏	122	118	Grey Crag	638	2093	497072	FE	_____
❏	123	119	Causey Pike	637	2089	218209	NW	_____
❏	124	120	Little Hart Crag	637	2089	387100	E	_____
❏	125	121	Mungrisdale Common	633	2077	312292	N	_____
❏	126	122	Starling Dodd	633	2076	142158	W	_____
❏	127	123	Seathwaite Fell	632	2073	227097	S	_____
❏	128		Rosthwaite Fell	630	2067	254114	S	_____
❏	129	124	Yewbarrow	628	2060	173085	W	_____
❏	130	125	Birks	622	2040	380144	E	_____
❏	131		Walna Scar	621	2037	258963	S	_____
❏	132	126	Hartsop Dodd	618	2027	411118	FE	_____
❏	133	127	Great Borne	616	2020	124164	W	_____
❏	134	128	Heron Pike	612	2007	356083	E	_____
❏	135	129	Illgill Head	609	1998	169049	S	_____
❏	136	130	High Seat	608	1994	287180	C	_____
❏	137	*	Black Combe	600	1968	135855	S	_____
❏	138	131	Hay Stacks	597	1958	193131	W	_____
❏	139	132	Bleaberry Fell	590	1935	286196	C	_____
❏	140	133	Shipman Knotts	587	1926	472063	FE	_____
❏	141	134	Brae Fell	586	1922	289352	N	_____
❏	142	135	Middle Fell	582	1909	151072	W	_____
❏	143	136	Ard Crags	581	1906	207198	NW	_____
❏	144	137	Hartsop Above How	580	1902	384120	E	_____
❏	145	138	Maiden Moor	576	1889	237182	NW	_____
❏	146	139	The Nab	576	1889	434152	FE	_____
❏	147	140	Blake Fell	573	1879	110197	W	_____
❏	148	*	Whitfell	573	1879	159930	S	_____
❏	149	141	Sergeant's Crag	571	1873	274114	C	_____
❏	150	142	Outerside	568	1863	211215	NW	_____
❏	151	143	Angletarn Pikes	567	1860	413148	FE	_____
❏	152	144	Brock Crags	561	1840	417136	FE	_____
❏	153	145	Knott Rigg	556	1824	197189	NW	_____
❏	154	146	Steel Fell	553	1814	319111	C	_____
❏	155	147	Lord's Seat	552	1811	204266	NW	_____
❏	156	148	Meal Fell	550	1804	283337	N	_____
❏	157	149	Tarn Crag (Easedale)	550	1804	303093	C	_____
❏	158	*	Buck Barrow	549	1801	152910	S	_____
❏	159	150	Hard Knott	549	1801	232024	S	_____
❏	160		Carling Knott	544	1784	117203	W	_____
❏	161	151	Blea Rigg	541	1774	301078	C	_____
❏	162	152	Lank Rigg	541	1774	092120	W	_____
❏	163	153	Bessyboot	540	1771	258125	S	_____

	FRCC No.	AW No.	Fell	Metres	Feet	Grid ref	Section	Date
❑	164	154	Calf Crag	537	1761	301104	C	_____
❑	165	155	Great Mell Fell	537	1760	397254	E	_____
❑	166	156	Whin Rigg	535	1755	152034	S	_____
❑	167	157	Arthur's Pike	532	1745	461207	FE	_____
❑	168	*	High Wether Howe	531	1742	516109	FE	_____
❑	169	*	Caw	529	1735	230945	S	_____
❑	170	158	Gavel Fell	526	1725	117185	W	_____
❑	171	159	Great Cockup	526	1725	273333	N	_____
❑	172	160	Whinlatter	525	1722	197249	NW	_____
❑	173	161	Bonscale Pike	524	1719	450200	FE	_____
❑	174	162	Crag Fell	523	1715	097144	W	_____
❑	175	163	Souther Fell	522	1712	355291	N	_____
❑	176	164	Eagle Crag	520	1706	276121	C	_____
❑	177	165	High Hartsop Dodd	519	1702	393107	E	_____
❑	178	166	Sallows	516	1691	437040	FE	_____
❑	179	167	High Tove	515	1689	289165	C	_____
❑	180	168	Mellbreak	512	1679	149186	W	_____
❑	181	169	Broom Fell	511	1676	196270	NW	_____
❑	182	170	Beda Head	509	1669	428170	FE	_____
❑	183	171	Hen Comb	509	1669	132181	W	_____
❑	184	172	Low Pike	508	1666	374078	E	_____
❑	185	173	Little Mell Fell	505	1657	423240	E	_____
❑	186	*	Hare Shaw	503	1650	497131	FE	_____
❑	187	174	Dodd	502	1646	244273	N	_____
❑	188	175	Stone Arthur	500	1640	348092	E	_____
❑	189	*	Stainton Pike	497	1632	153943	S	_____
❑	190	*	Yoadcastle	494	1610	157952	S	_____
❑	191	176	Green Crag	489	1604	200983	S	_____
❑	192	177	Grike	488	1601	085141	W	_____
❑	193	178	Wansfell	487	1597	404053	FE	_____
❑	194	179	Longlands Fell	483	1584	276354	N	_____
❑	195	180	Sour Howes	483	1584	428032	FE	_____
❑	196	181	Gowbarrow Fell	481	1579	407218	E	_____
❑	197	182	Armboth Fell	479	1571	297160	C	_____
❑	198	*	Hesk Fell	477	1564	176947	S	_____
❑	199	183	Burnbank Fell	475	1558	110209	W	_____
❑	200	184	Lingmoor Fell	469	1538	303046	S	_____
❑	201	185	Barf	468	1536	214268	NW	_____
❑	202	186	Raven Crag	461	1512	303187	C	_____
❑	203	187	Graystones/Kirk Fell	456	1496	178264	NW	_____
❑	204	188	Great Crag	456	1496	269147	C	_____
❑	205	189	Barrow	455	1492	227218	NW	_____
❑	206	190	Cat Bells	451	1479	244199	NW	_____

	FRCC No.	AW No.	Fell	Metres	Feet	Grid ref	Section	Date
❏	207	191	Binsey	447	1466	225355	N	_____
❏	208		Knock Murton	447	1466	095191	W	_____
❏	209	192	Glenridding Dodd	442	1450	381176	E	_____
❏	210	193	Nab Scar	440	1443	355072	E	_____
❏	211	194	Arnison Crag	433	1420	394150	E	_____
❏	212	195	Steel Knotts	432	1417	440181	FE	_____
❏	213	*	Brunt Knott	427	1400	484006	FE	_____
❏	214	*	Great Worm Crag	427	1400	194969	S	_____
❏	215	*	Green Quarter Fell	426	1397	469041	FE	_____
❏	216	196	Low Fell	423	1387	137226	W	_____
❏	217	197	Buckbarrow	420	1377	136058	W	_____
❏	218	198	Gibson Knott	420	1377	319099	C	_____
❏	219	199	Fellbarrow	416	1364	132242	W	_____
❏	220	200	Grange Fell	410	1345	264162	C	_____
❏	221	201	Helm Crag	405	1328	327093	C	_____
❏	222	*	Whiteside Pike	397	1302	521016	FE	_____
❏	223	202	Silver How	394	1292	325066	C	_____
❏	224	203	Hallin Fell	388	1271	433198	FE	_____
❏	225	204	Walla Crag	379	1243	277213	C	_____
❏	226	*	Heughscar Hill	375	1230	488231	FE	_____
❏	227	*	Stickle Pike	375	1230	212927	S	_____
❏	228	205	Ling Fell	373	1223	180286	NW	_____
❏	229	*	The Pike	370	1214	186934	S	_____
❏	230	206	Latrigg	368	1207	279247	N	_____
❏	231	207	Troutbeck Tongue	364	1194	422064	FE	_____
❏	232	208	Sale Fell	359	1177	194297	NW	_____
❏	233	209	Rannerdale Knotts	355	1164	167182	NW	_____
❏	234	210	High Rigg	354	1161	309220	C	_____
❏	235	*	Knipescar Common	342	1131	527191	FE	_____
❏	236		Swainson Knott	340	1115	079083	W	_____
❏	237	211	Loughrigg Fell	335	1099	347051	C	_____
❏	238	*	Top o'Selside	335	1099	309919	S	_____
❏	239	212	Black Fell	323	1059	340016	S	_____
❏	240	*	Gummer's How	321	1054	390885	S	_____
❏	241	213	Holme Fell	317	1040	315006	S	_____
❏	242	*	Carron Crag	314	1030	325943	S	_____
❏	243	*	Ponsonby Fell	310	1017	082071	W	_____
❏	244	214	Castle Crag	290	951	249159	NW	_____

Index of fells

References in **bold** denote principal entries. Other references denote extensions to other walks where the particular fell may also be climbed.

Index of starting points

This index can be used to identify possible walking routes from your known starting point, usually in a valley base. Entries in **bold** denote principal route descriptions in the text. Those in ordinary type indicate a text reference to an alternative approach route.

The Fell and Rock Climbing Club

The Fell and Rock Climbing Club is the leading membership organisation for mountaineers interested in walking and climbing in the Lake District. The Club was formed in November 1906 at Coniston and within a year had attracted over 170 men and women. Today there are more than 1100 members living throughout Britain and abroad.

Fell and Rock members are active in many mountain ranges. The Club arranges an annual programme of meets throughout the Lakes, Scotland, Peak District, Wales and southern England as well as to the Alps. Members also arrange their own walking, climbing, skiing and trekking parties to the Alps, Himalaya and mountain areas throughout the world.

Members and their families are able to use the Club's climbing huts – of which there are currently five in the Lakes and one in Scotland – and three cottages. Reciprocal arrangements exist to use the huts of several other clubs throughout the world.

The Club owns an important library of mountaineering literature which may be consulted by non-members. It is based within the main library at the University of Lancaster to whom application should be made. There is also an extensive photographic archive as well as collections of documents and artefacts relating to mountaineering history available for inspection at various museums and archives.

A bi-annual *Journal* of mountaineering interest is published by the Club and, since 1921, the Fell and Rock has regularly published a definitive series of rock climbing guides to the Lake District which are available from climbing shops and bookshops or by mail order.

The objectives of the Club extend to the general protection of the amenities of the Lake District and to the promotion of the general interests of mountaineers.

Membership of the Club is open to mountaineers with a strong interest in the Lake District and who support the purposes of the Club. Prospective members are proposed by existing members who are familiar with their experience and mountaineering competence.

The Fell and Rock Climbing Club and The Ernest Press offer a range of books for people interested in the mountains. Most of these titles can be obtained from good bookshops, or direct from their respective publisher.

Fell and Rock Climbing Club publications

Climbing Guides:
Scafell, Wasdale and Eskdale 13.00
Borrowdale 13.00
Dow, Duddon and Slate 13.00
Gable and Pillar 13.00
Langdale 13.00
Buttermere and Eastern Crags 13.00
Fell and Rock *Journal* (state year) .. 10.00

For post and packaging, please add 10% (minimum £1.50) (UK only).

Please send orders, accompanied by a cheque or postal order payable to 'FRCC' to:
The Archway, 17 St John Street, Keswick, Cumbria CA12 5AE

Ernest Press publications

Heart of Lakeland by LJ Oppenheimer 4.95
Packhorse Bridges of the Lake District by
M Hartwell 6.95
Whensoever by Frank Card 17.95
The Undiscovered Country by P Bartlett 13.95
Tight Rope by Dennis Gray 9.95
The First Munroist by P Drummond and
I Mitchell 13.95

For post and packaging, please add 10% (minimum 50p) (UK only).

Please send orders, accompanied by a cheque or postal order payable to 'The Ernest Press' to:
1 Thomas Street, Holyhead, Gwynedd LL65 1RR

Credits

This list identifies the respective author and photographer for each contribution to this guide. All maps are credited to Clive Beveridge, Paul Hudson, Adrian Wiszniewski and Tim Pickles. All other uncredited text is written by the editors.

Page	Author	Photographer	Page	Author	Photographer
Cover		Colin Fearnley	47	June Parker	Ron Kenyon
ii		Jill Aldersley	48	June Parker	Bill Comstive
viii		Ernest Shepherd	49	June Parker	Bill Comstive
			50	June Parker	June Parker
x		Richard Gibbens	51		Richard Gibbens
			52	Alasdair Pettifer	Brian Cosby
Introduction			53	Ron and Chris Lyon	Iain Whitmey
1		Richard Gibbens	54	Alasdair Pettifer	June Parker
2	Editors	Stella Berkeley	55	June Parker	Jill Aldersley
5		Irene Farrington	56	Dave Gregory	Paul Exley
6	Editors		57	Irene Farrington	Irene Farrington
7	John Moore		58	Dave Gregory	Jill Aldersley
9	Bill Comstive	June Parker	59	Dave Gregory	June Parker
11	Bill Roberts	June Parker	60	Adrian Wisznieski	Irene Farrington
13	June Parker		61	Dave Gregory	Dave Gregory
			62	Alasdair Pettifer	Richard Gibbens
Eastern Fells			63	Alasdair Pettifer	Alan Parker
15	Editors		64	Richard Coatsworth	Paul Exley
16	Tom Price	June Parker	65	C Beveridge / S Loxam	June Parker
17	June Parker	Les Shore			
18	Chris Craggs	Chris Craggs	**Central Fells**		
19	Chris Craggs	Chris Craggs	67	Editors	
20	June Parker	Colin Fearnley	68	Tim Pickles	Alick Woods
21	June Parker	Alan Parker	69	Tom Price	June Parker
22	June Parker	June Parker	70	Tim Pickles	June Parker
23	June Parker	Les Shore	71	Tim Pickles	Ron Kenyon
24	Adrian Wiszniewski	Iain Whitmey	72	Tim Pickles	Ernest Shepherd
25	Ron Kenyon	June Parker	73	Tim Pickles	June Parker
26	June Parker	Richard Gibbens	74	Neil Dowie	June Parker
27		June Parker	75	Maureen Linton	Ernest Shepherd
28	Ron Kenyon	Les Shore	76	June Parker	June Parker
29		Richard Gibbens	77	Maureen Linton	Richard Gibbens
30	Ron Kenyon	Richard Gibbens	78	Cath and Paul Exley	Stella Berkeley
31	June Parker	June Parker	79		Richard Gibbens
32	Paul Hudson	Colin Fearnley	80	Bill Comstive	Iain Whitmey
33	Ron and Chris Lyon	Ernest Shepherd	81	Bill Comstive	Colin Wells
34	June Parker	June Parker	82	Richard Coatsworth	Irene Farrington
35	June Parker	Peter Hodgkiss	83	Bill Roberts	Alan Parker
36	Tim Pickles	Richard Gibbens			
37	Tim Pickles	Irene Farrington	**Southern Fells**		
			85	Editors	
Far Eastern Fells			86	Cath and Paul Exley	Brian Cosby
39	Editors		87	Cath and Paul Exley	Al Phizacklea
40	Ron Kenyon	June Parker	88	Richard Barnes	Peter Hodgkiss
41	Ron Kenyon	Colin Fearnley	89	Tim Pickles	Richard Gibbens
42	June Parker	June Parker	90	C Beveridge / S Loxam	Richard Gibbens
43	June Parker	June Parker	91		Richard Gibbens
44	Ron Kenyon	Stephen Reid	92	Tom Price	Peter Fleming
45	June Parker	Alan Parker	93	Pauline Sweet	Bill Comstive
46	June Parker	Colin Fearnley	94	Chris Craggs	Stella Berkeley

Page	Author	Photographer
95	Cath and Paul Exley	Chris Craggs
96	Chris Craggs	Jill Aldersley
97	Richard Coatsworth	Chris Craggs
98	Hatty Harris	Paul Exley
99	Hatty Harris	Alan Parker
100	Hatty Harris	Brian Cosby
101		Ernest Shepherd
102	Hatty Harris	Peter Fleming
103	Hatty Harris	Jill Aldersley
104	Tom Price	Richard Gibbens
105	Les Shore	Jill Aldersley
106	Tom Price	June Parker
107	Tom Price	Peter Fleming
108	Iain and Brenda Whitmey	Iain Whitmey
109	Iain and Brenda Whitmey	June Parker
110	Iain and Brenda Whitmey	June Parker
111	Hatty Harris	Iain Whitmey
112		Bill Comstive
113	Pauline Sweet	Ron Kenyon
114	Bill Comstive	Bill Comstive
115	June Parker	Irene Farrington
116	Iain and Brenda Whitmey	Peter Fleming
117	Richard Barnes	Irene Farrington

Northern Fells

119	Editors	
120		Brian Cosby
121	Tim Pickles	June Parker
122	Chris Craggs	Richard Gibbens
123		Peter Fleming
124	Tim Pickles	Stan Thompson
125	Tim Pickles	June Parker
126	Paul Hudson	Richard Gibbens
127	Bill Roberts	Colin Fearnley
128	Ron Kenyon	June Parker
129	Bill Roberts	Bill Comstive
130	Bill Roberts	Alick Woods
131	Bill Roberts	Alan Parker
132	Tim Pickles	June Parker
133	Bill Roberts	Alan Parker

North Western Fells

135	Editors	
136	June Parker	June Parker
137	Adrian Wiszniewski	June Parker
138	Adrian Wiszniewski	June Parker
139	Adrian Wiszniewski	June Parker
140	Tim Pickles	Alan Parker
141	Bill Roberts	Les Shore
142	June Parker	Alick Woods
143	Alan Slater	Peter Fleming
144	C Beveridge / S Loxam	Andy Coatsworth
145	Andy Coatsworth	Andy Coatsworth
146	Tim Pickles	Richard Gibbens
147	Tim Pickles	Ron Kenyon
148	Tim Pickles	Peter Hodgkiss

Page	Author	Photographer
149	Tim Pickles	June Parker
150	Tim Pickles	Brian Cosby
151	Richard Barnes	Peter Fleming
152	Richard Barnes	Peter Fleming
153	Tim Pickles	Alick Woods

Western Fells

155	Editors	
156		Ernest Shepherd
157	Don Greenop	Jack Carswell
158	Cath and Paul Exley	June Parker
159	John Slater	Ron Kenyon
160	Don Greenop	Brian Cosby
161	Cath and Paul Exley	June Parker
162	Richard Barnes	Colin Fearnley
163	June Parker	Stephen Reid
164	Tim Pickles	Ernest Shepherd
165	Richard Barnes	Ernest Shepherd
166	Tim Pickles	Peter Hodgkiss
167	Roy and Norma Precious	Roy Precious
168	Tim Pickles	Peter Fleming
169		Ernest Shepherd
170	Don Greenop	Ernest Shepherd
171		Colin Fearnley
172	June Parker	Peter Fleming
173	C Beveridge / S Loxam	Alan Parker
174	Tim Pickles	Jill Aldersley
175	John Slater	Les Shore
176	C Beveridge / S Loxam	Don Greenop
177	Les Shore	Alan Parker

Reference Section

178		Richard Gibbens
180	Editors	Alan Parker
181		Richard Gibbens
182	Editors	June Parker
184	Editors	Ron Kenyon
185	David Staton	Richard Gibbens
187	Tim Pickles	Ron Kenyon
188	Ron Kenyon	Andy Coatsworth
189	Editors	
190	Editors	
191		Richard Gibbens
192	Editors	
193	Editors	Al Phizacklea
194		Ron Kenyon
195		Richard Gibbens
196	Editors	
197		Richard Gibbens
198	Editors	
199		Richard Gibbens
200	Editors	
212		Ron Kenyon
213	Editors	
214		Richard Gibbens
Cover		Peter Fleming

FELL & ROCK CLIMBING CLUB

IN GLORIOUS & HAPPY MEMORY OF THOSE
WHOSE NAMES ARE INSCRIBED BELOW—
MEMBERS OF THIS CLUB WHO DIED FOR
THEIR COUNTRY IN THE EUROPEAN WAR
1914–1918 THESE FELLS WERE ACQUIRED
BY THEIR FELLOW-MEMBERS & BY THEM
VESTED IN THE NATIONAL TRUST FOR
THE USE & ENJOYMENT OF THE PEOPLE
OF OUR LAND FOR ALL TIME:—
J.S.BAINBRIDGE: J.G.BEAN: H.S.P.BLAIR:
A.J.CLAY: J.N.FLETCHER: W.H.B.GROSS:
E.HARTLEY: S.W.HERFORD: S.F.JEFFCOAT:
E.B.LEES: S.J.LINZELL: L.J.OPPENHEIMER:
A.J.PRICHARD: A.M.RIMER: R.B.SANDERSON:
H.H.SUMOSBY: C.G.TURNER: B.H.WHITTY:
A.J.WHITWORTH: C.S.WORTHINGTON:

The Gable Memorial